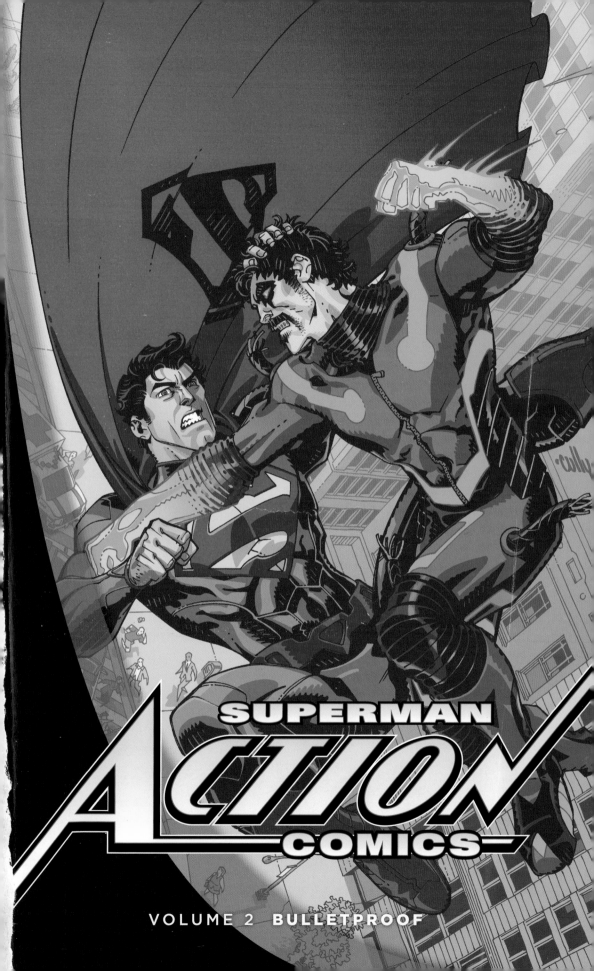

SUPERMAN

ACTION COMICS

VOLUME 2 BULLETPROOF

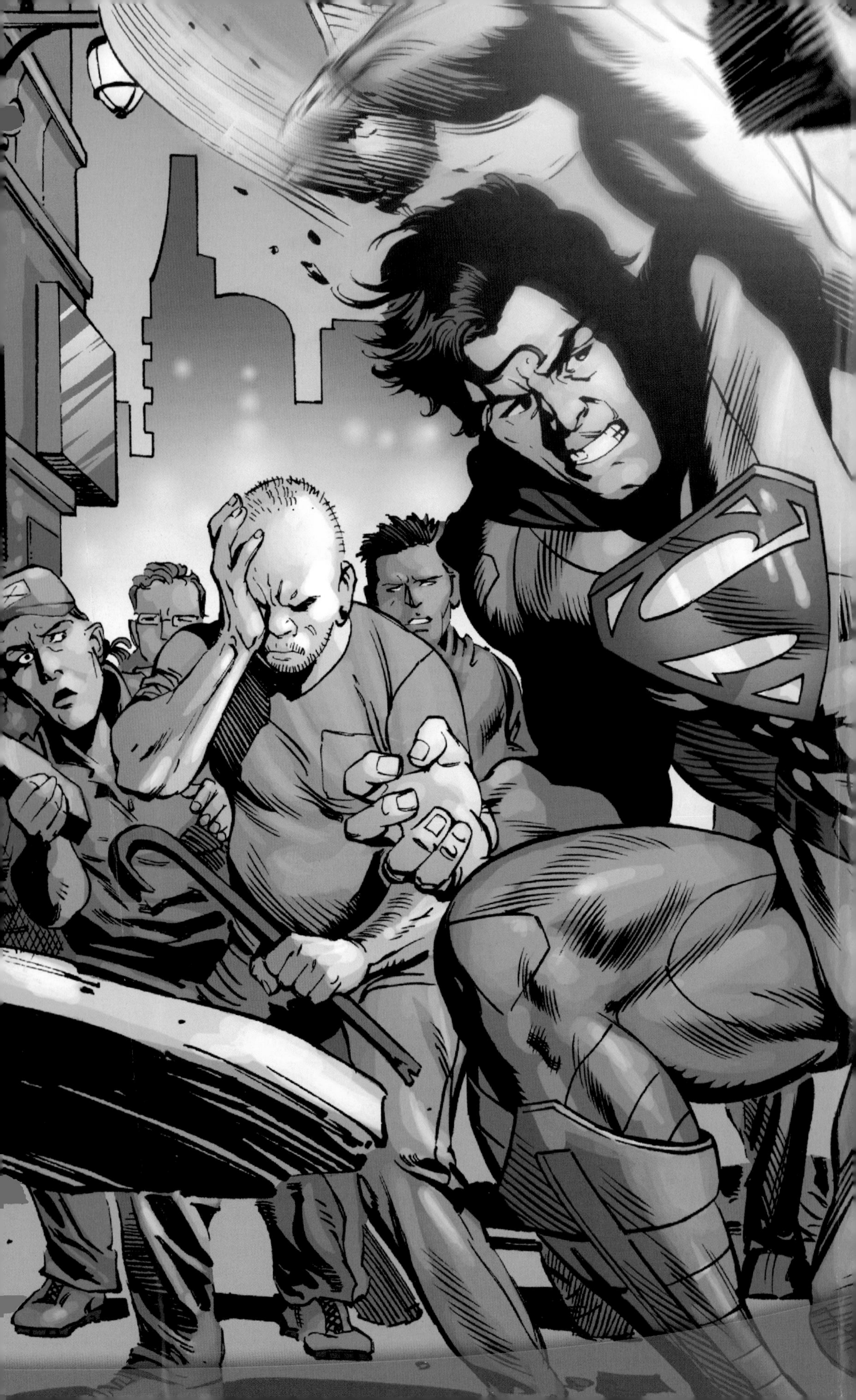

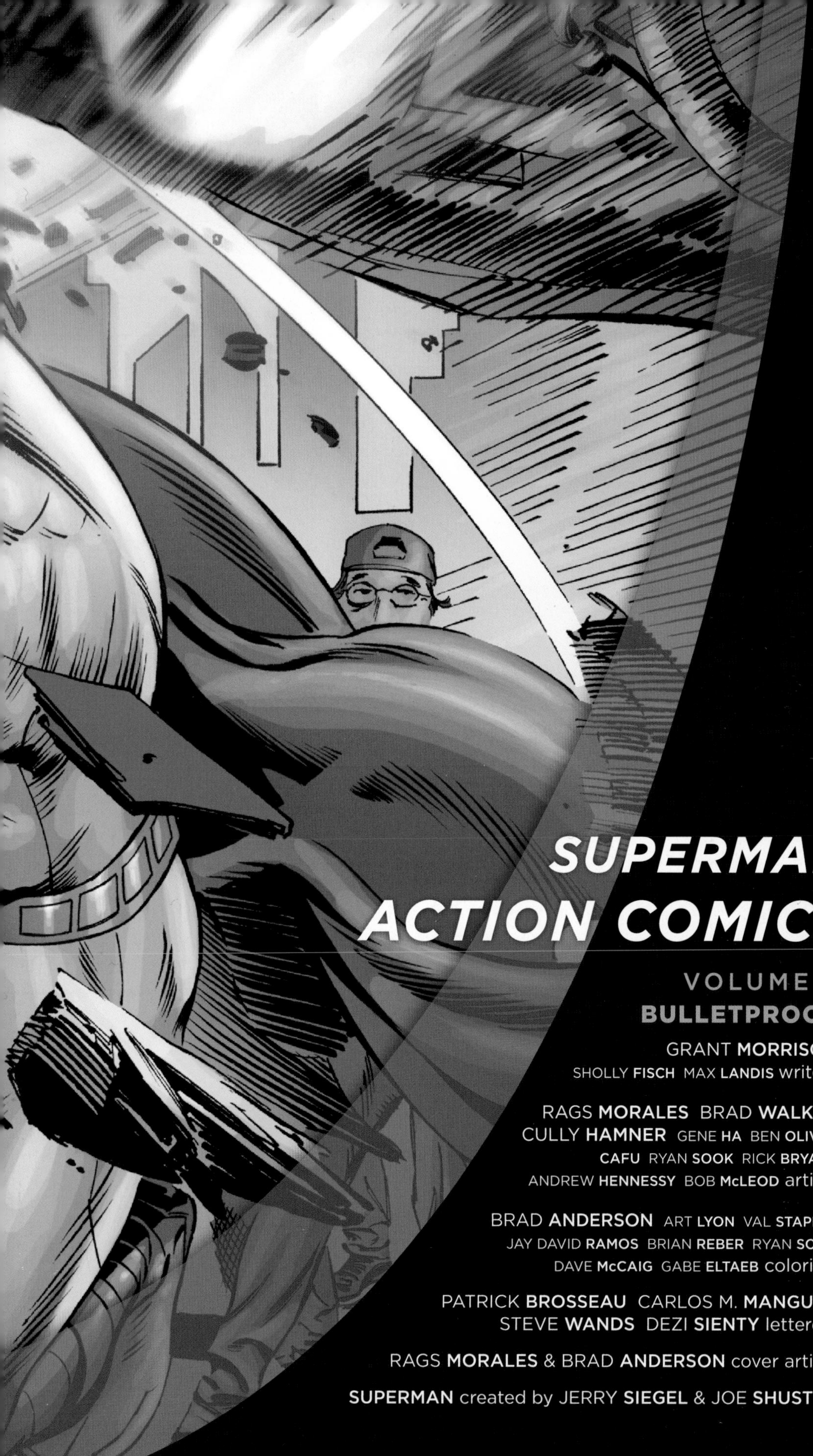

SUPERMAN ACTION COMICS

VOLUME 2
BULLETPROOF

GRANT **MORRISON**
SHOLLY **FISCH** MAX **LANDIS** writers

RAGS **MORALES** BRAD **WALKER**
CULLY **HAMNER** GENE **HA** BEN **OLIVER**
CAFU RYAN **SOOK** RICK **BRYANT**
ANDREW **HENNESSY** BOB **McLEOD** artists

BRAD **ANDERSON** ART **LYON** VAL **STAPLES**
JAY DAVID **RAMOS** BRIAN **REBER** RYAN **SOOK**
DAVE **McCAIG** GABE **ELTAEB** colorists

PATRICK **BROSSEAU** CARLOS M. **MANGUAL**
STEVE **WANDS** DEZI **SIENTY** letterers

RAGS **MORALES** & BRAD **ANDERSON** cover artists

SUPERMAN created by JERRY **SIEGEL** & JOE **SHUSTER**

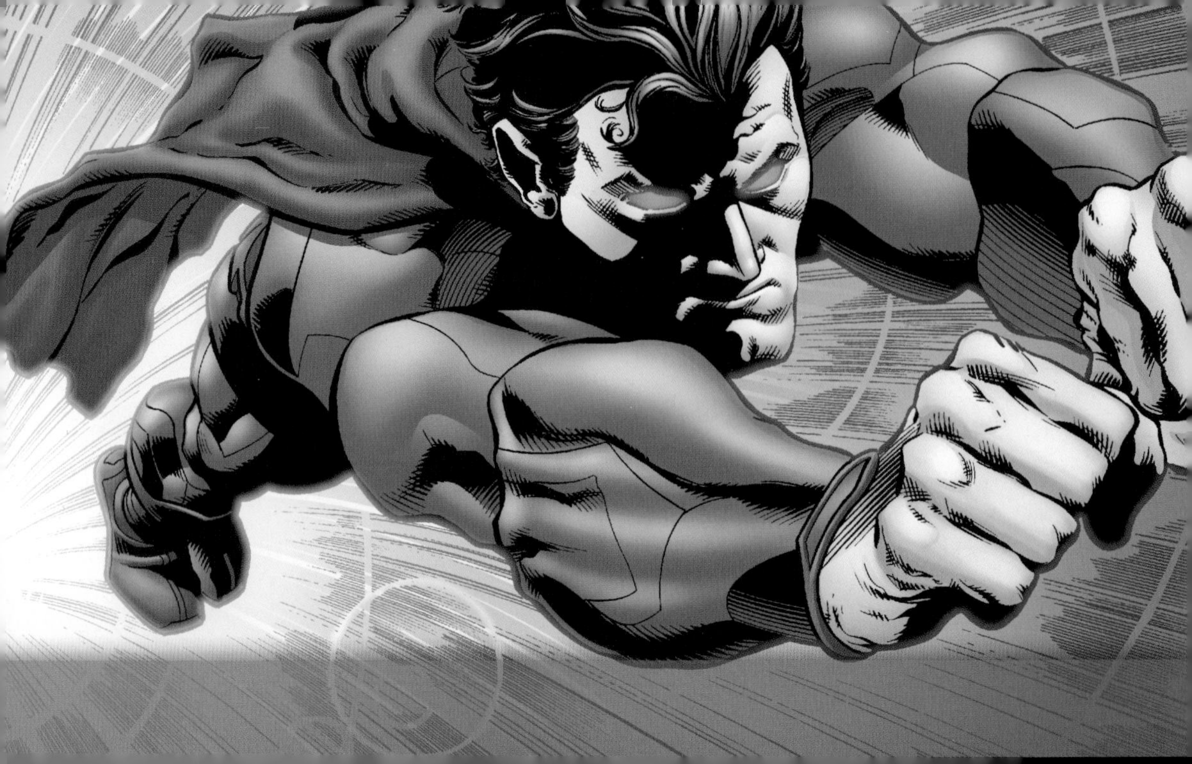

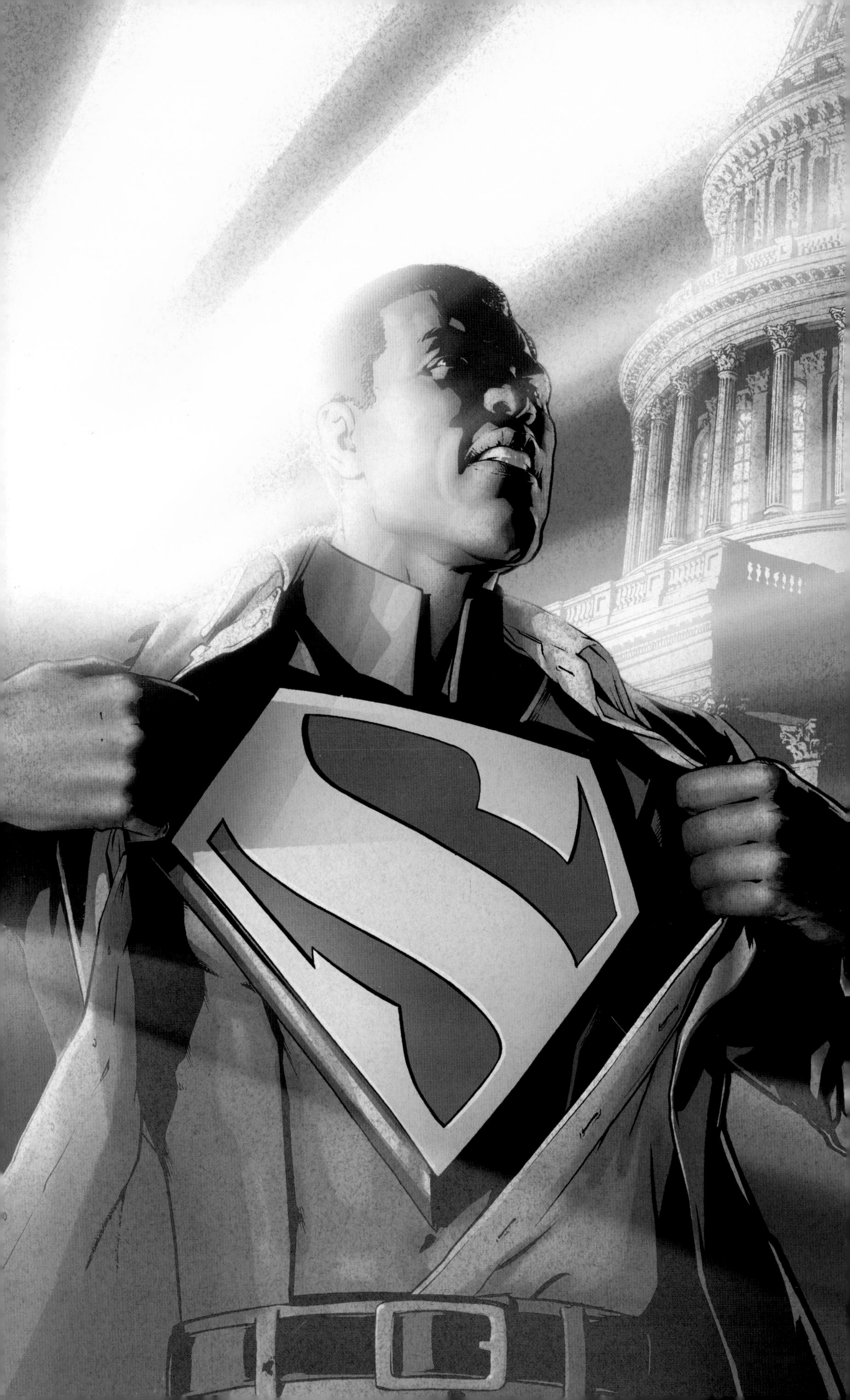

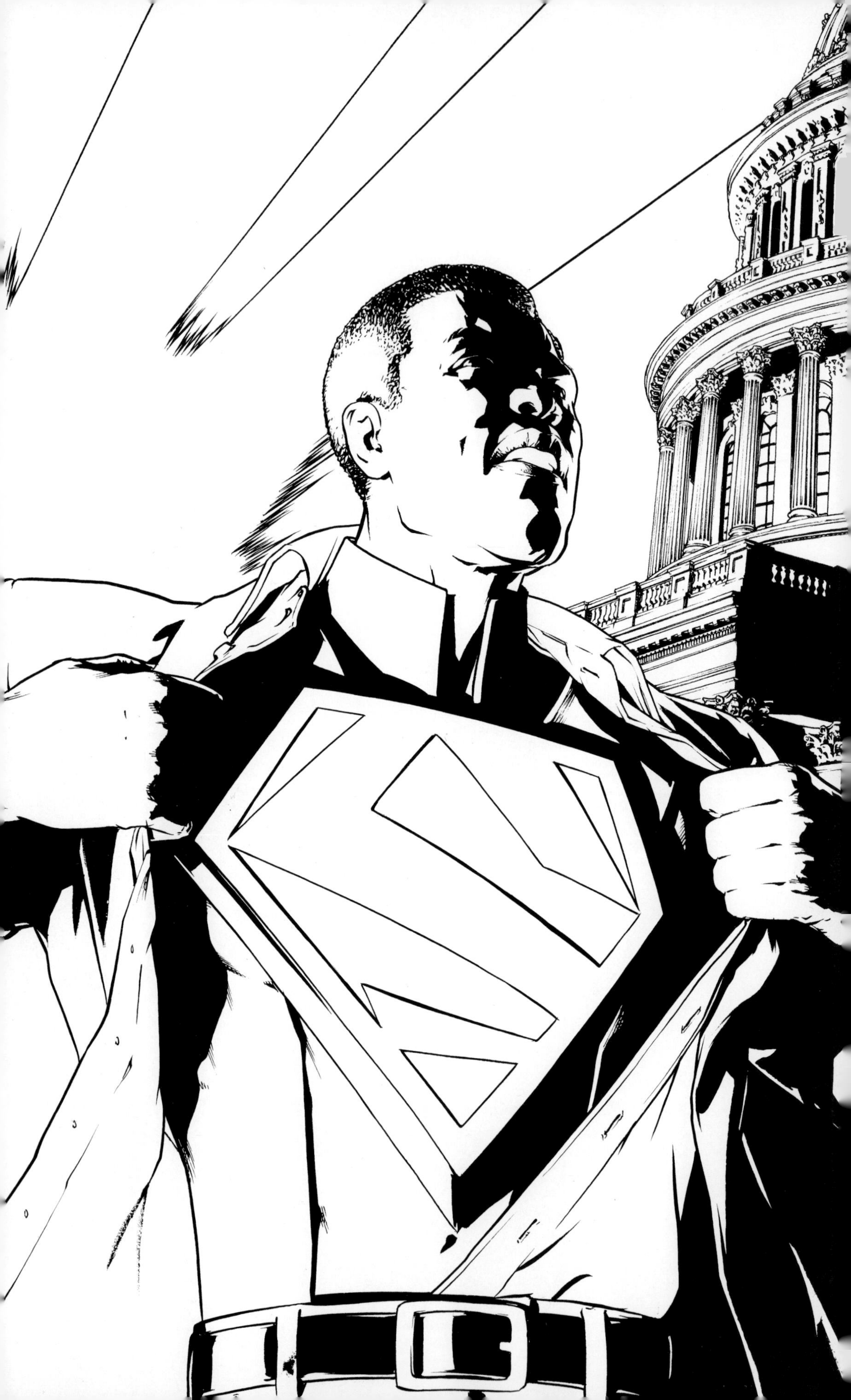

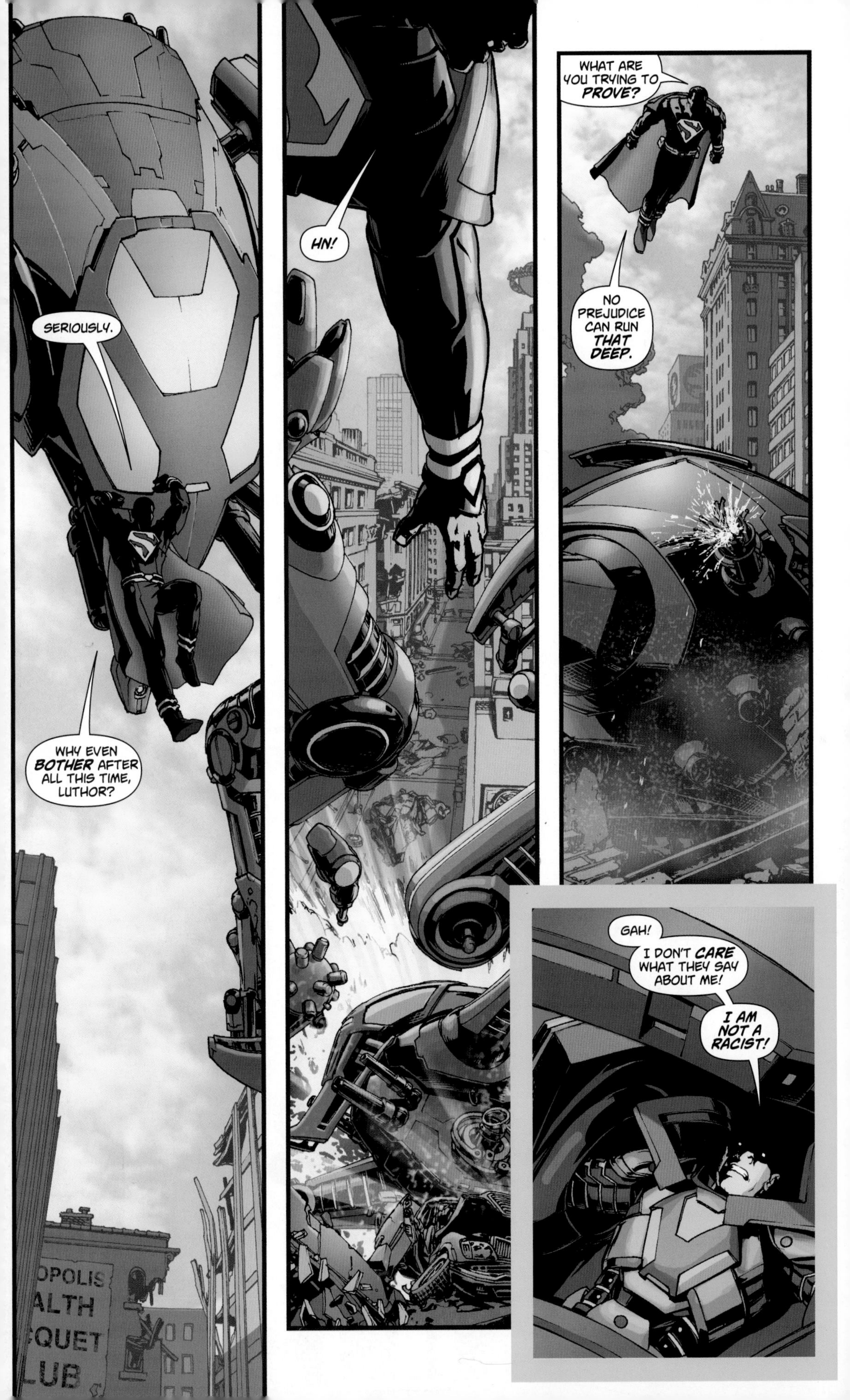
SERIOUSLY.
WHY EVEN BOTHER AFTER ALL THIS TIME, LUTHOR?
OPOLIS ALTH CQUET LUB
HN!
WHAT ARE YOU TRYING TO PROVE?
NO PREJUDICE CAN RUN THAT DEEP.
GAH!
I DON'T CARE WHAT THEY SAY ABOUT ME!
I AM NOT A RACIST!

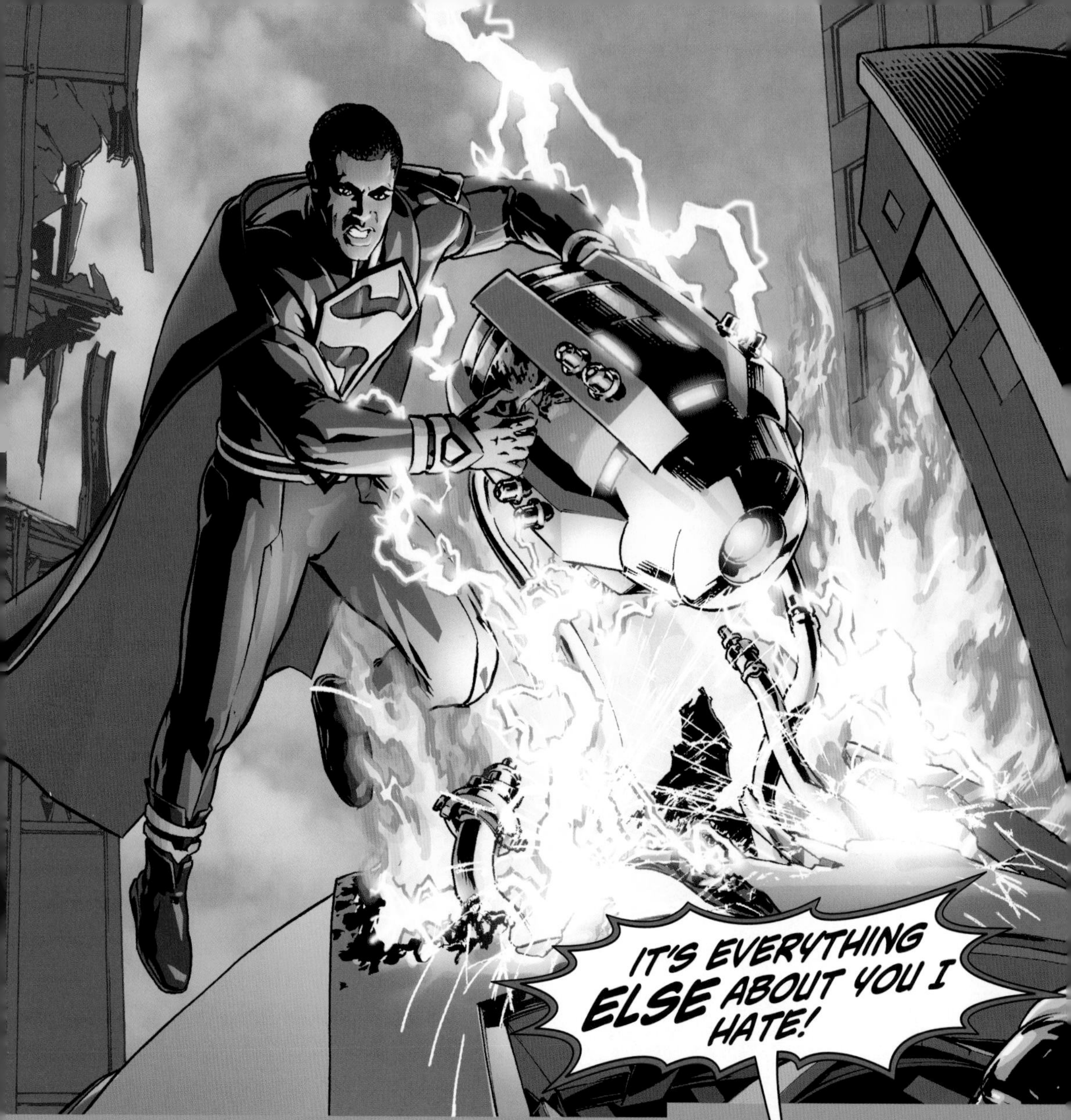
IT'S EVERYTHING ELSE ABOUT YOU I HATE!

THE CURSE OF SUPERMAN

GRANT MORRISION WRITER
GENE HA ARTIST ART LYON COLORIST
PATRICK BROSSEAU LETTERER GENE HA & ART LYON COVER
RAGS MORALES & BRAD ANDERSON VARIANT COVER
WIL MOSS ASSOCIATE EDITOR MATT IDELSON EDITOR
SUPERMAN CREATED BY JERRY SIEGEL & JOE SHUSTER

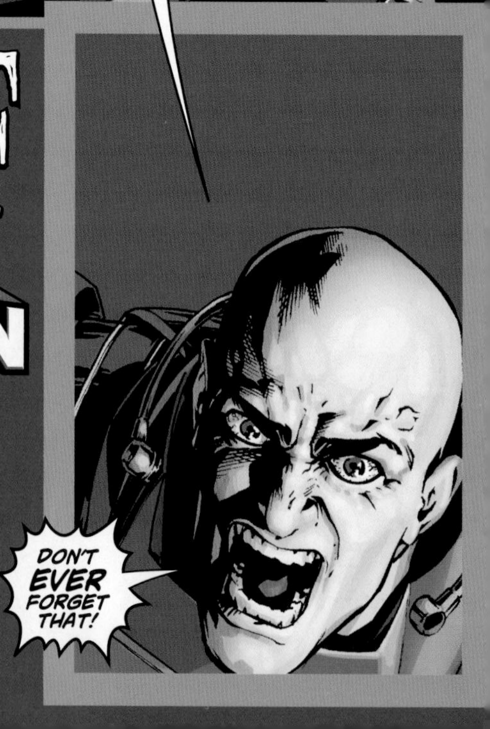
DON'T EVER FORGET THAT!

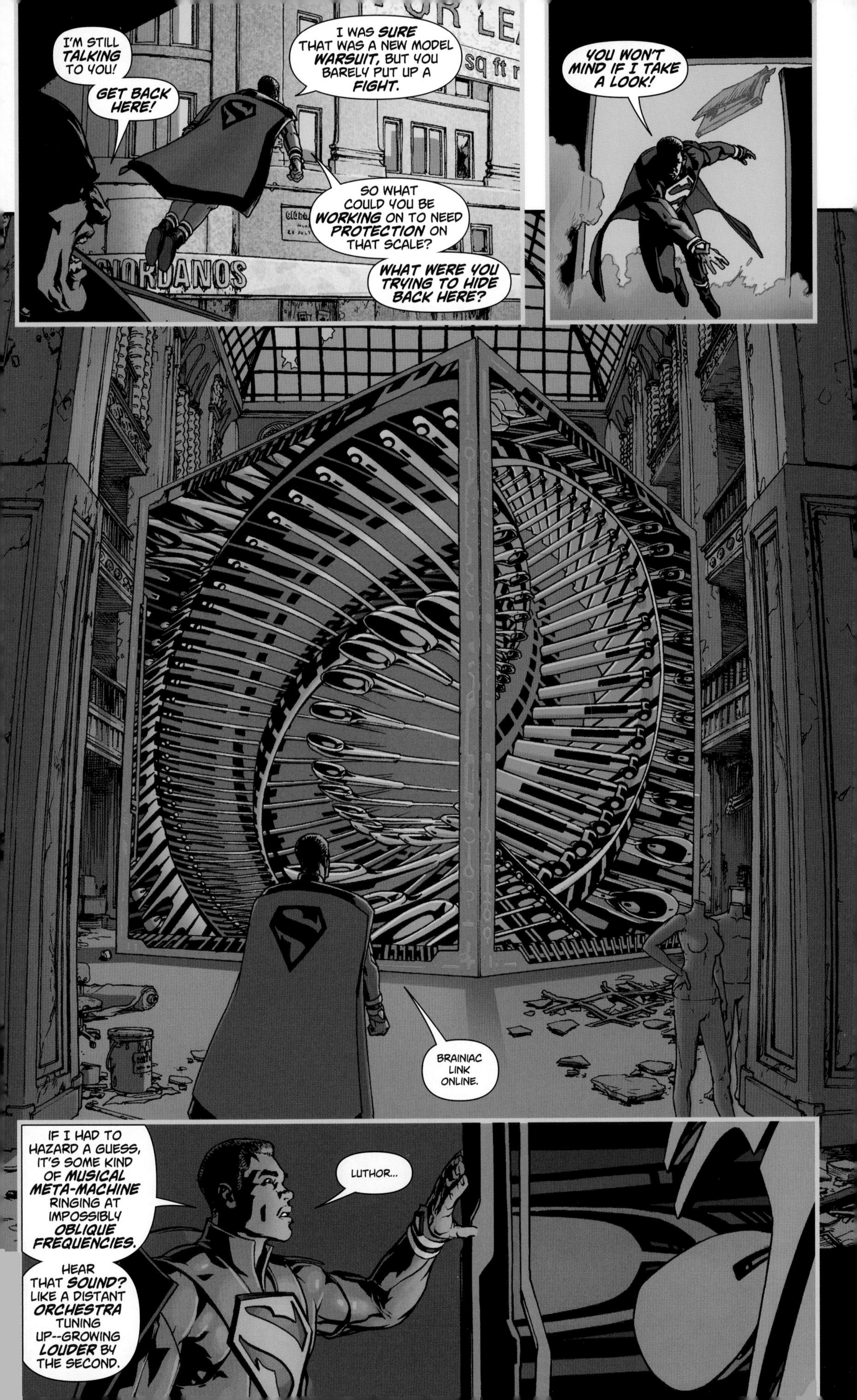
I'M STILL TALKING TO YOU!
GET BACK HERE!
I WAS SURE THAT WAS A NEW MODEL WARSUIT, BUT YOU BARELY PUT UP A FIGHT.
SO WHAT COULD YOU BE WORKING ON TO NEED PROTECTION ON THAT SCALE?
WHAT WERE YOU TRYING TO HIDE BACK HERE?
YOU WON'T MIND IF I TAKE A LOOK!
BRAINIAC LINK ONLINE.
IF I HAD TO HAZARD A GUESS, IT'S SOME KIND OF MUSICAL META-MACHINE RINGING AT IMPOSSIBLY OBLIQUE FREQUENCIES.
LUTHOR...
HEAR THAT SOUND? LIKE A DISTANT ORCHESTRA TUNING UP--GROWING LOUDER BY THE SECOND.

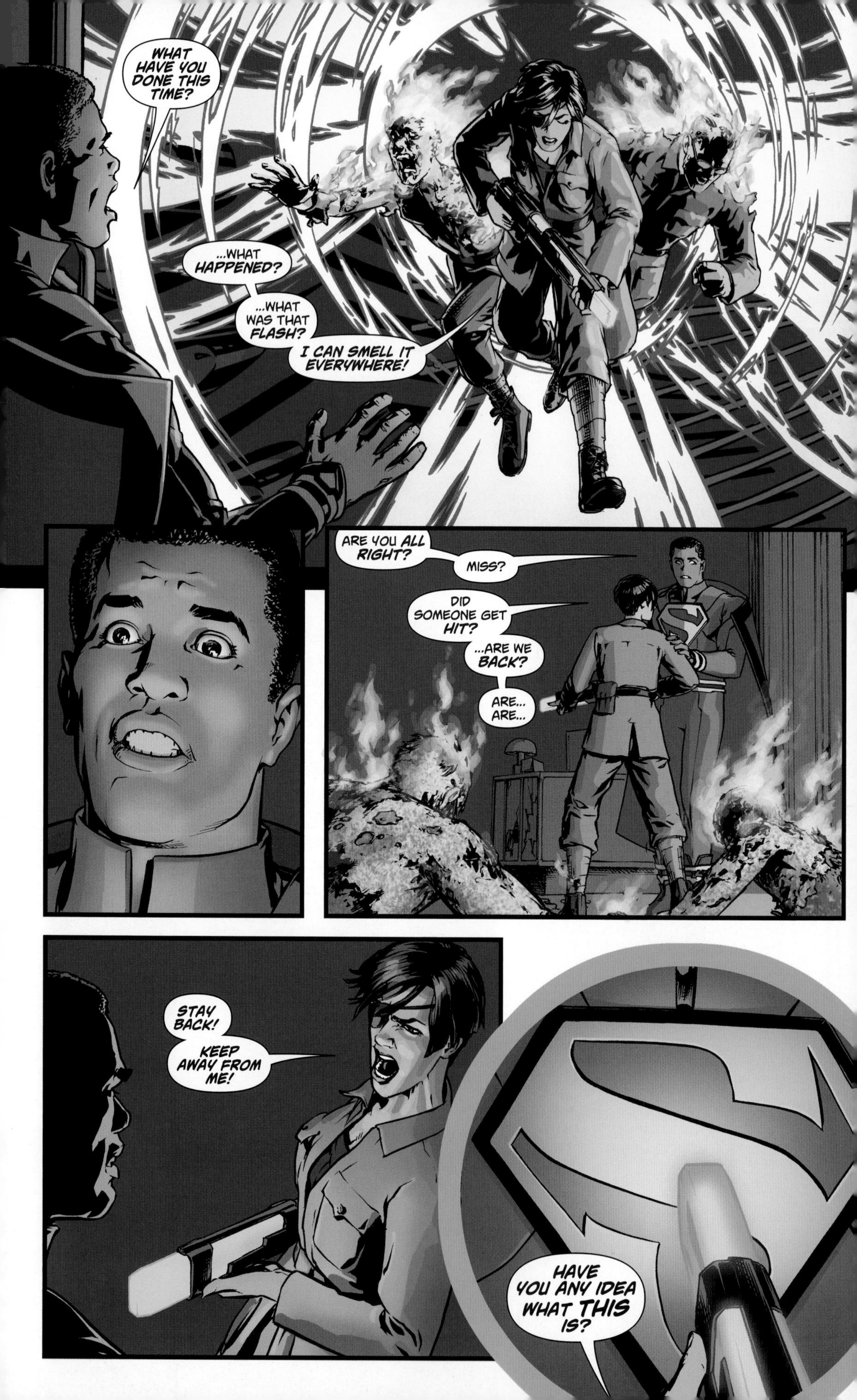
WHAT HAVE YOU DONE THIS TIME?
...WHAT HAPPENED?
...WHAT WAS THAT FLASH?
I CAN SMELL IT EVERYWHERE!
ARE YOU ALL RIGHT?
MISS?
DID SOMEONE GET HIT?
...ARE WE BACK?
ARE... ARE...
STAY BACK!
KEEP AWAY FROM ME!
HAVE YOU ANY IDEA WHAT THIS IS?

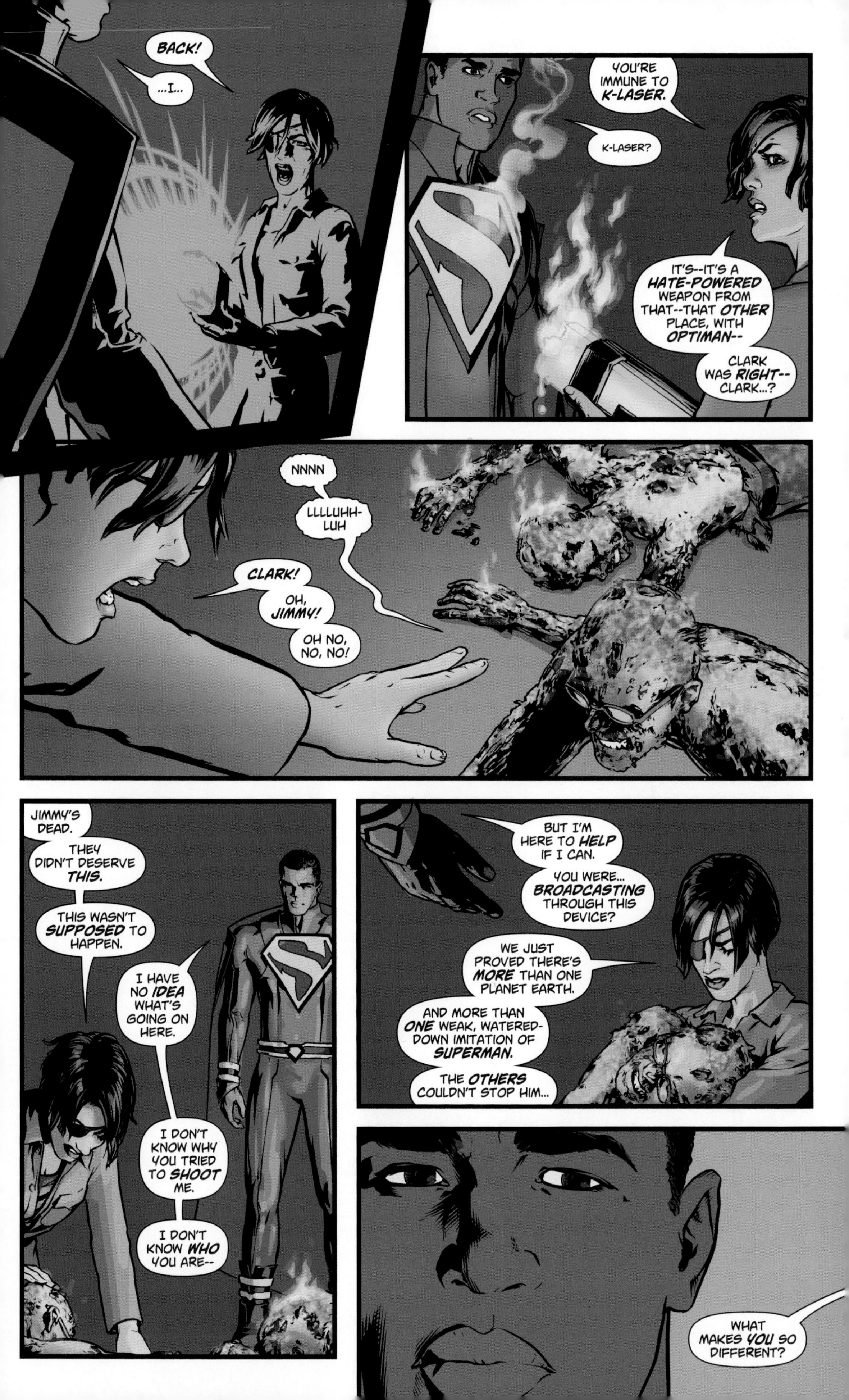
BACK!
...I...
YOU'RE IMMUNE TO K-LASER.
K-LASER?
IT'S--IT'S A HATE-POWERED WEAPON FROM THAT--THAT OTHER PLACE, WITH OPTIMAN--
CLARK WAS RIGHT-- CLARK...?
NNNN
LLLLUHH-LUH
CLARK!
OH, JIMMY!
OH NO, NO, NO!
JIMMY'S DEAD.
THEY DIDN'T DESERVE THIS.
THIS WASN'T SUPPOSED TO HAPPEN.
I HAVE NO IDEA WHAT'S GOING ON HERE.
I DON'T KNOW WHY YOU TRIED TO SHOOT ME.
I DON'T KNOW WHO YOU ARE--
BUT I'M HERE TO HELP IF I CAN.
YOU WERE... BROADCASTING THROUGH THIS DEVICE?
WE JUST PROVED THERE'S MORE THAN ONE PLANET EARTH.
AND MORE THAN ONE WEAK, WATERED-DOWN IMITATION OF SUPERMAN.
THE OTHERS COULDN'T STOP HIM...
WHAT MAKES YOU SO DIFFERENT?

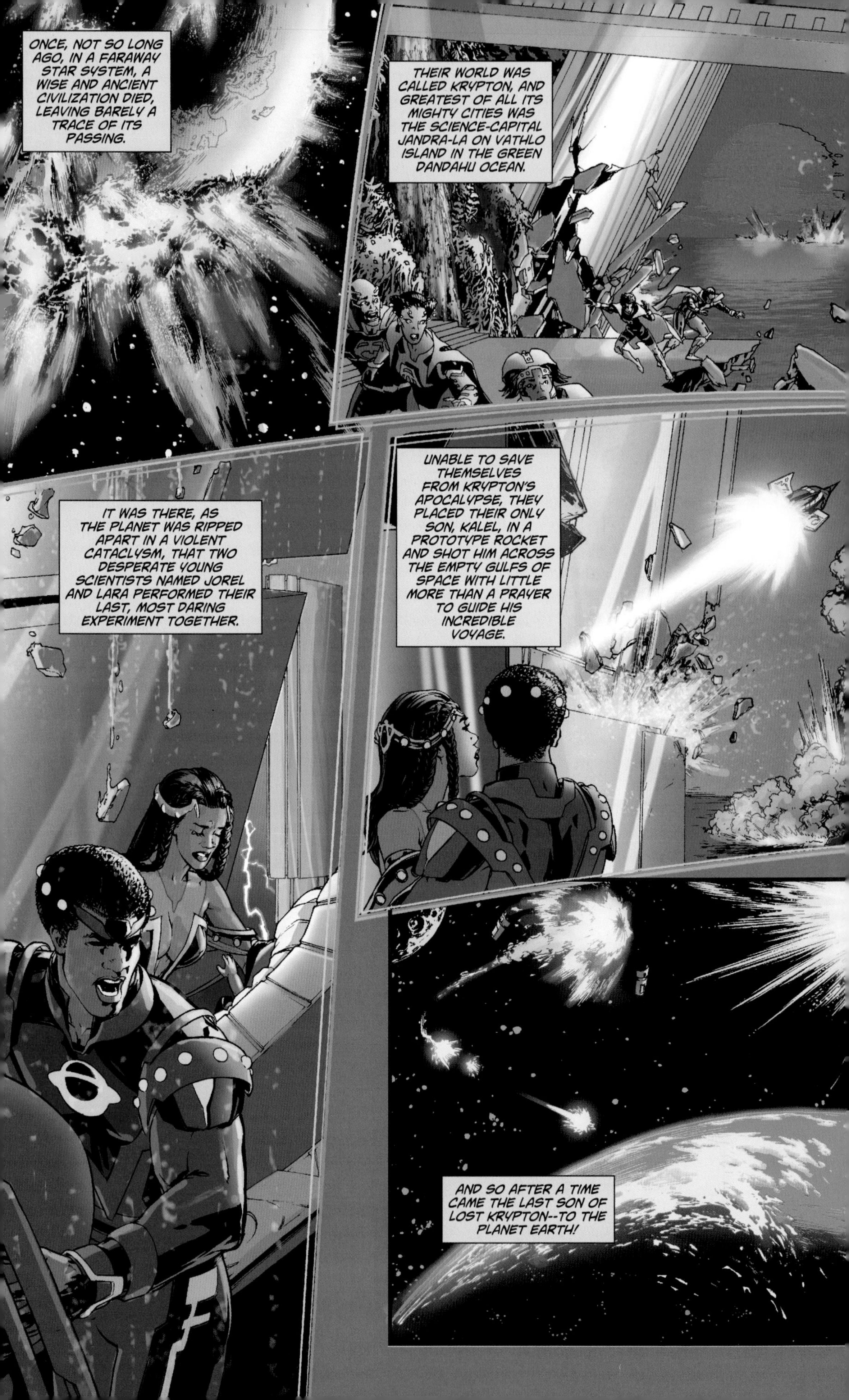
ONCE, NOT SO LONG AGO, IN A FARAWAY STAR SYSTEM, A WISE AND ANCIENT CIVILIZATION DIED, LEAVING BARELY A TRACE OF ITS PASSING.
THEIR WORLD WAS CALLED KRYPTON, AND GREATEST OF ALL ITS MIGHTY CITIES WAS THE SCIENCE-CAPITAL JANDRA-LA ON VATHLO ISLAND IN THE GREEN DANDAHU OCEAN.
IT WAS THERE, AS THE PLANET WAS RIPPED APART IN A VIOLENT CATACLYSM, THAT TWO DESPERATE YOUNG SCIENTISTS NAMED JOREL AND LARA PERFORMED THEIR LAST, MOST DARING EXPERIMENT TOGETHER.
UNABLE TO SAVE THEMSELVES FROM KRYPTON'S APOCALYPSE, THEY PLACED THEIR ONLY SON, KALEL, IN A PROTOTYPE ROCKET AND SHOT HIM ACROSS THE EMPTY GULFS OF SPACE WITH LITTLE MORE THAN A PRAYER TO GUIDE HIS INCREDIBLE VOYAGE.
AND SO AFTER A TIME CAME THE LAST SON OF LOST KRYPTON--TO THE PLANET EARTH!

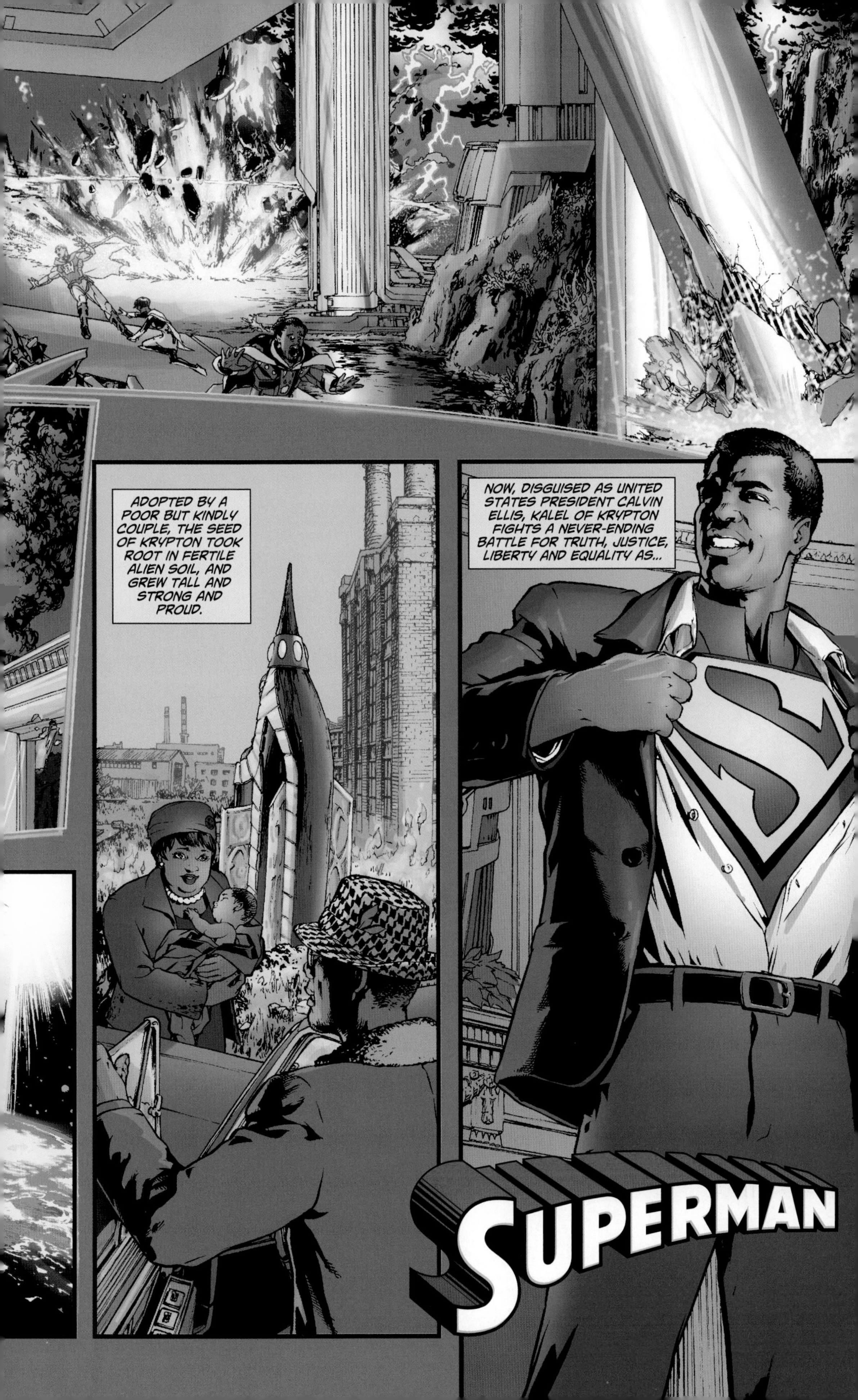
ADOPTED BY A POOR BUT KINDLY COUPLE, THE SEED OF KRYPTON TOOK ROOT IN FERTILE ALIEN SOIL, AND GREW TALL AND STRONG AND PROUD.
NOW, DISGUISED AS UNITED STATES PRESIDENT CALVIN ELLIS, KALEL OF KRYPTON FIGHTS A NEVER-ENDING BATTLE FOR TRUTH, JUSTICE, LIBERTY AND EQUALITY AS...
SUPERMAN

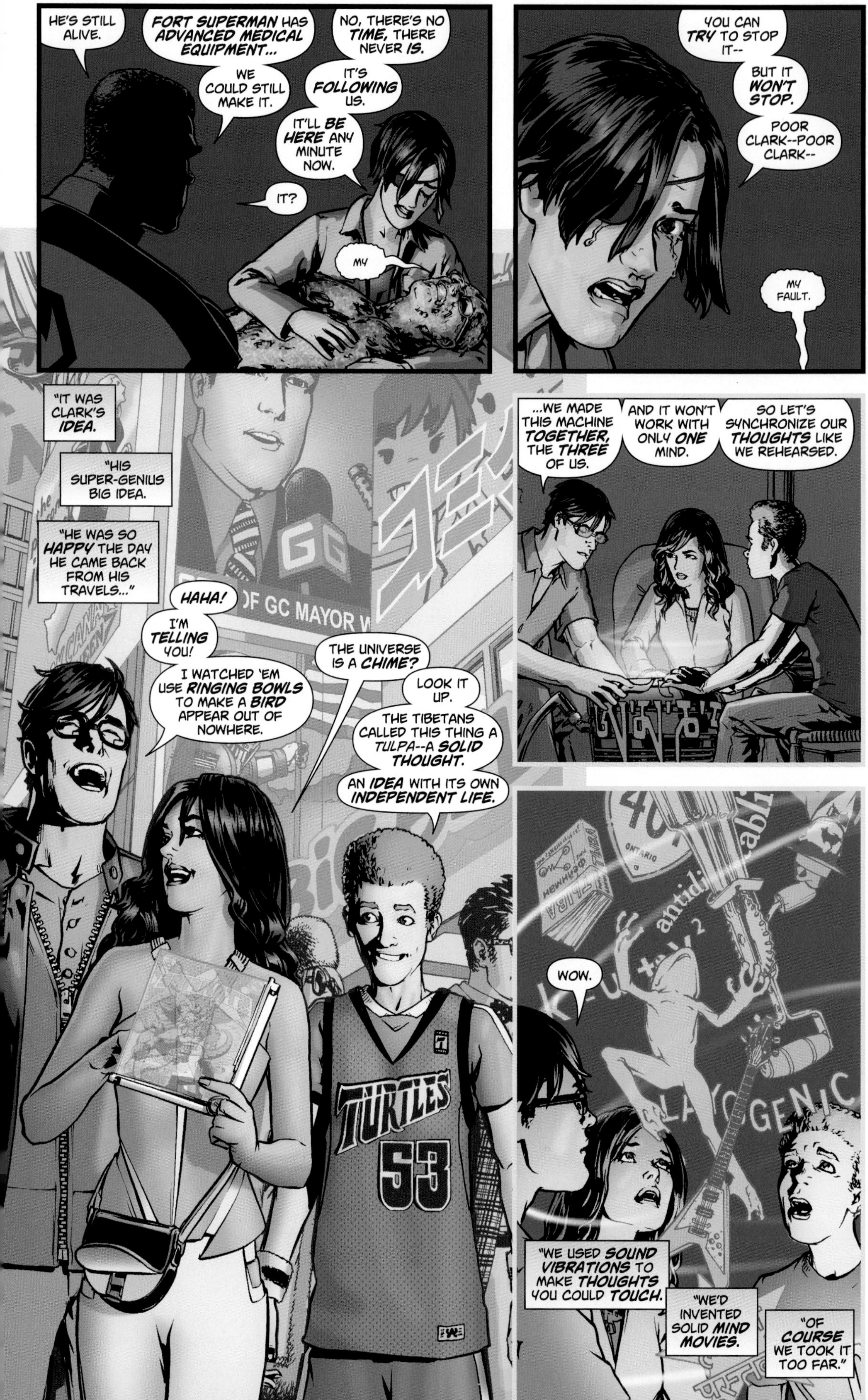

HE'S STILL ALIVE.
FORT SUPERMAN HAS ADVANCED MEDICAL EQUIPMENT...
WE COULD STILL MAKE IT.
NO, THERE'S NO TIME, THERE NEVER IS.
IT'S FOLLOWING US.
IT'LL BE HERE ANY MINUTE NOW.
IT?
MY
YOU CAN TRY TO STOP IT--
BUT IT WON'T STOP.
POOR CLARK--POOR CLARK--
MY FAULT.
"IT WAS CLARK'S IDEA.
"HIS SUPER-GENIUS BIG IDEA.
"HE WAS SO HAPPY THE DAY HE CAME BACK FROM HIS TRAVELS..."
OF GC MAYOR W
HAHA!
I'M TELLING YOU!
I WATCHED 'EM USE RINGING BOWLS TO MAKE A BIRD APPEAR OUT OF NOWHERE.
THE UNIVERSE IS A CHIME?
LOOK IT UP.
THE TIBETANS CALLED THIS THING A TULPA--A SOLID THOUGHT.
AN IDEA WITH ITS OWN INDEPENDENT LIFE.
TURTLES
53
...WE MADE THIS MACHINE TOGETHER, THE THREE OF US.
AND IT WON'T WORK WITH ONLY ONE MIND.
SO LET'S SYNCHRONIZE OUR THOUGHTS LIKE WE REHEARSED.
ONTARIO
antidi
WOW.
GENIC
"WE USED SOUND VIBRATIONS TO MAKE THOUGHTS YOU COULD TOUCH.
"WE'D INVENTED SOLID MIND MOVIES.
"OF COURSE WE TOOK IT TOO FAR."

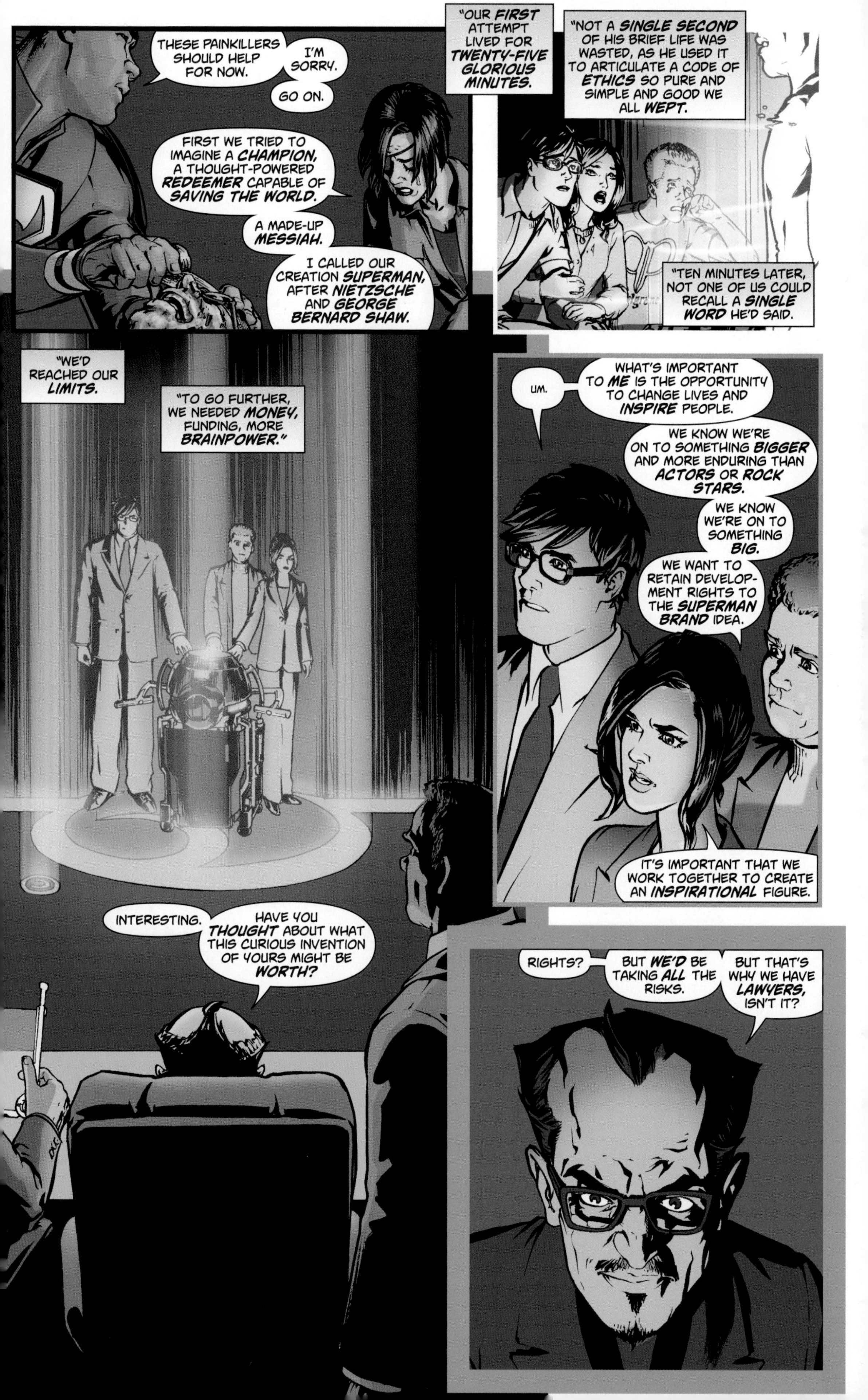
THESE PAINKILLERS SHOULD HELP FOR NOW.
I'M SORRY.
GO ON.
FIRST WE TRIED TO IMAGINE A CHAMPION, A THOUGHT-POWERED REDEEMER CAPABLE OF SAVING THE WORLD.
A MADE-UP MESSIAH.
I CALLED OUR CREATION SUPERMAN, AFTER NIETZSCHE AND GEORGE BERNARD SHAW.
"OUR FIRST ATTEMPT LIVED FOR TWENTY-FIVE GLORIOUS MINUTES.
"NOT A SINGLE SECOND OF HIS BRIEF LIFE WAS WASTED, AS HE USED IT TO ARTICULATE A CODE OF ETHICS SO PURE AND SIMPLE AND GOOD WE ALL WEPT.
"TEN MINUTES LATER, NOT ONE OF US COULD RECALL A SINGLE WORD HE'D SAID.
"WE'D REACHED OUR LIMITS.
"TO GO FURTHER, WE NEEDED MONEY, FUNDING, MORE BRAINPOWER."
UM.
WHAT'S IMPORTANT TO ME IS THE OPPORTUNITY TO CHANGE LIVES AND INSPIRE PEOPLE.
WE KNOW WE'RE ON TO SOMETHING BIGGER AND MORE ENDURING THAN ACTORS OR ROCK STARS.
WE KNOW WE'RE ON TO SOMETHING BIG.
WE WANT TO RETAIN DEVELOPMENT RIGHTS TO THE SUPERMAN BRAND IDEA.
IT'S IMPORTANT THAT WE WORK TOGETHER TO CREATE AN INSPIRATIONAL FIGURE.
INTERESTING.
HAVE YOU THOUGHT ABOUT WHAT THIS CURIOUS INVENTION OF YOURS MIGHT BE WORTH?
RIGHTS?
BUT WE'D BE TAKING ALL THE RISKS.
BUT THAT'S WHY WE HAVE LAWYERS, ISN'T IT?

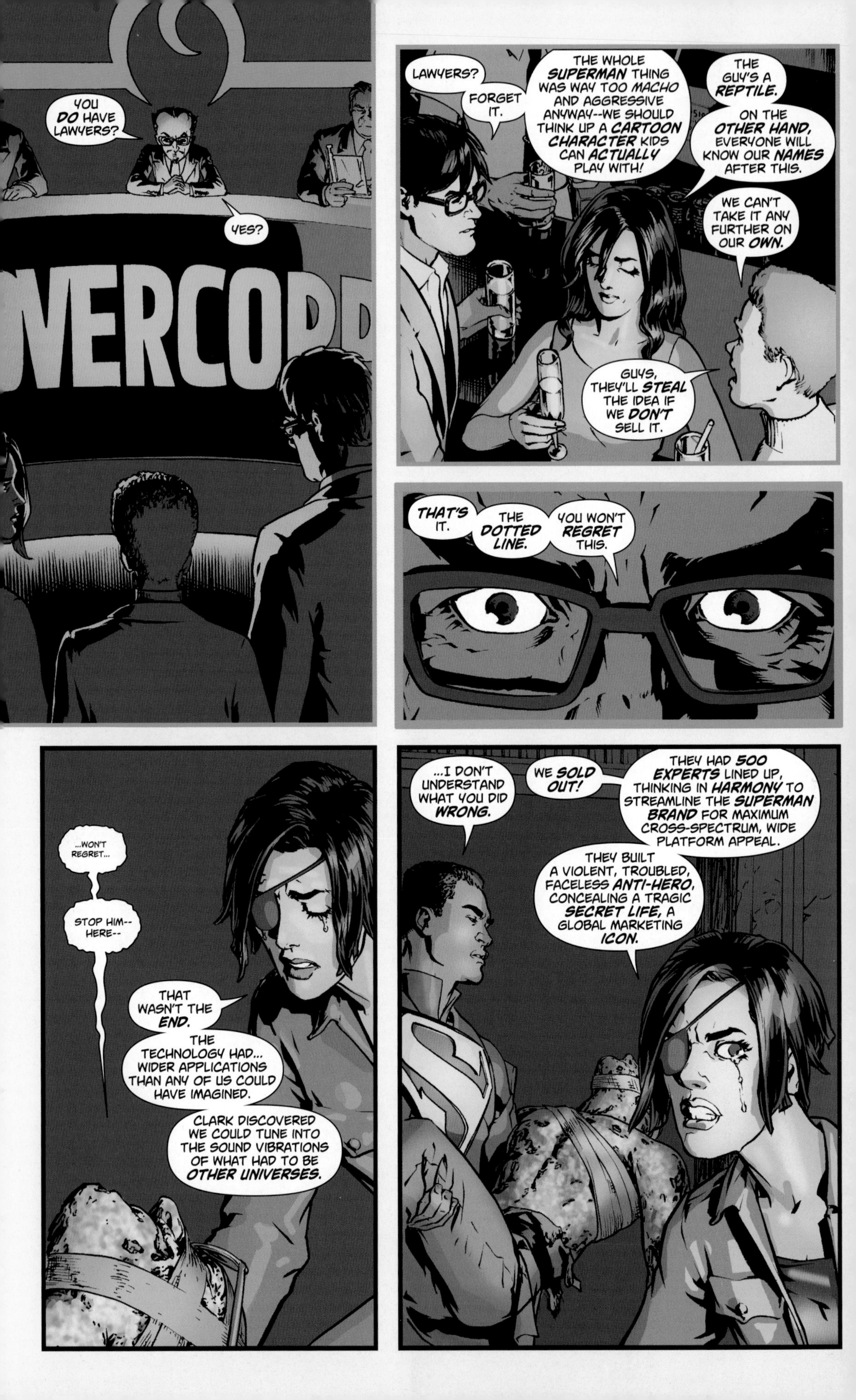
YOU DO HAVE LAWYERS?
YES?
VERCOR
LAWYERS?
FORGET IT.
THE WHOLE SUPERMAN THING WAS WAY TOO MACHO AND AGGRESSIVE ANYWAY--WE SHOULD THINK UP A CARTOON CHARACTER KIDS CAN ACTUALLY PLAY WITH!
THE GUY'S A REPTILE.
ON THE OTHER HAND, EVERYONE WILL KNOW OUR NAMES AFTER THIS.
WE CAN'T TAKE IT ANY FURTHER ON OUR OWN.
GUYS, THEY'LL STEAL THE IDEA IF WE DON'T SELL IT.
THAT'S IT.
THE DOTTED LINE.
YOU WON'T REGRET THIS.
...WON'T REGRET...
STOP HIM-- HERE--
THAT WASN'T THE END.
THE TECHNOLOGY HAD... WIDER APPLICATIONS THAN ANY OF US COULD HAVE IMAGINED.
CLARK DISCOVERED WE COULD TUNE INTO THE SOUND VIBRATIONS OF WHAT HAD TO BE OTHER UNIVERSES.
...I DON'T UNDERSTAND WHAT YOU DID WRONG.
WE SOLD OUT!
THEY HAD 500 EXPERTS LINED UP, THINKING IN HARMONY TO STREAMLINE THE SUPERMAN BRAND FOR MAXIMUM CROSS-SPECTRUM, WIDE PLATFORM APPEAL.
THEY BUILT A VIOLENT, TROUBLED, FACELESS ANTI-HERO, CONCEALING A TRAGIC SECRET LIFE, A GLOBAL MARKETING ICON.

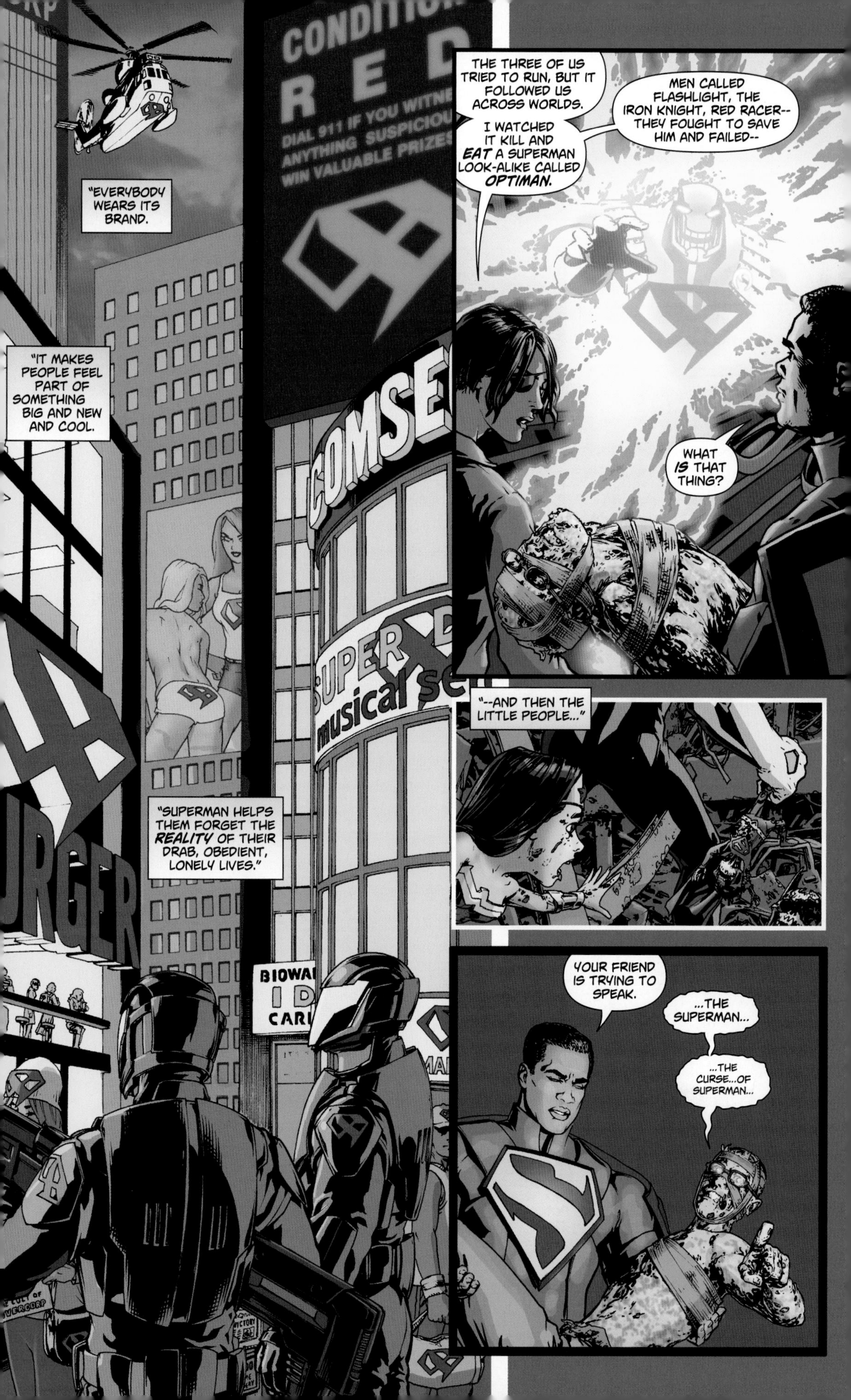
CONDITION
R E D
DIAL 911 IF YOU WITNE
ANYTHING SUSPICIOU
WIN VALUABLE PRIZES
"EVERYBODY WEARS ITS BRAND.
"IT MAKES PEOPLE FEEL PART OF SOMETHING BIG AND NEW AND COOL.
COMSE
SUPER
musical se
"SUPERMAN HELPS THEM FORGET THE REALITY OF THEIR DRAB, OBEDIENT, LONELY LIVES."
URGER
BIOWA
CAR
THE THREE OF US TRIED TO RUN, BUT IT FOLLOWED US ACROSS WORLDS.
I WATCHED IT KILL AND EAT A SUPERMAN LOOK-ALIKE CALLED OPTIMAN.
MEN CALLED FLASHLIGHT, THE IRON KNIGHT, RED RACER-- THEY FOUGHT TO SAVE HIM AND FAILED--
WHAT IS THAT THING?
"--AND THEN THE LITTLE PEOPLE..."
YOUR FRIEND IS TRYING TO SPEAK.
...THE SUPERMAN...
...THE CURSE...OF SUPERMAN...

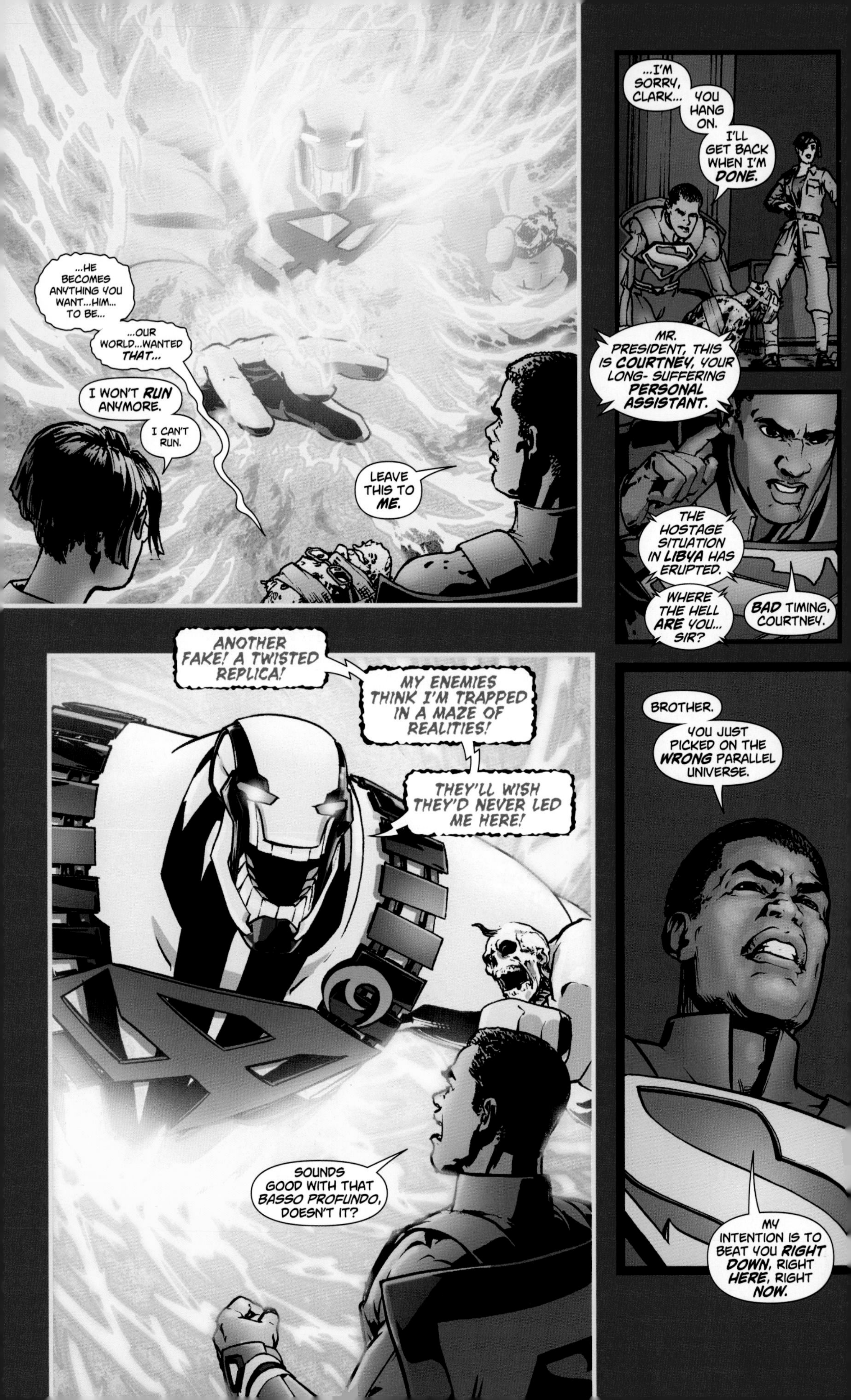
...HE BECOMES ANYTHING YOU WANT...HIM... TO BE...
...OUR WORLD...WANTED *THAT...*
I WON'T ***RUN*** ANYMORE.
I CAN'T RUN.
LEAVE THIS TO ***ME.***
...I'M SORRY, CLARK...
YOU HANG ON.
I'LL GET BACK WHEN I'M ***DONE.***
MR. PRESIDENT, THIS IS **COURTNEY**, YOUR LONG- SUFFERING **PERSONAL ASSISTANT.**
THE HOSTAGE SITUATION IN **LIBYA** HAS ERUPTED.
WHERE THE HELL **ARE** YOU... SIR?
BAD TIMING, COURTNEY.
ANOTHER FAKE! A TWISTED REPLICA!
MY ENEMIES THINK I'M TRAPPED IN A MAZE OF REALITIES!
THEY'LL WISH THEY'D NEVER LED ME HERE!
SOUNDS GOOD WITH THAT BASSO PROFUNDO, DOESN'T IT?
BROTHER.
YOU JUST PICKED ON THE ***WRONG*** PARALLEL UNIVERSE.
MY INTENTION IS TO BEAT YOU ***RIGHT DOWN***, RIGHT ***HERE***, RIGHT ***NOW.***

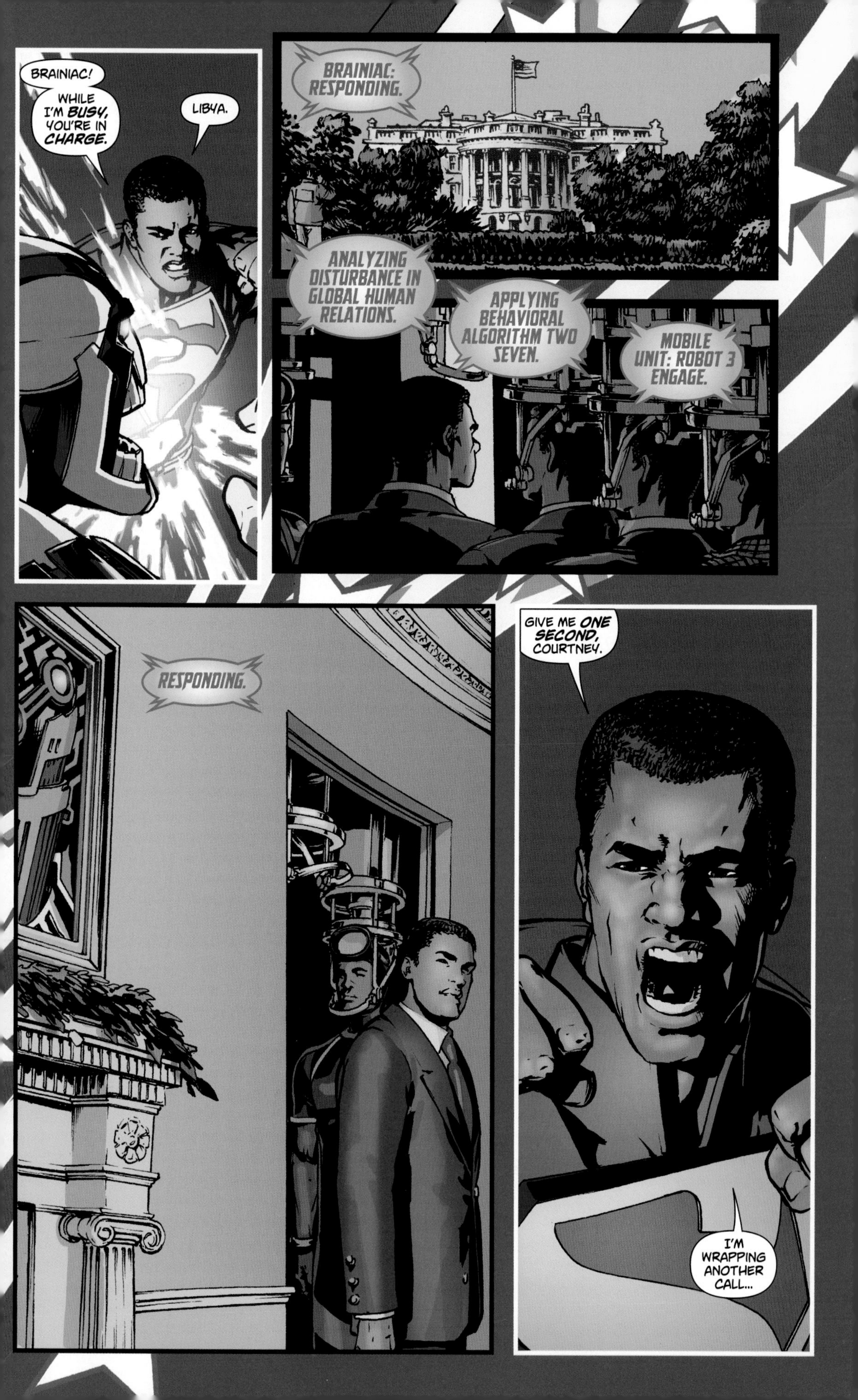
BRAINIAC! WHILE I'M *BUSY,* YOU'RE IN *CHARGE.*
LIBYA.
BRAINIAC: RESPONDING.
ANALYZING DISTURBANCE IN GLOBAL HUMAN RELATIONS.
APPLYING BEHAVIORAL ALGORITHM TWO SEVEN.
MOBILE UNIT: ROBOT 3 ENGAGE.
RESPONDING.
GIVE ME *ONE SECOND,* COURTNEY.
I'M WRAPPING ANOTHER CALL...

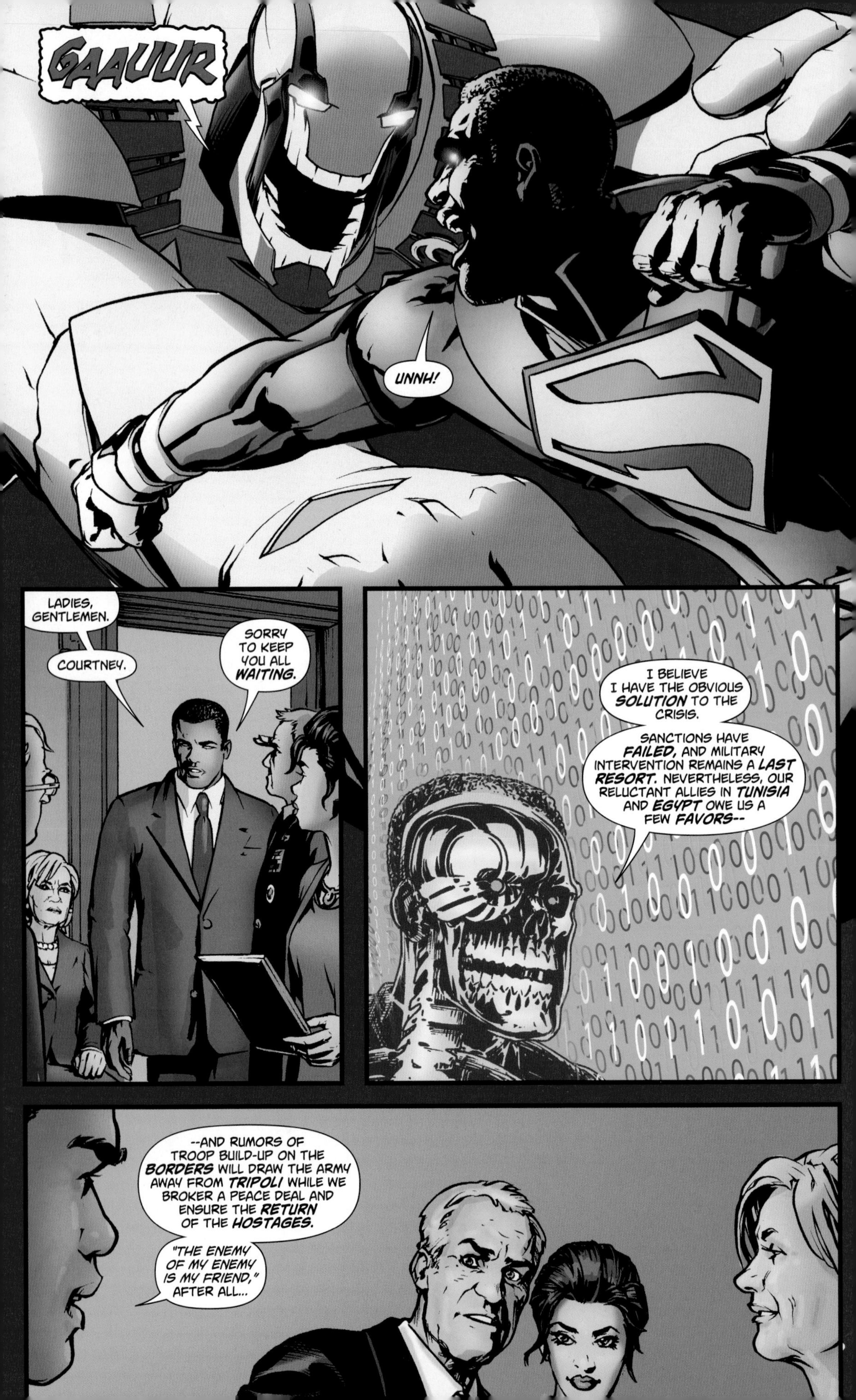
GAAUUR
UNNH!
LADIES, GENTLEMEN.
COURTNEY.
SORRY TO KEEP YOU ALL WAITING.
I BELIEVE I HAVE THE OBVIOUS SOLUTION TO THE CRISIS.
SANCTIONS HAVE FAILED, AND MILITARY INTERVENTION REMAINS A LAST RESORT. NEVERTHELESS, OUR RELUCTANT ALLIES IN TUNISIA AND EGYPT OWE US A FEW FAVORS--
--AND RUMORS OF TROOP BUILD-UP ON THE BORDERS WILL DRAW THE ARMY AWAY FROM TRIPOLI WHILE WE BROKER A PEACE DEAL AND ENSURE THE RETURN OF THE HOSTAGES.
"THE ENEMY OF MY ENEMY IS MY FRIEND," AFTER ALL...

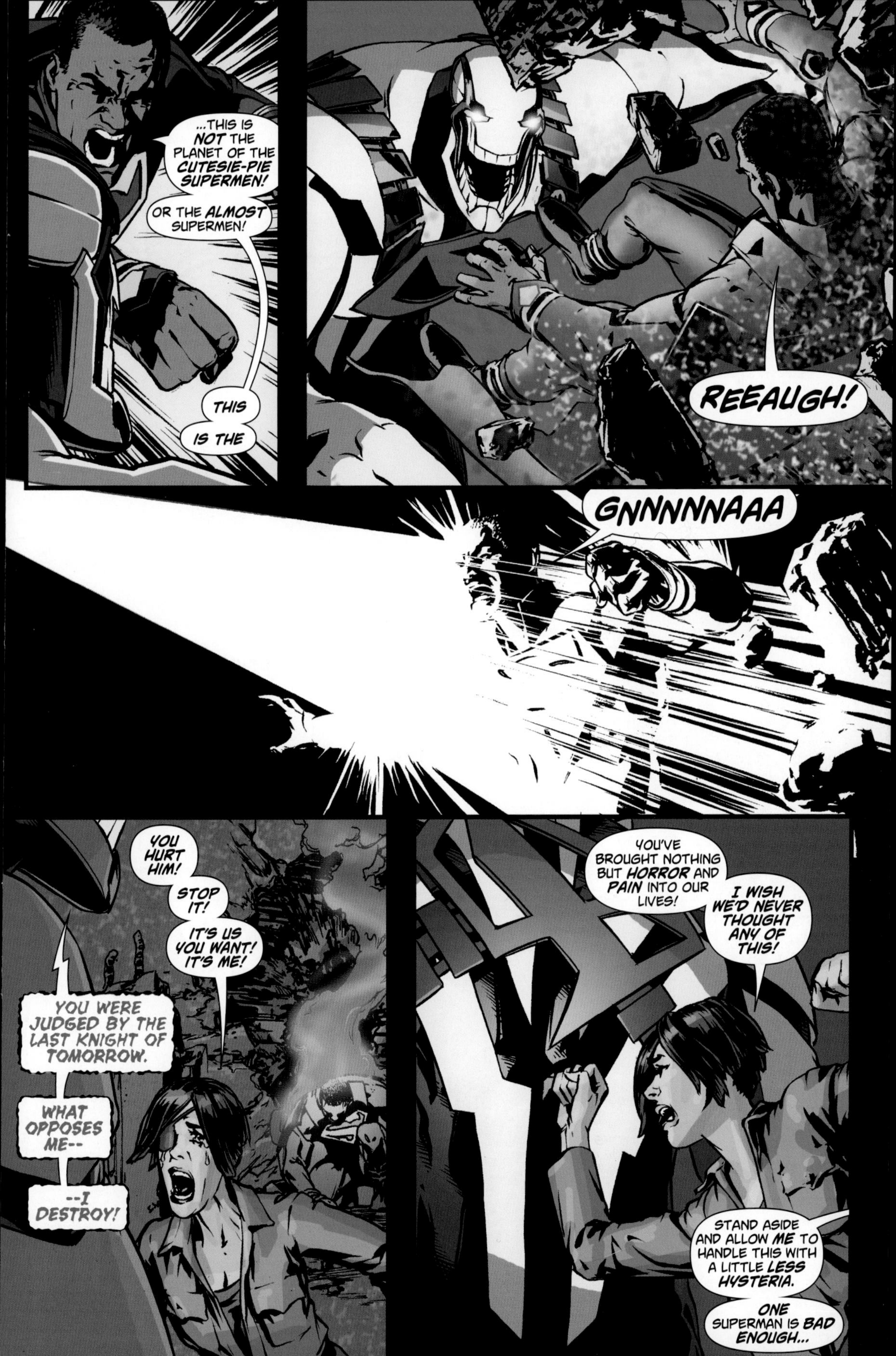
...THIS IS NOT THE PLANET OF THE CUTESIE-PIE SUPERMEN!
OR THE ALMOST SUPERMEN!
THIS
IS THE
REEAUGH!
GNNNNNAAA
YOU HURT HIM!
STOP IT!
IT'S US YOU WANT! IT'S ME!
YOU WERE JUDGED BY THE LAST KNIGHT OF TOMORROW.
WHAT OPPOSES ME--
--I DESTROY!
YOU'VE BROUGHT NOTHING BUT HORROR AND PAIN INTO OUR LIVES!
I WISH WE'D NEVER THOUGHT ANY OF THIS!
STAND ASIDE AND ALLOW ME TO HANDLE THIS WITH A LITTLE LESS HYSTERIA.
ONE SUPERMAN IS BAD ENOUGH...

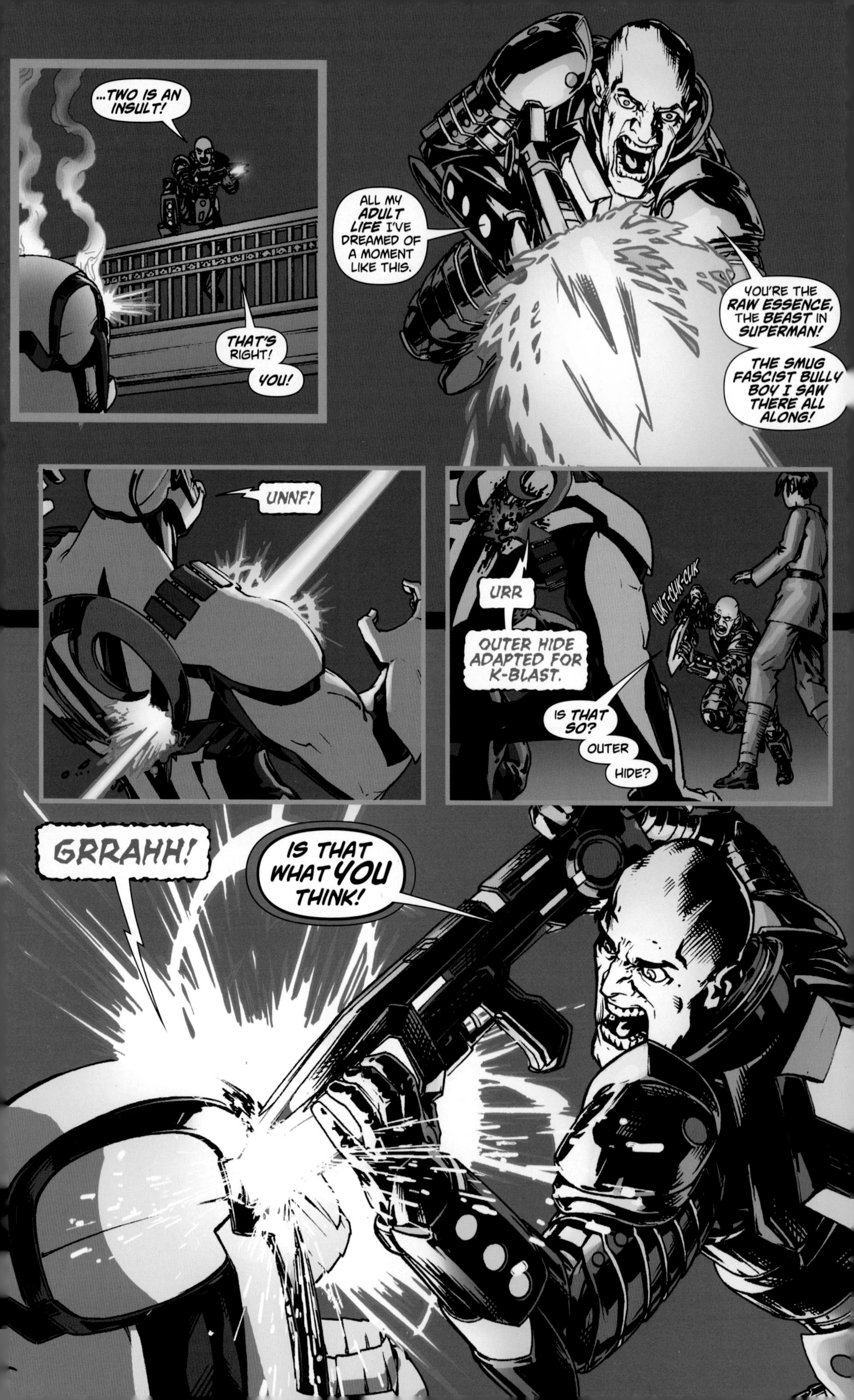

...TWO IS AN INSULT!
THAT'S RIGHT!
YOU!
ALL MY ADULT LIFE I'VE DREAMED OF A MOMENT LIKE THIS.
YOU'RE THE RAW ESSENCE, THE BEAST IN SUPERMAN!
THE SMUG FASCIST BULLY BOY I SAW THERE ALL ALONG!
UNNF!
URR
OUTER HIDE ADAPTED FOR K-BLAST.
CLIKT-CLIK-CLIK
IS THAT SO?
OUTER
HIDE?
GRRAHH!
IS THAT WHAT YOU THINK!

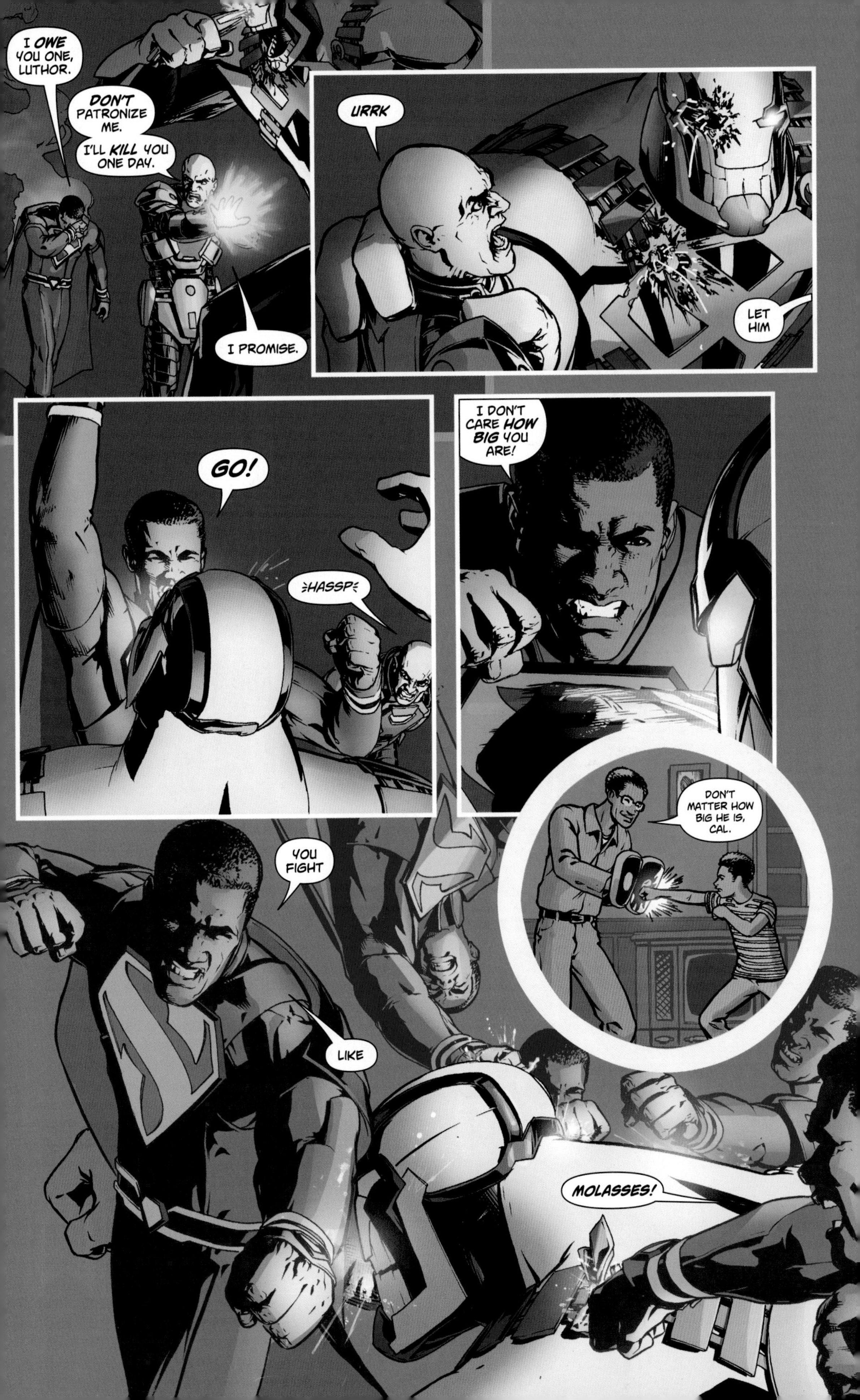
I OWE YOU ONE, LUTHOR.
DON'T PATRONIZE ME.
I'LL KILL YOU ONE DAY.
I PROMISE.
URRK
LET HIM
GO!
HASSP
I DON'T CARE HOW BIG YOU ARE!
DON'T MATTER HOW BIG HE IS, CAL.
YOU FIGHT
LIKE
MOLASSES!

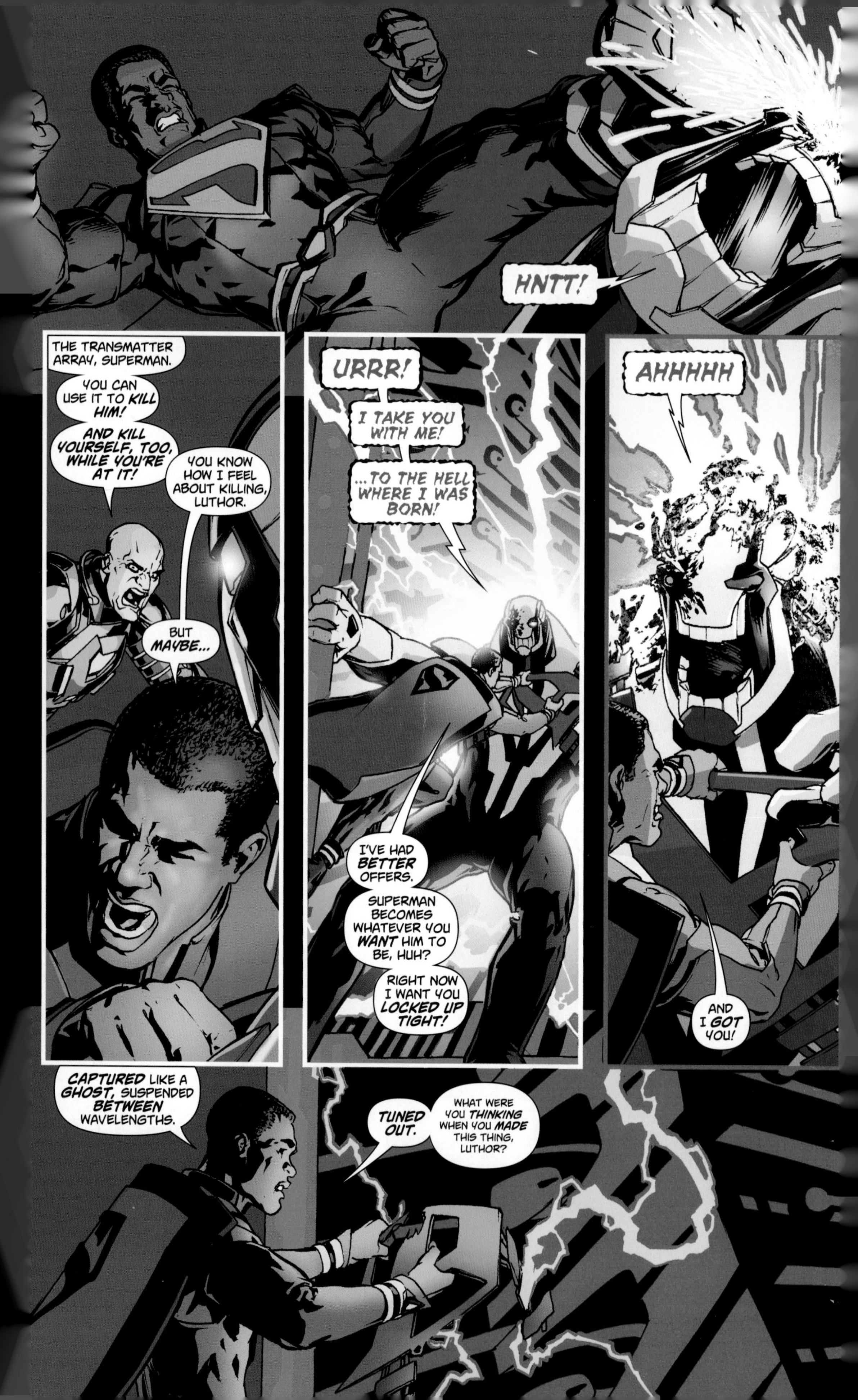
HNTT!
THE TRANSMATTER ARRAY, SUPERMAN.
YOU CAN USE IT TO KILL HIM!
AND KILL YOURSELF, TOO, WHILE YOU'RE AT IT!
YOU KNOW HOW I FEEL ABOUT KILLING, LUTHOR.
BUT MAYBE...
URRR!
I TAKE YOU WITH ME!
...TO THE HELL WHERE I WAS BORN!
I'VE HAD BETTER OFFERS.
SUPERMAN BECOMES WHATEVER YOU WANT HIM TO BE, HUH?
RIGHT NOW I WANT YOU LOCKED UP TIGHT!
AHHHHH
AND I GOT YOU!
CAPTURED LIKE A GHOST, SUSPENDED BETWEEN WAVELENGTHS.
TUNED OUT.
WHAT WERE YOU THINKING WHEN YOU MADE THIS THING, LUTHOR?

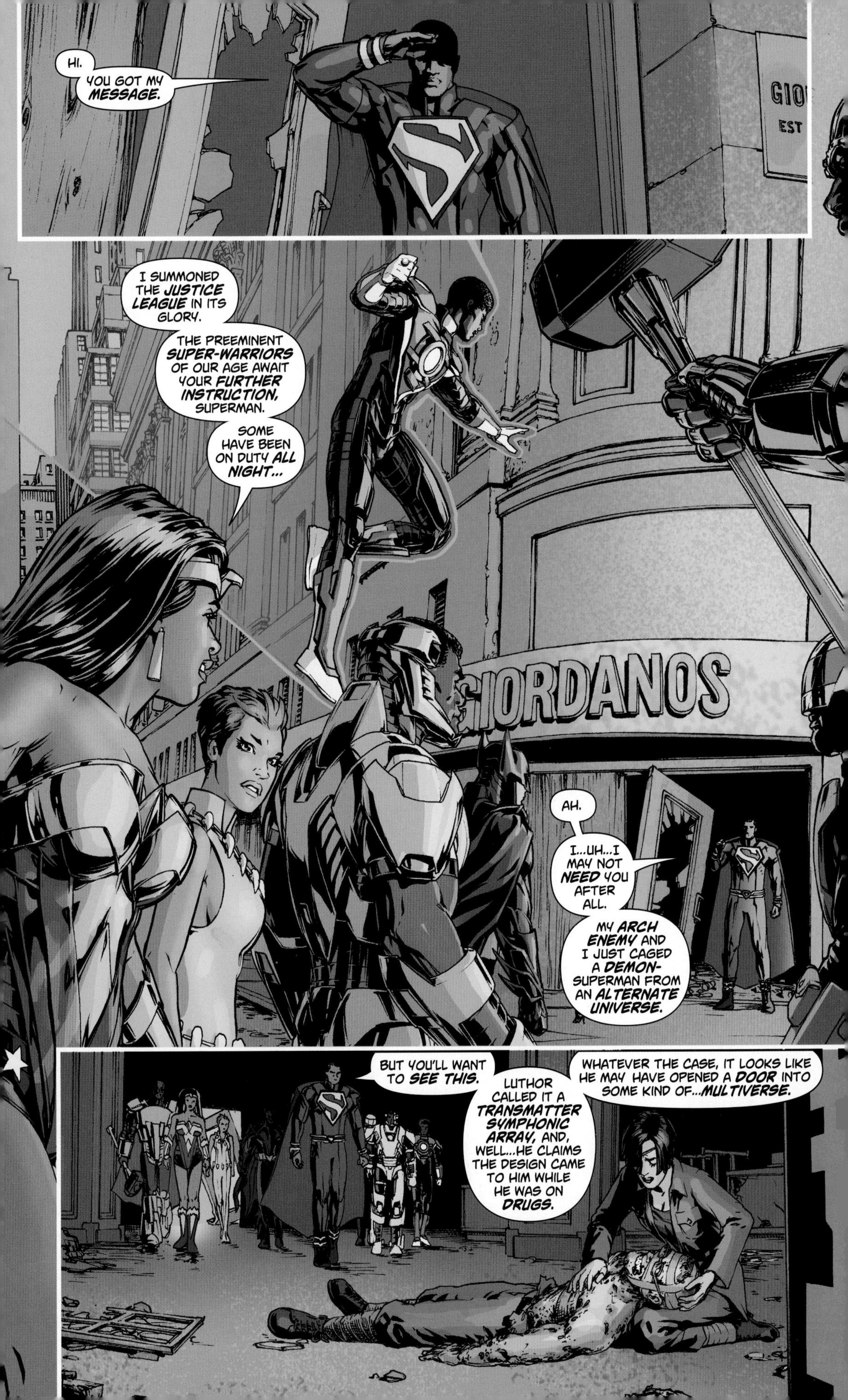
HI.
YOU GOT MY MESSAGE.
I SUMMONED THE JUSTICE LEAGUE IN ITS GLORY.
THE PREEMINENT SUPER-WARRIORS OF OUR AGE AWAIT YOUR FURTHER INSTRUCTION, SUPERMAN.
SOME HAVE BEEN ON DUTY ALL NIGHT...
GIORDANOS
AH.
I...UH...I MAY NOT NEED YOU AFTER ALL.
MY ARCH ENEMY AND I JUST CAGED A DEMON-SUPERMAN FROM AN ALTERNATE UNIVERSE.
BUT YOU'LL WANT TO SEE THIS.
LUTHOR CALLED IT A TRANSMATTER SYMPHONIC ARRAY, AND, WELL...HE CLAIMS THE DESIGN CAME TO HIM WHILE HE WAS ON DRUGS.
WHATEVER THE CASE, IT LOOKS LIKE HE MAY HAVE OPENED A DOOR INTO SOME KIND OF...MULTIVERSE.

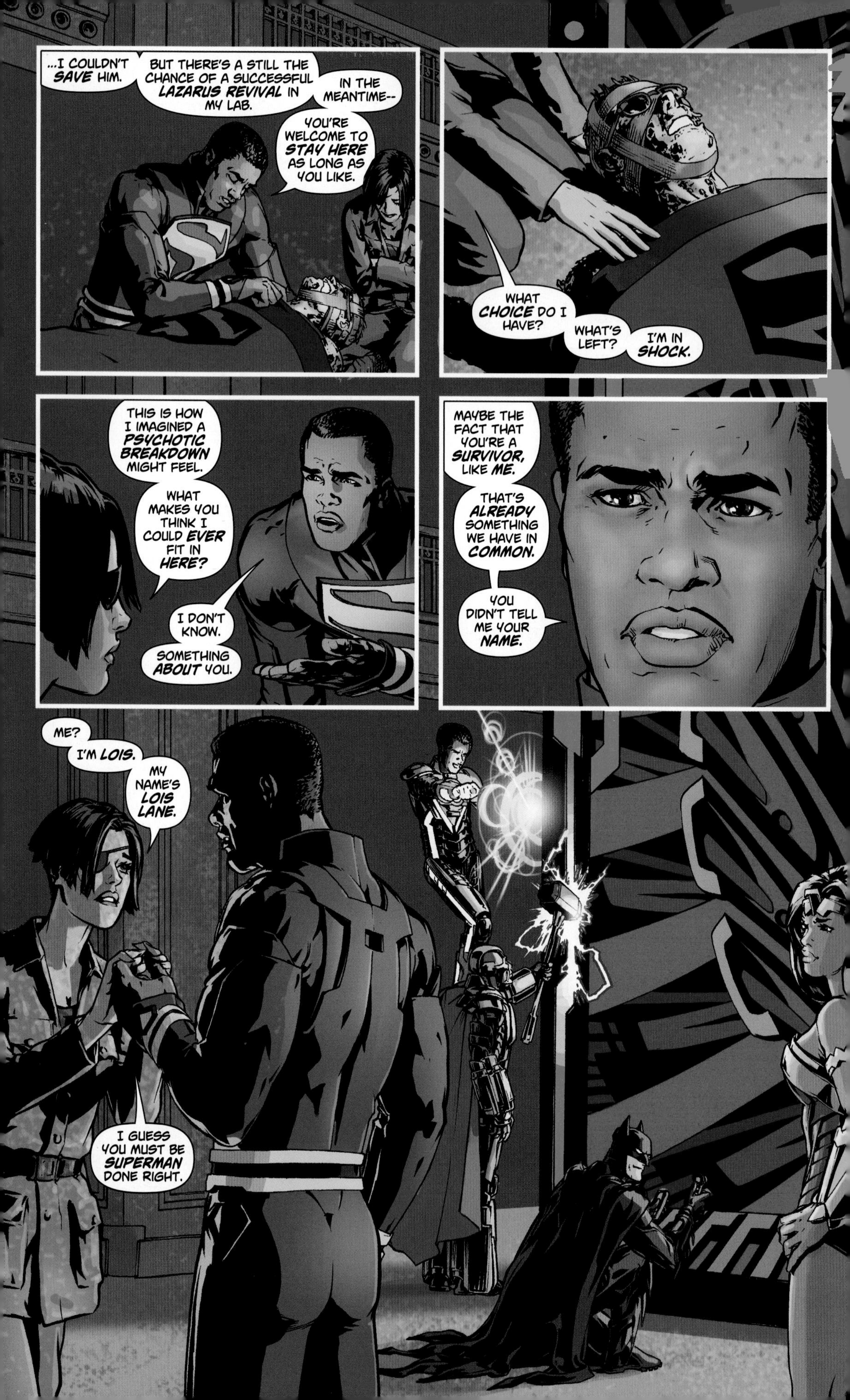
...I COULDN'T SAVE HIM.
BUT THERE'S A STILL THE CHANCE OF A SUCCESSFUL LAZARUS REVIVAL IN MY LAB.
IN THE MEANTIME--
YOU'RE WELCOME TO STAY HERE AS LONG AS YOU LIKE.
WHAT CHOICE DO I HAVE?
WHAT'S LEFT?
I'M IN SHOCK.
THIS IS HOW I IMAGINED A PSYCHOTIC BREAKDOWN MIGHT FEEL.
WHAT MAKES YOU THINK I COULD EVER FIT IN HERE?
I DON'T KNOW.
SOMETHING ABOUT YOU.
MAYBE THE FACT THAT YOU'RE A SURVIVOR, LIKE ME.
THAT'S ALREADY SOMETHING WE HAVE IN COMMON.
YOU DIDN'T TELL ME YOUR NAME.
ME?
I'M LOIS.
MY NAME'S LOIS LANE.
I GUESS YOU MUST BE SUPERMAN DONE RIGHT.

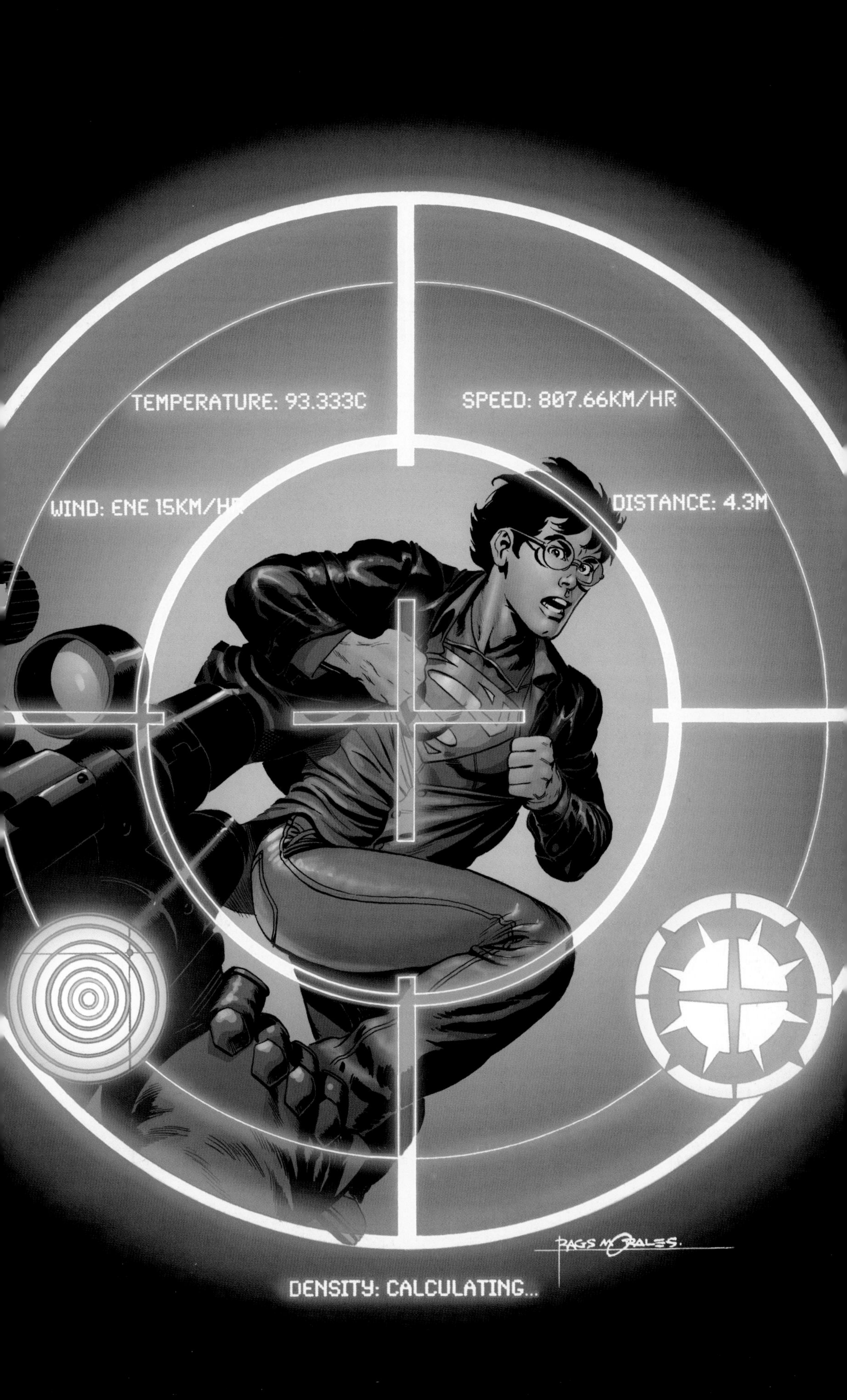
TEMPERATURE: 93.333C
SPEED: 807.66KM/HR
WIND: ENE 15KM/HR
DISTANCE: 4.3M
RAGS MORALES.
DENSITY: CALCULATING...

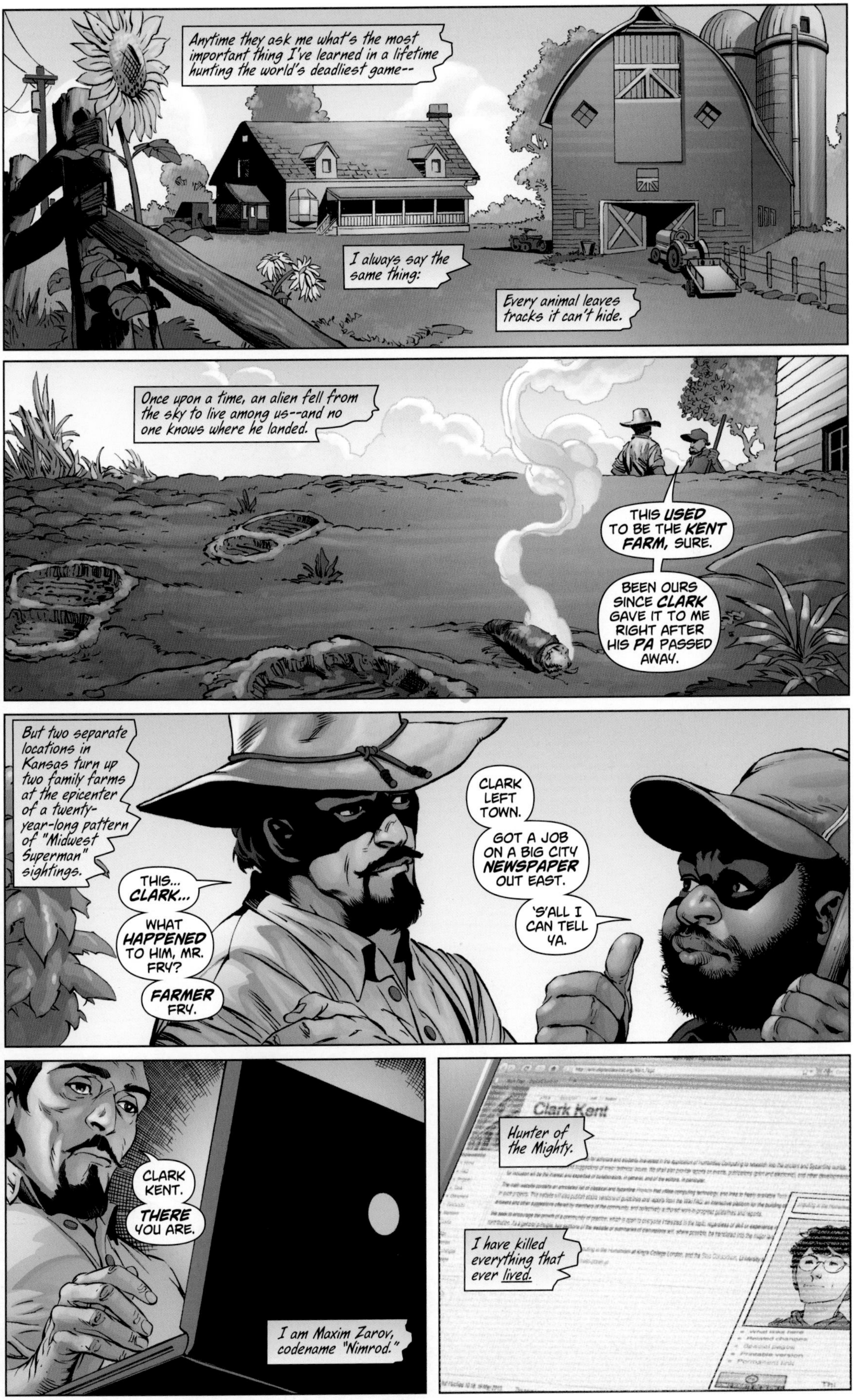
Anytime they ask me what's the most important thing I've learned in a lifetime hunting the world's deadliest game--
I always say the same thing:
Every animal leaves tracks it can't hide.
Once upon a time, an alien fell from the sky to live among us--and no one knows where he landed.
THIS USED TO BE THE KENT FARM, SURE.
BEEN OURS SINCE CLARK GAVE IT TO ME RIGHT AFTER HIS PA PASSED AWAY.
But two separate locations in Kansas turn up two family farms at the epicenter of a twenty-year-long pattern of "Midwest Superman" sightings.
THIS... CLARK...
WHAT HAPPENED TO HIM, MR. FRY?
FARMER FRY.
CLARK LEFT TOWN.
GOT A JOB ON A BIG CITY NEWSPAPER OUT EAST.
'S'ALL I CAN TELL YA.
CLARK KENT.
THERE YOU ARE.
I am Maxim Zarov, codename "Nimrod."
Clark Kent
Hunter of the Mighty.
I have killed everything that ever lived.

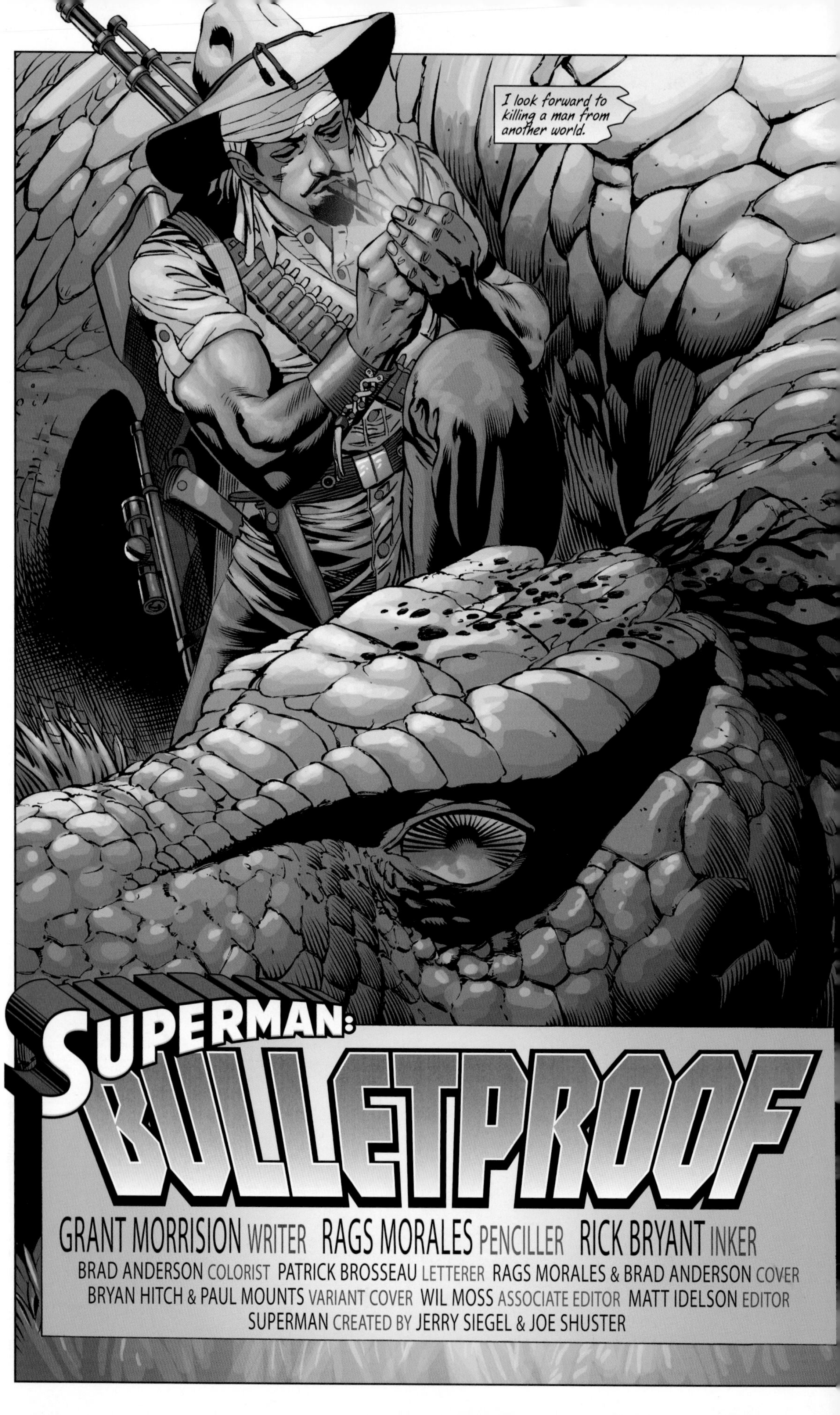

I look forward to killing a man from another world.
SUPERMAN: BULLETPROOF
GRANT MORRISION WRITER RAGS MORALES PENCILLER RICK BRYANT INKER
BRAD ANDERSON COLORIST PATRICK BROSSEAU LETTERER RAGS MORALES & BRAD ANDERSON COVER
BRYAN HITCH & PAUL MOUNTS VARIANT COVER WIL MOSS ASSOCIATE EDITOR MATT IDELSON EDITOR
SUPERMAN CREATED BY JERRY SIEGEL & JOE SHUSTER

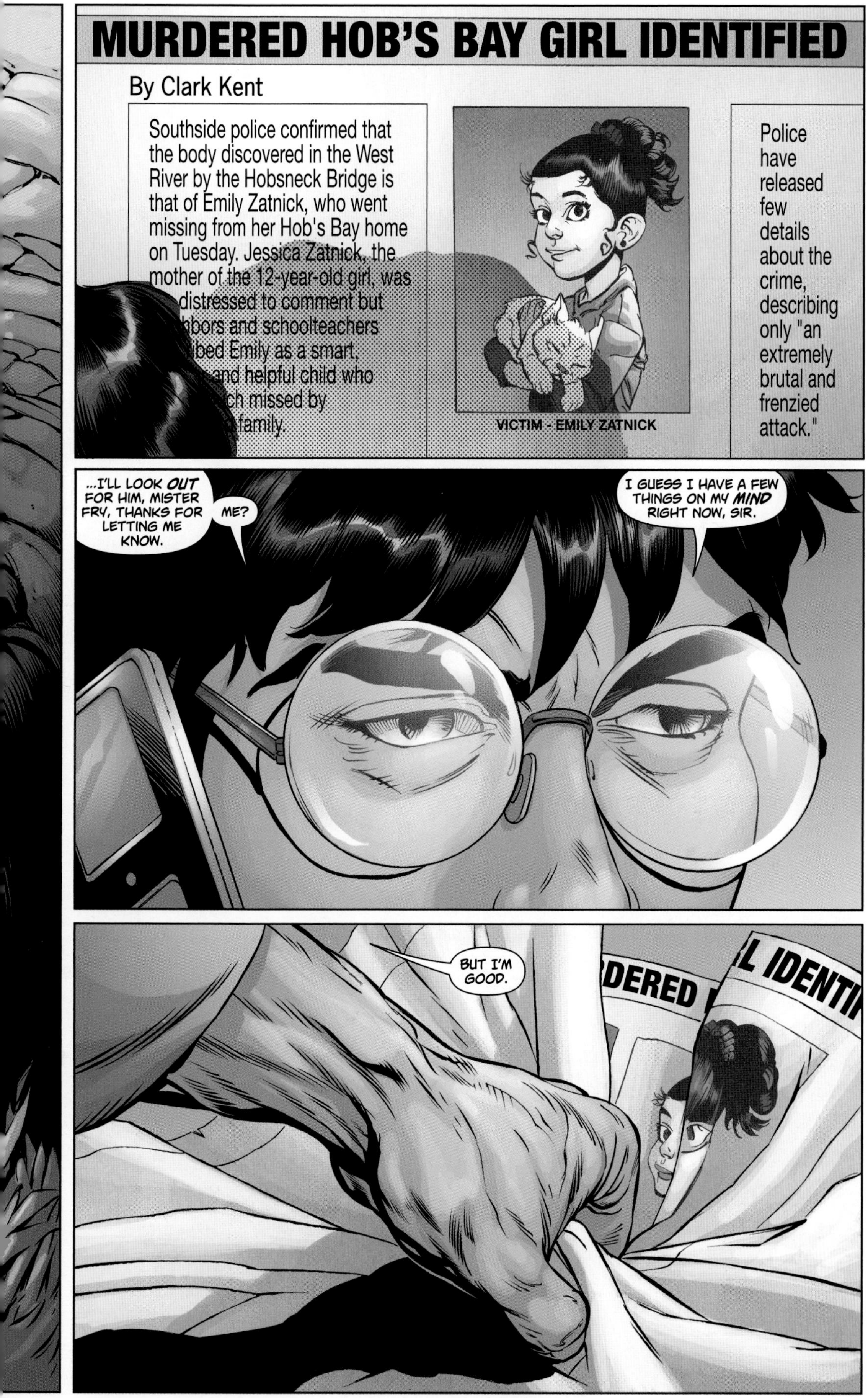
MURDERED HOB'S BAY GIRL IDENTIFIED
By Clark Kent
Southside police confirmed that the body discovered in the West River by the Hobsneck Bridge is that of Emily Zatnick, who went missing from her Hob's Bay home on Tuesday. Jessica Zatnick, the mother of the 12-year-old girl, was
distressed to comment but
bors and schoolteachers
ibed Emily as a smart,
and helpful child who
ch missed by
family.
VICTIM - EMILY ZATNICK
Police have released few details about the crime, describing only "an extremely brutal and frenzied attack."
...I'LL LOOK OUT FOR HIM, MISTER FRY, THANKS FOR LETTING ME KNOW.
ME?
I GUESS I HAVE A FEW THINGS ON MY MIND RIGHT NOW, SIR.
BUT I'M GOOD.
RDERED
L IDENTI

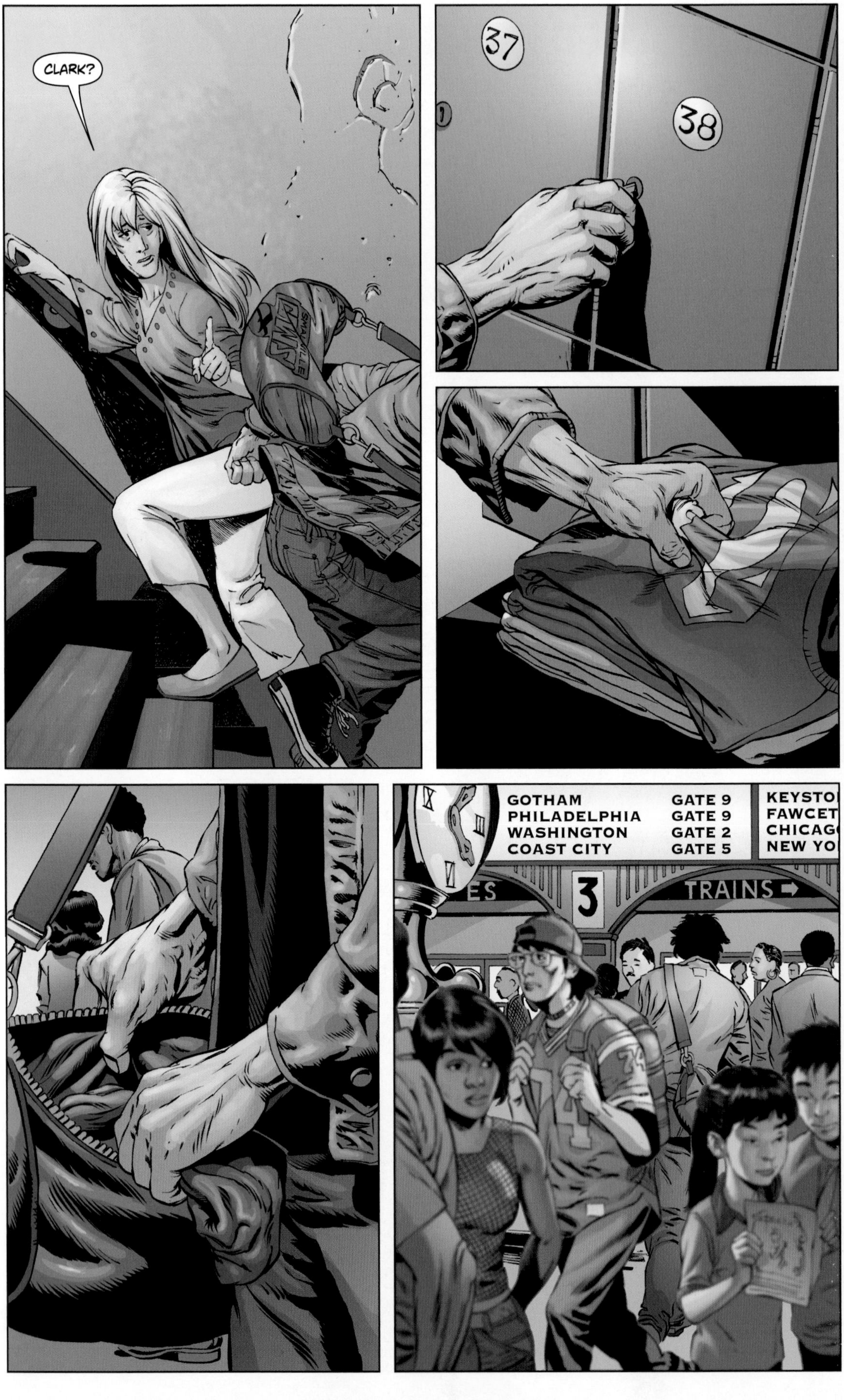
CLARK?
37
38
SMALLVILLE
GOTHAM GATE 9
PHILADELPHIA GATE 9
WASHINGTON GATE 2
COAST CITY GATE 5
3
TRAINS

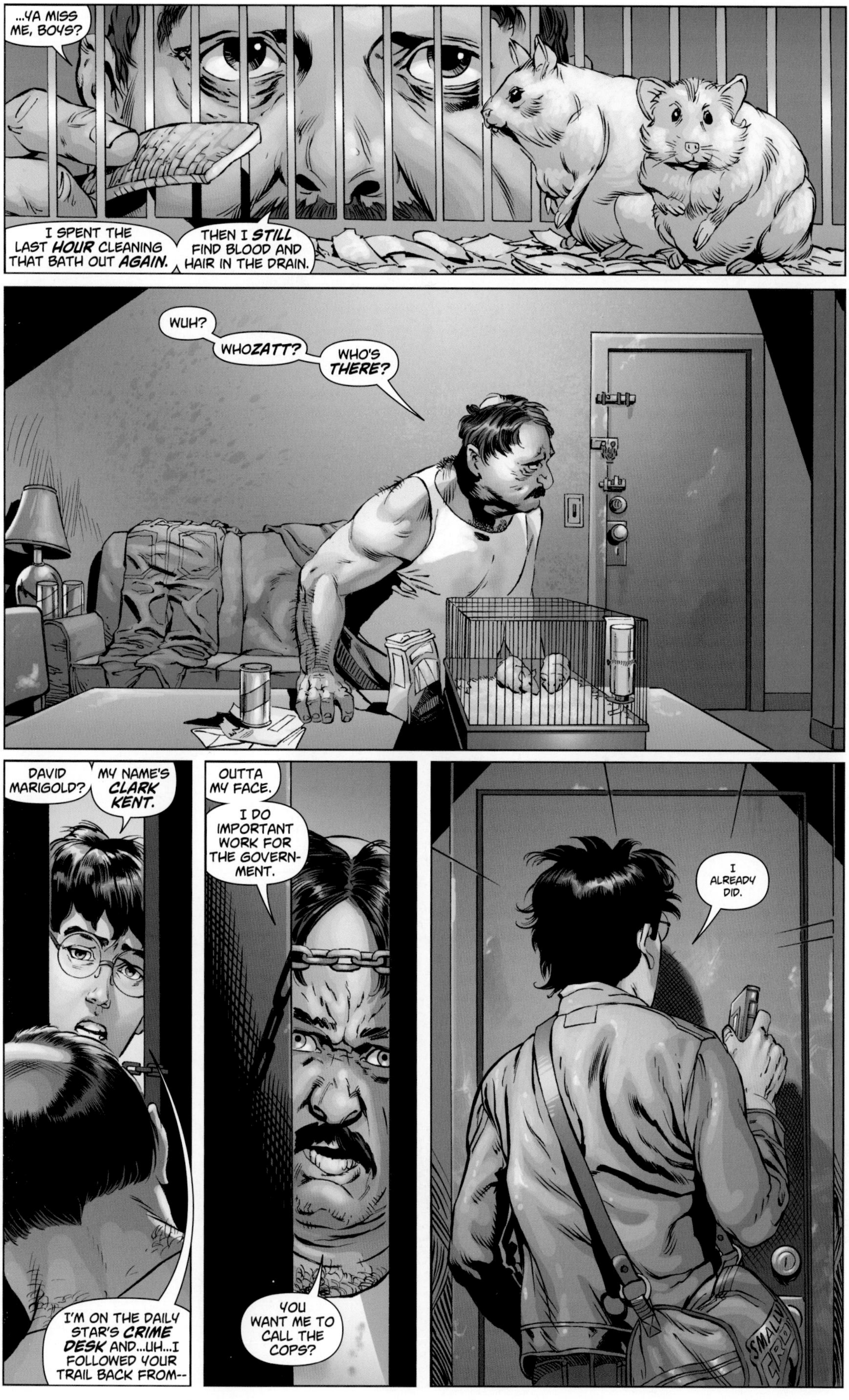
...YA MISS ME, BOYS?
I SPENT THE LAST HOUR CLEANING THAT BATH OUT AGAIN.
THEN I STILL FIND BLOOD AND HAIR IN THE DRAIN.
WUH?
WHOZATT?
WHO'S THERE?
DAVID MARIGOLD?
MY NAME'S CLARK KENT.
I'M ON THE DAILY STAR'S CRIME DESK AND...UH...I FOLLOWED YOUR TRAIL BACK FROM--
OUTTA MY FACE.
I DO IMPORTANT WORK FOR THE GOVERNMENT.
YOU WANT ME TO CALL THE COPS?
I ALREADY DID.

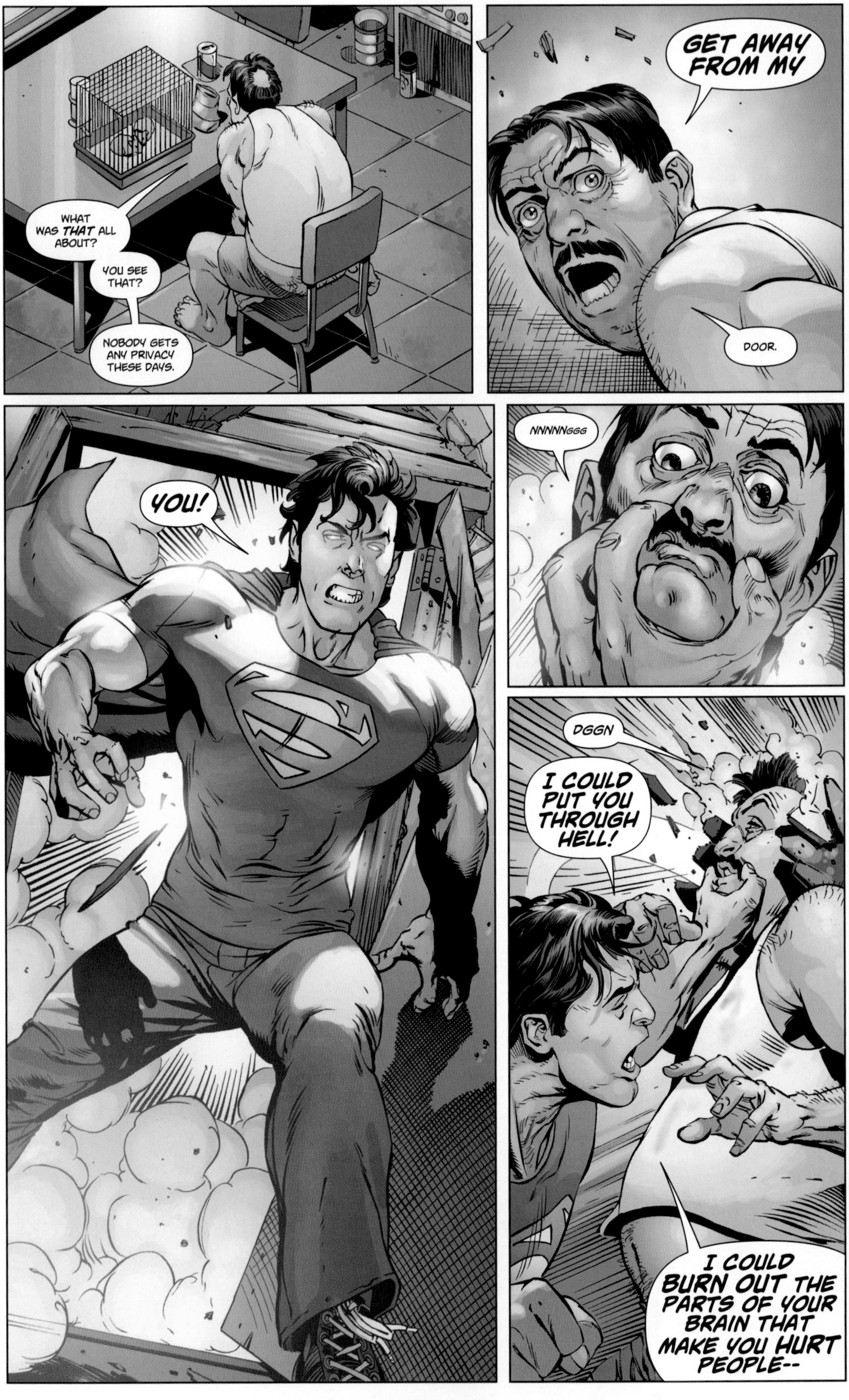
WHAT WAS THAT ALL ABOUT?
YOU SEE THAT?
NOBODY GETS ANY PRIVACY THESE DAYS.
GET AWAY FROM MY
DOOR.
YOU!
NNNNNGGG
DGGN
I COULD PUT YOU THROUGH HELL!
I COULD BURN OUT THE PARTS OF YOUR BRAIN THAT MAKE YOU HURT PEOPLE--

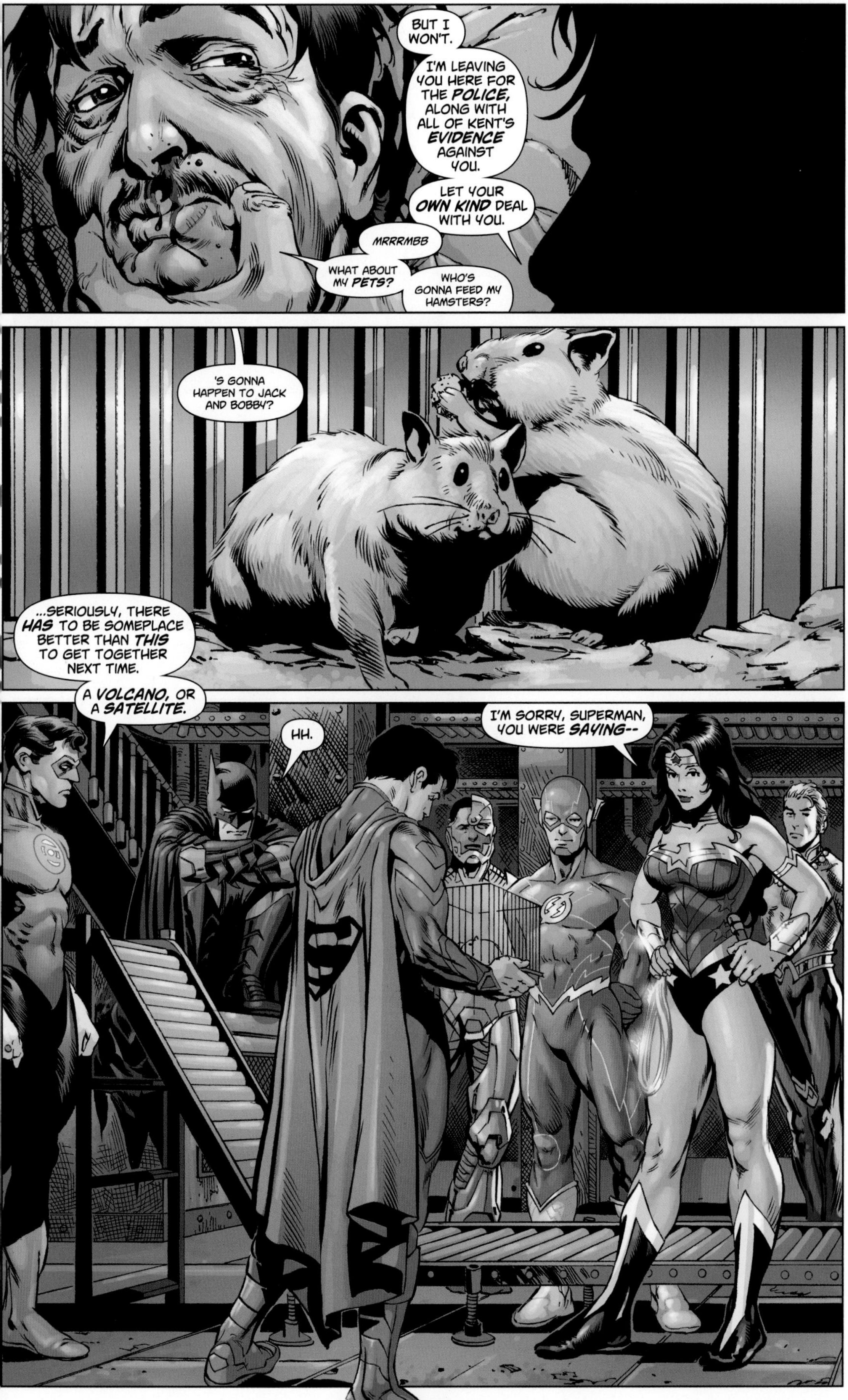
BUT I WON'T.
I'M LEAVING YOU HERE FOR THE POLICE, ALONG WITH ALL OF KENT'S EVIDENCE AGAINST YOU.
LET YOUR OWN KIND DEAL WITH YOU.
MRRRMBB
WHAT ABOUT MY PETS?
WHO'S GONNA FEED MY HAMSTERS?
'S GONNA HAPPEN TO JACK AND BOBBY?
...SERIOUSLY, THERE HAS TO BE SOMEPLACE BETTER THAN THIS TO GET TOGETHER NEXT TIME.
A VOLCANO, OR A SATELLITE.
HH.
I'M SORRY, SUPERMAN, YOU WERE SAYING--

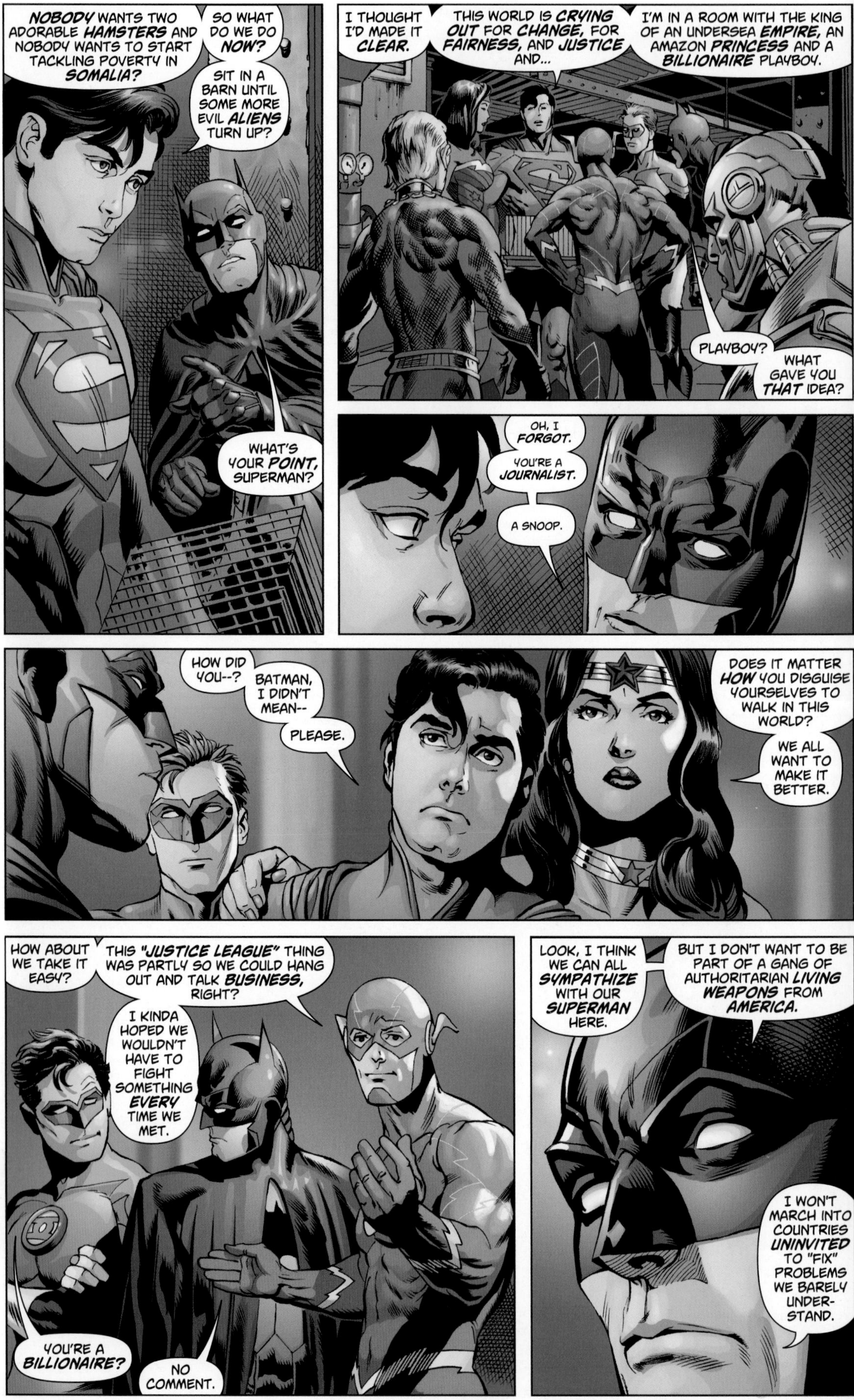
NOBODY WANTS TWO ADORABLE HAMSTERS AND NOBODY WANTS TO START TACKLING POVERTY IN SOMALIA?
SO WHAT DO WE DO NOW?
SIT IN A BARN UNTIL SOME MORE EVIL ALIENS TURN UP?
WHAT'S YOUR POINT, SUPERMAN?
I THOUGHT I'D MADE IT CLEAR.
THIS WORLD IS CRYING OUT FOR CHANGE, FOR FAIRNESS, AND JUSTICE AND...
I'M IN A ROOM WITH THE KING OF AN UNDERSEA EMPIRE, AN AMAZON PRINCESS AND A BILLIONAIRE PLAYBOY.
PLAYBOY?
WHAT GAVE YOU THAT IDEA?
OH, I FORGOT.
YOU'RE A JOURNALIST.
A SNOOP.
HOW DID YOU--?
BATMAN, I DIDN'T MEAN--
PLEASE.
DOES IT MATTER HOW YOU DISGUISE YOURSELVES TO WALK IN THIS WORLD?
WE ALL WANT TO MAKE IT BETTER.
HOW ABOUT WE TAKE IT EASY?
THIS "JUSTICE LEAGUE" THING WAS PARTLY SO WE COULD HANG OUT AND TALK BUSINESS, RIGHT?
I KINDA HOPED WE WOULDN'T HAVE TO FIGHT SOMETHING EVERY TIME WE MET.
YOU'RE A BILLIONAIRE?
NO COMMENT.
LOOK, I THINK WE CAN ALL SYMPATHIZE WITH OUR SUPERMAN HERE.
BUT I DON'T WANT TO BE PART OF A GANG OF AUTHORITARIAN LIVING WEAPONS FROM AMERICA.
I WON'T MARCH INTO COUNTRIES UNINVITED TO "FIX" PROBLEMS WE BARELY UNDER-STAND.

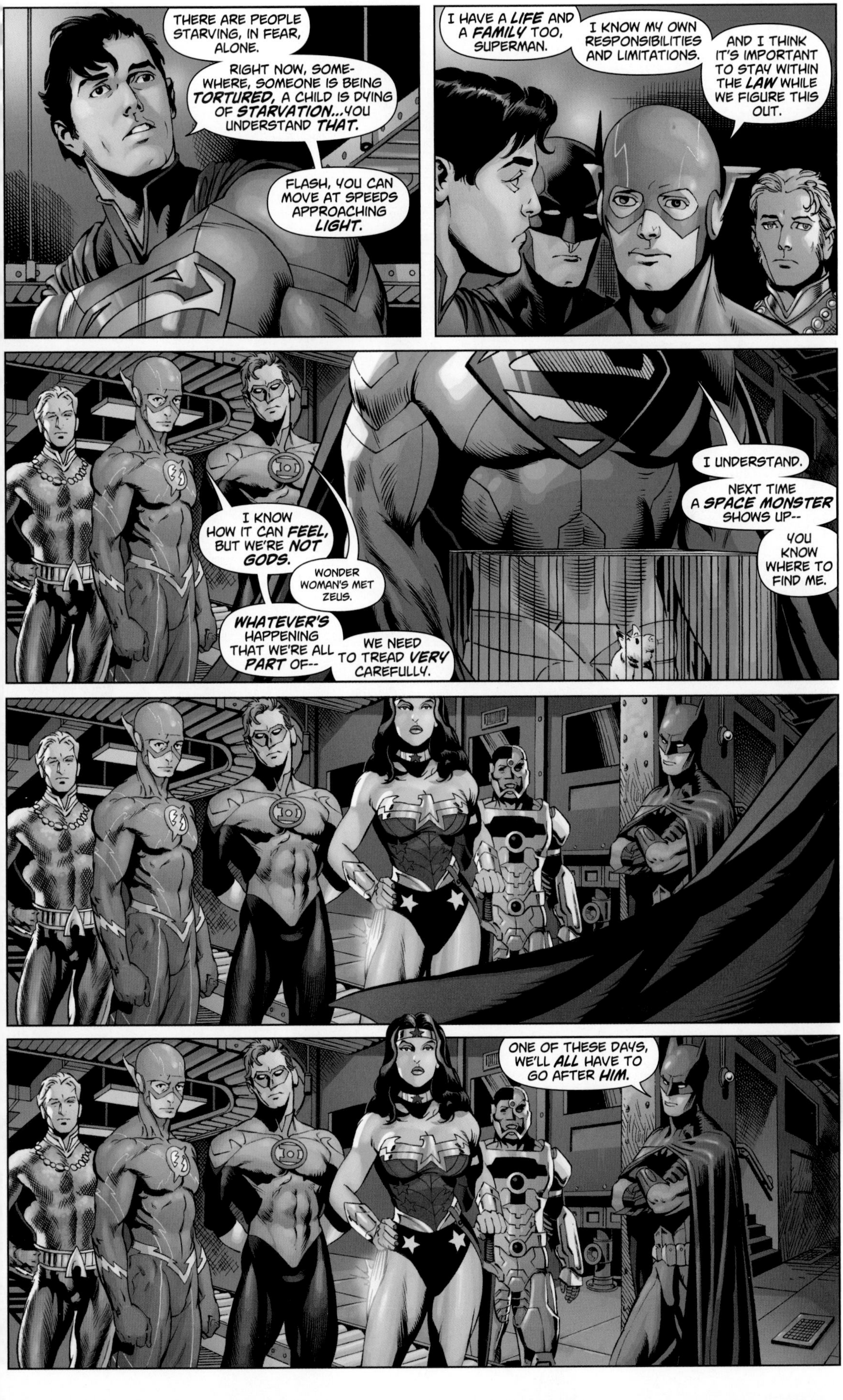
THERE ARE PEOPLE STARVING, IN FEAR, ALONE.
RIGHT NOW, SOMEWHERE, SOMEONE IS BEING TORTURED, A CHILD IS DYING OF STARVATION...YOU UNDERSTAND THAT.
FLASH, YOU CAN MOVE AT SPEEDS APPROACHING LIGHT.
I HAVE A LIFE AND A FAMILY TOO, SUPERMAN.
I KNOW MY OWN RESPONSIBILITIES AND LIMITATIONS.
AND I THINK IT'S IMPORTANT TO STAY WITHIN THE LAW WHILE WE FIGURE THIS OUT.
I KNOW HOW IT CAN FEEL, BUT WE'RE NOT GODS.
WONDER WOMAN'S MET ZEUS.
WHATEVER'S HAPPENING THAT WE'RE ALL PART OF--
WE NEED TO TREAD VERY CAREFULLY.
I UNDERSTAND.
NEXT TIME A SPACE MONSTER SHOWS UP--
YOU KNOW WHERE TO FIND ME.
ONE OF THESE DAYS, WE'LL ALL HAVE TO GO AFTER HIM.

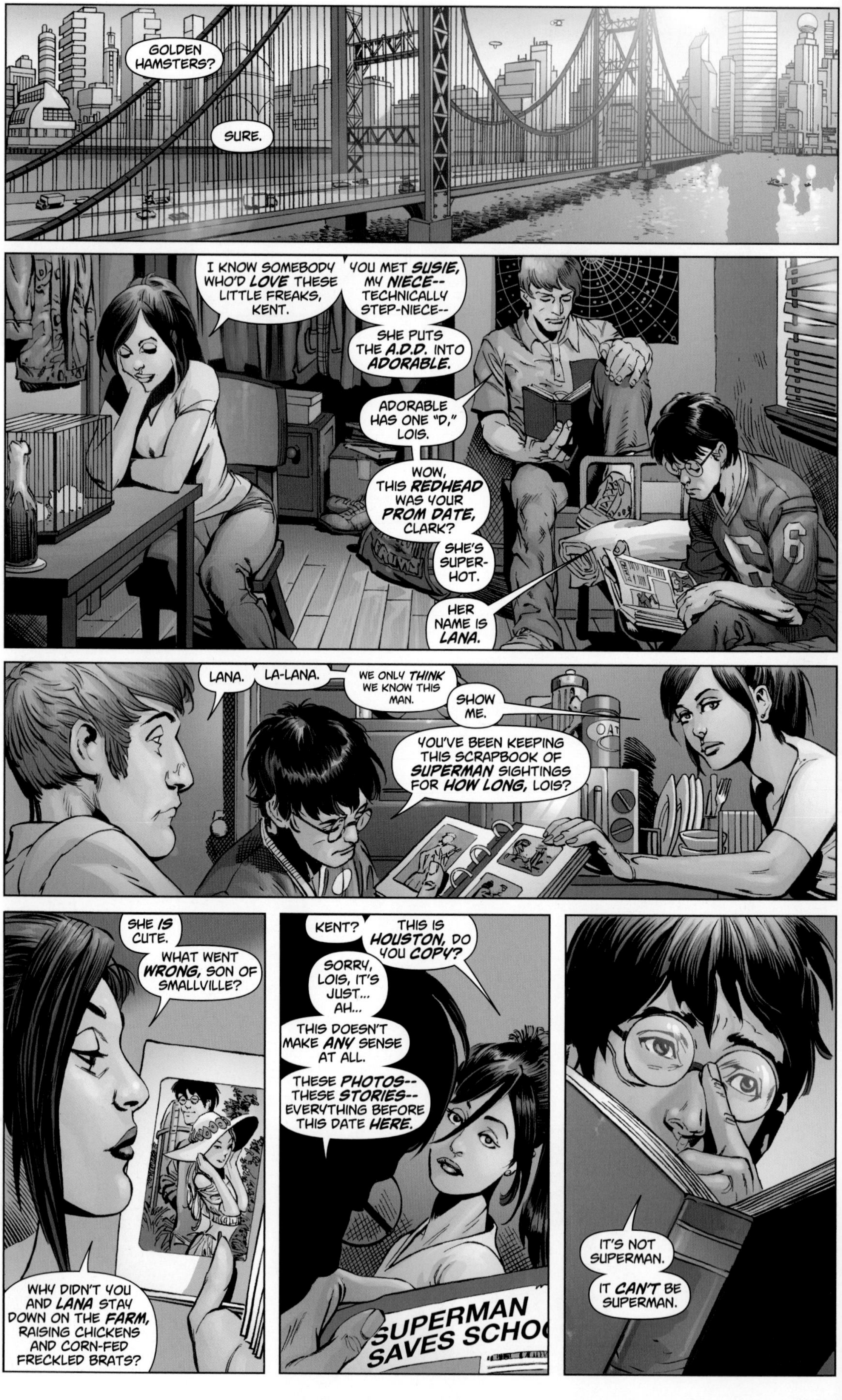
GOLDEN HAMSTERS?
SURE.
I KNOW SOMEBODY WHO'D LOVE THESE LITTLE FREAKS, KENT.
YOU MET SUSIE, MY NIECE-- TECHNICALLY STEP-NIECE--
SHE PUTS THE A.D.D. INTO ADORABLE.
ADORABLE HAS ONE "D," LOIS.
WOW, THIS REDHEAD WAS YOUR PROM DATE, CLARK?
SHE'S SUPER-HOT.
HER NAME IS LANA.
LANA.
LA-LANA.
WE ONLY THINK WE KNOW THIS MAN.
SHOW ME.
YOU'VE BEEN KEEPING THIS SCRAPBOOK OF SUPERMAN SIGHTINGS FOR HOW LONG, LOIS?
SHE IS CUTE.
WHAT WENT WRONG, SON OF SMALLVILLE?
WHY DIDN'T YOU AND LANA STAY DOWN ON THE FARM, RAISING CHICKENS AND CORN-FED FRECKLED BRATS?
KENT?
THIS IS HOUSTON, DO YOU COPY?
SORRY, LOIS, IT'S JUST... AH...
THIS DOESN'T MAKE ANY SENSE AT ALL.
THESE PHOTOS-- THESE STORIES-- EVERYTHING BEFORE THIS DATE HERE.
SUPERMAN SAVES SCHO
IT'S NOT SUPERMAN.
IT CAN'T BE SUPERMAN.

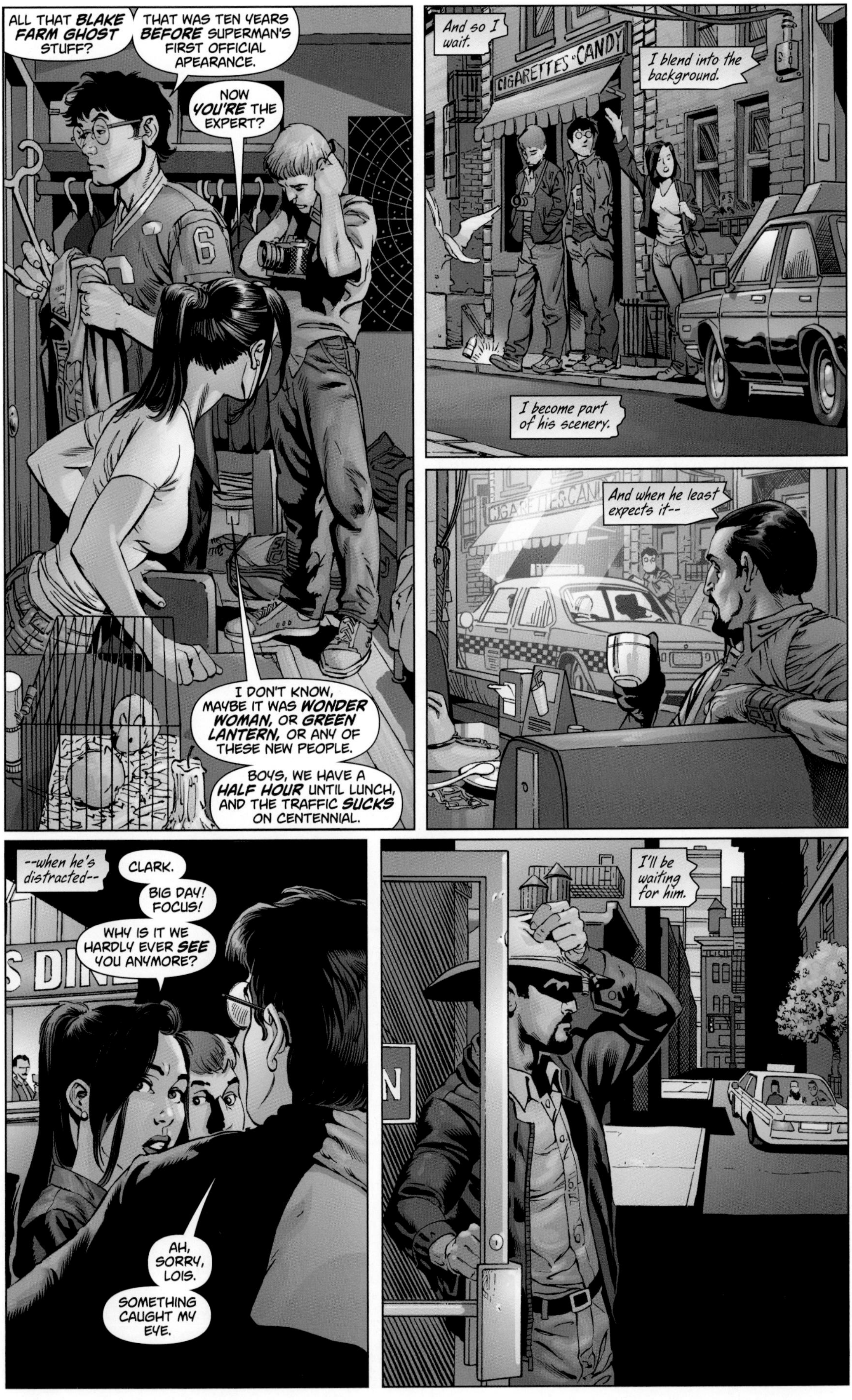
ALL THAT BLAKE FARM GHOST STUFF?
THAT WAS TEN YEARS BEFORE SUPERMAN'S FIRST OFFICIAL APEARANCE.
NOW YOU'RE THE EXPERT?
I DON'T KNOW, MAYBE IT WAS WONDER WOMAN, OR GREEN LANTERN, OR ANY OF THESE NEW PEOPLE.
BOYS, WE HAVE A HALF HOUR UNTIL LUNCH, AND THE TRAFFIC SUCKS ON CENTENNIAL.
And so I wait.
CIGARETTES CANDY
I blend into the background.
I become part of his scenery.
And when he least expects it--
--when he's distracted--
CLARK.
BIG DAY! FOCUS!
WHY IS IT WE HARDLY EVER SEE YOU ANYMORE?
AH, SORRY, LOIS.
SOMETHING CAUGHT MY EYE.
I'll be waiting for him.

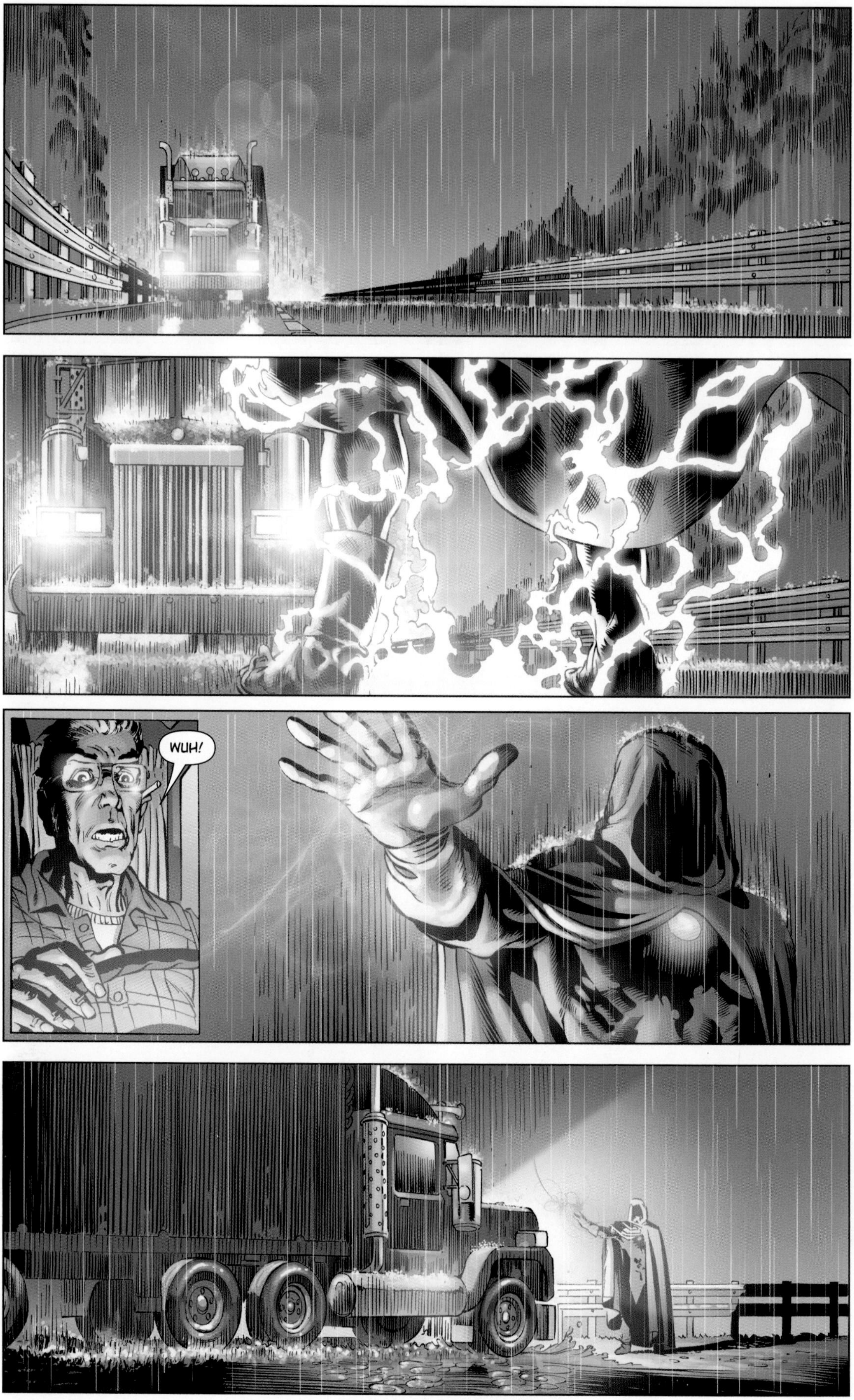
WUH!

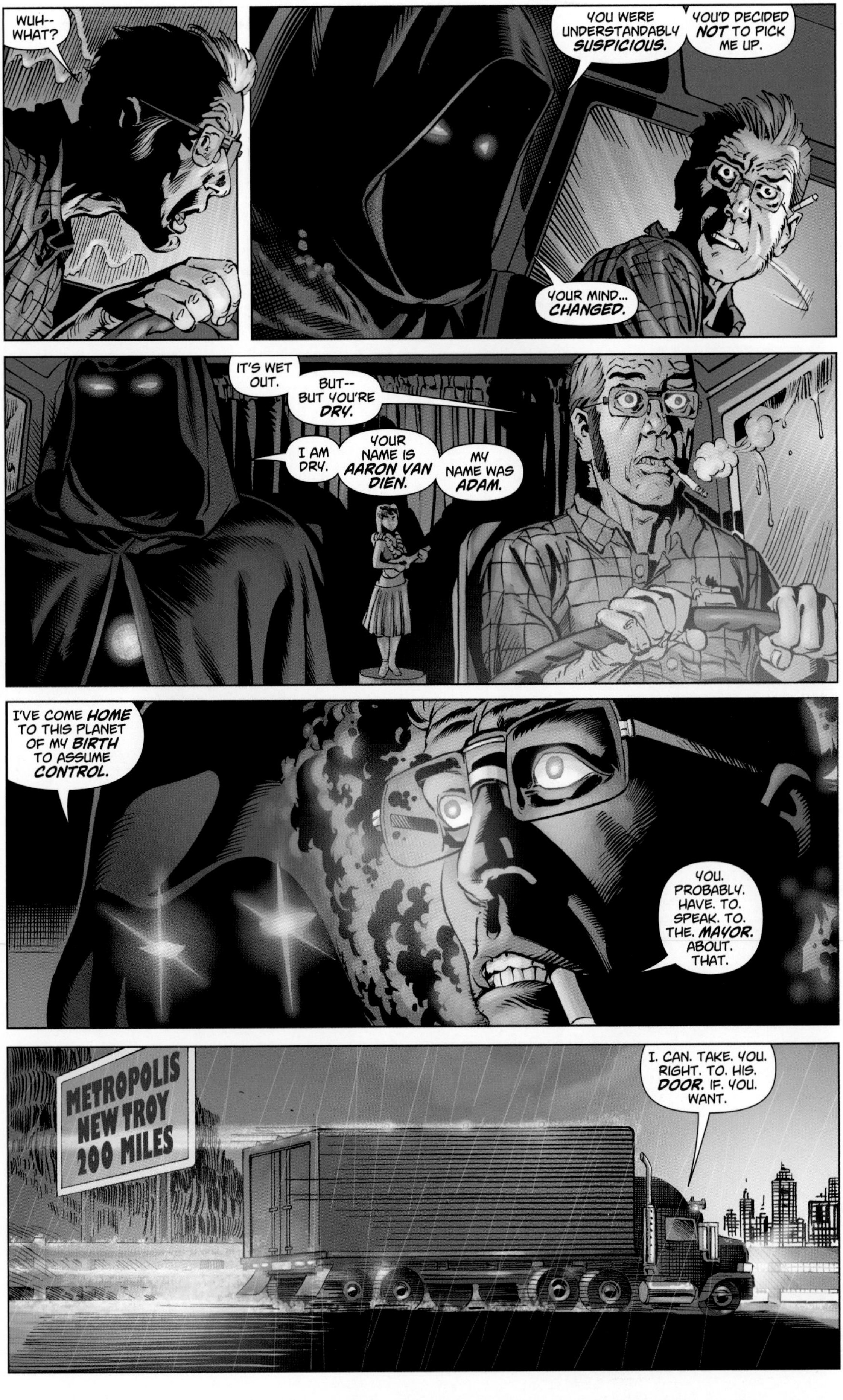
WUH--
WHAT?
YOU WERE UNDERSTANDABLY **SUSPICIOUS.**
YOU'D DECIDED **NOT** TO PICK ME UP.
YOUR MIND... **CHANGED.**
IT'S WET OUT.
BUT-- BUT YOU'RE **DRY.**
I AM DRY.
YOUR NAME IS **AARON VAN DIEN.**
MY NAME WAS **ADAM.**
I'VE COME **HOME** TO THIS PLANET OF MY **BIRTH** TO ASSUME **CONTROL.**
YOU. PROBABLY. HAVE. TO. SPEAK. TO. THE. **MAYOR.** ABOUT. THAT.
METROPOLIS NEW TROY 200 MILES
I. CAN. TAKE. YOU. RIGHT. TO. HIS. **DOOR.** IF. YOU. WANT.

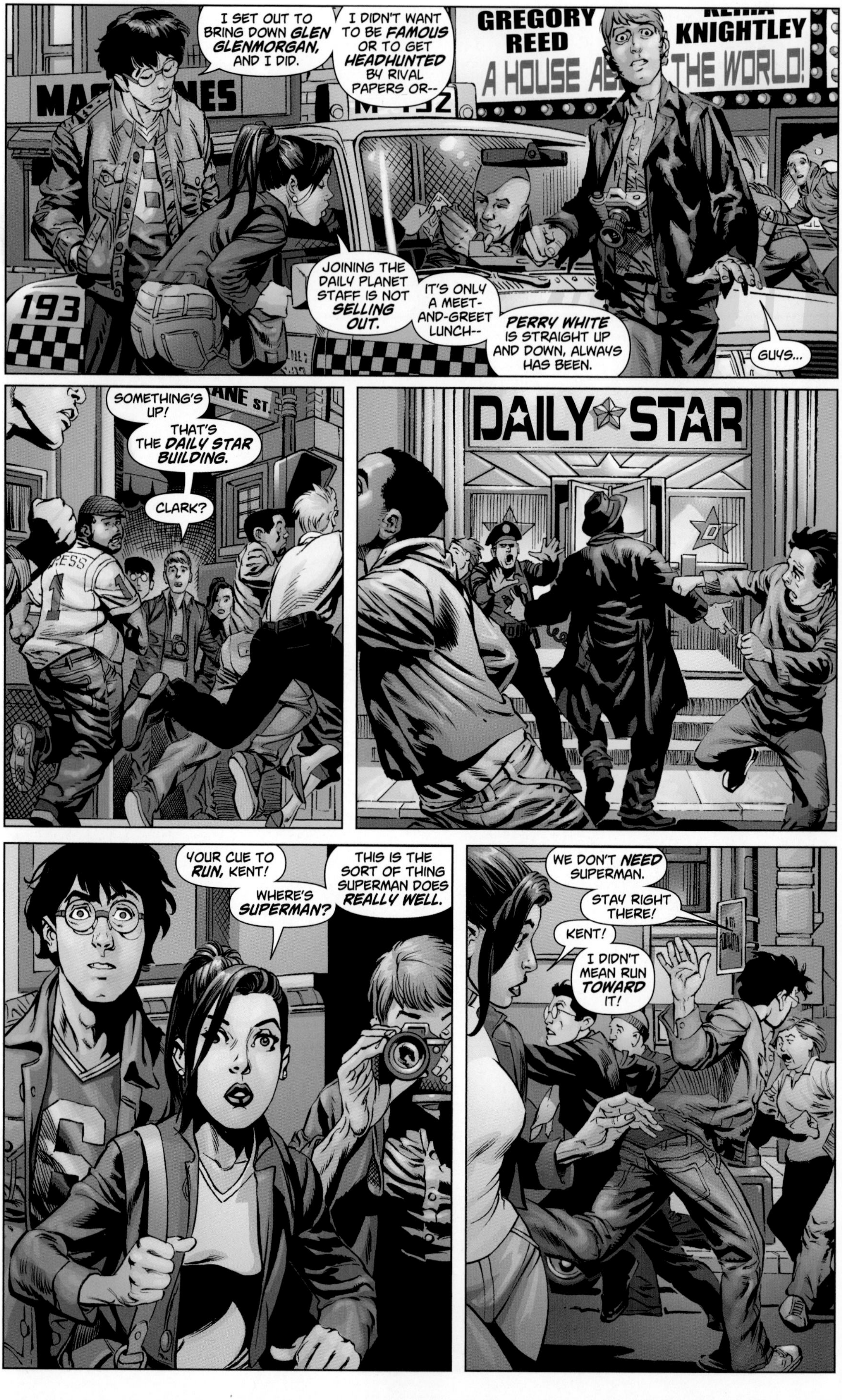

MAGAZINES
I SET OUT TO BRING DOWN GLEN GLENMORGAN, AND I DID.
I DIDN'T WANT TO BE FAMOUS OR TO GET HEADHUNTED BY RIVAL PAPERS OR--
GREGORY REED
KNIGHTLEY
A HOUSE AB
THE WORLD!
193
JOINING THE DAILY PLANET STAFF IS NOT SELLING OUT.
IT'S ONLY A MEET-AND-GREET LUNCH--
PERRY WHITE IS STRAIGHT UP AND DOWN, ALWAYS HAS BEEN.
GUYS...
SOMETHING'S UP!
THAT'S THE DAILY STAR BUILDING.
CLARK?
DAILY STAR
YOUR CUE TO RUN, KENT!
WHERE'S SUPERMAN?
THIS IS THE SORT OF THING SUPERMAN DOES REALLY WELL.
WE DON'T NEED SUPERMAN.
STAY RIGHT THERE!
KENT!
I DIDN'T MEAN RUN TOWARD IT!

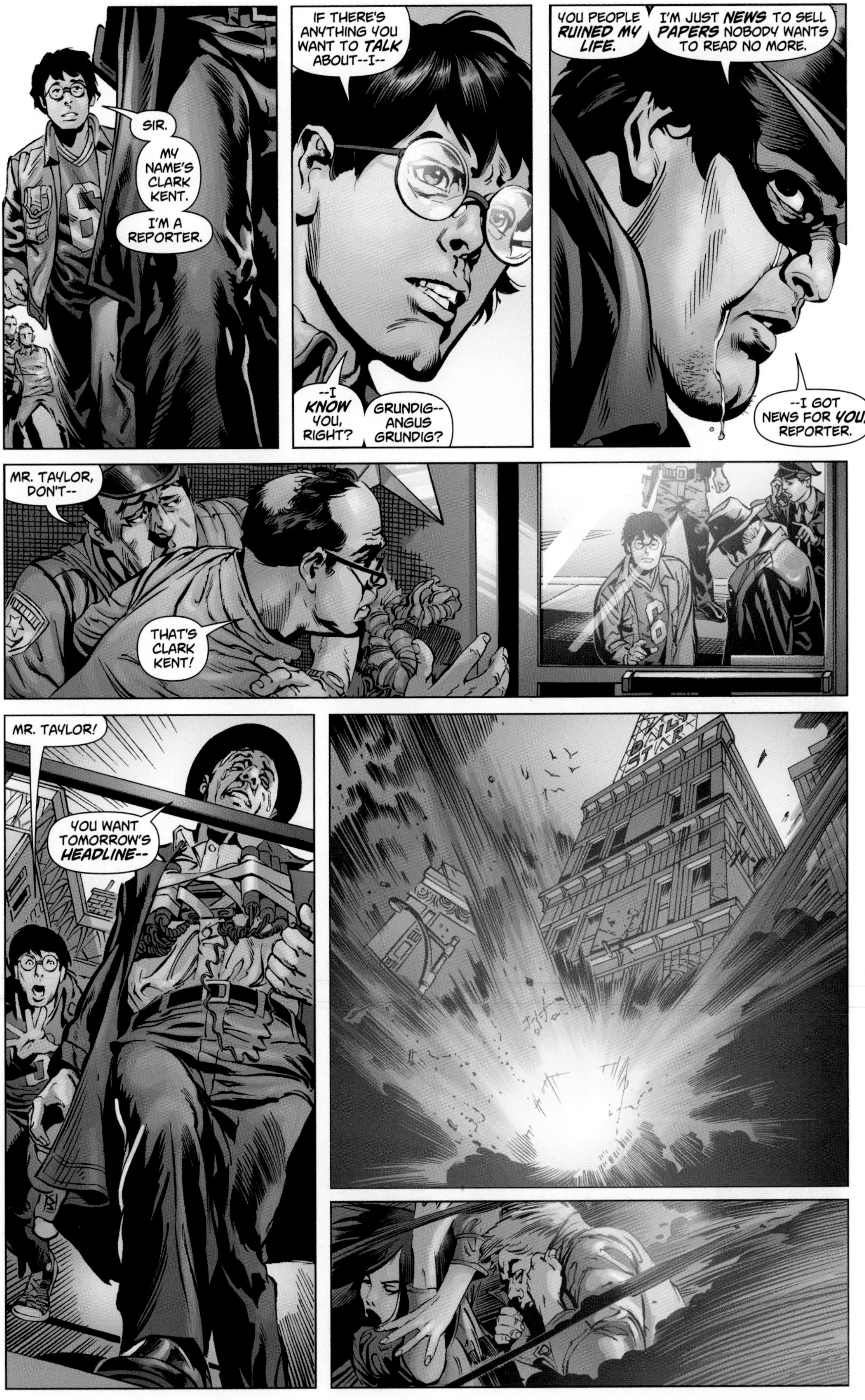
SIR.
MY NAME'S CLARK KENT.
I'M A REPORTER.
IF THERE'S ANYTHING YOU WANT TO TALK ABOUT--I--
--I KNOW YOU, RIGHT?
GRUNDIG--ANGUS GRUNDIG?
YOU PEOPLE RUINED MY LIFE.
I'M JUST NEWS TO SELL PAPERS NOBODY WANTS TO READ NO MORE.
--I GOT NEWS FOR YOU, REPORTER.
MR. TAYLOR, DON'T--
THAT'S CLARK KENT!
MR. TAYLOR!
YOU WANT TOMORROW'S HEADLINE--

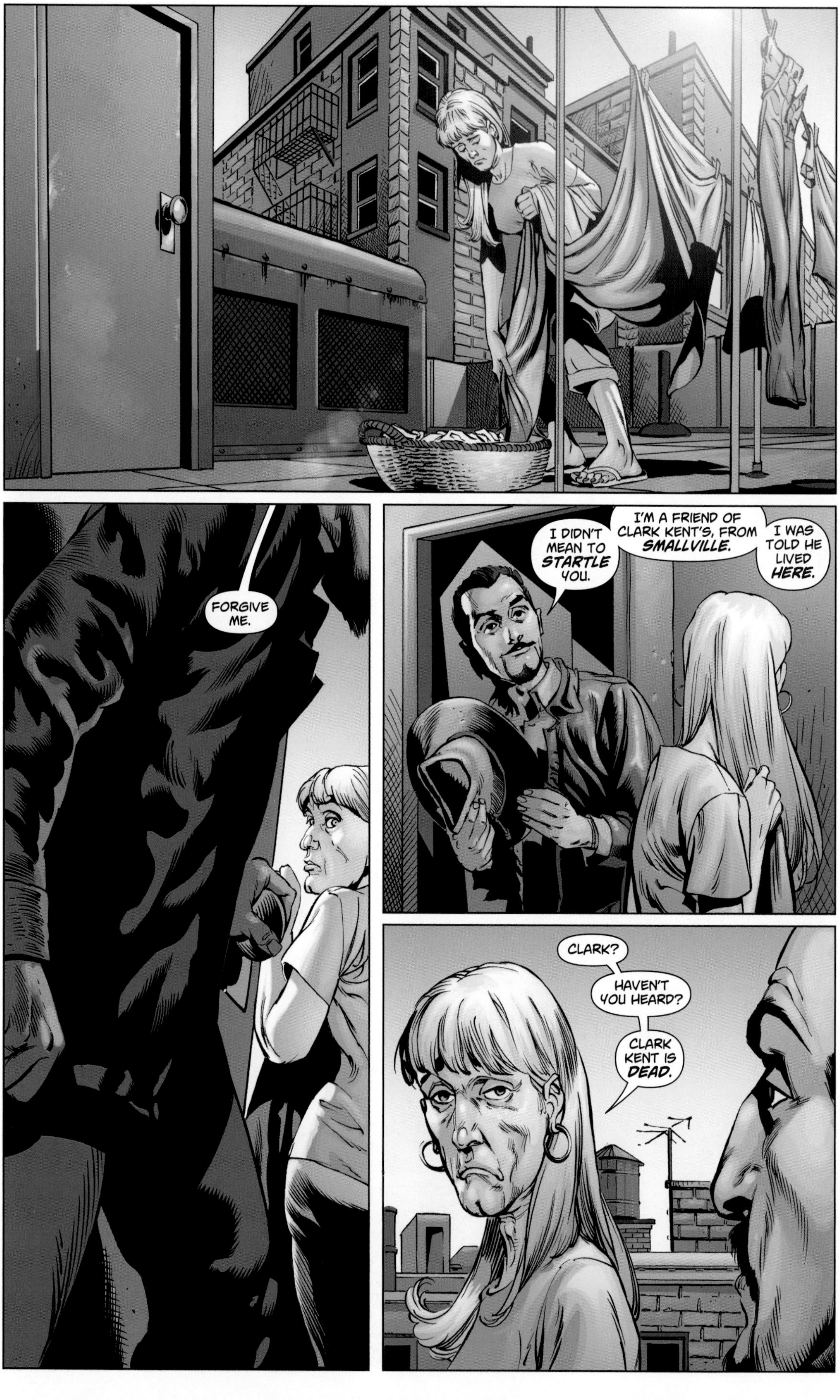
FORGIVE ME.
I DIDN'T MEAN TO STARTLE YOU.
I'M A FRIEND OF CLARK KENT'S, FROM SMALLVILLE.
I WAS TOLD HE LIVED HERE.
CLARK?
HAVEN'T YOU HEARD?
CLARK KENT IS DEAD.

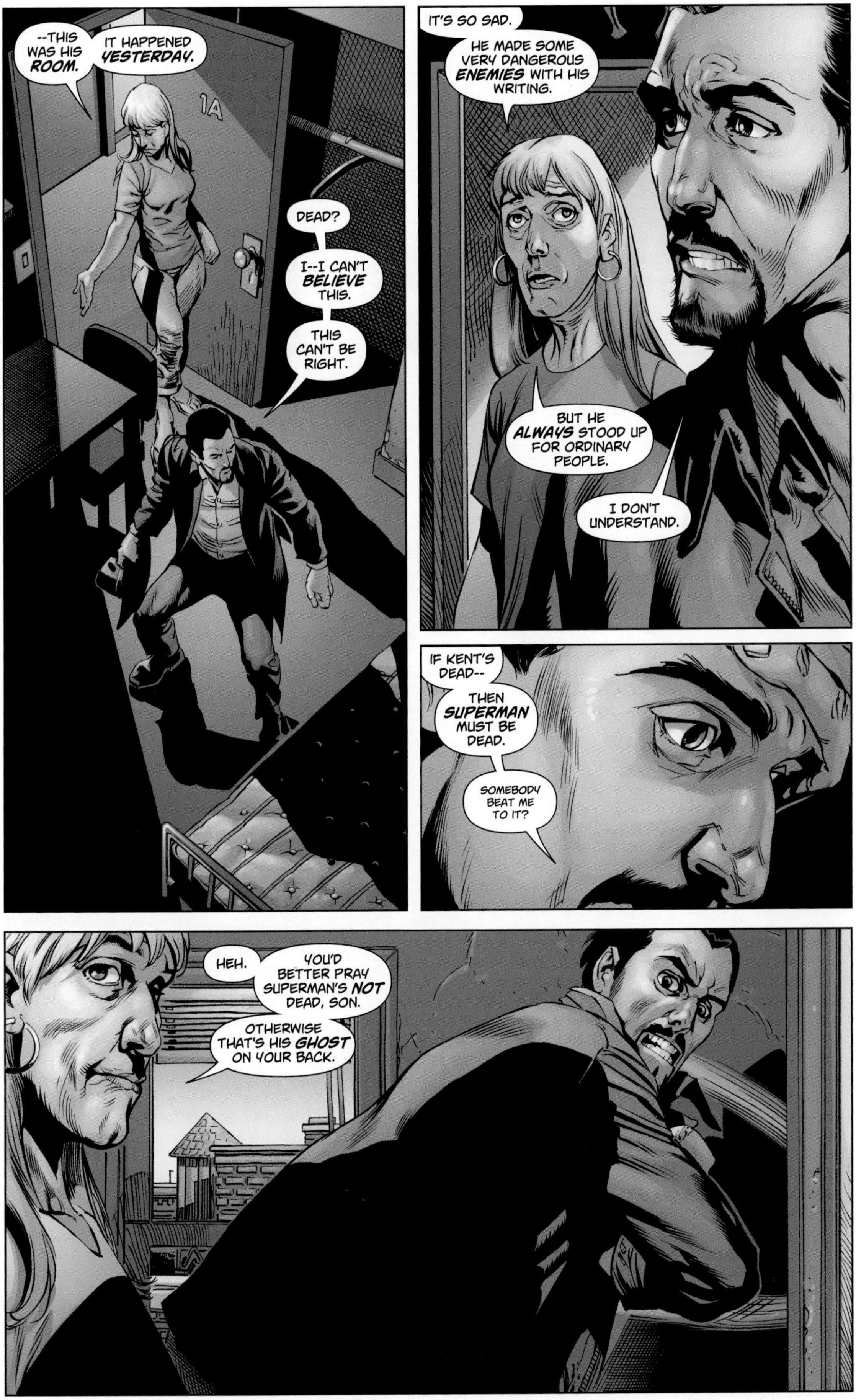
--THIS WAS HIS ROOM.
IT HAPPENED YESTERDAY.
DEAD?
I--I CAN'T BELIEVE THIS.
THIS CAN'T BE RIGHT.
IT'S SO SAD.
HE MADE SOME VERY DANGEROUS ENEMIES WITH HIS WRITING.
BUT HE ALWAYS STOOD UP FOR ORDINARY PEOPLE.
I DON'T UNDERSTAND.
IF KENT'S DEAD--
THEN SUPERMAN MUST BE DEAD.
SOMEBODY BEAT ME TO IT?
HEH.
YOU'D BETTER PRAY SUPERMAN'S NOT DEAD, SON.
OTHERWISE THAT'S HIS GHOST ON YOUR BACK.

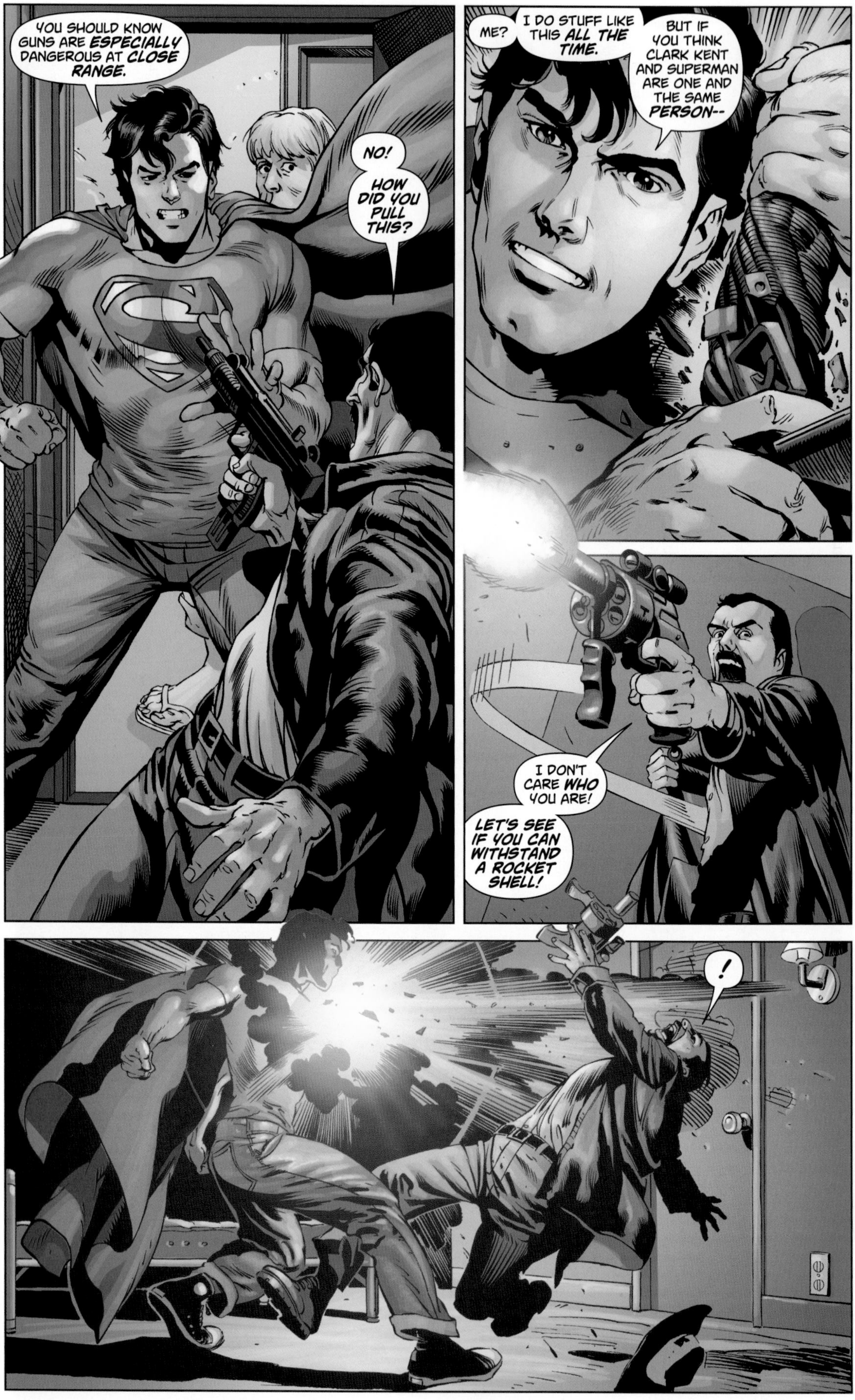
YOU SHOULD KNOW GUNS ARE ESPECIALLY DANGEROUS AT CLOSE RANGE.
NO!
HOW DID YOU PULL THIS?
ME?
I DO STUFF LIKE THIS ALL THE TIME.
BUT IF YOU THINK CLARK KENT AND SUPERMAN ARE ONE AND THE SAME PERSON--
I DON'T CARE WHO YOU ARE!
LET'S SEE IF YOU CAN WITHSTAND A ROCKET SHELL!
!

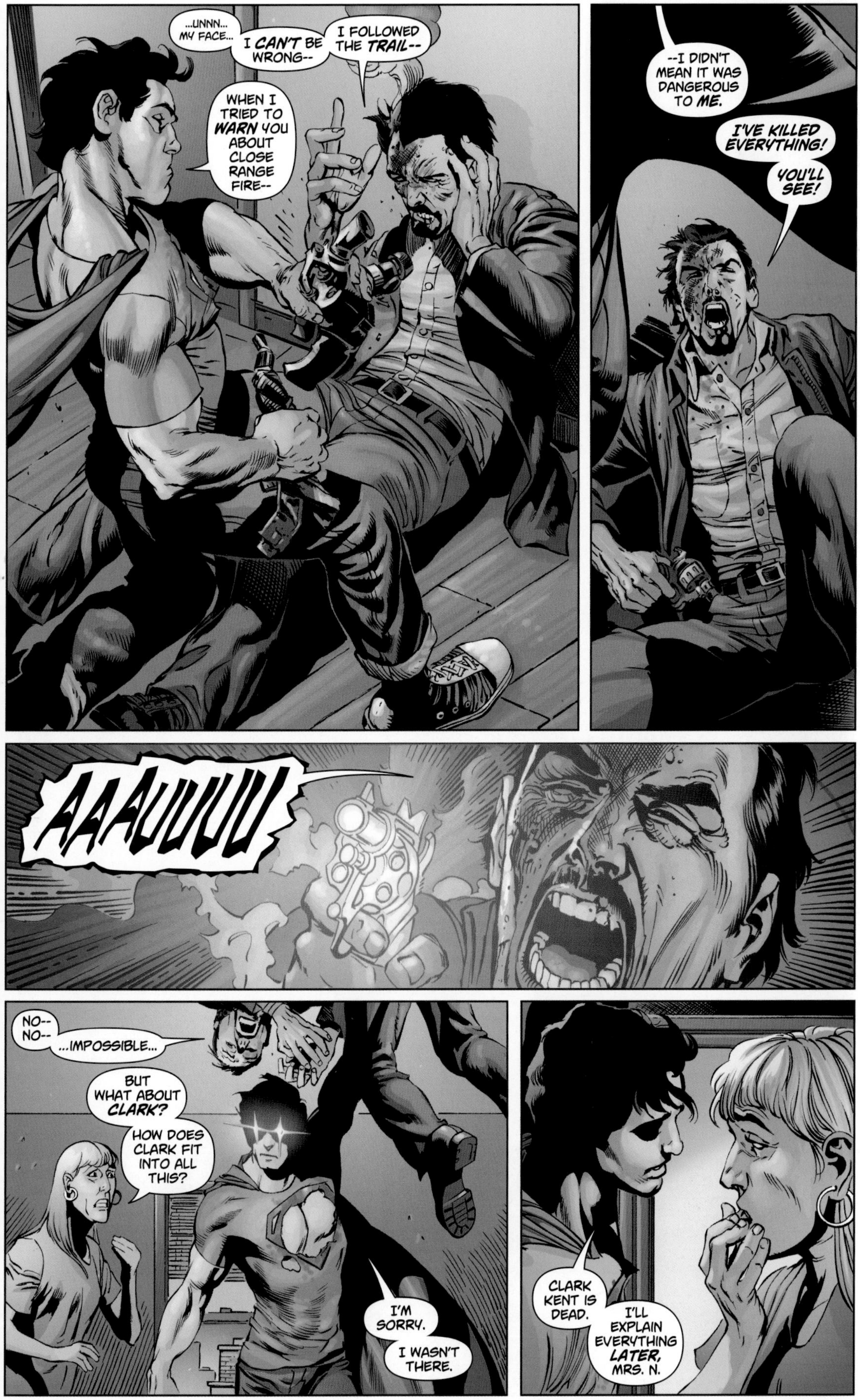
...UNNN... MY FACE...
I CAN'T BE WRONG--
I FOLLOWED THE TRAIL--
WHEN I TRIED TO WARN YOU ABOUT CLOSE RANGE FIRE--
--I DIDN'T MEAN IT WAS DANGEROUS TO ME.
I'VE KILLED EVERYTHING!
YOU'LL SEE!
AAAUUUUU
NO-- NO--
...IMPOSSIBLE...
BUT WHAT ABOUT CLARK?
HOW DOES CLARK FIT INTO ALL THIS?
I'M SORRY.
I WASN'T THERE.
CLARK KENT IS DEAD.
I'LL EXPLAIN EVERYTHING LATER, MRS. N.

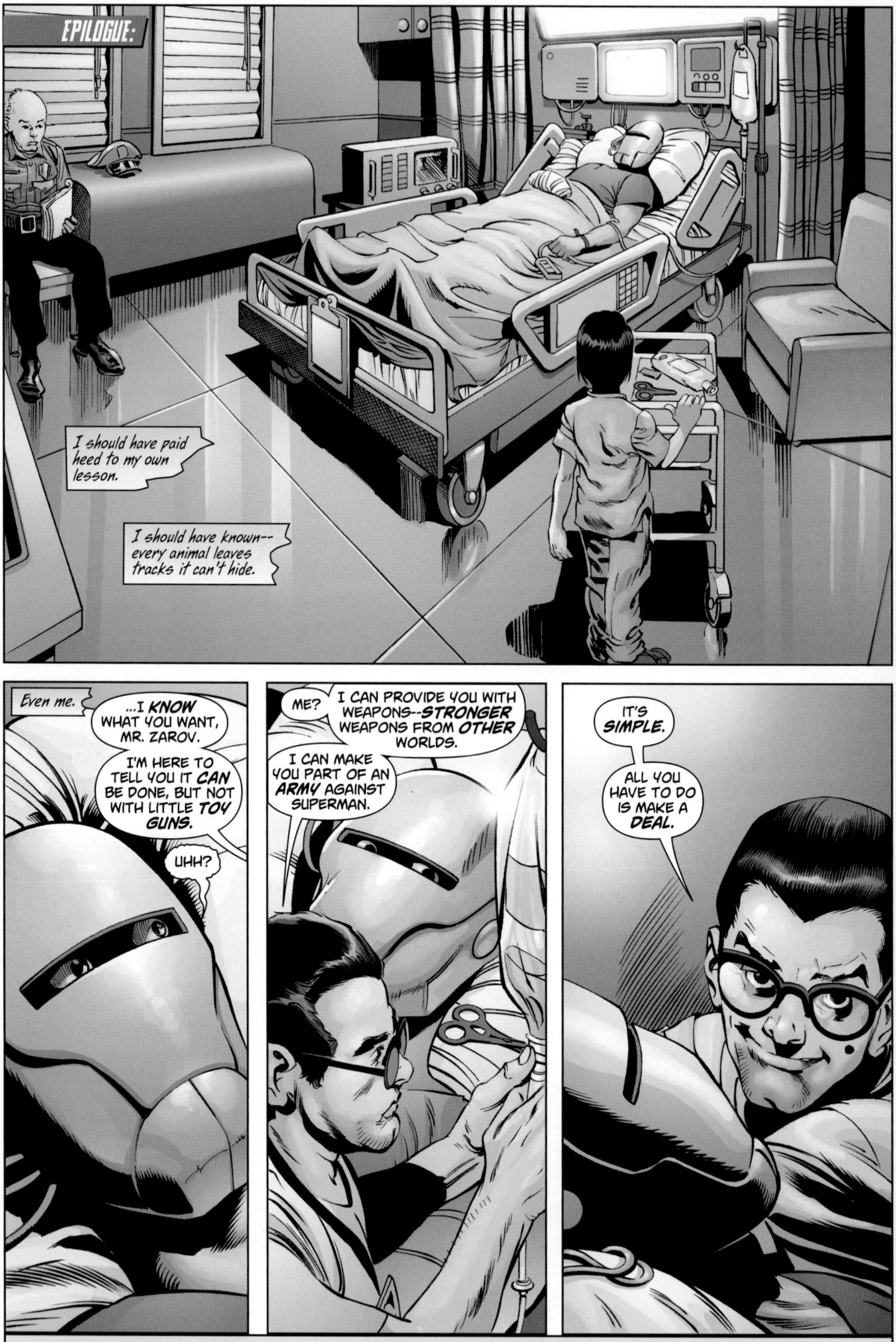
EPILOGUE:
I should have paid heed to my own lesson.
I should have known-- every animal leaves tracks it can't hide.
Even me.
...I KNOW WHAT YOU WANT, MR. ZAROV.
I'M HERE TO TELL YOU IT CAN BE DONE, BUT NOT WITH LITTLE TOY GUNS.
UHH?
ME?
I CAN PROVIDE YOU WITH WEAPONS--STRONGER WEAPONS FROM OTHER WORLDS.
I CAN MAKE YOU PART OF AN ARMY AGAINST SUPERMAN.
IT'S SIMPLE.
ALL YOU HAVE TO DO IS MAKE A DEAL.

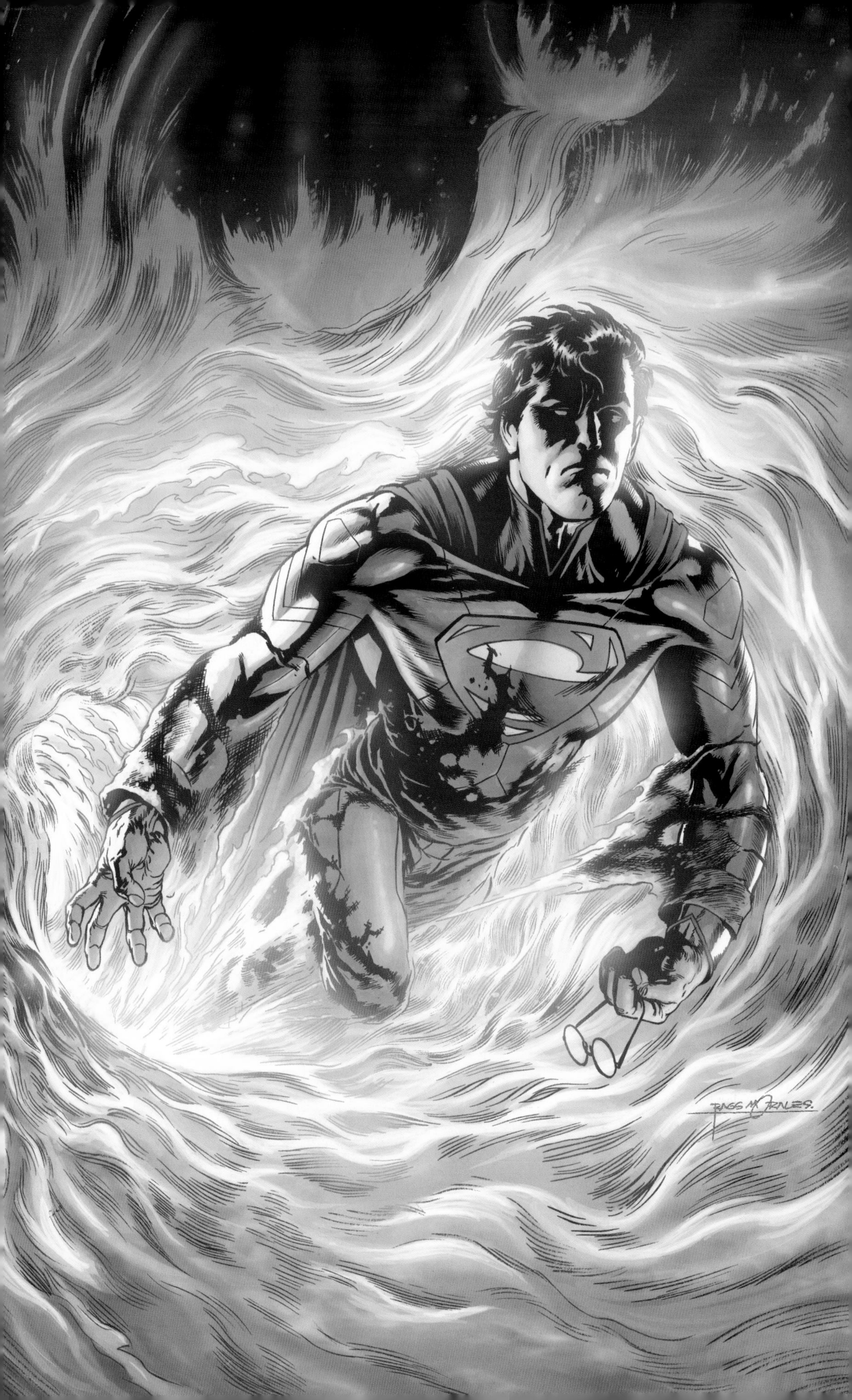

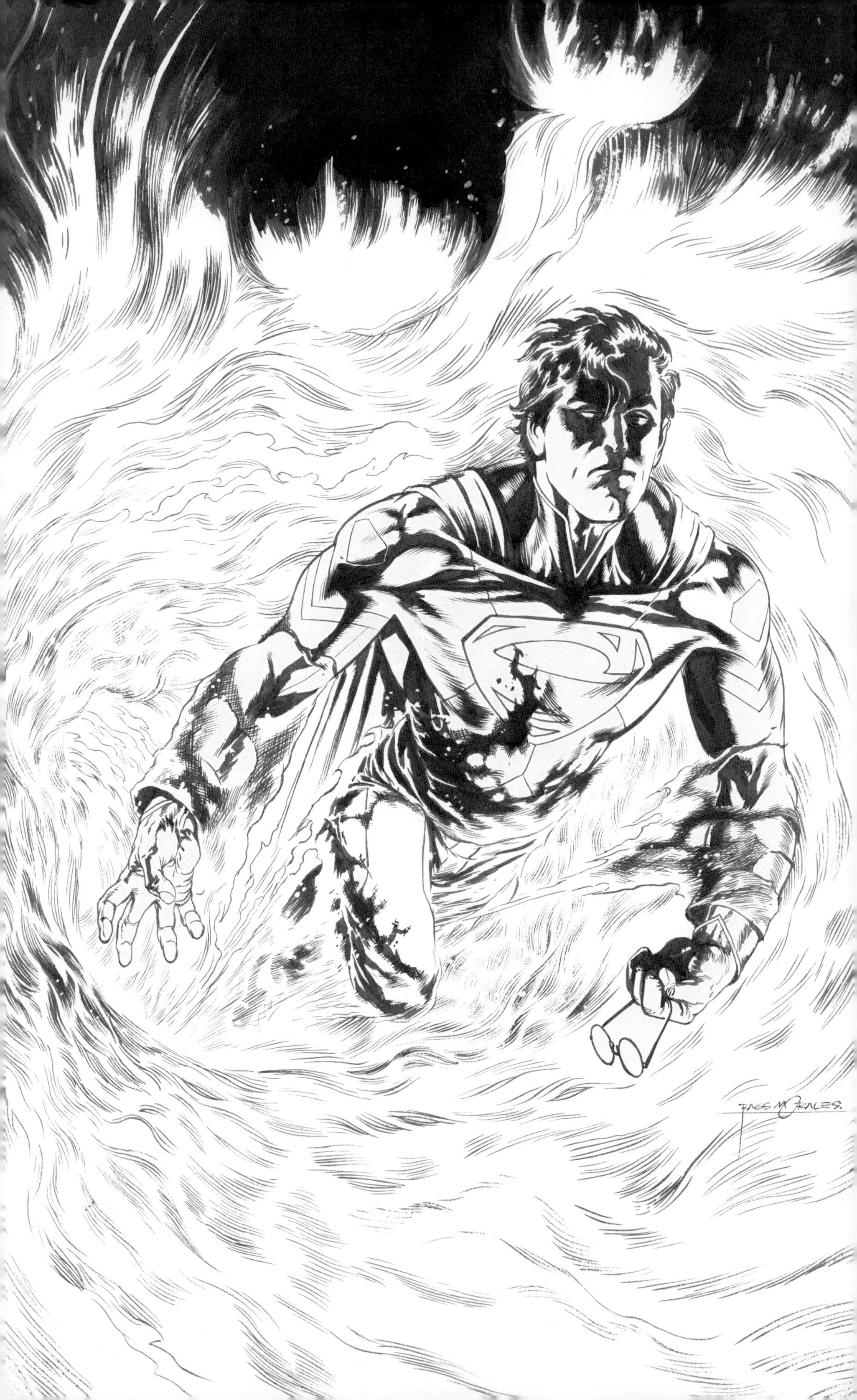

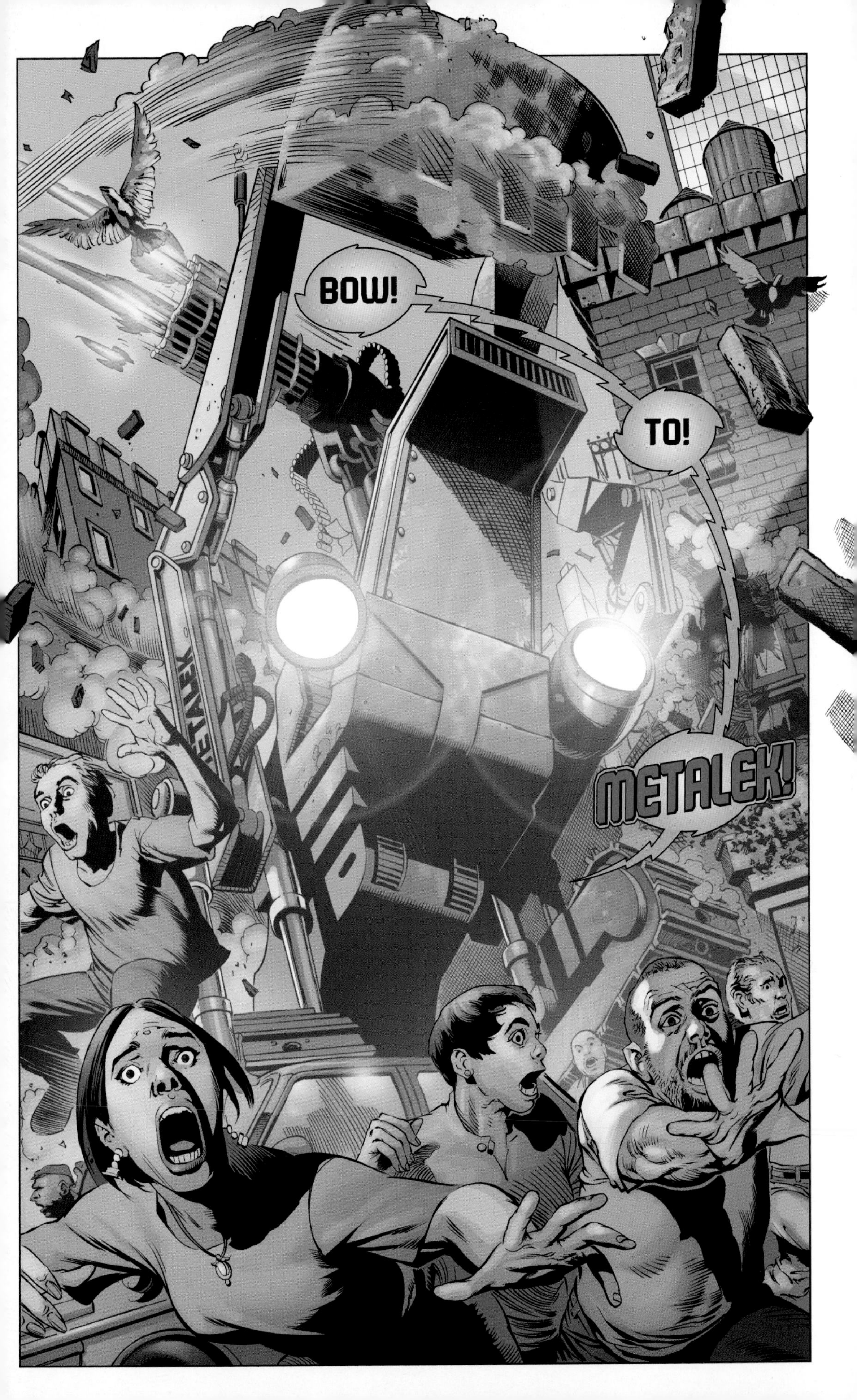
BOW!
TO!
METALEK!
METALEK

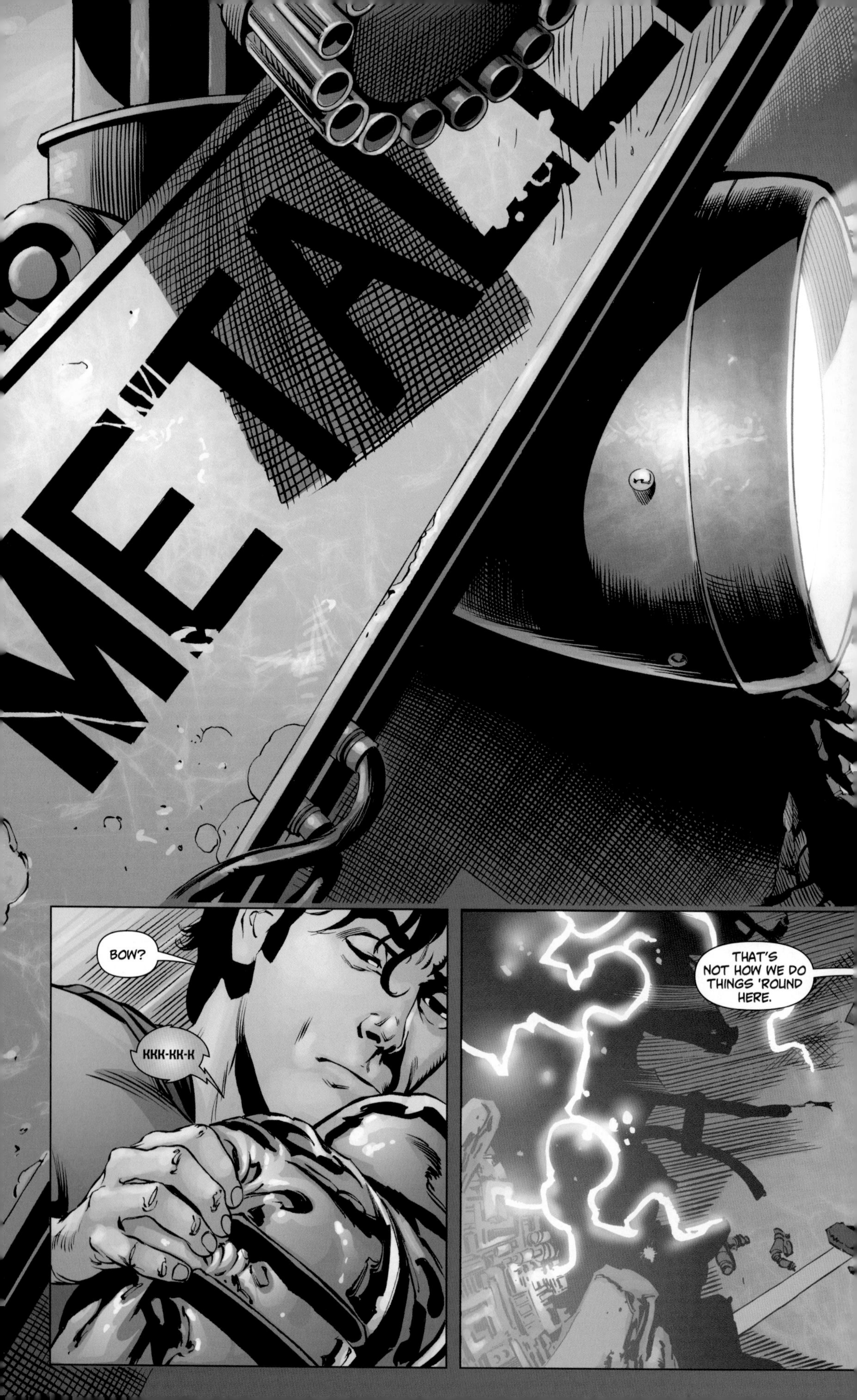
METAL
BOW?
KKK-KK-K
THAT'S NOT HOW WE DO THINGS 'ROUND HERE.

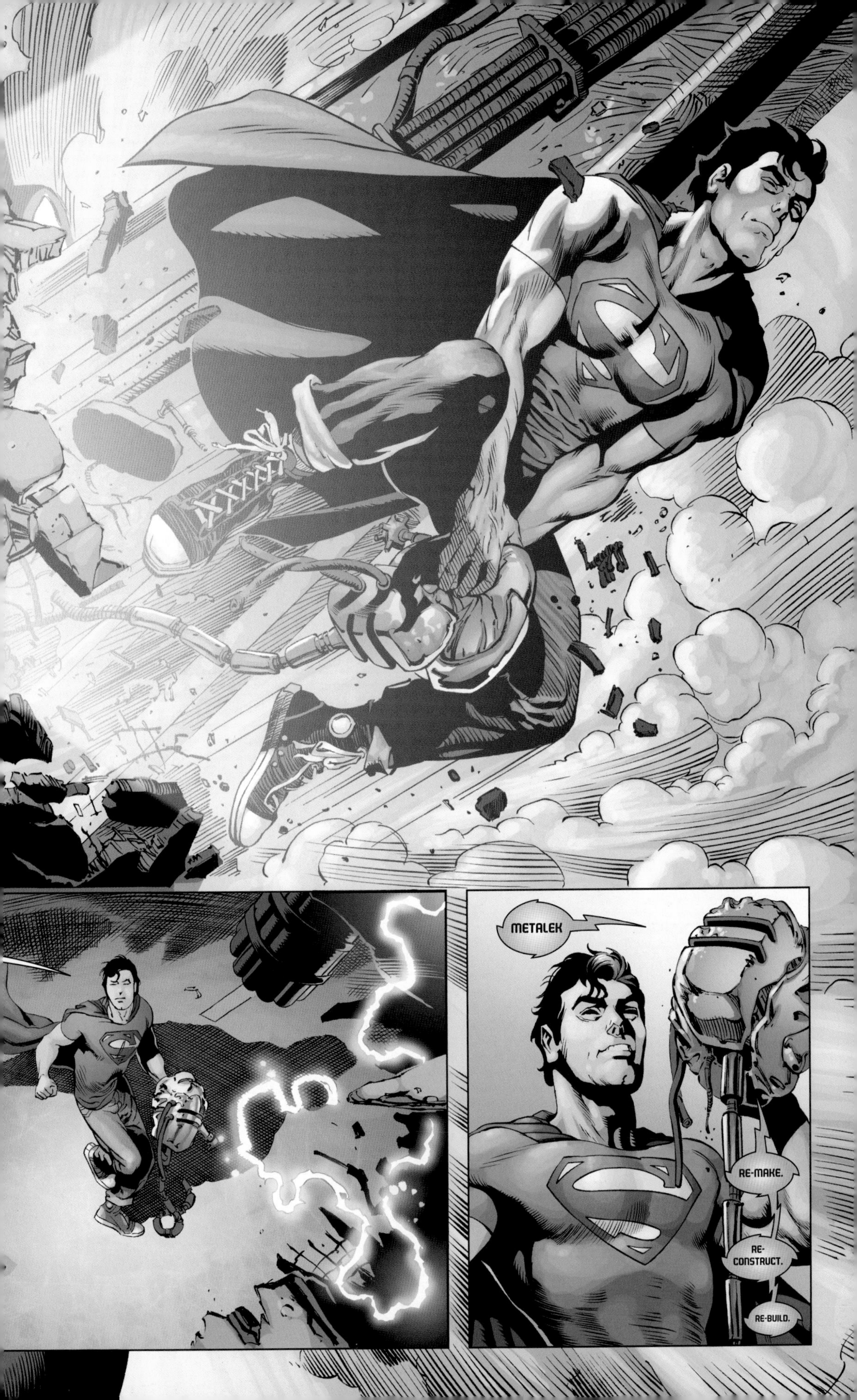
METALEK
RE-MAKE.
RE-CONSTRUCT.
RE-BUILD.

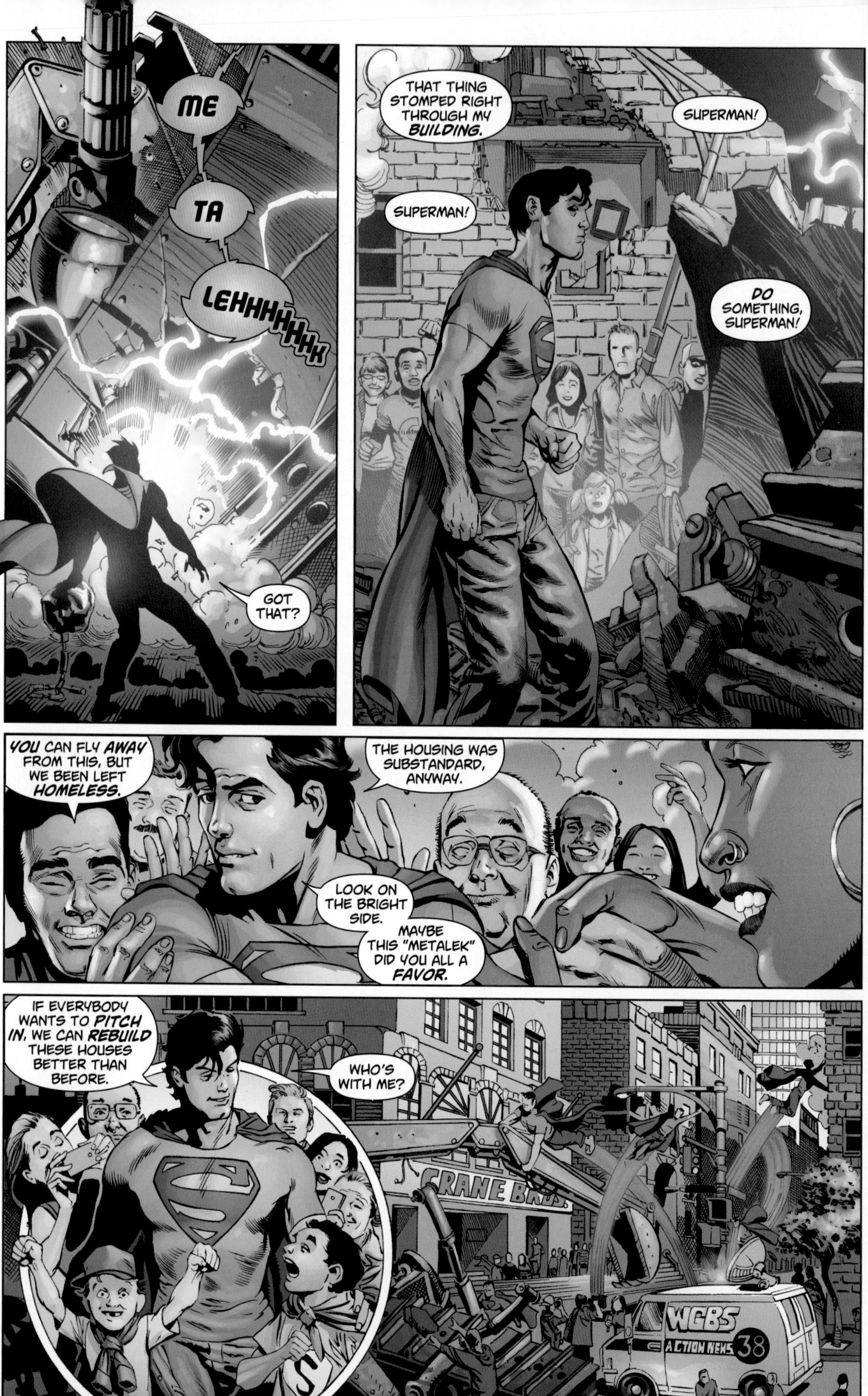
ME
TA
LEHHHHHHHK
GOT THAT?
THAT THING STOMPED RIGHT THROUGH MY BUILDING.
SUPERMAN!
SUPERMAN!
DO SOMETHING, SUPERMAN!
YOU CAN FLY AWAY FROM THIS, BUT WE BEEN LEFT HOMELESS.
THE HOUSING WAS SUBSTANDARD, ANYWAY.
LOOK ON THE BRIGHT SIDE.
MAYBE THIS "METALEK" DID YOU ALL A FAVOR.
IF EVERYBODY WANTS TO PITCH IN, WE CAN REBUILD THESE HOUSES BETTER THAN BEFORE.
WHO'S WITH ME?
CRANE BROS.
WGBS
ACTION NEWS 38

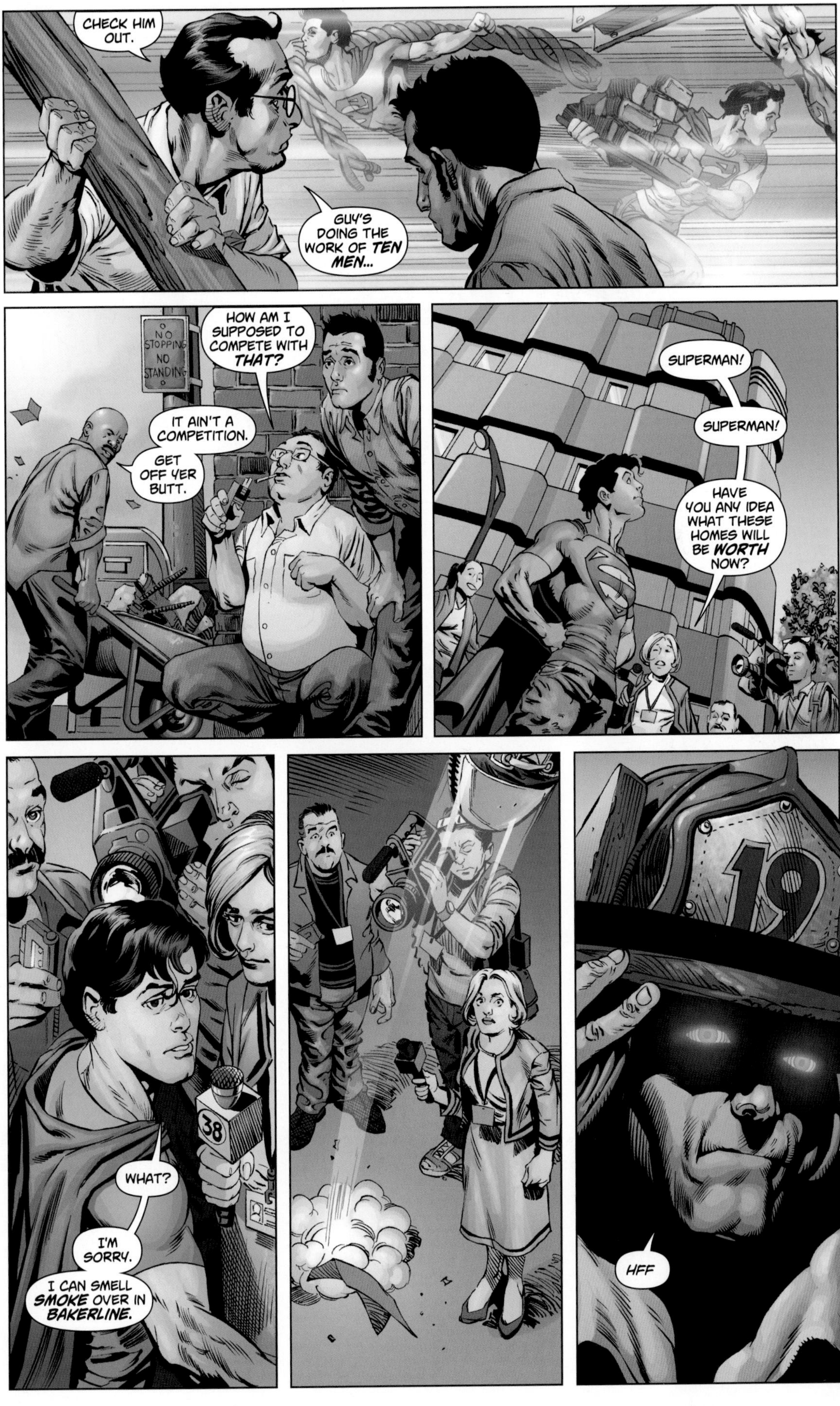
CHECK HIM OUT.
GUY'S DOING THE WORK OF TEN MEN...
NO STOPPING NO STANDING
HOW AM I SUPPOSED TO COMPETE WITH THAT?
IT AIN'T A COMPETITION.
GET OFF YER BUTT.
SUPERMAN!
SUPERMAN!
HAVE YOU ANY IDEA WHAT THESE HOMES WILL BE WORTH NOW?
WHAT?
I'M SORRY.
I CAN SMELL SMOKE OVER IN BAKERLINE.
HFF

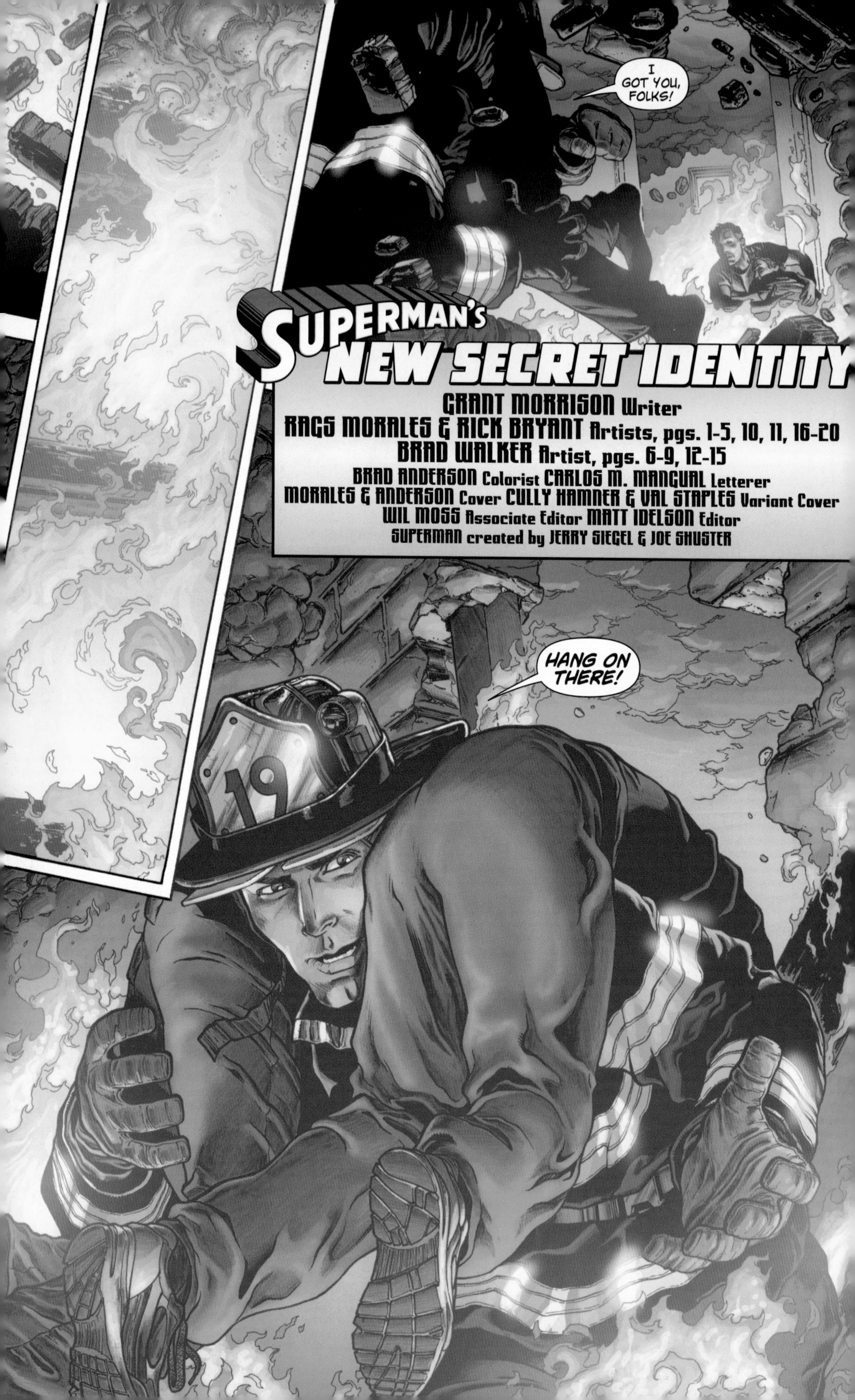
I GOT YOU, FOLKS!
SUPERMAN'S NEW SECRET IDENTITY
GRANT MORRISON Writer
RAGS MORALES & RICK BRYANT Artists, pgs. 1-5, 10, 11, 16-20
BRAD WALKER Artist, pgs. 6-9, 12-15
BRAD ANDERSON Colorist CARLOS M. MANGUAL Letterer
MORALES & ANDERSON Cover CULLY HAMNER & VAL STAPLES Variant Cover
WIL MOSS Associate Editor MATT IDELSON Editor
SUPERMAN created by JERRY SIEGEL & JOE SHUSTER
HANG ON THERE!

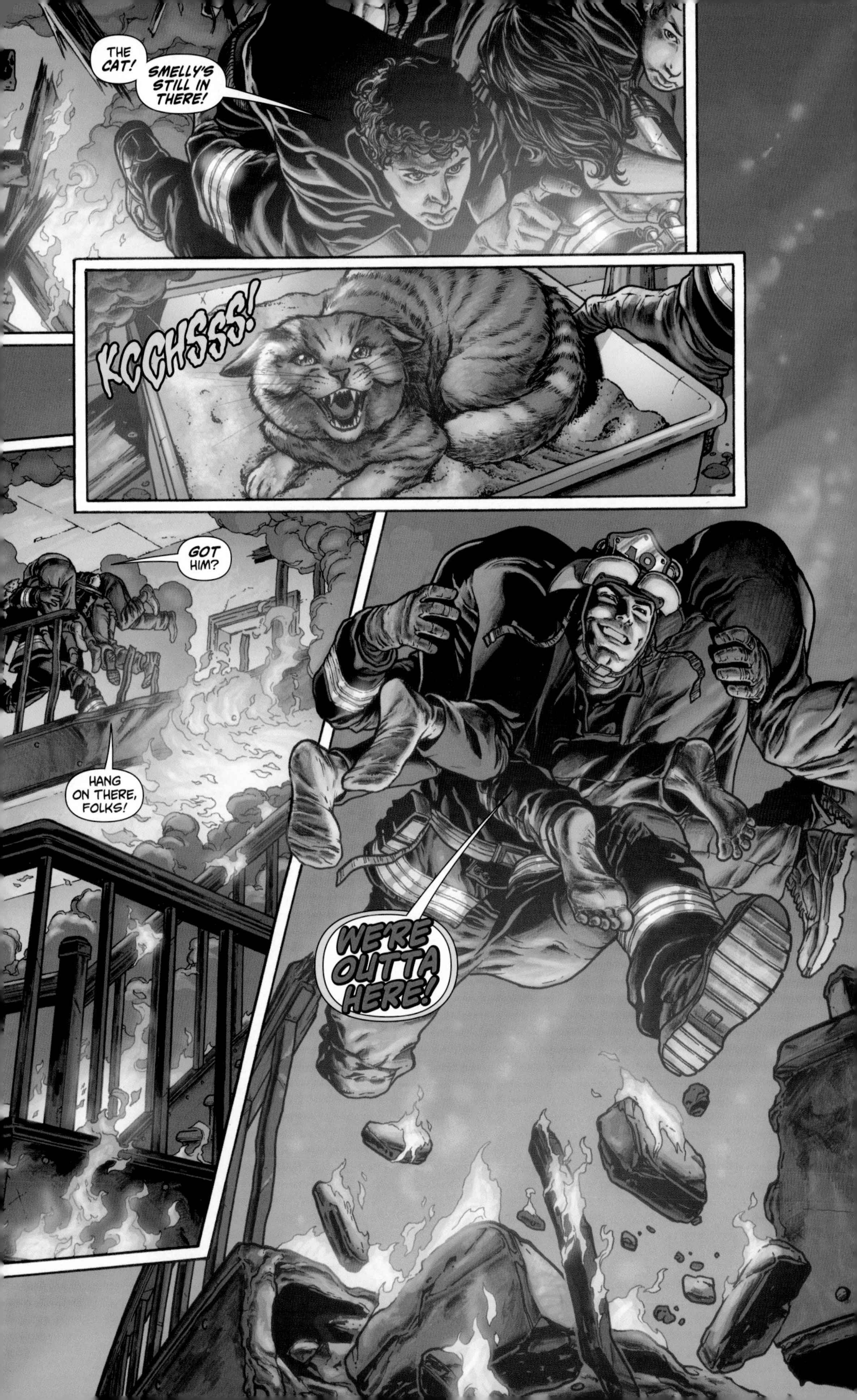
THE CAT!
SMELLY'S STILL IN THERE!
KCCHSSS!
GOT HIM?
HANG ON THERE, FOLKS!
WE'RE OUTTA HERE!

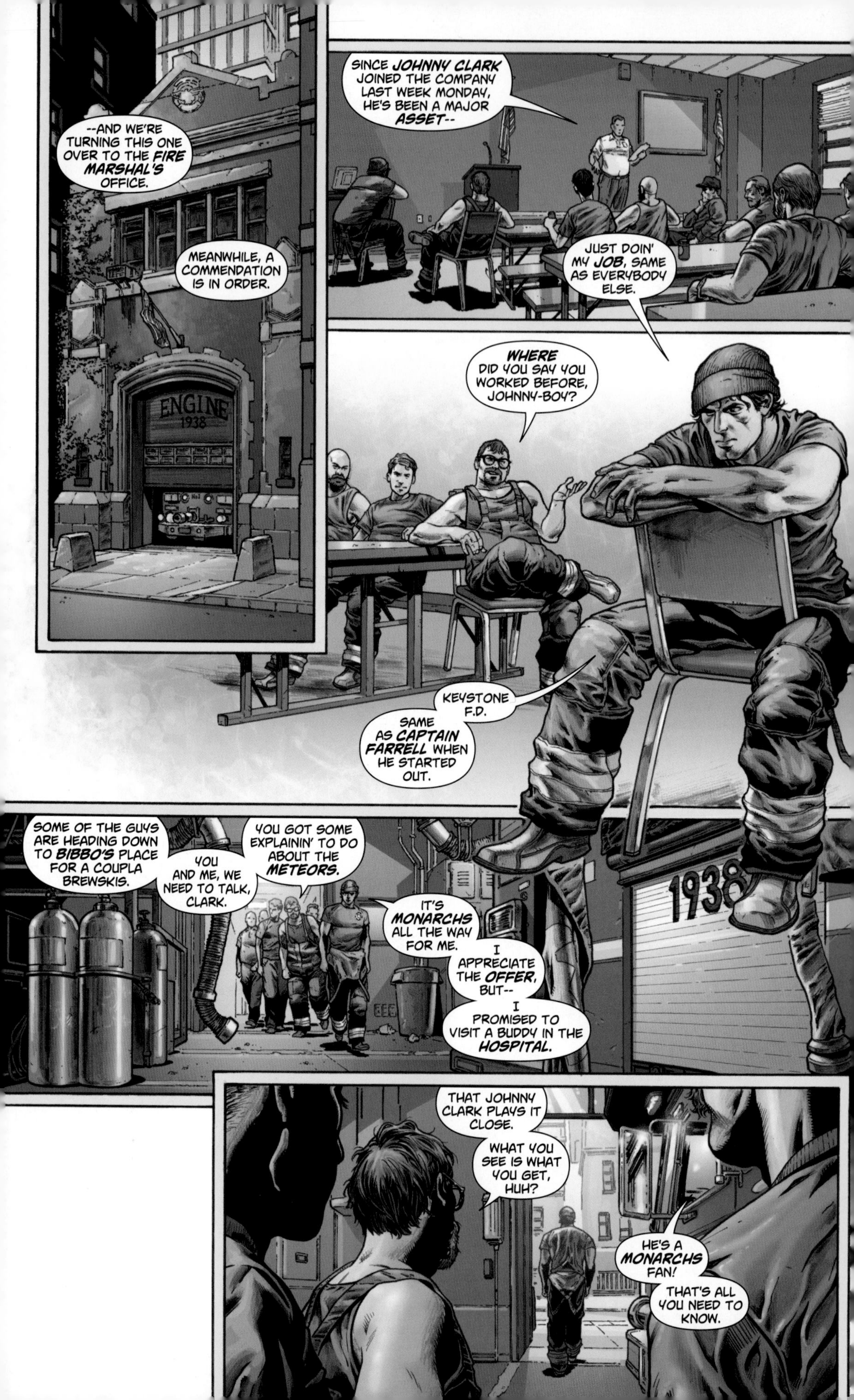

--AND WE'RE TURNING THIS ONE OVER TO THE FIRE MARSHAL'S OFFICE.
MEANWHILE, A COMMENDATION IS IN ORDER.
ENGINE 1938
SINCE JOHNNY CLARK JOINED THE COMPANY LAST WEEK MONDAY, HE'S BEEN A MAJOR ASSET--
JUST DOIN' MY JOB, SAME AS EVERYBODY ELSE.
WHERE DID YOU SAY YOU WORKED BEFORE, JOHNNY-BOY?
KEYSTONE F.D.
SAME AS CAPTAIN FARRELL WHEN HE STARTED OUT.
SOME OF THE GUYS ARE HEADING DOWN TO BIBBO'S PLACE FOR A COUPLA BREWSKIS.
YOU AND ME, WE NEED TO TALK, CLARK.
YOU GOT SOME EXPLAININ' TO DO ABOUT THE METEORS.
IT'S MONARCHS ALL THE WAY FOR ME.
I APPRECIATE THE OFFER, BUT--
I PROMISED TO VISIT A BUDDY IN THE HOSPITAL.
1938
THAT JOHNNY CLARK PLAYS IT CLOSE.
WHAT YOU SEE IS WHAT YOU GET, HUH?
HE'S A MONARCHS FAN!
THAT'S ALL YOU NEED TO KNOW.

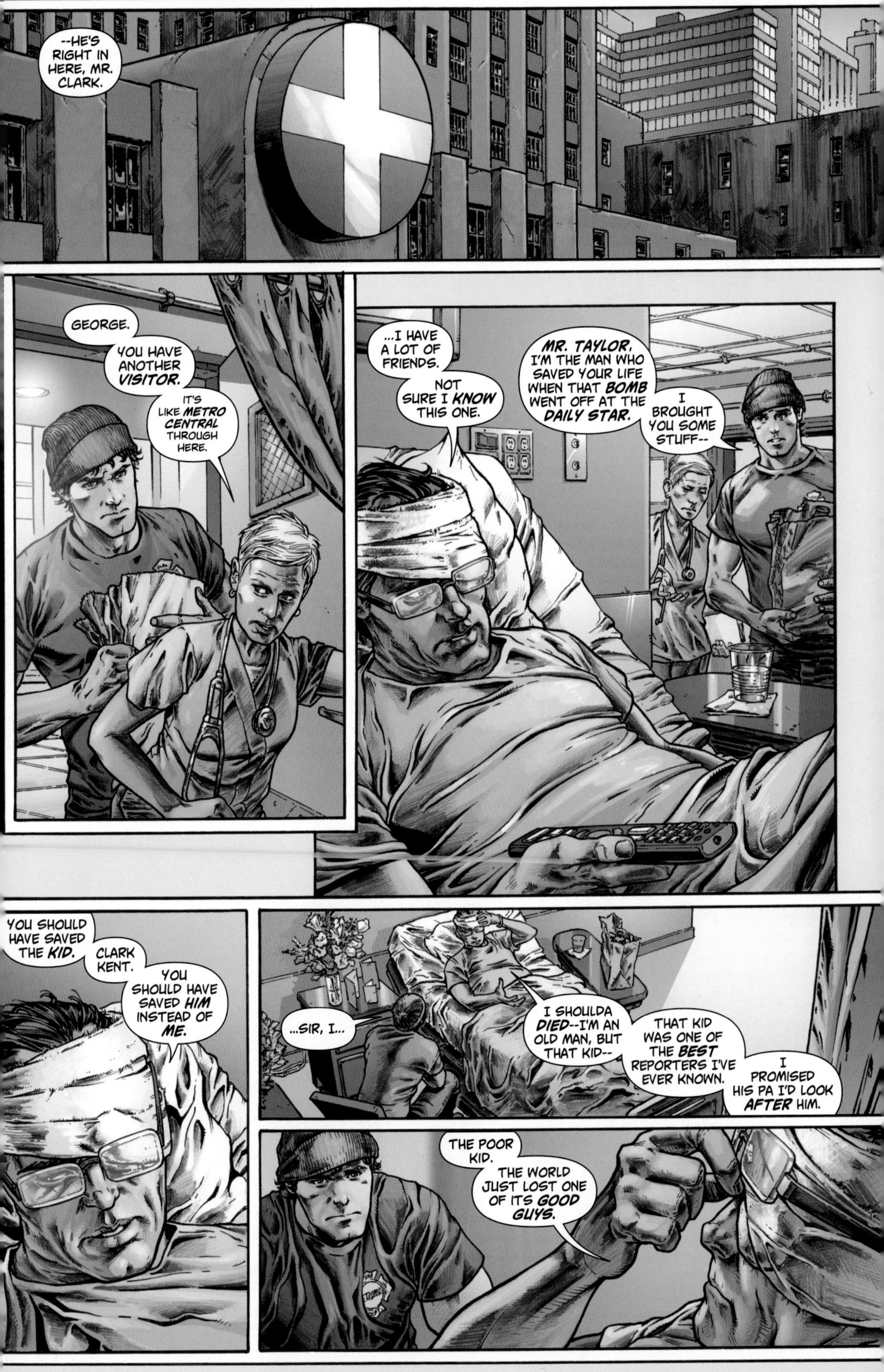
--HE'S RIGHT IN HERE, MR. CLARK.
GEORGE.
YOU HAVE ANOTHER VISITOR.
IT'S LIKE METRO CENTRAL THROUGH HERE.
...I HAVE A LOT OF FRIENDS.
NOT SURE I KNOW THIS ONE.
MR. TAYLOR, I'M THE MAN WHO SAVED YOUR LIFE WHEN THAT BOMB WENT OFF AT THE DAILY STAR.
I BROUGHT YOU SOME STUFF--
YOU SHOULD HAVE SAVED THE KID.
CLARK KENT.
YOU SHOULD HAVE SAVED HIM INSTEAD OF ME.
...SIR, I...
I SHOULDA DIED--I'M AN OLD MAN, BUT THAT KID--
THAT KID WAS ONE OF THE BEST REPORTERS I'VE EVER KNOWN.
I PROMISED HIS PA I'D LOOK AFTER HIM.
THE POOR KID.
THE WORLD JUST LOST ONE OF ITS GOOD GUYS.

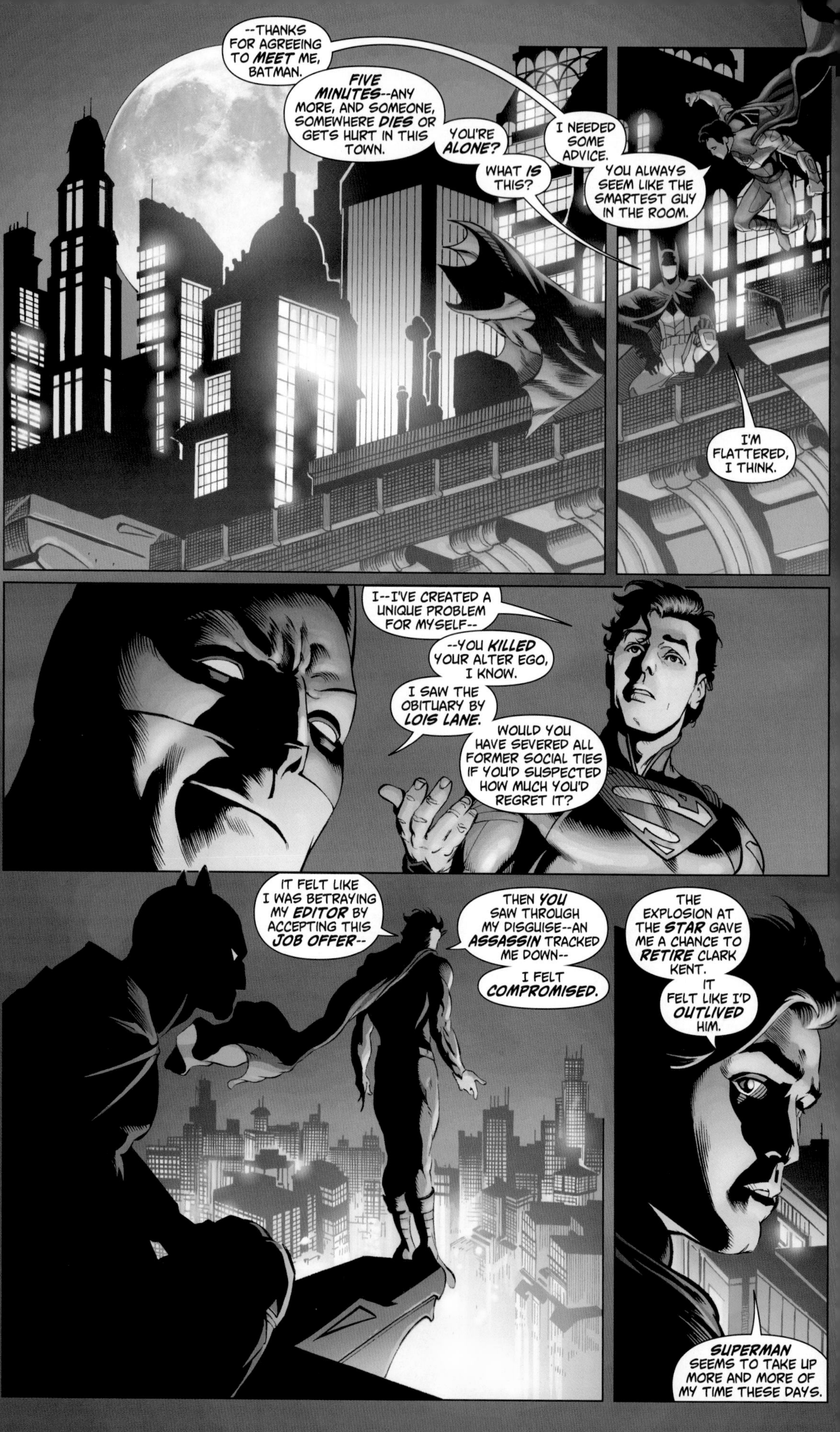
--THANKS FOR AGREEING TO MEET ME, BATMAN.
FIVE MINUTES--ANY MORE, AND SOMEONE, SOMEWHERE DIES OR GETS HURT IN THIS TOWN.
YOU'RE ALONE?
WHAT IS THIS?
I NEEDED SOME ADVICE.
YOU ALWAYS SEEM LIKE THE SMARTEST GUY IN THE ROOM.
I'M FLATTERED, I THINK.
I--I'VE CREATED A UNIQUE PROBLEM FOR MYSELF--
--YOU KILLED YOUR ALTER EGO, I KNOW.
I SAW THE OBITUARY BY LOIS LANE.
WOULD YOU HAVE SEVERED ALL FORMER SOCIAL TIES IF YOU'D SUSPECTED HOW MUCH YOU'D REGRET IT?
IT FELT LIKE I WAS BETRAYING MY EDITOR BY ACCEPTING THIS JOB OFFER--
THEN YOU SAW THROUGH MY DISGUISE--AN ASSASSIN TRACKED ME DOWN--
I FELT COMPROMISED.
THE EXPLOSION AT THE STAR GAVE ME A CHANCE TO RETIRE CLARK KENT.
IT FELT LIKE I'D OUTLIVED HIM.
SUPERMAN SEEMS TO TAKE UP MORE AND MORE OF MY TIME THESE DAYS.

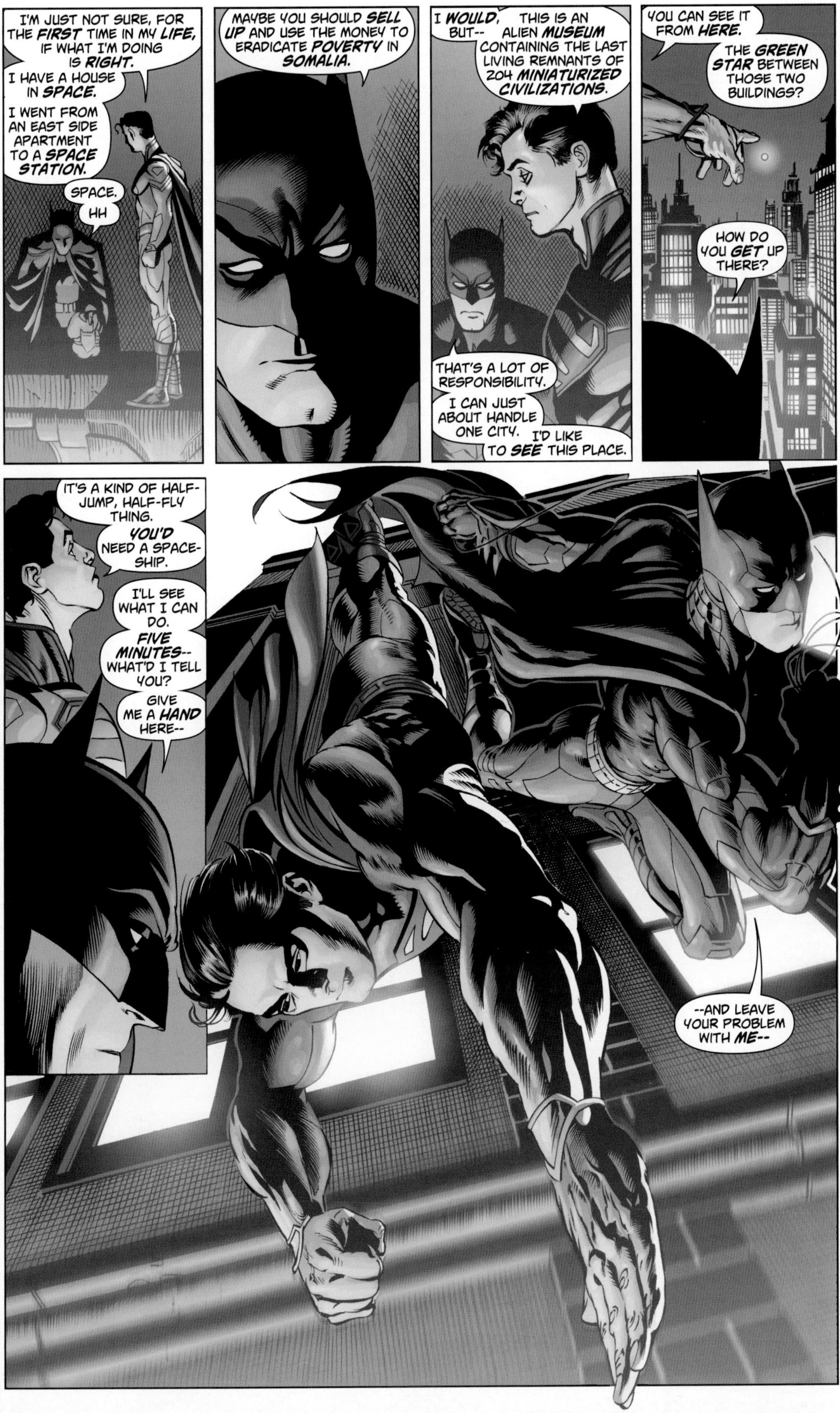
I'M JUST NOT SURE, FOR THE FIRST TIME IN MY LIFE, IF WHAT I'M DOING IS RIGHT.
I HAVE A HOUSE IN SPACE.
I WENT FROM AN EAST SIDE APARTMENT TO A SPACE STATION.
SPACE.
HH
MAYBE YOU SHOULD SELL UP AND USE THE MONEY TO ERADICATE POVERTY IN SOMALIA.
I WOULD, BUT--
THIS IS AN ALIEN MUSEUM CONTAINING THE LAST LIVING REMNANTS OF 204 MINIATURIZED CIVILIZATIONS.
THAT'S A LOT OF RESPONSIBILITY.
I CAN JUST ABOUT HANDLE ONE CITY.
I'D LIKE TO SEE THIS PLACE.
YOU CAN SEE IT FROM HERE.
THE GREEN STAR BETWEEN THOSE TWO BUILDINGS?
HOW DO YOU GET UP THERE?
IT'S A KIND OF HALF-JUMP, HALF-FLY THING.
YOU'D NEED A SPACE-SHIP.
I'LL SEE WHAT I CAN DO.
FIVE MINUTES-- WHAT'D I TELL YOU?
GIVE ME A HAND HERE--
--AND LEAVE YOUR PROBLEM WITH ME--

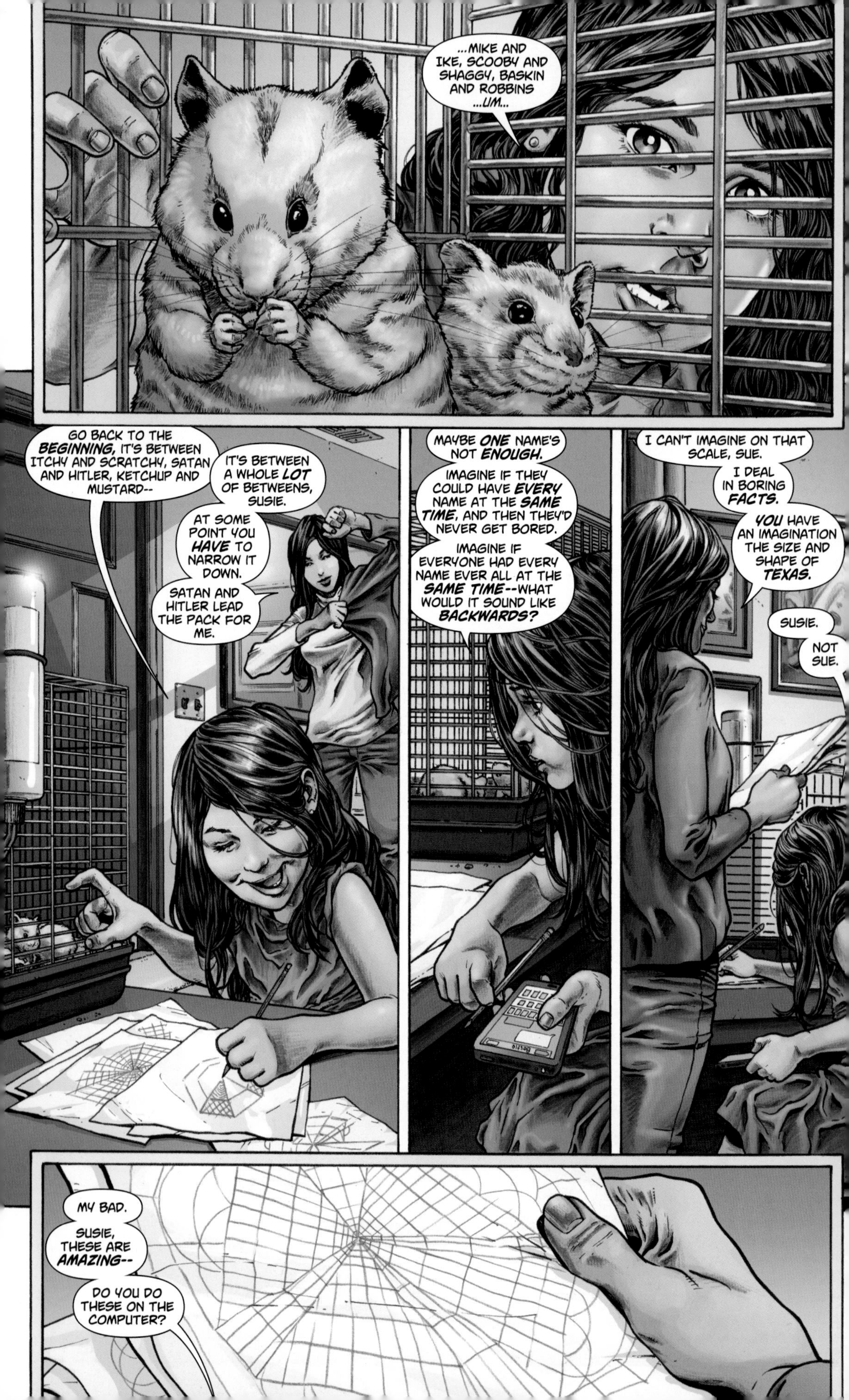
...MIKE AND IKE, SCOOBY AND SHAGGY, BASKIN AND ROBBINS ...UM...
GO BACK TO THE BEGINNING, IT'S BETWEEN ITCHY AND SCRATCHY, SATAN AND HITLER, KETCHUP AND MUSTARD--
IT'S BETWEEN A WHOLE LOT OF BETWEENS, SUSIE.
AT SOME POINT YOU HAVE TO NARROW IT DOWN.
SATAN AND HITLER LEAD THE PACK FOR ME.
MAYBE ONE NAME'S NOT ENOUGH.
IMAGINE IF THEY COULD HAVE EVERY NAME AT THE SAME TIME, AND THEN THEY'D NEVER GET BORED.
IMAGINE IF EVERYONE HAD EVERY NAME EVER ALL AT THE SAME TIME--WHAT WOULD IT SOUND LIKE BACKWARDS?
I CAN'T IMAGINE ON THAT SCALE, SUE.
I DEAL IN BORING FACTS.
YOU HAVE AN IMAGINATION THE SIZE AND SHAPE OF TEXAS.
SUSIE.
NOT SUE.
MY BAD.
SUSIE, THESE ARE AMAZING--
DO YOU DO THESE ON THE COMPUTER?

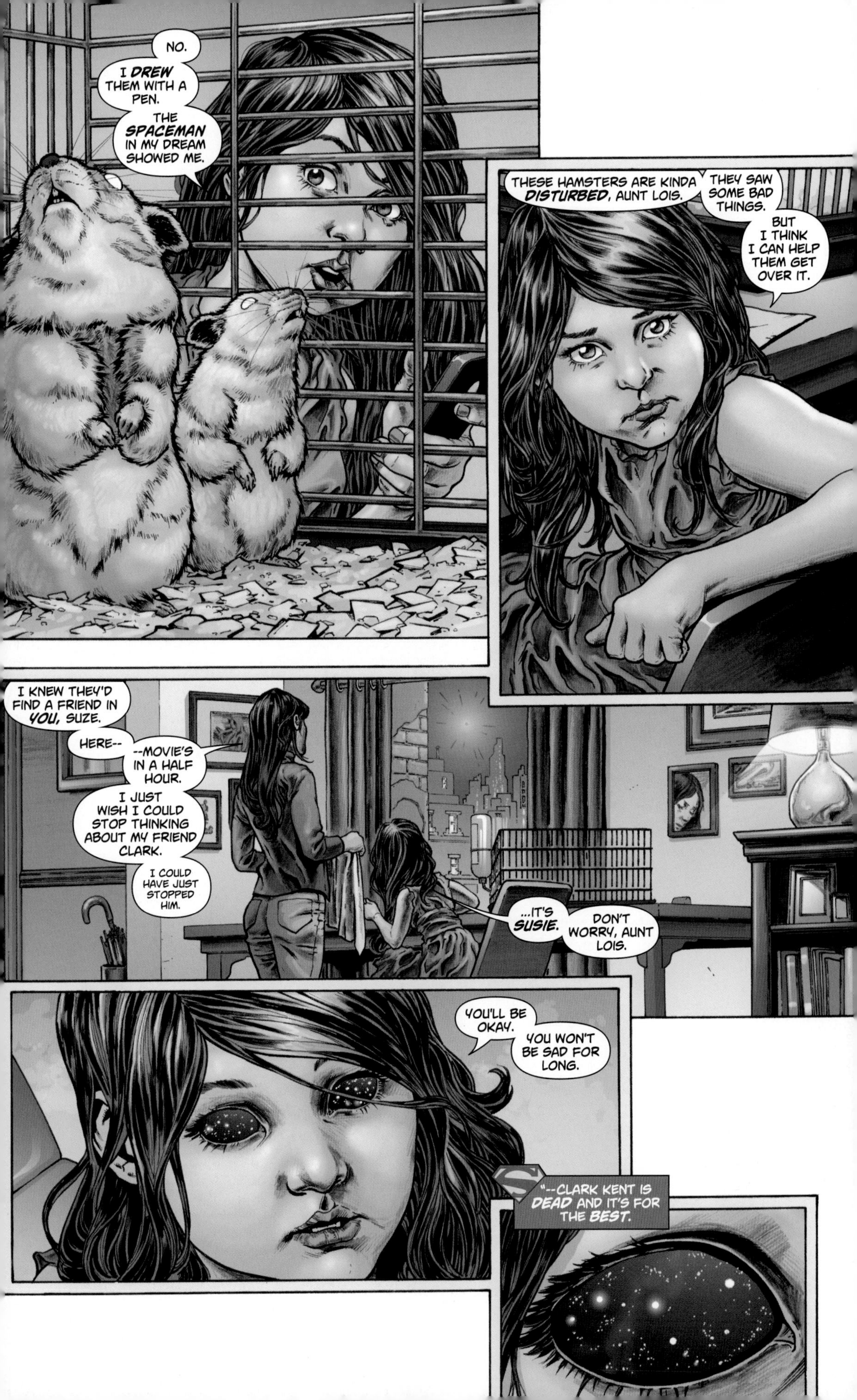
NO.
I DREW THEM WITH A PEN.
THE SPACEMAN IN MY DREAM SHOWED ME.
THESE HAMSTERS ARE KINDA DISTURBED, AUNT LOIS.
THEY SAW SOME BAD THINGS.
BUT I THINK I CAN HELP THEM GET OVER IT.
I KNEW THEY'D FIND A FRIEND IN YOU, SUZE.
HERE--
--MOVIE'S IN A HALF HOUR.
I JUST WISH I COULD STOP THINKING ABOUT MY FRIEND CLARK.
I COULD HAVE JUST STOPPED HIM.
...IT'S SUSIE.
DON'T WORRY, AUNT LOIS.
YOU'LL BE OKAY.
YOU WON'T BE SAD FOR LONG.
"--CLARK KENT IS DEAD AND IT'S FOR THE BEST.

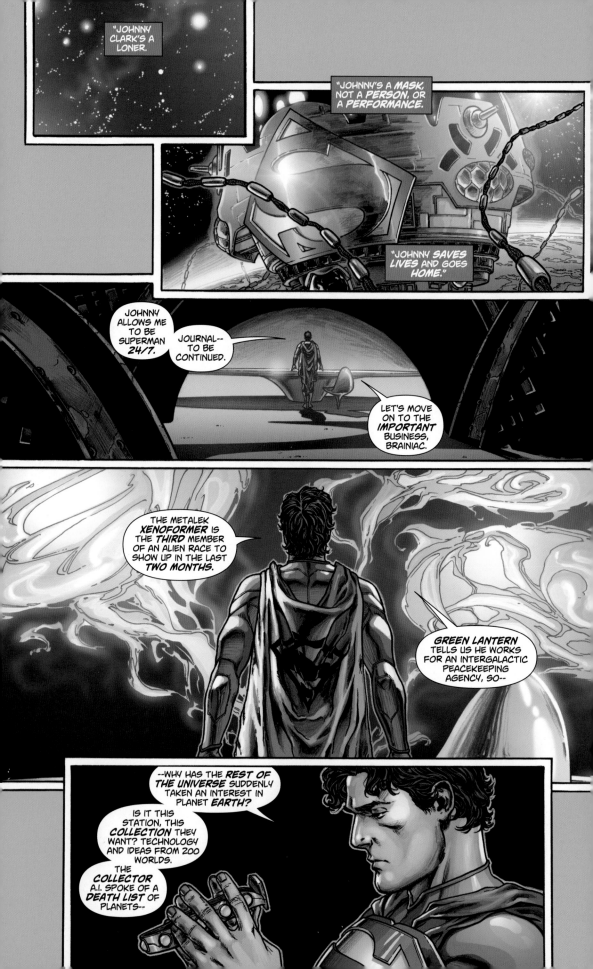

"JOHNNY CLARK'S A LONER.

"JOHNNY'S A *MASK*, NOT A *PERSON*, OR A *PERFORMANCE*.

"JOHNNY *SAVES LIVES* AND GOES *HOME*."

JOHNNY ALLOWS ME TO BE SUPERMAN 24/7.

JOURNAL-- TO BE CONTINUED.

LET'S MOVE ON TO THE *IMPORTANT* BUSINESS, BRAINIAC.

THE METALEK *XENOFORMER* IS THE *THIRD* MEMBER OF AN ALIEN RACE TO SHOW UP IN THE LAST *TWO MONTHS*.

GREEN LANTERN TELLS US HE WORKS FOR AN INTERGALACTIC PEACEKEEPING AGENCY, SO--

--WHY HAS THE *REST OF THE UNIVERSE* SUDDENLY TAKEN AN INTEREST IN PLANET *EARTH?*

IS IT THIS STATION, THIS *COLLECTION* THEY WANT? TECHNOLOGY AND IDEAS FROM 200 WORLDS.

THE *COLLECTOR* A.I. SPOKE OF A *DEATH LIST* OF PLANETS--

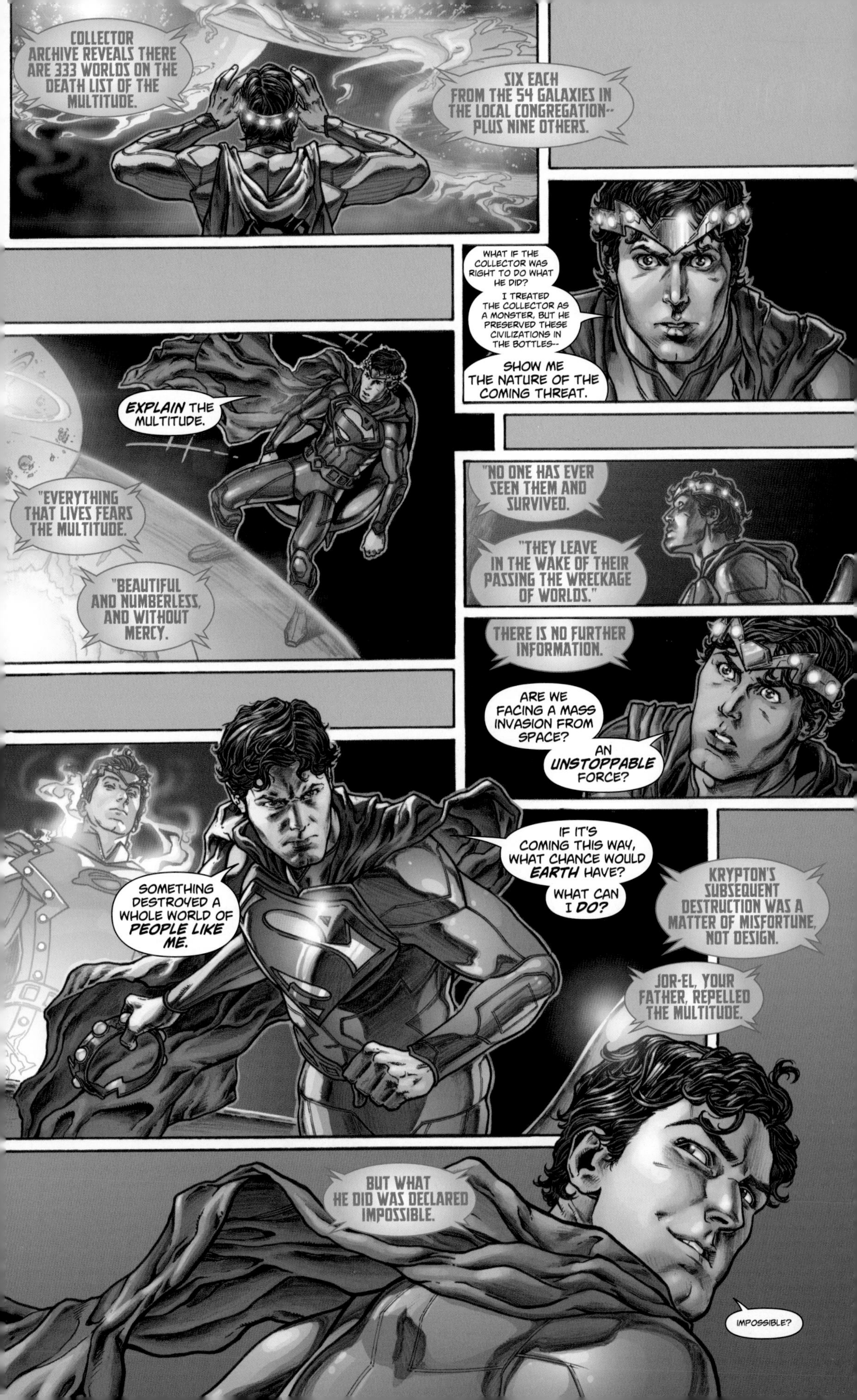
COLLECTOR ARCHIVE REVEALS THERE ARE 333 WORLDS ON THE DEATH LIST OF THE MULTITUDE.
SIX EACH FROM THE 54 GALAXIES IN THE LOCAL CONGREGATION-- PLUS NINE OTHERS.
WHAT IF THE COLLECTOR WAS RIGHT TO DO WHAT HE DID?
I TREATED THE COLLECTOR AS A MONSTER, BUT HE PRESERVED THESE CIVILIZATIONS IN THE BOTTLES--
SHOW ME THE NATURE OF THE COMING THREAT.
EXPLAIN THE MULTITUDE.
"EVERYTHING THAT LIVES FEARS THE MULTITUDE.
"BEAUTIFUL AND NUMBERLESS, AND WITHOUT MERCY.
"NO ONE HAS EVER SEEN THEM AND SURVIVED.
"THEY LEAVE IN THE WAKE OF THEIR PASSING THE WRECKAGE OF WORLDS."
THERE IS NO FURTHER INFORMATION.
ARE WE FACING A MASS INVASION FROM SPACE?
AN UNSTOPPABLE FORCE?
SOMETHING DESTROYED A WHOLE WORLD OF PEOPLE LIKE ME.
IF IT'S COMING THIS WAY, WHAT CHANCE WOULD EARTH HAVE?
WHAT CAN I DO?
KRYPTON'S SUBSEQUENT DESTRUCTION WAS A MATTER OF MISFORTUNE, NOT DESIGN.
JOR-EL, YOUR FATHER, REPELLED THE MULTITUDE.
BUT WHAT HE DID WAS DECLARED IMPOSSIBLE.
IMPOSSIBLE?

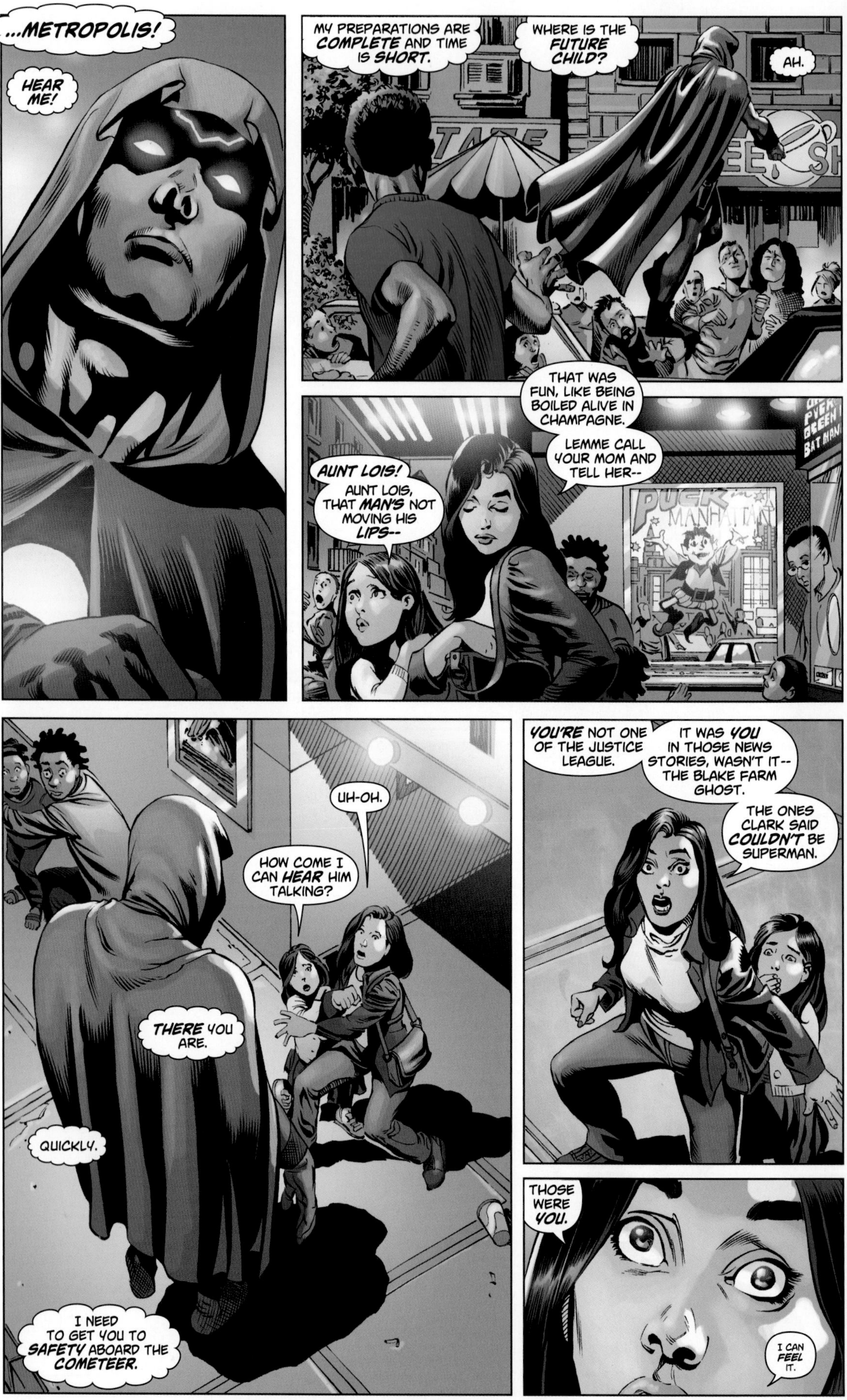

...METROPOLIS!
HEAR ME!
MY PREPARATIONS ARE COMPLETE AND TIME IS SHORT.
WHERE IS THE FUTURE CHILD?
AH.
THAT WAS FUN, LIKE BEING BOILED ALIVE IN CHAMPAGNE.
LEMME CALL YOUR MOM AND TELL HER--
AUNT LOIS!
AUNT LOIS, THAT MAN'S NOT MOVING HIS LIPS--
PUCK in MANHATTAN
UH-OH.
HOW COME I CAN HEAR HIM TALKING?
THERE YOU ARE.
QUICKLY.
I NEED TO GET YOU TO SAFETY ABOARD THE COMETEER.
YOU'RE NOT ONE OF THE JUSTICE LEAGUE.
IT WAS YOU IN THOSE NEWS STORIES, WASN'T IT-- THE BLAKE FARM GHOST.
THE ONES CLARK SAID COULDN'T BE SUPERMAN.
THOSE WERE YOU.
I CAN FEEL IT.

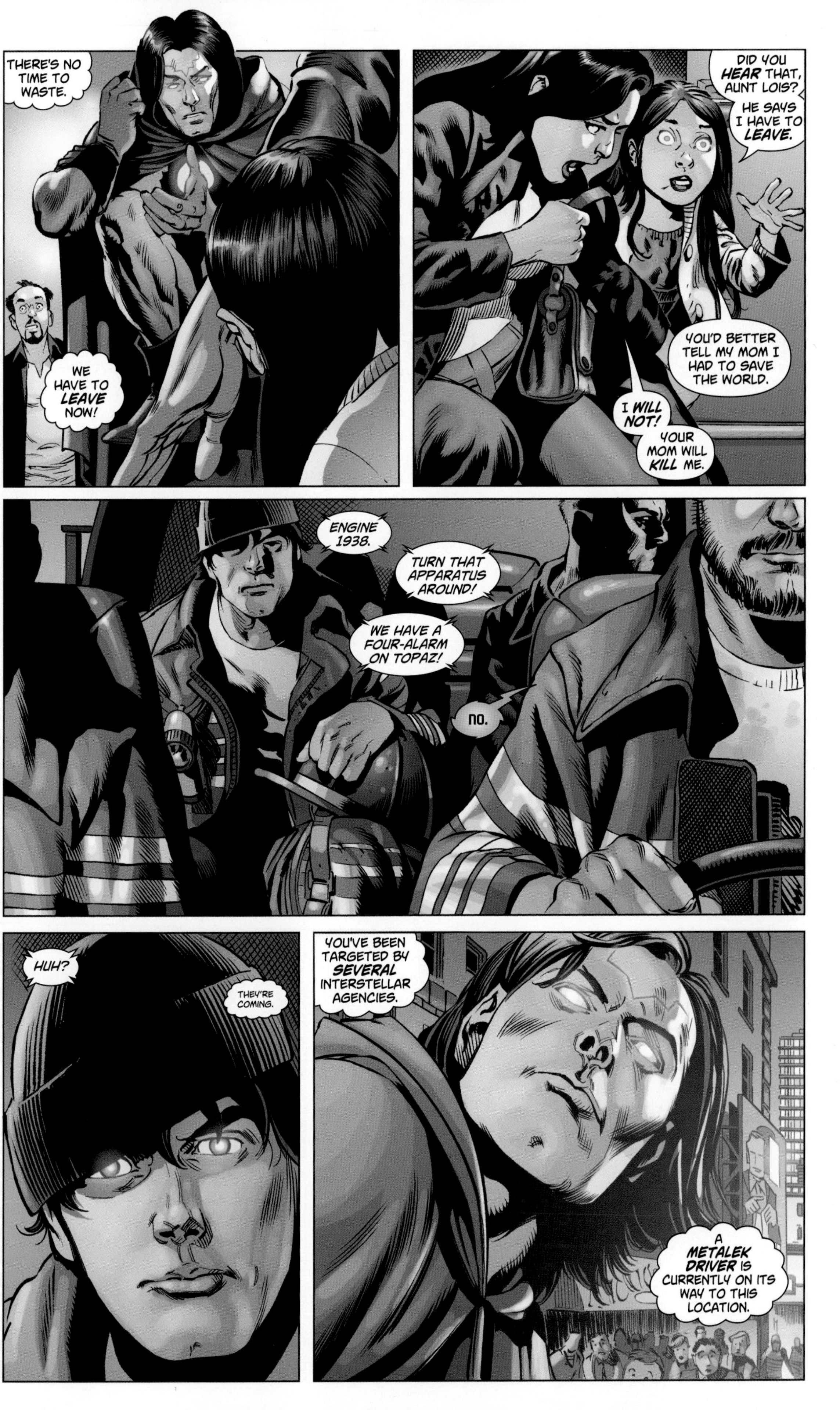
THERE'S NO TIME TO WASTE.
WE HAVE TO LEAVE NOW!
DID YOU HEAR THAT, AUNT LOIS?
HE SAYS I HAVE TO LEAVE.
YOU'D BETTER TELL MY MOM I HAD TO SAVE THE WORLD.
I WILL NOT!
YOUR MOM WILL KILL ME.
ENGINE 1938.
TURN THAT APPARATUS AROUND!
WE HAVE A FOUR-ALARM ON TOPAZ!
NO.
HUH?
THEY'RE COMING.
YOU'VE BEEN TARGETED BY SEVERAL INTERSTELLAR AGENCIES.
A METALEK DRIVER IS CURRENTLY ON ITS WAY TO THIS LOCATION.

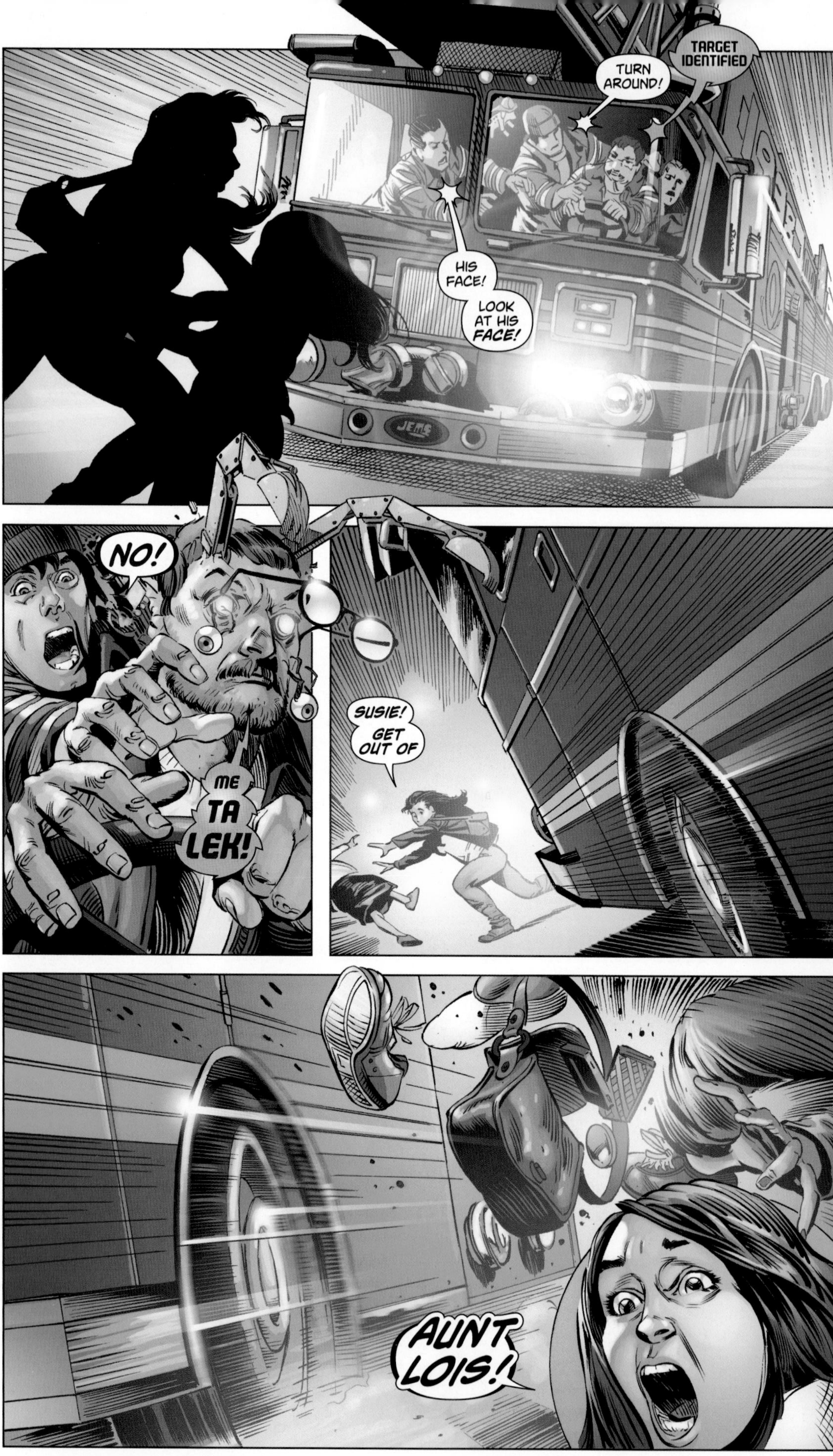
TARGET IDENTIFIED
TURN AROUND!
HIS FACE!
LOOK AT HIS FACE!
NO!
ME TA LEK!
SUSIE! GET OUT OF
AUNT LOIS!

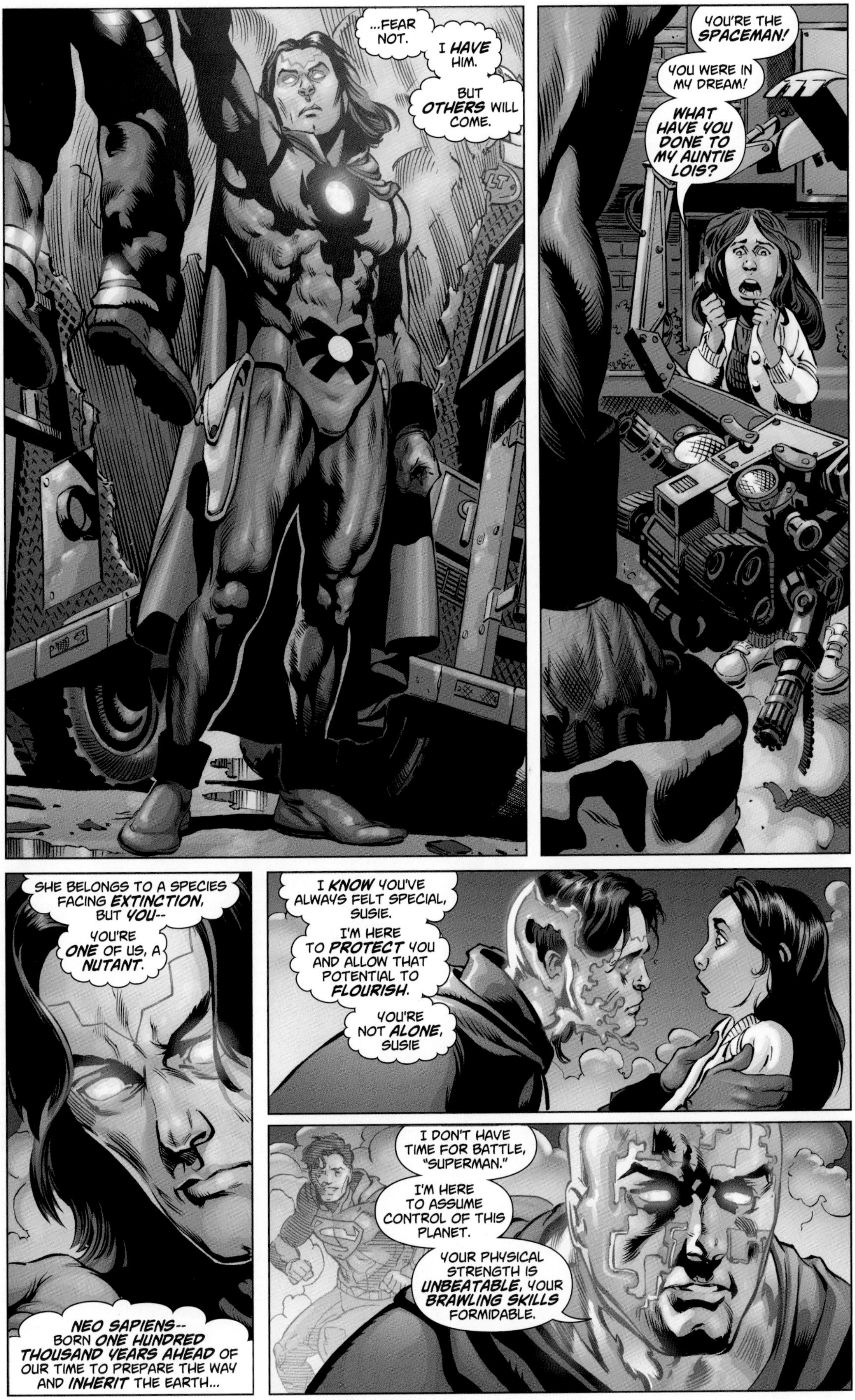
...FEAR NOT.
I HAVE HIM.
BUT OTHERS WILL COME.
YOU'RE THE SPACEMAN!
YOU WERE IN MY DREAM!
WHAT HAVE YOU DONE TO MY AUNTIE LOIS?
SHE BELONGS TO A SPECIES FACING EXTINCTION, BUT YOU--
YOU'RE ONE OF US, A NUTANT.
NEO SAPIENS-- BORN ONE HUNDRED THOUSAND YEARS AHEAD OF OUR TIME TO PREPARE THE WAY AND INHERIT THE EARTH...
I KNOW YOU'VE ALWAYS FELT SPECIAL, SUSIE.
I'M HERE TO PROTECT YOU AND ALLOW THAT POTENTIAL TO FLOURISH.
YOU'RE NOT ALONE, SUSIE
I DON'T HAVE TIME FOR BATTLE, "SUPERMAN."
I'M HERE TO ASSUME CONTROL OF THIS PLANET.
YOUR PHYSICAL STRENGTH IS UNBEATABLE, YOUR BRAWLING SKILLS FORMIDABLE.

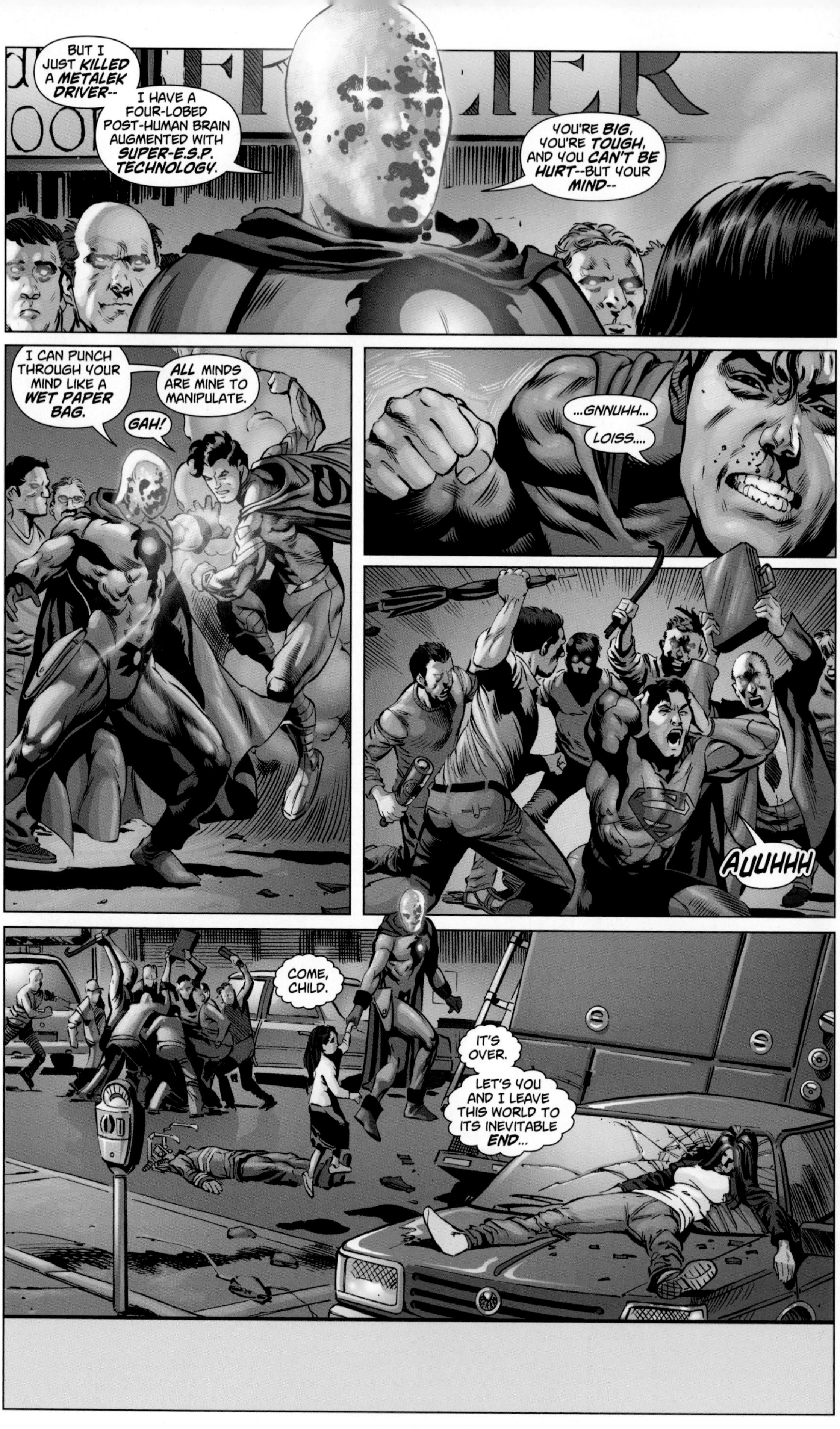
BUT I JUST KILLED A METALEK DRIVER--
I HAVE A FOUR-LOBED POST-HUMAN BRAIN AUGMENTED WITH SUPER-E.S.P. TECHNOLOGY.
YOU'RE BIG, YOU'RE TOUGH, AND YOU CAN'T BE HURT--BUT YOUR MIND--
I CAN PUNCH THROUGH YOUR MIND LIKE A WET PAPER BAG.
ALL MINDS ARE MINE TO MANIPULATE.
GAH!
...GNNUHH...
LOISS....
AUUHHH
COME, CHILD.
IT'S OVER.
LET'S YOU AND I LEAVE THIS WORLD TO ITS INEVITABLE END...

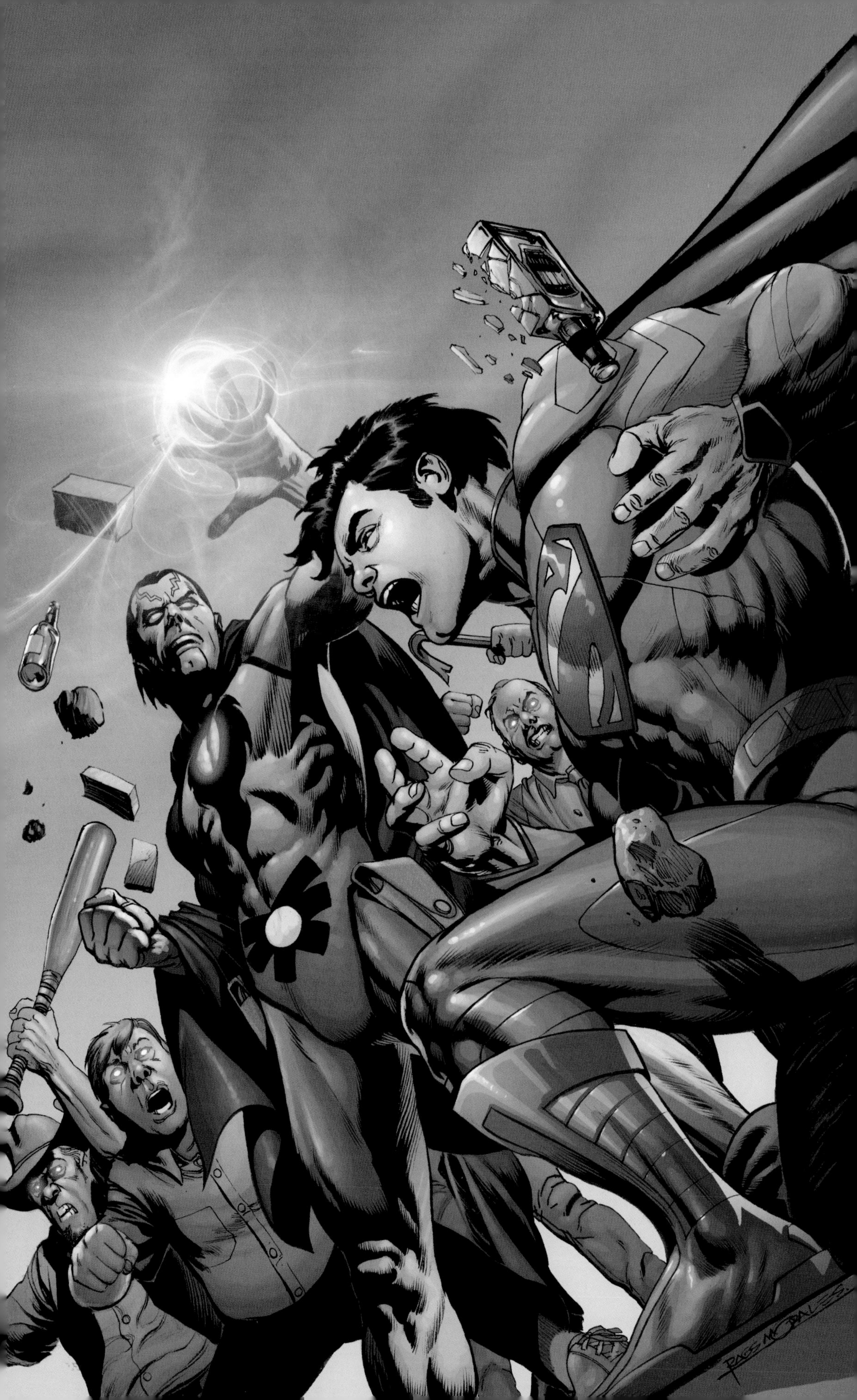

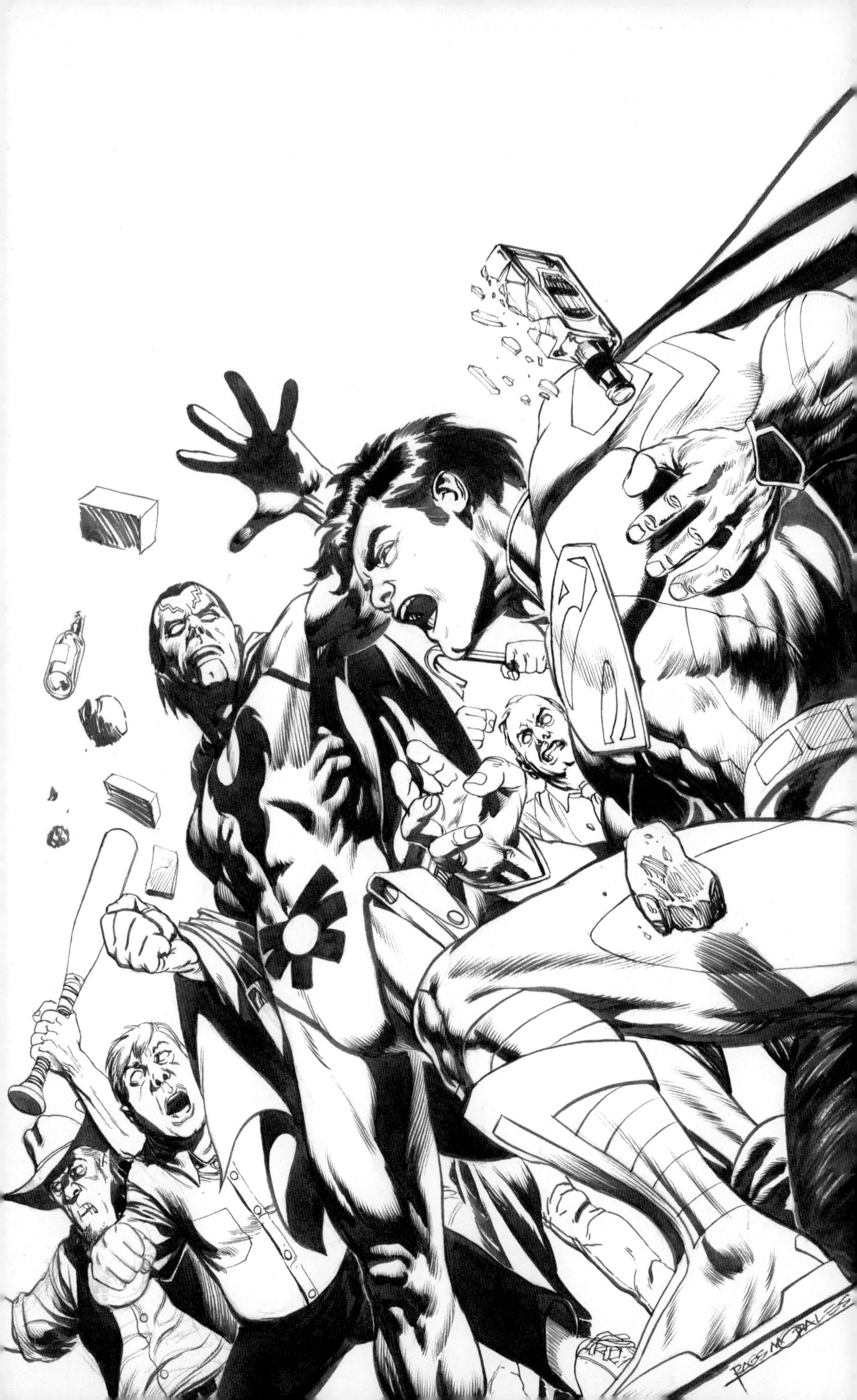
RAGS MORALES

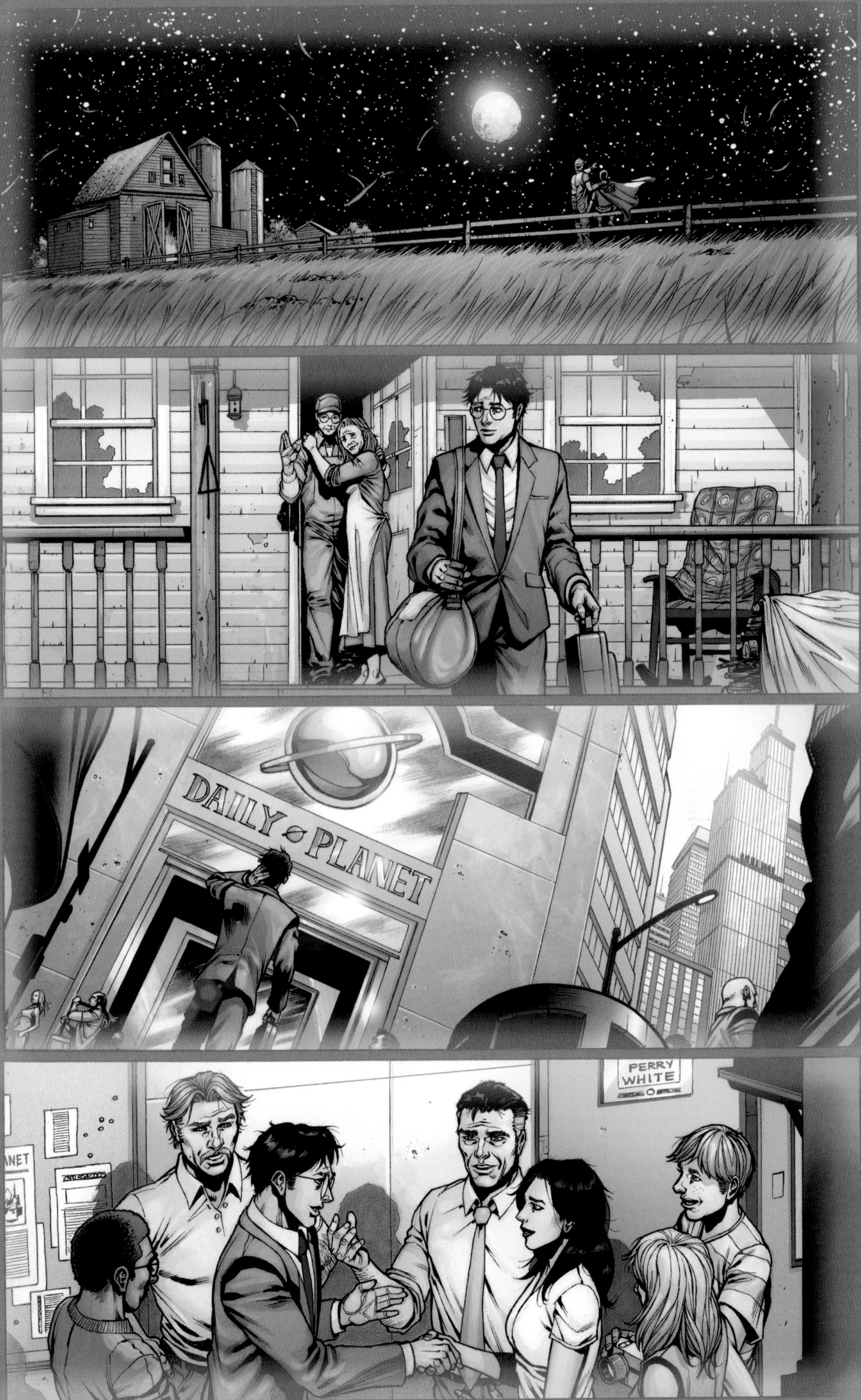
DAILY PLANET
PERRY WHITE

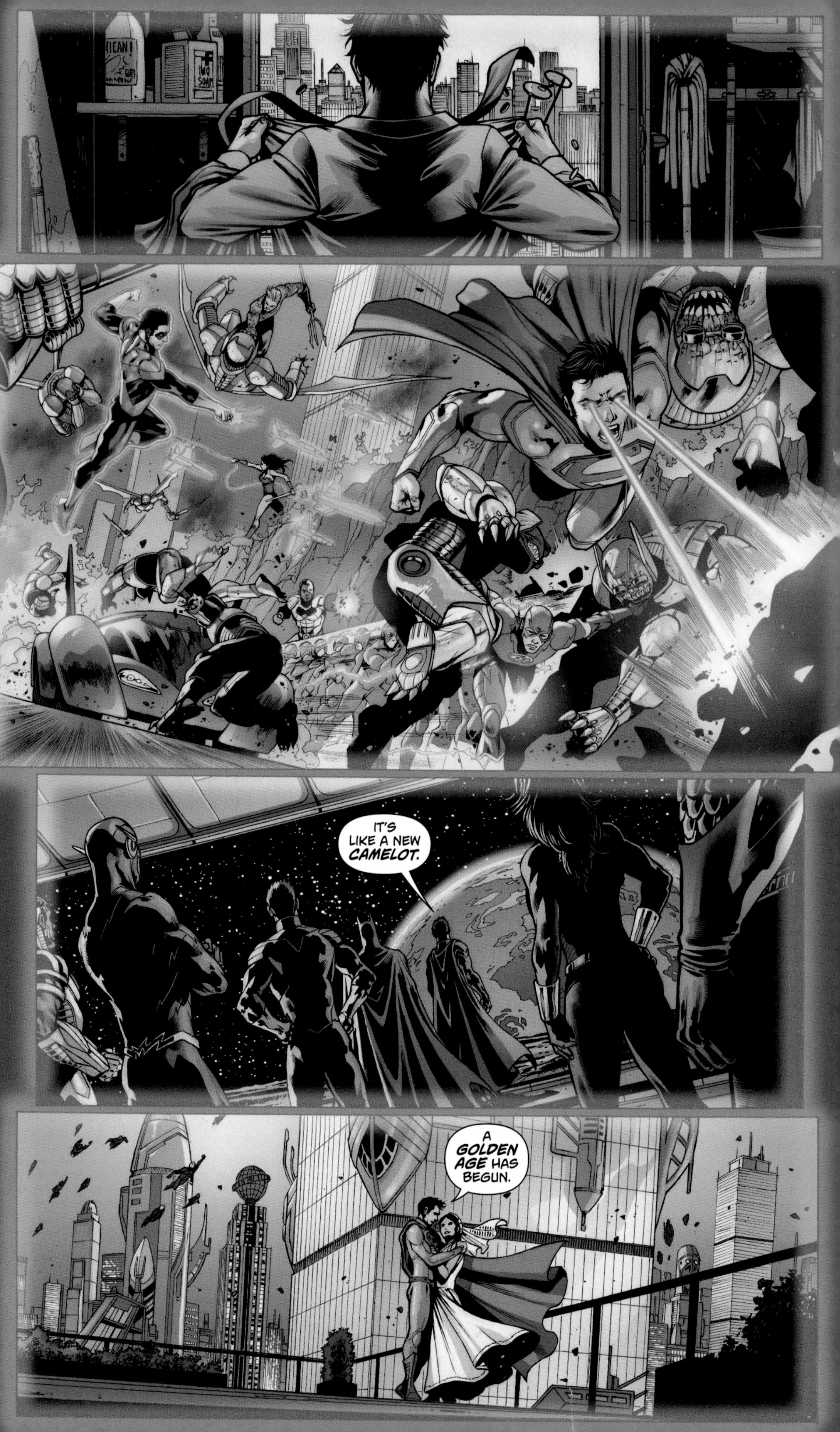
IT'S LIKE A NEW CAMELOT.
A GOLDEN AGE HAS BEGUN.

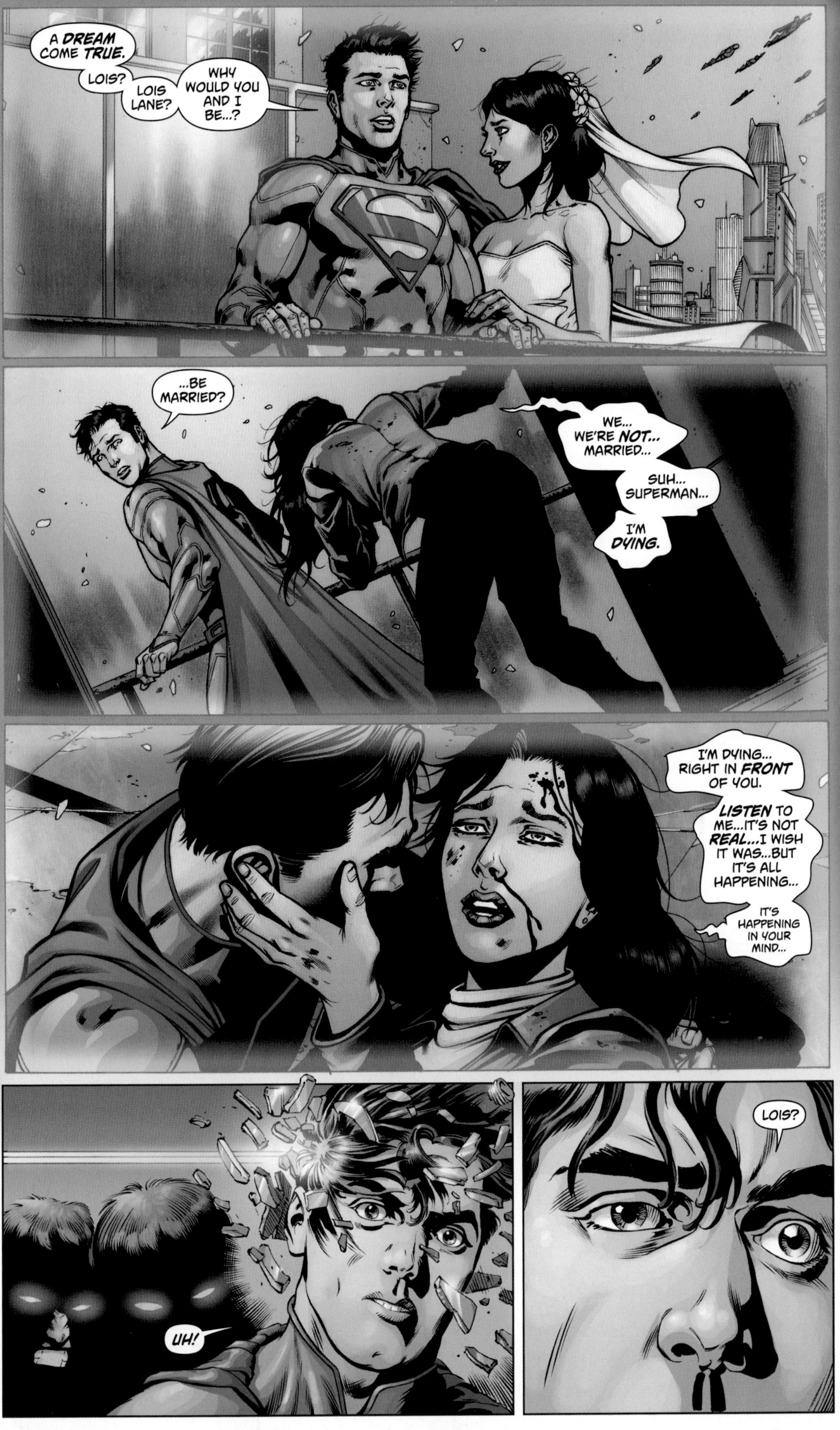
A DREAM COME TRUE.
LOIS?
LOIS LANE?
WHY WOULD YOU AND I BE...?
...BE MARRIED?
WE... WE'RE NOT... MARRIED...
SUH... SUPERMAN...
I'M DYING.
I'M DYING... RIGHT IN FRONT OF YOU.
LISTEN TO ME...IT'S NOT REAL...I WISH IT WAS...BUT IT'S ALL HAPPENING...
IT'S HAPPENING IN YOUR MIND...
UH!
LOIS?

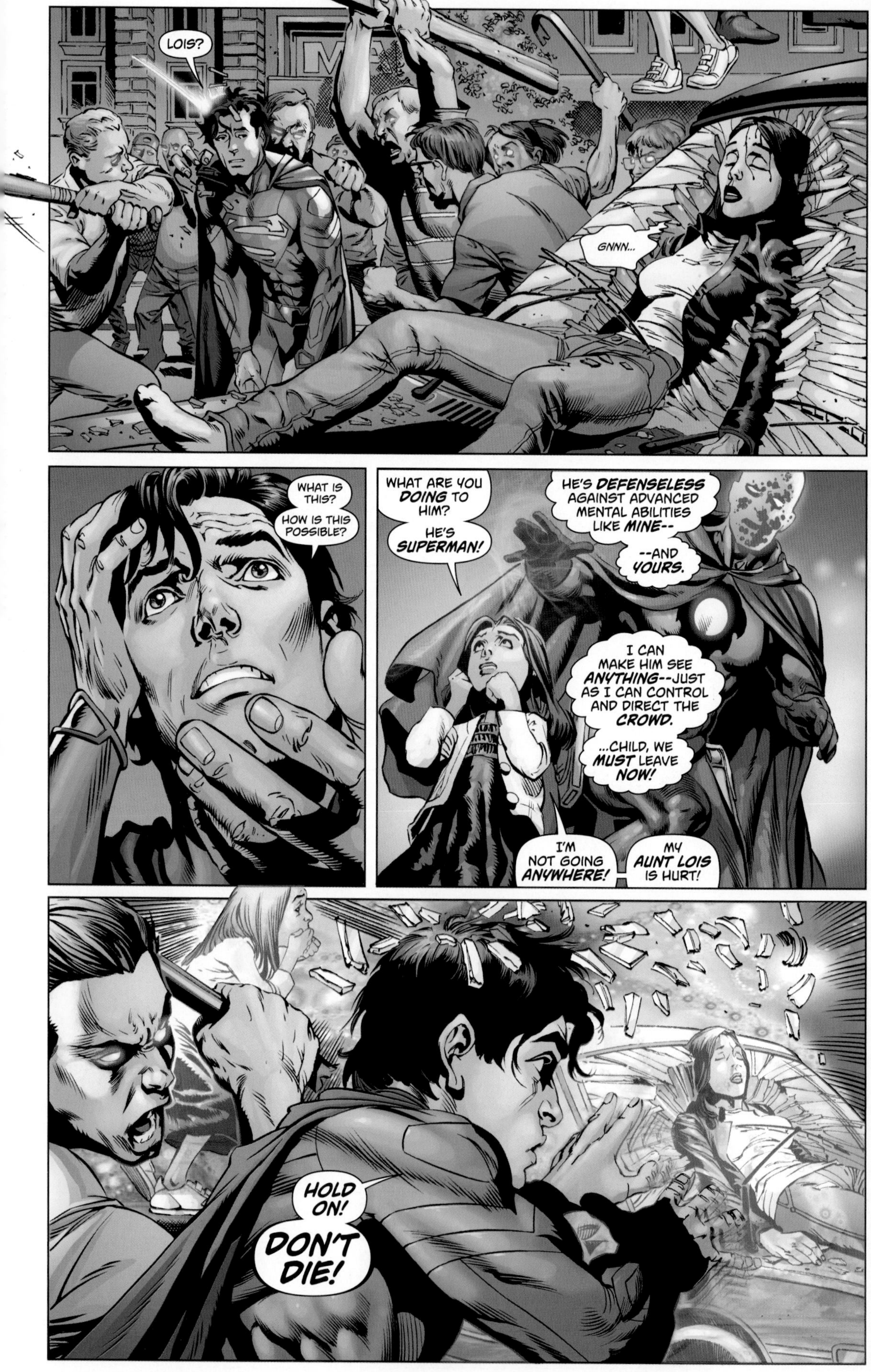
LOIS?
GNNN...
WHAT IS THIS?
HOW IS THIS POSSIBLE?
WHAT ARE YOU DOING TO HIM?
HE'S SUPERMAN!
HE'S DEFENSELESS AGAINST ADVANCED MENTAL ABILITIES LIKE MINE--
--AND YOURS.
I CAN MAKE HIM SEE ANYTHING--JUST AS I CAN CONTROL AND DIRECT THE CROWD.
...CHILD, WE MUST LEAVE NOW!
I'M NOT GOING ANYWHERE!
MY AUNT LOIS IS HURT!
HOLD ON!
DON'T DIE!

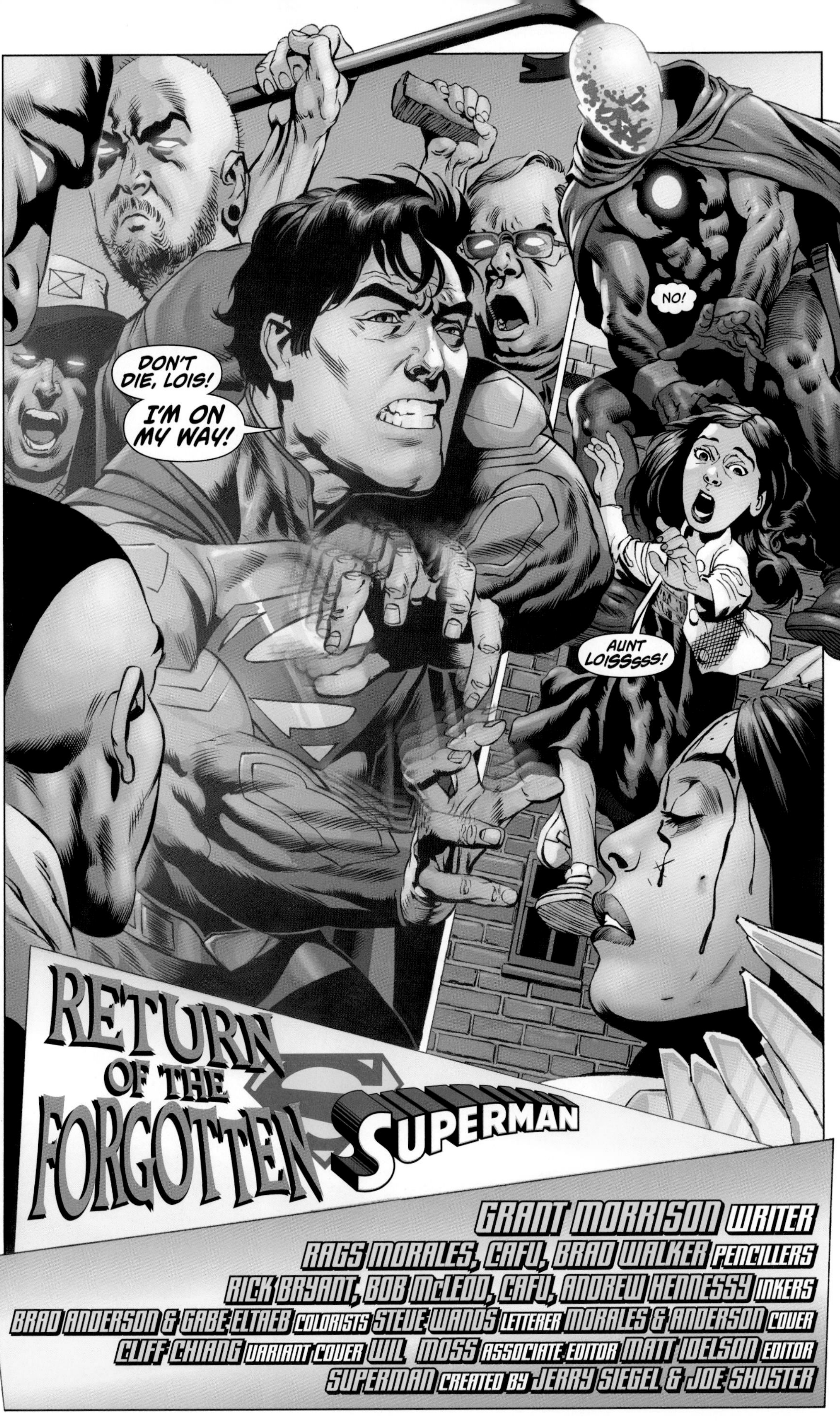
NO!
DON'T DIE, LOIS!
I'M ON MY WAY!
AUNT LOISSSSS!
RETURN OF THE FORGOTTEN
SUPERMAN
GRANT MORRISON WRITER
RAGS MORALES, CAFU, BRAD WALKER PENCILLERS
RICK BRYANT, BOB McLEOD, CAFU, ANDREW HENNESSY INKERS
BRAD ANDERSON & GABE ELTAEB COLORISTS STEVE WANDS LETTERER MORALES & ANDERSON COVER
CLIFF CHIANG VARIANT COVER WIL MOSS ASSOCIATE EDITOR MATT IDELSON EDITOR
SUPERMAN CREATED BY JERRY SIEGEL & JOE SHUSTER

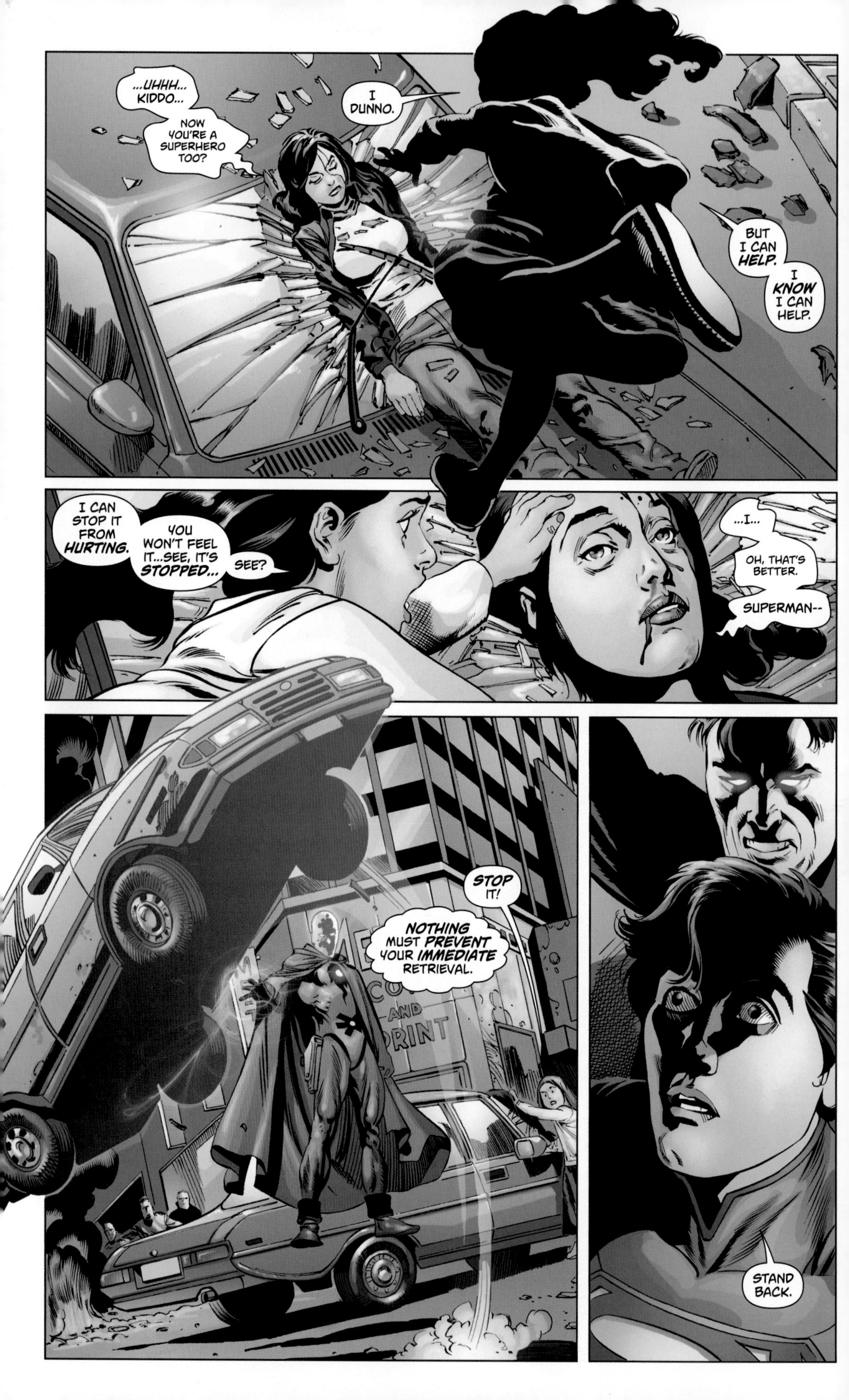
...UHHH... KIDDO...
NOW YOU'RE A SUPERHERO TOO?
I DUNNO.
BUT I CAN HELP.
I KNOW I CAN HELP.
I CAN STOP IT FROM HURTING.
YOU WON'T FEEL IT...SEE, IT'S STOPPED...
SEE?
...I...
OH, THAT'S BETTER.
SUPERMAN--
STOP IT!
NOTHING MUST PREVENT YOUR IMMEDIATE RETRIEVAL.
AND
STAND BACK.

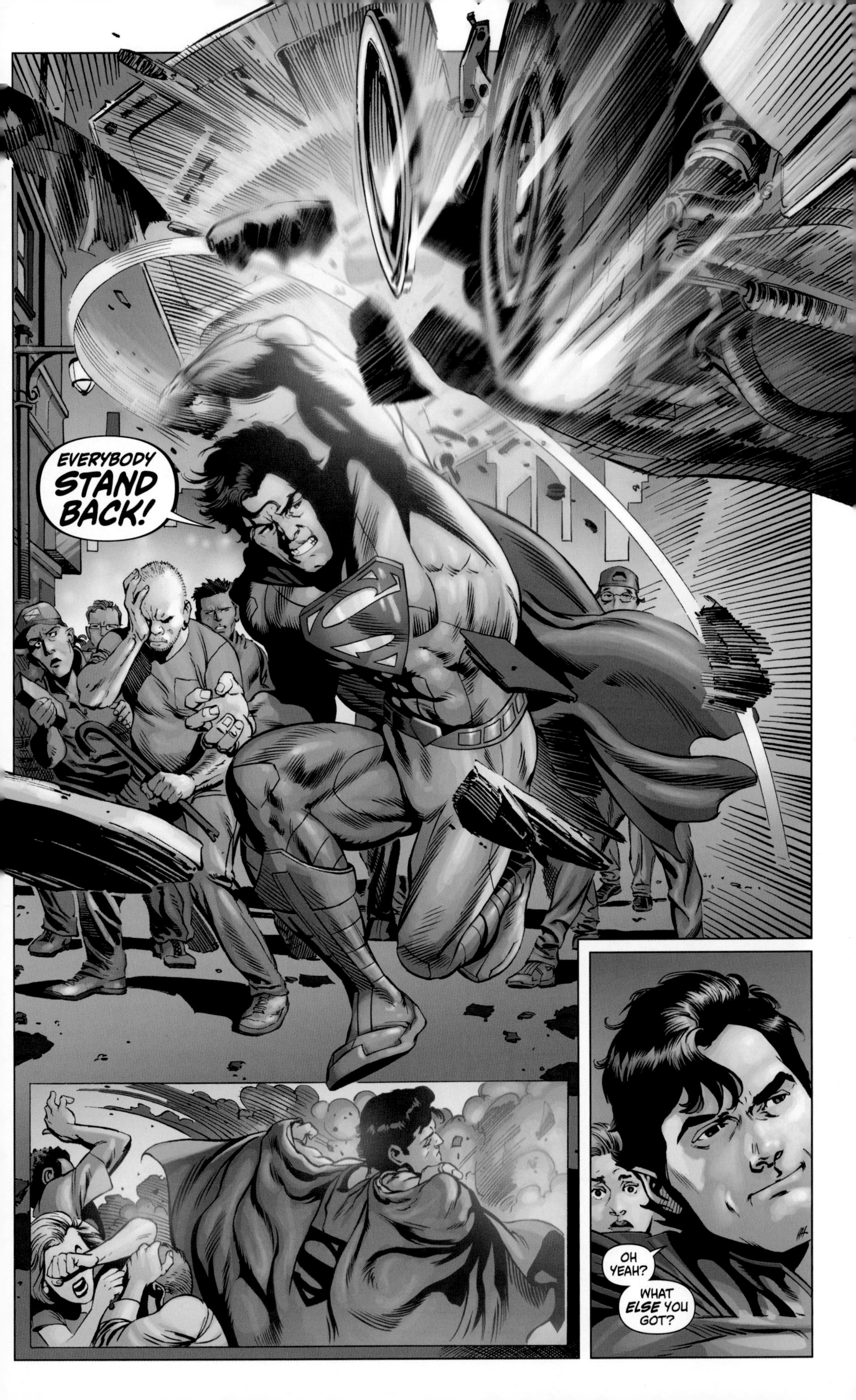
EVERYBODY STAND BACK!
OH YEAH?
WHAT ELSE YOU GOT?

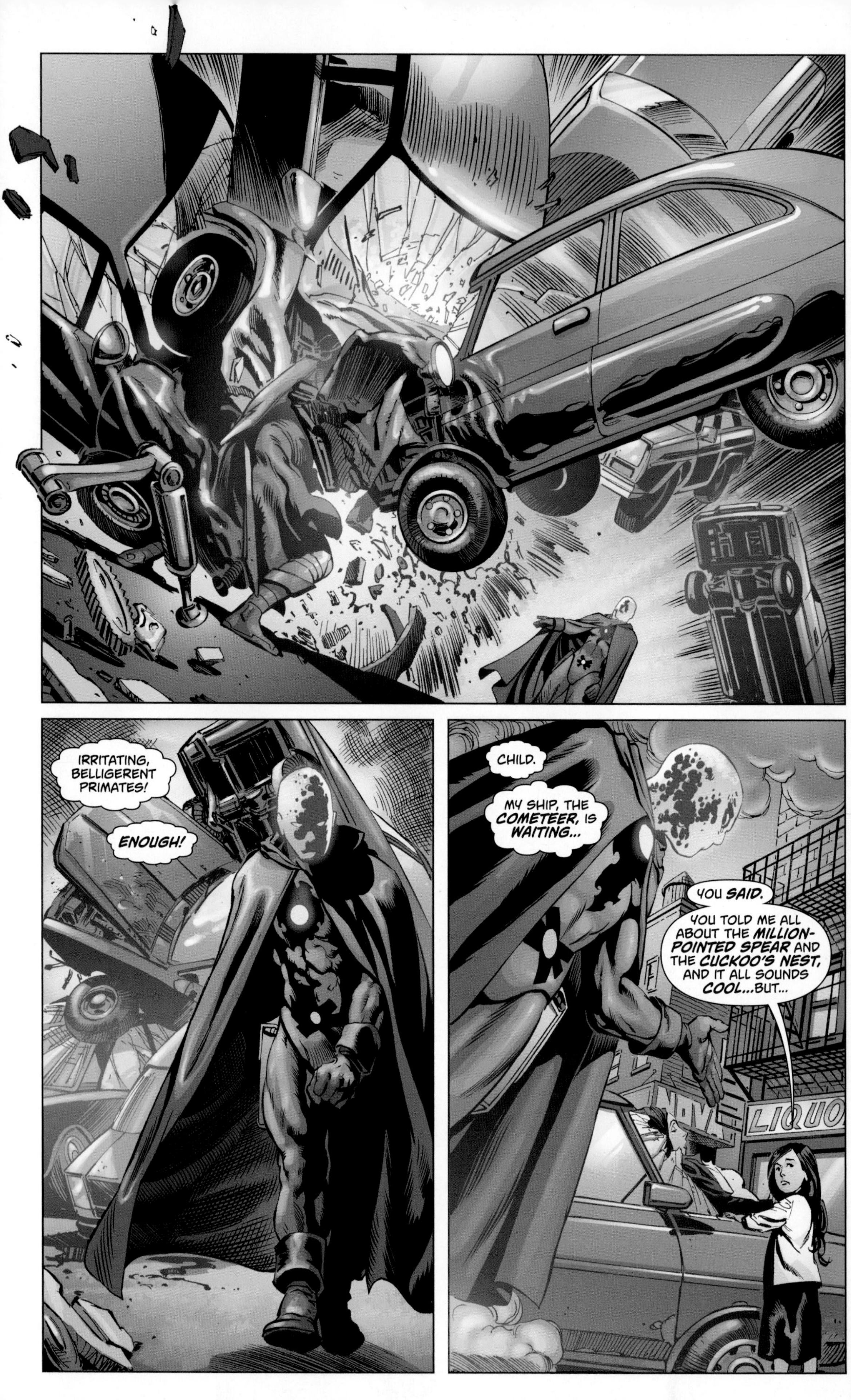
IRRITATING, BELLIGERENT PRIMATES!
ENOUGH!
CHILD.
MY SHIP, THE COMETEER, IS WAITING...
YOU SAID.
YOU TOLD ME ALL ABOUT THE MILLION-POINTED SPEAR AND THE CUCKOO'S NEST, AND IT ALL SOUNDS COOL...BUT...
LIQUO

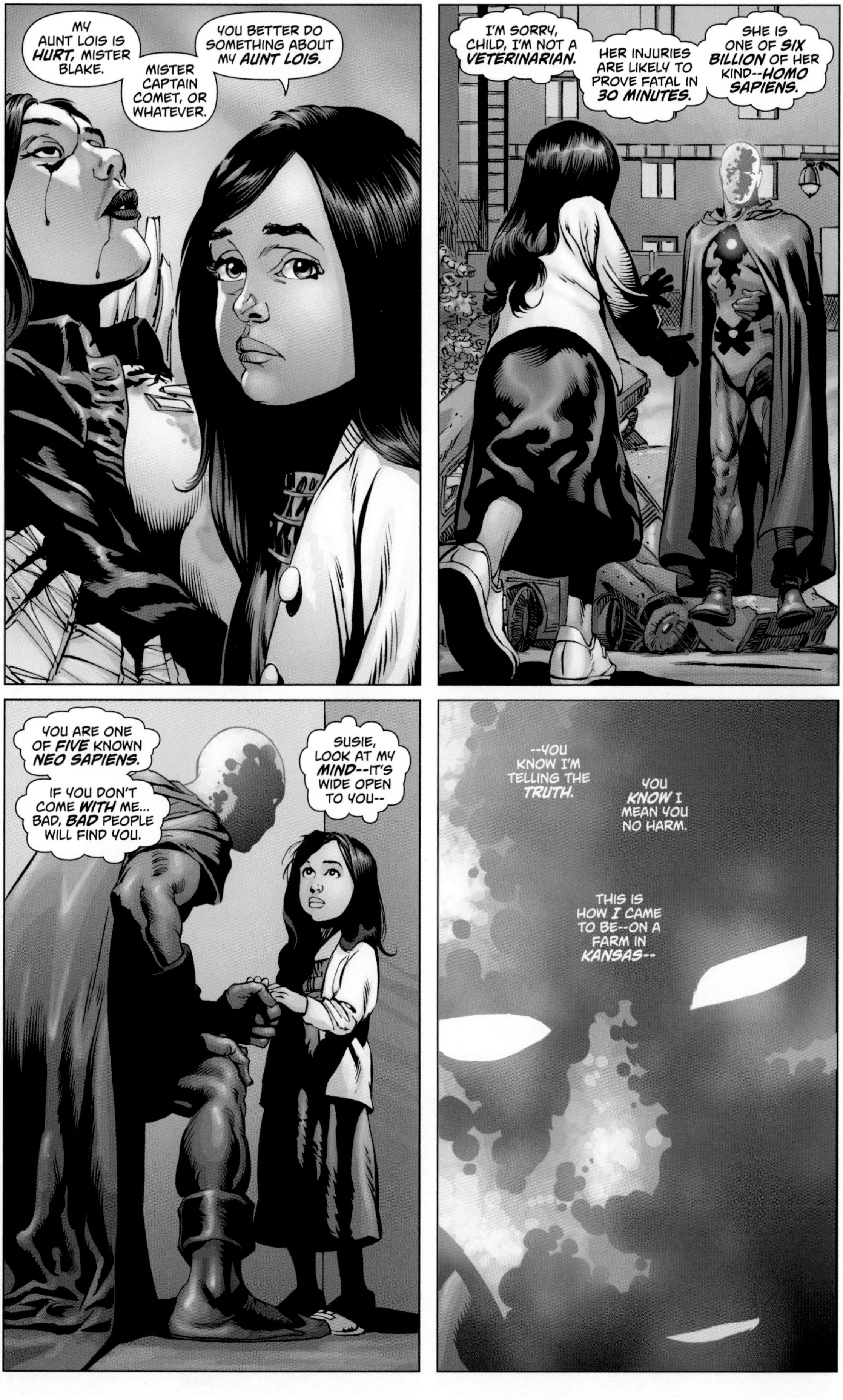
MY AUNT LOIS IS HURT, MISTER BLAKE.
MISTER CAPTAIN COMET, OR WHATEVER.
YOU BETTER DO SOMETHING ABOUT MY AUNT LOIS.
I'M SORRY, CHILD, I'M NOT A VETERINARIAN.
HER INJURIES ARE LIKELY TO PROVE FATAL IN 30 MINUTES.
SHE IS ONE OF SIX BILLION OF HER KIND--HOMO SAPIENS.
YOU ARE ONE OF FIVE KNOWN NEO SAPIENS.
IF YOU DON'T COME WITH ME... BAD, BAD PEOPLE WILL FIND YOU.
SUSIE, LOOK AT MY MIND--IT'S WIDE OPEN TO YOU--
--YOU KNOW I'M TELLING THE TRUTH.
YOU KNOW I MEAN YOU NO HARM.
THIS IS HOW I CAME TO BE--ON A FARM IN KANSAS--

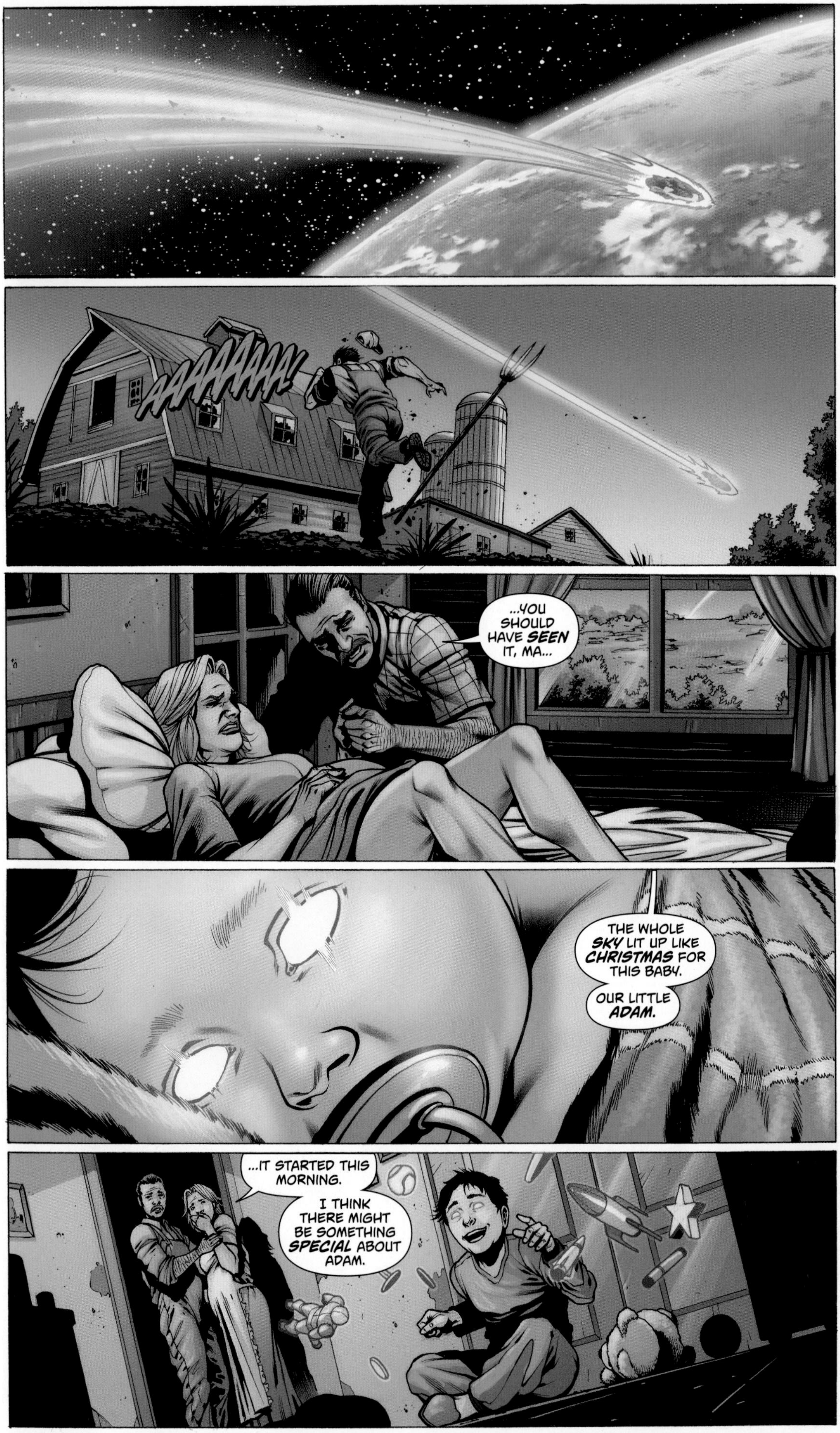
AAAAAAAA!
...YOU SHOULD HAVE SEEN IT, MA...
THE WHOLE SKY LIT UP LIKE CHRISTMAS FOR THIS BABY.
OUR LITTLE ADAM.
...IT STARTED THIS MORNING.
I THINK THERE MIGHT BE SOMETHING SPECIAL ABOUT ADAM.

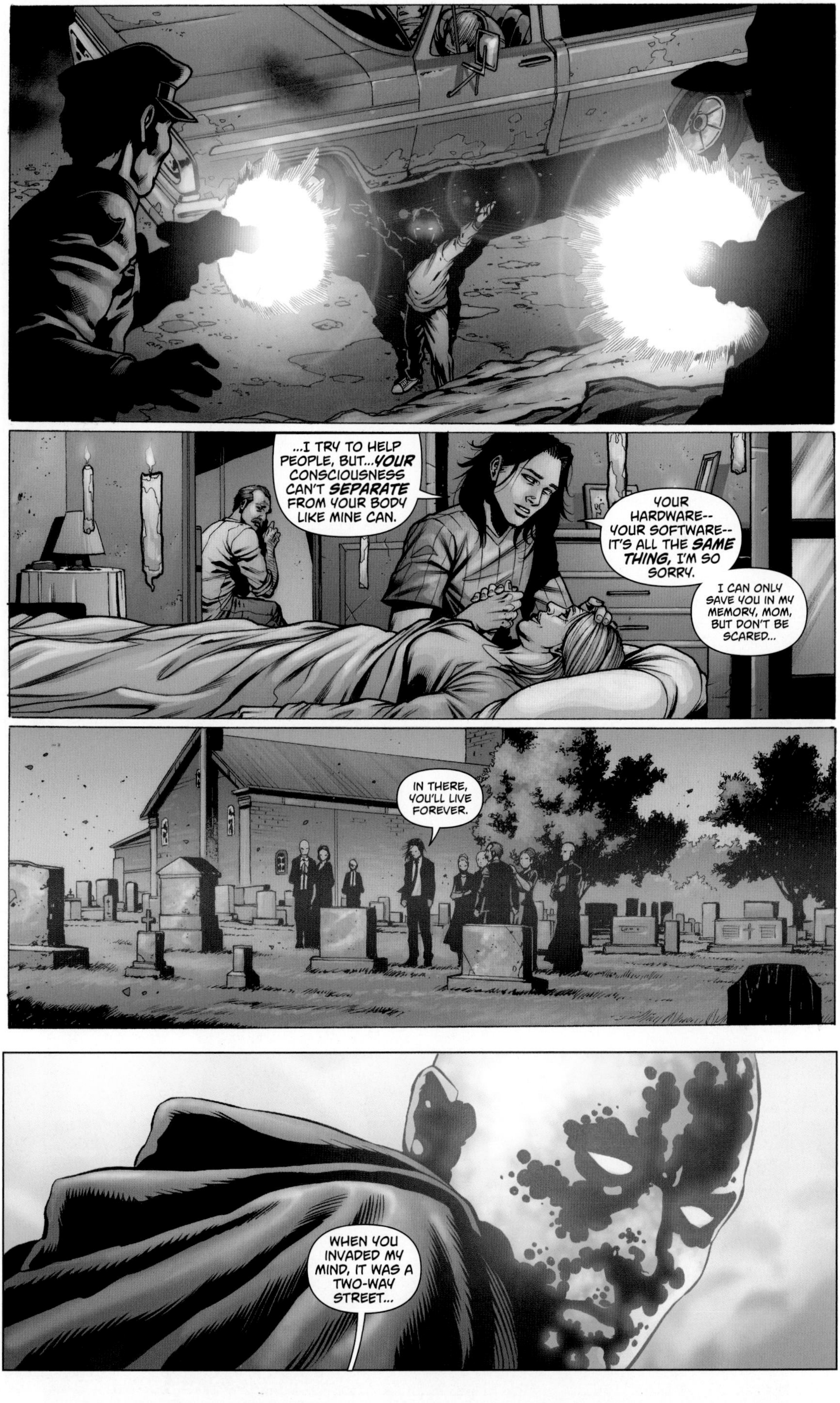
...I TRY TO HELP PEOPLE, BUT...YOUR CONSCIOUSNESS CAN'T SEPARATE FROM YOUR BODY LIKE MINE CAN.
YOUR HARDWARE--YOUR SOFTWARE--IT'S ALL THE SAME THING, I'M SO SORRY.
I CAN ONLY SAVE YOU IN MY MEMORY, MOM, BUT DON'T BE SCARED...
IN THERE, YOU'LL LIVE FOREVER.
WHEN YOU INVADED MY MIND, IT WAS A TWO-WAY STREET...

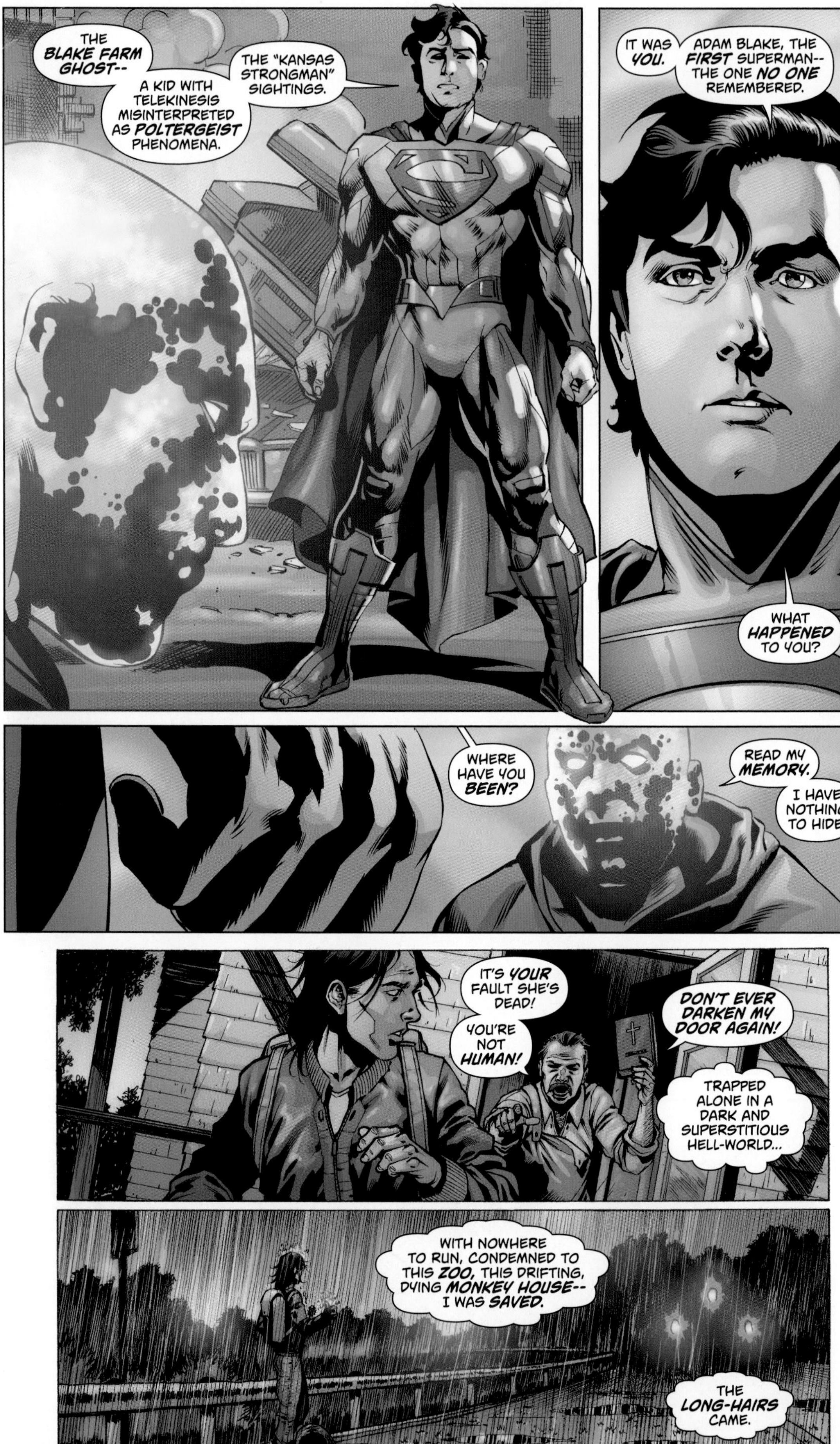

THE BLAKE FARM GHOST--
A KID WITH TELEKINESIS MISINTERPRETED AS POLTERGEIST PHENOMENA.
THE "KANSAS STRONGMAN" SIGHTINGS.
IT WAS YOU.
ADAM BLAKE, THE FIRST SUPERMAN-- THE ONE NO ONE REMEMBERED.
WHAT HAPPENED TO YOU?
WHERE HAVE YOU BEEN?
READ MY MEMORY.
I HAVE NOTHING TO HIDE.
IT'S YOUR FAULT SHE'S DEAD!
YOU'RE NOT HUMAN!
DON'T EVER DARKEN MY DOOR AGAIN!
TRAPPED ALONE IN A DARK AND SUPERSTITIOUS HELL-WORLD...
WITH NOWHERE TO RUN, CONDEMNED TO THIS ZOO, THIS DRIFTING, DYING MONKEY HOUSE-- I WAS SAVED.
THE LONG-HAIRS CAME.

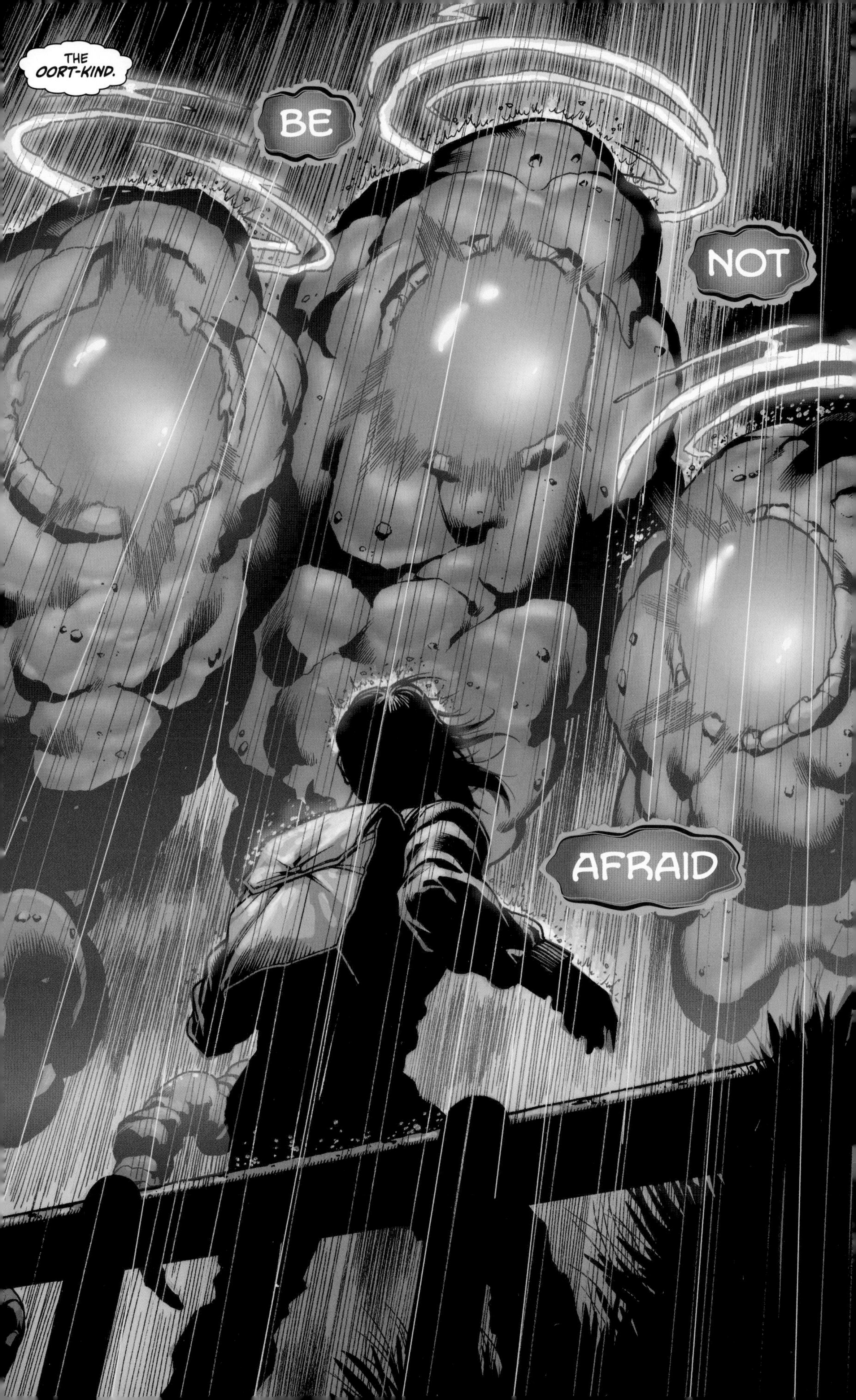
THE OORT-KIND.
BE
NOT
AFRAID

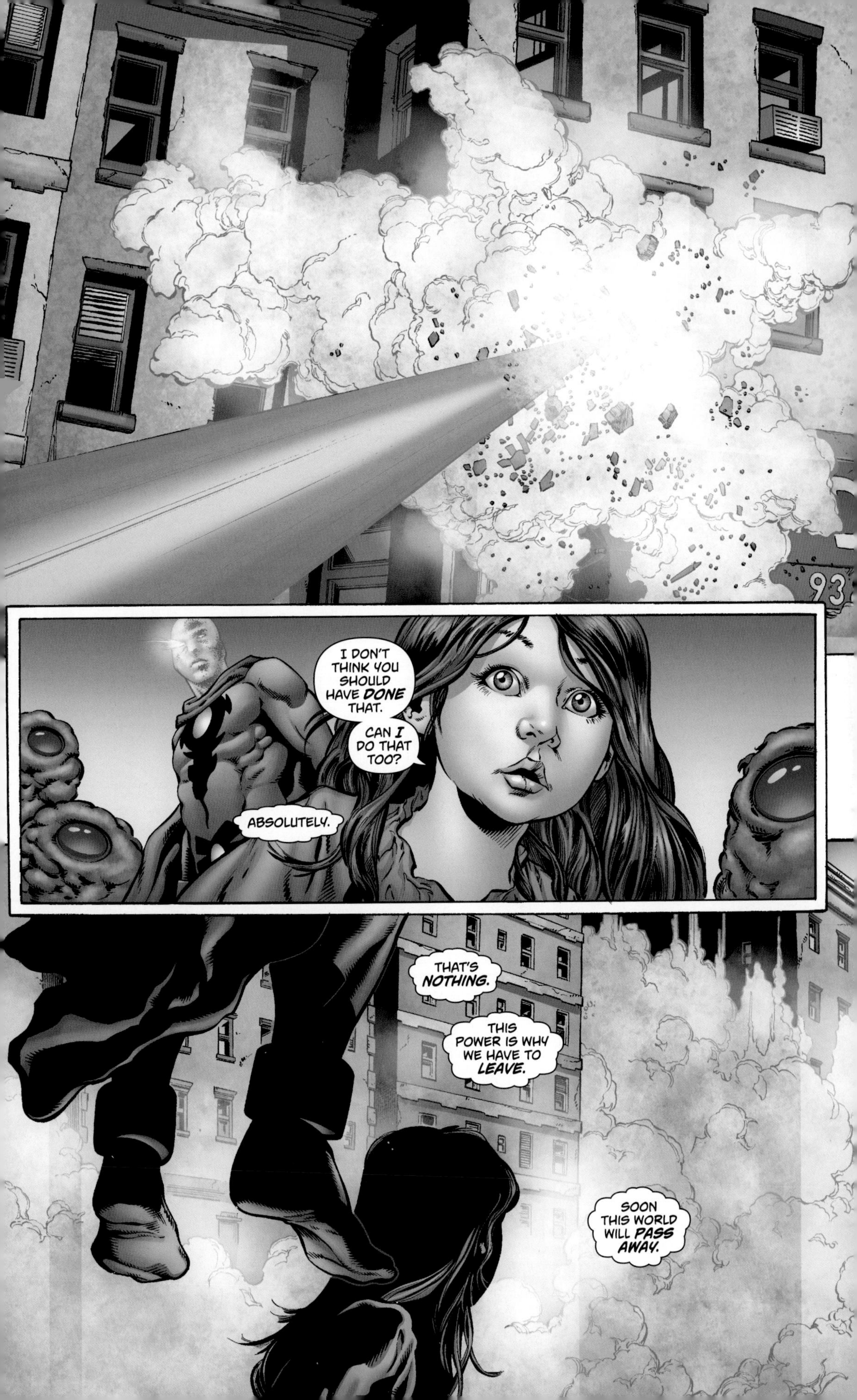

93
I DON'T THINK YOU SHOULD HAVE DONE THAT.
CAN I DO THAT TOO?
ABSOLUTELY.
THAT'S NOTHING.
THIS POWER IS WHY WE HAVE TO LEAVE.
SOON THIS WORLD WILL PASS AWAY.

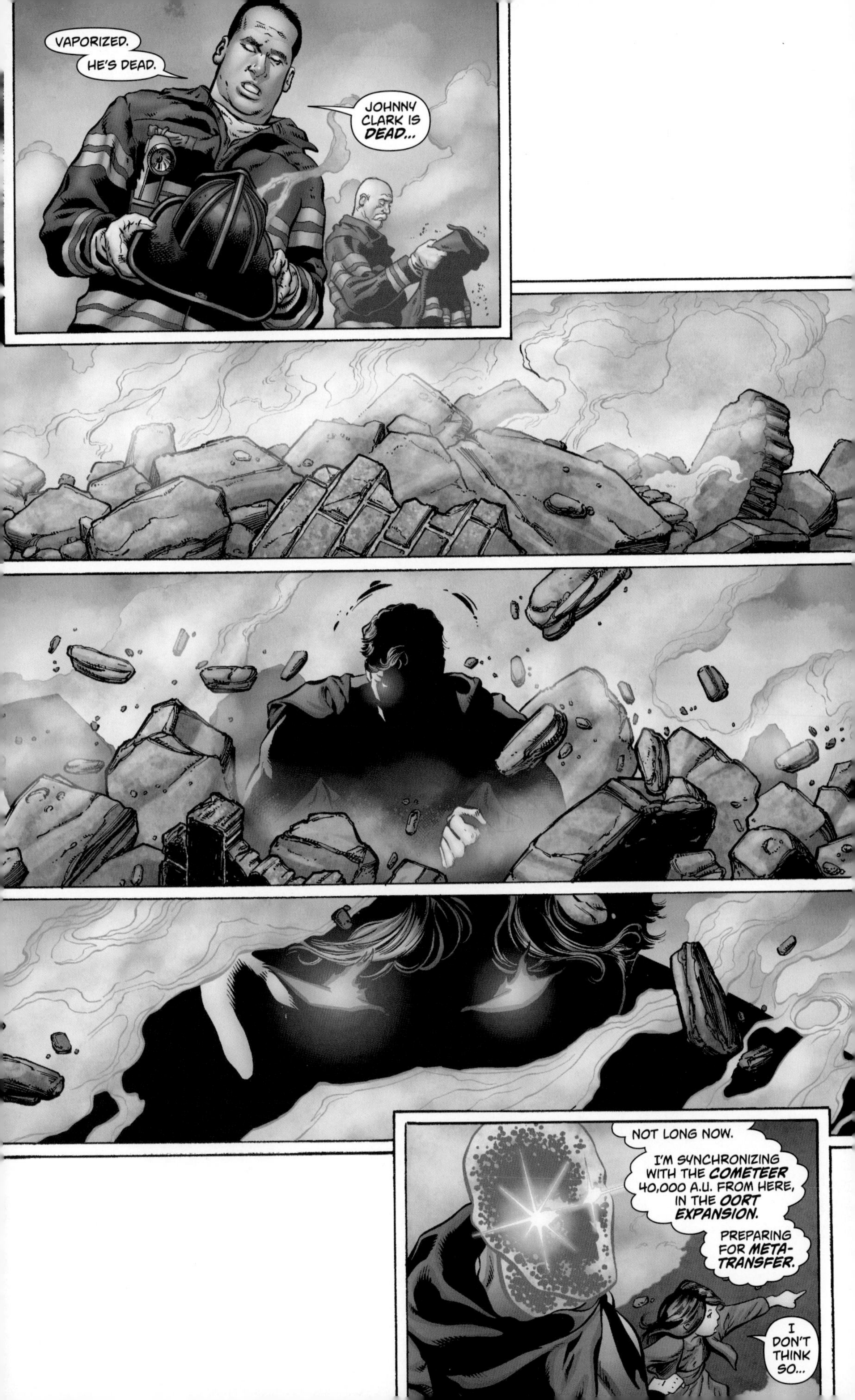

VAPORIZED.
HE'S DEAD.
JOHNNY CLARK IS DEAD...
NOT LONG NOW.
I'M SYNCHRONIZING WITH THE COMETEER 40,000 A.U. FROM HERE, IN THE OORT EXPANSION.
PREPARING FOR META-TRANSFER.
I DON'T THINK SO...

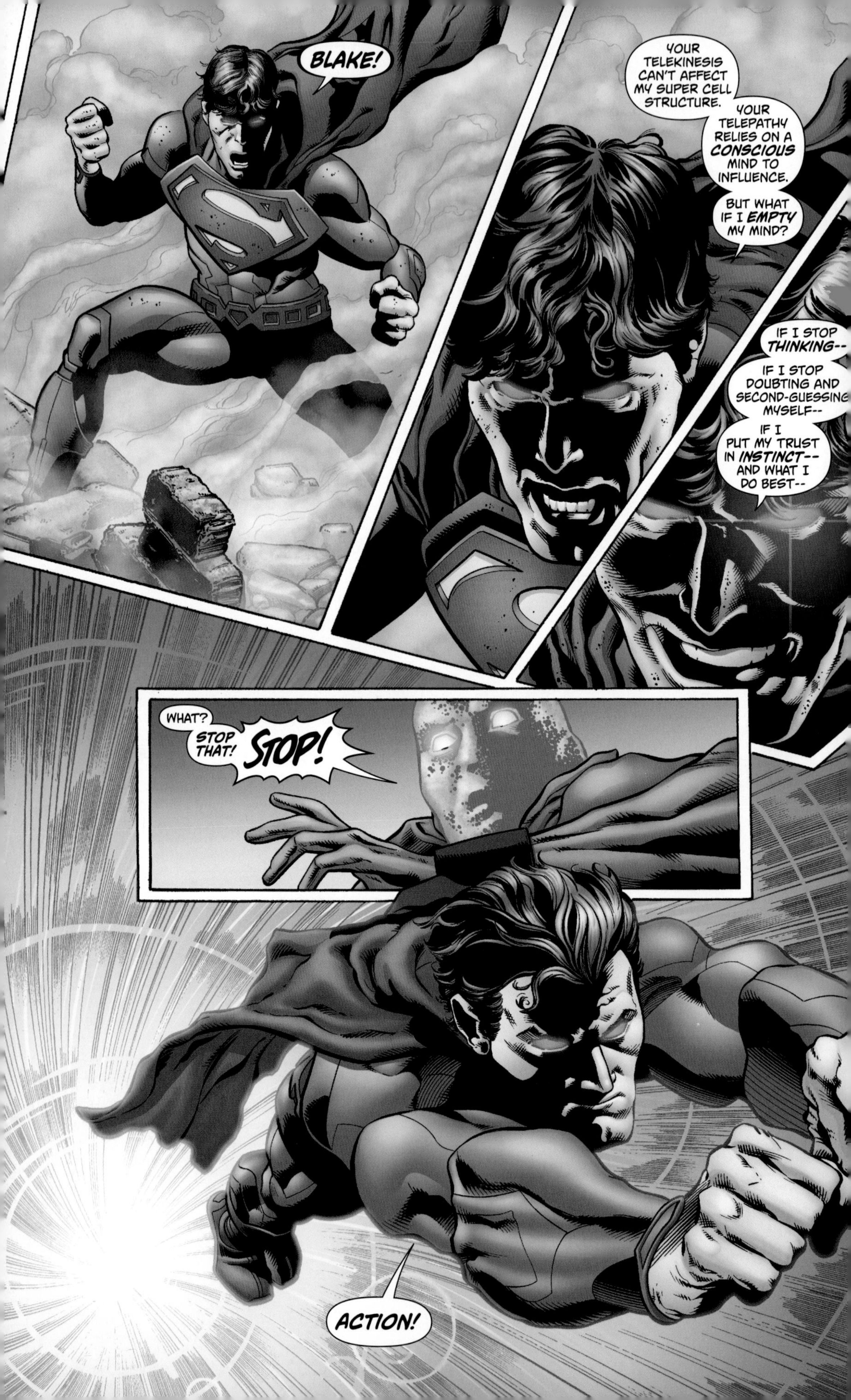
BLAKE!
YOUR TELEKINESIS CAN'T AFFECT MY SUPER CELL STRUCTURE.
YOUR TELEPATHY RELIES ON A CONSCIOUS MIND TO INFLUENCE.
BUT WHAT IF I EMPTY MY MIND?
IF I STOP THINKING--
IF I STOP DOUBTING AND SECOND-GUESSING MYSELF--
IF I PUT MY TRUST IN INSTINCT--
AND WHAT I DO BEST--
WHAT?
STOP THAT!
STOP!
ACTION!

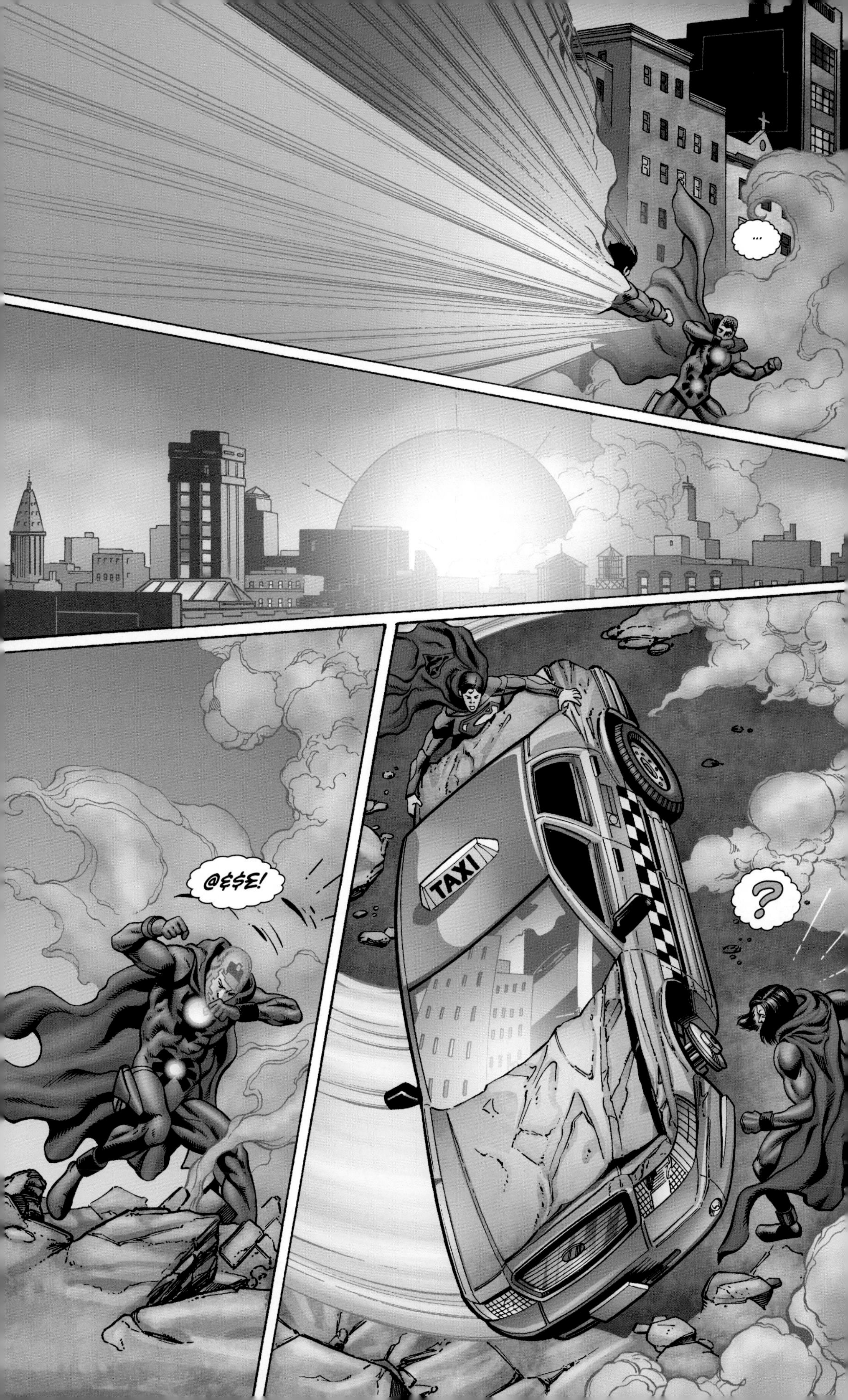
...
@¢$£!
TAXI
?

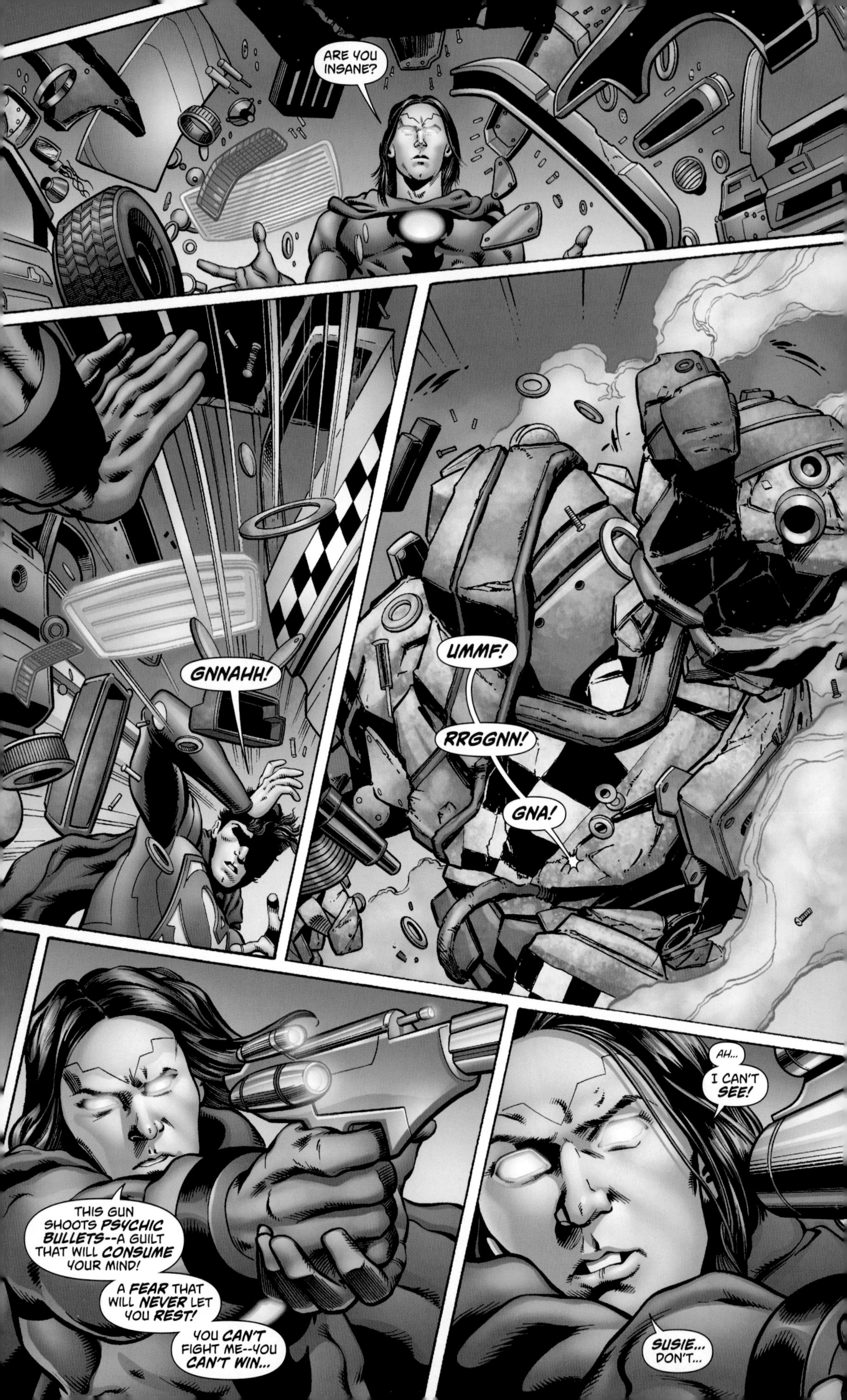
ARE YOU INSANE?
GNNAHH!
UMMF!
RRGGNN!
GNA!
THIS GUN SHOOTS PSYCHIC BULLETS--A GUILT THAT WILL CONSUME YOUR MIND!
A FEAR THAT WILL NEVER LET YOU REST!
YOU CAN'T FIGHT ME--YOU CAN'T WIN...
AH...
I CAN'T SEE!
SUSIE... DON'T...

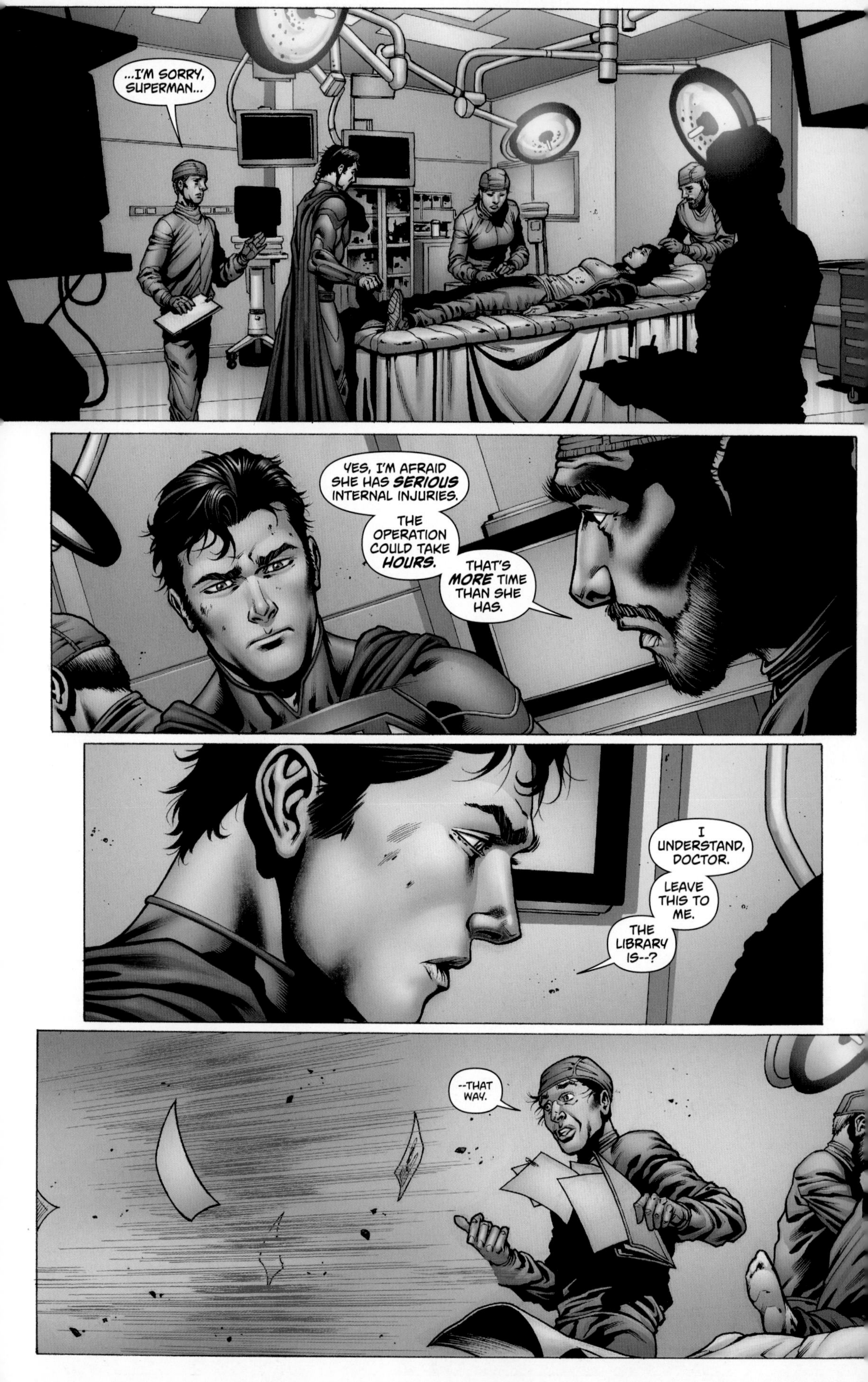
...I'M SORRY, SUPERMAN...
YES, I'M AFRAID SHE HAS SERIOUS INTERNAL INJURIES.
THE OPERATION COULD TAKE HOURS.
THAT'S MORE TIME THAN SHE HAS.
I UNDERSTAND, DOCTOR.
LEAVE THIS TO ME.
THE LIBRARY IS--?
--THAT WAY.

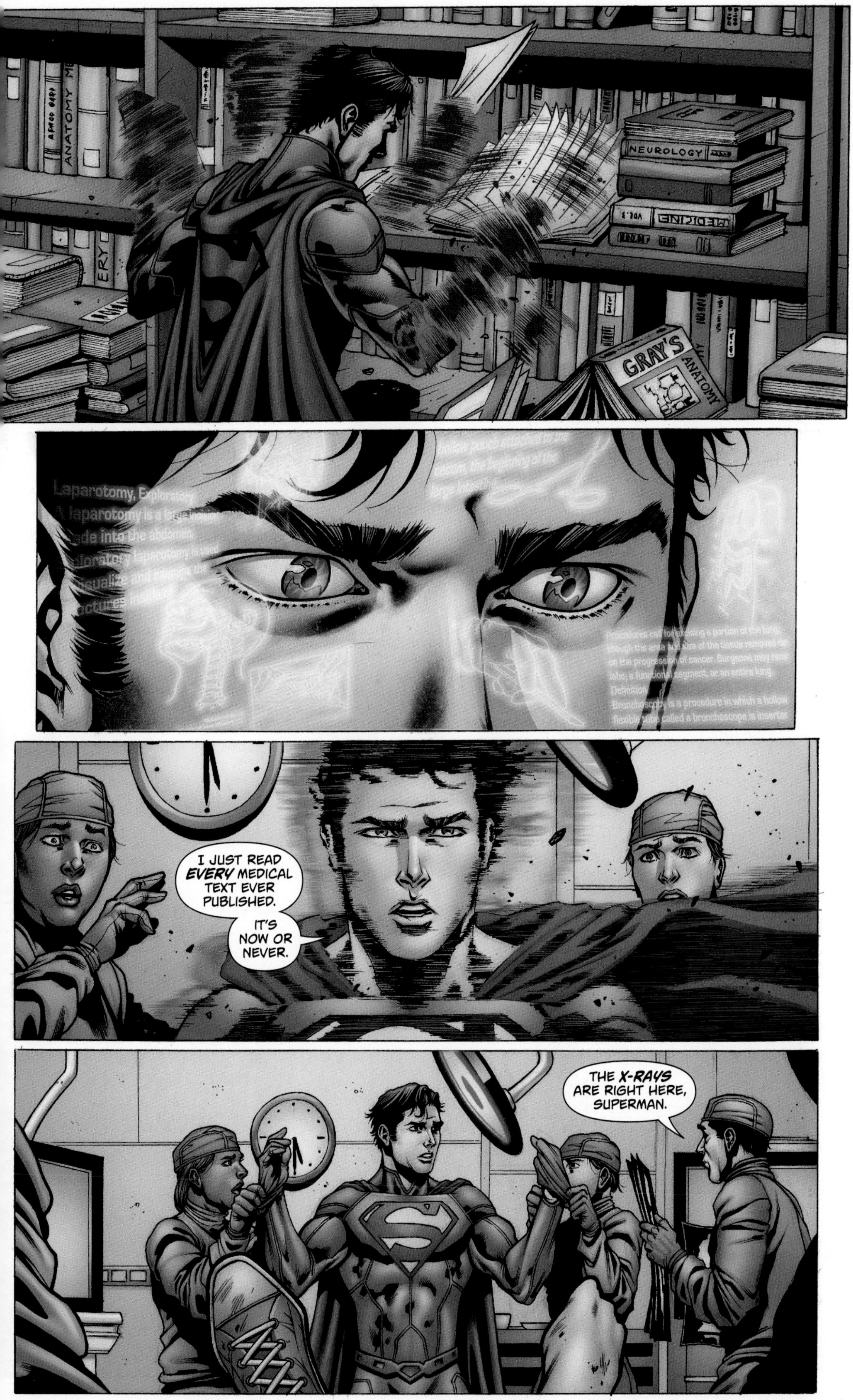
NEUROLOGY
GRAY'S ANATOMY
Laparotomy, Exploratory
I JUST READ EVERY MEDICAL TEXT EVER PUBLISHED.
IT'S NOW OR NEVER.
THE X-RAYS ARE RIGHT HERE, SUPERMAN.

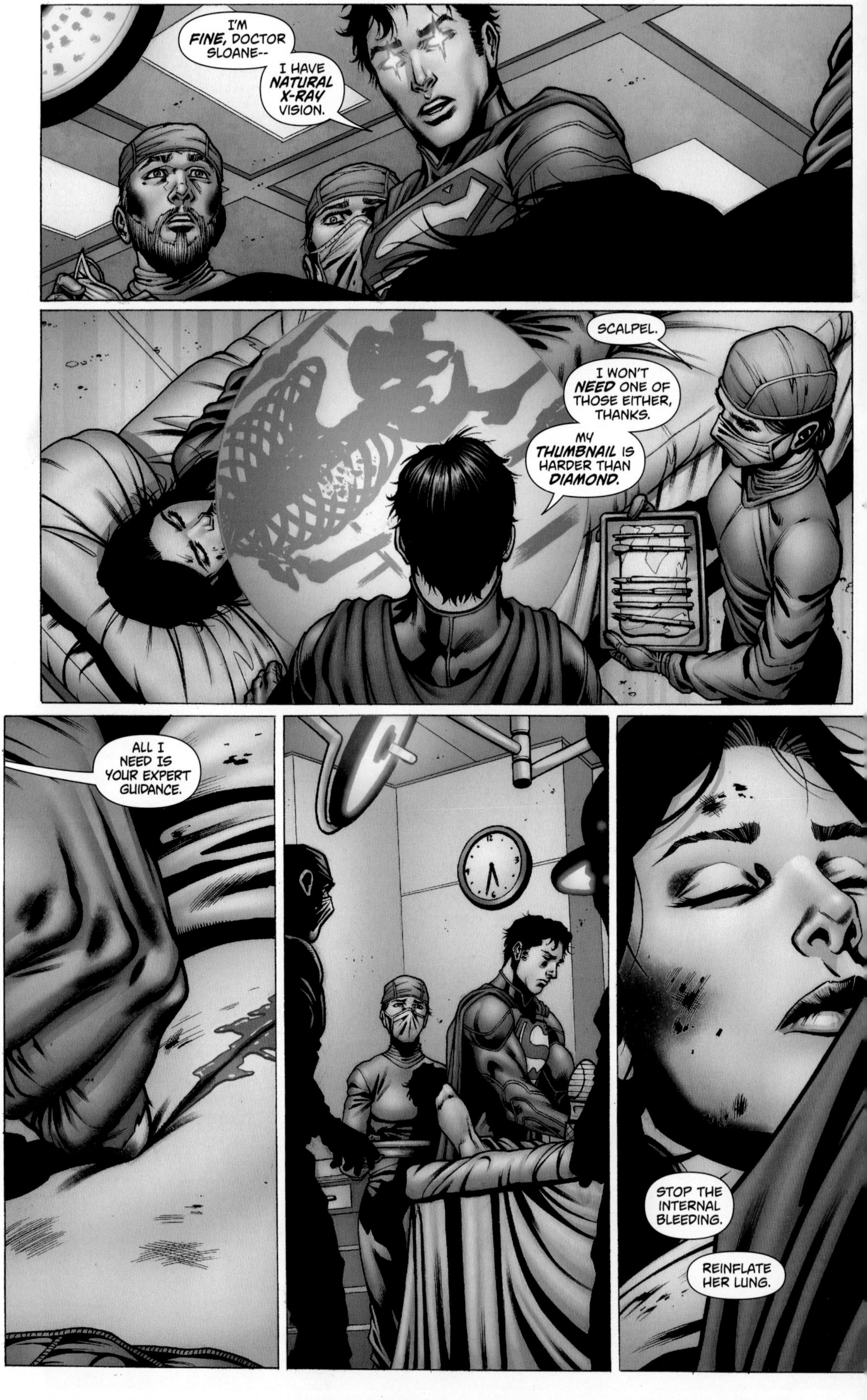
I'M FINE, DOCTOR SLOANE--
I HAVE NATURAL X-RAY VISION.
SCALPEL.
I WON'T NEED ONE OF THOSE EITHER, THANKS.
MY THUMBNAIL IS HARDER THAN DIAMOND.
ALL I NEED IS YOUR EXPERT GUIDANCE.
STOP THE INTERNAL BLEEDING.
REINFLATE HER LUNG.

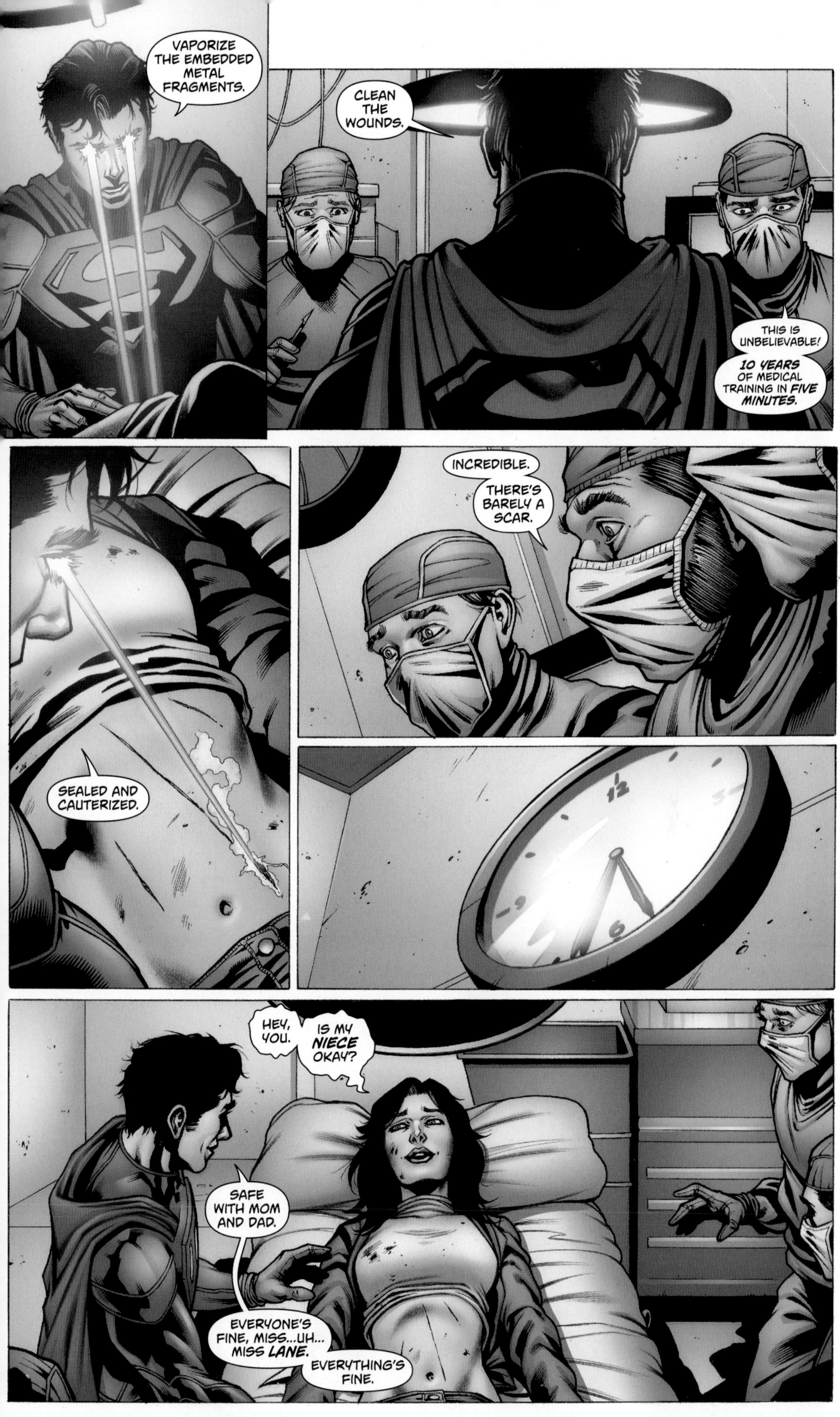
VAPORIZE THE EMBEDDED METAL FRAGMENTS.
CLEAN THE WOUNDS.
THIS IS UNBELIEVABLE!
10 YEARS OF MEDICAL TRAINING IN FIVE MINUTES.
SEALED AND CAUTERIZED.
INCREDIBLE.
THERE'S BARELY A SCAR.
HEY, YOU.
IS MY NIECE OKAY?
SAFE WITH MOM AND DAD.
EVERYONE'S FINE, MISS...UH... MISS LANE.
EVERYTHING'S FINE.

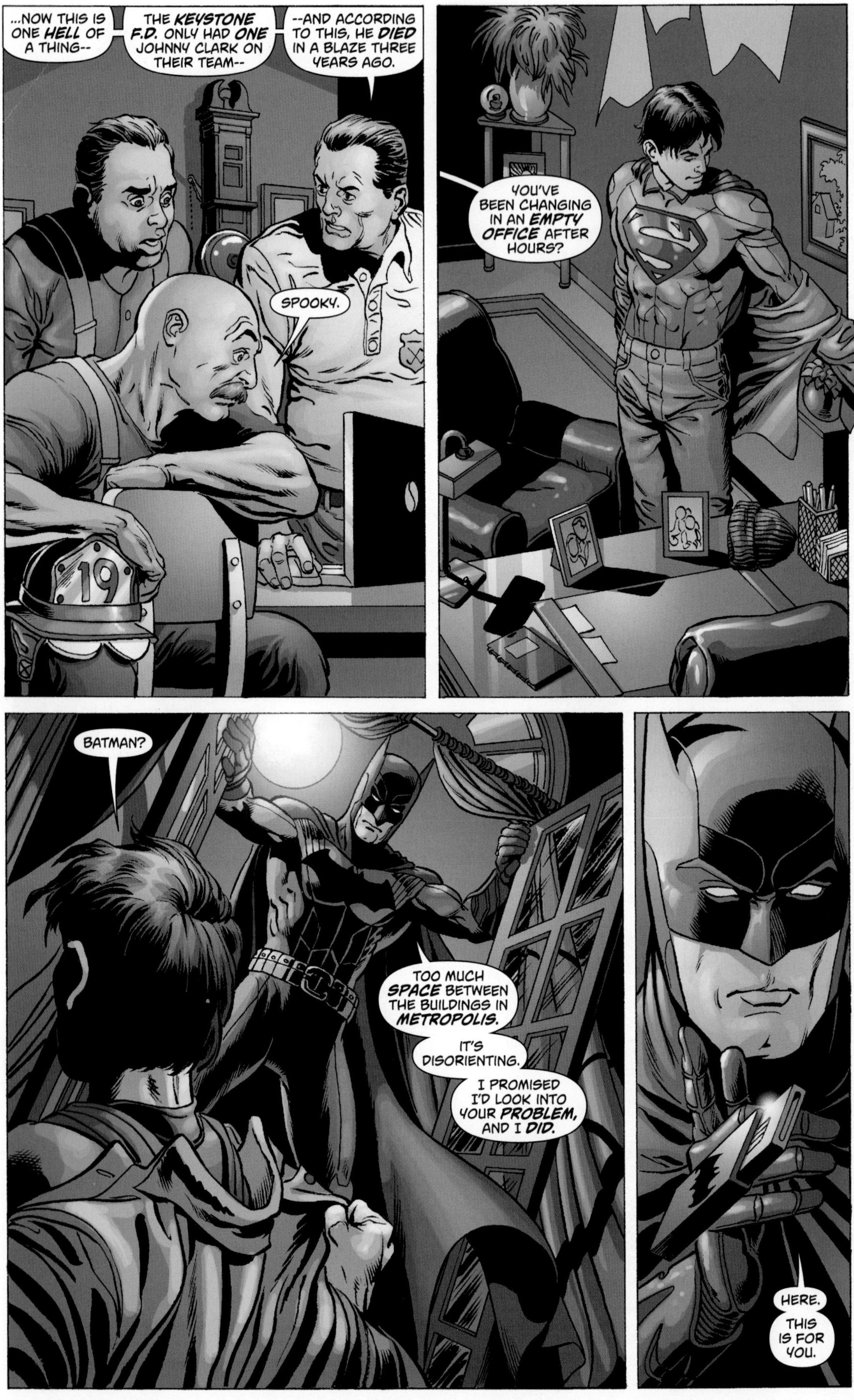
...NOW THIS IS ONE HELL OF A THING--
THE KEYSTONE F.D. ONLY HAD ONE JOHNNY CLARK ON THEIR TEAM--
--AND ACCORDING TO THIS, HE DIED IN A BLAZE THREE YEARS AGO.
SPOOKY.
YOU'VE BEEN CHANGING IN AN EMPTY OFFICE AFTER HOURS?
BATMAN?
TOO MUCH SPACE BETWEEN THE BUILDINGS IN METROPOLIS.
IT'S DISORIENTING.
I PROMISED I'D LOOK INTO YOUR PROBLEM, AND I DID.
HERE. THIS IS FOR YOU.

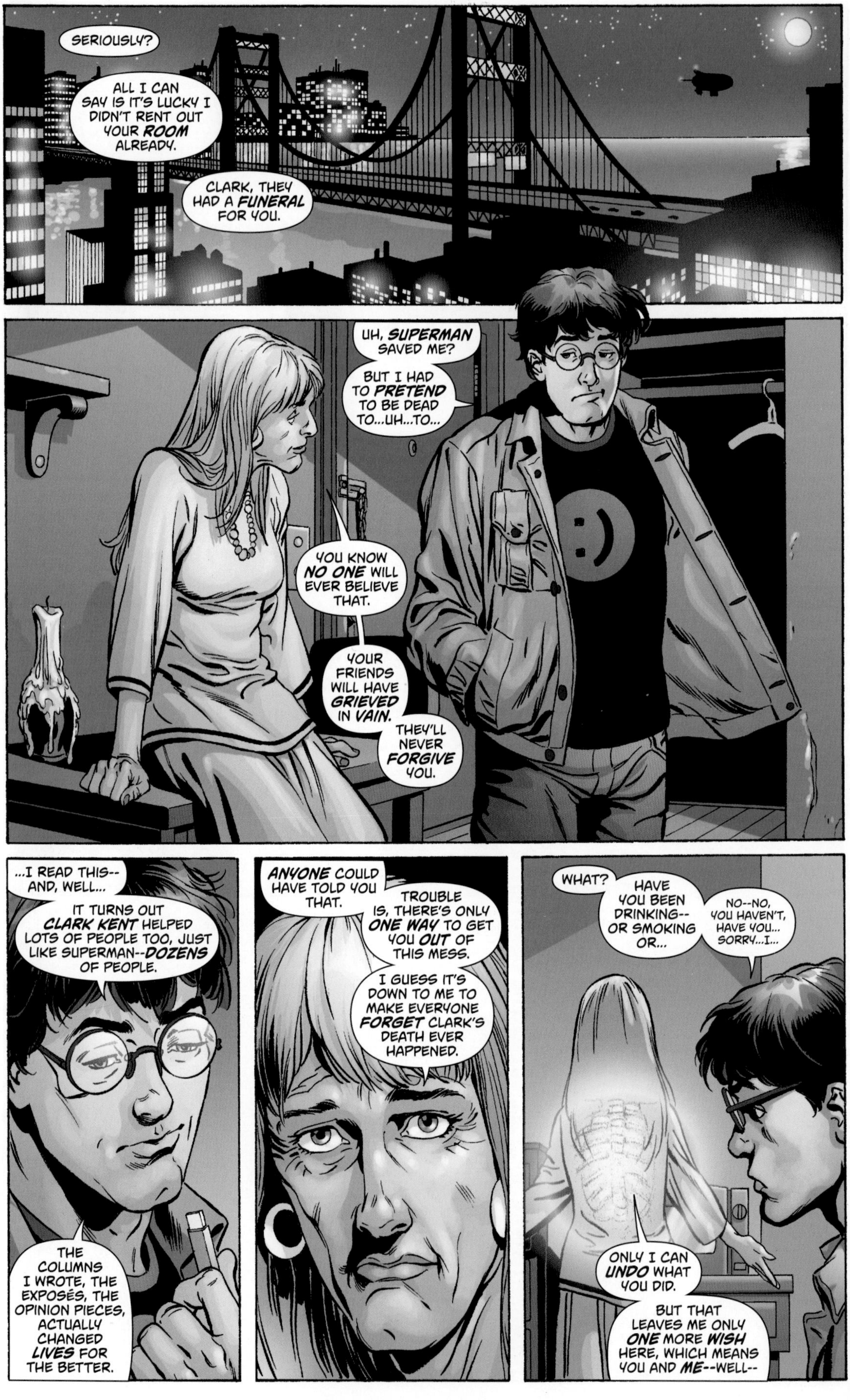
SERIOUSLY?
ALL I CAN SAY IS IT'S LUCKY I DIDN'T RENT OUT YOUR ROOM ALREADY.
CLARK, THEY HAD A FUNERAL FOR YOU.
UH, SUPERMAN SAVED ME?
BUT I HAD TO PRETEND TO BE DEAD TO...UH...TO...
YOU KNOW NO ONE WILL EVER BELIEVE THAT.
YOUR FRIENDS WILL HAVE GRIEVED IN VAIN.
THEY'LL NEVER FORGIVE YOU.
...I READ THIS-- AND, WELL...
IT TURNS OUT CLARK KENT HELPED LOTS OF PEOPLE TOO, JUST LIKE SUPERMAN--DOZENS OF PEOPLE.
THE COLUMNS I WROTE, THE EXPOSÉS, THE OPINION PIECES, ACTUALLY CHANGED LIVES FOR THE BETTER.
ANYONE COULD HAVE TOLD YOU THAT.
TROUBLE IS, THERE'S ONLY ONE WAY TO GET YOU OUT OF THIS MESS.
I GUESS IT'S DOWN TO ME TO MAKE EVERYONE FORGET CLARK'S DEATH EVER HAPPENED.
WHAT?
HAVE YOU BEEN DRINKING-- OR SMOKING OR...
NO--NO, YOU HAVEN'T, HAVE YOU... SORRY...I...
ONLY I CAN UNDO WHAT YOU DID.
BUT THAT LEAVES ME ONLY ONE MORE WISH HERE, WHICH MEANS YOU AND ME--WELL--

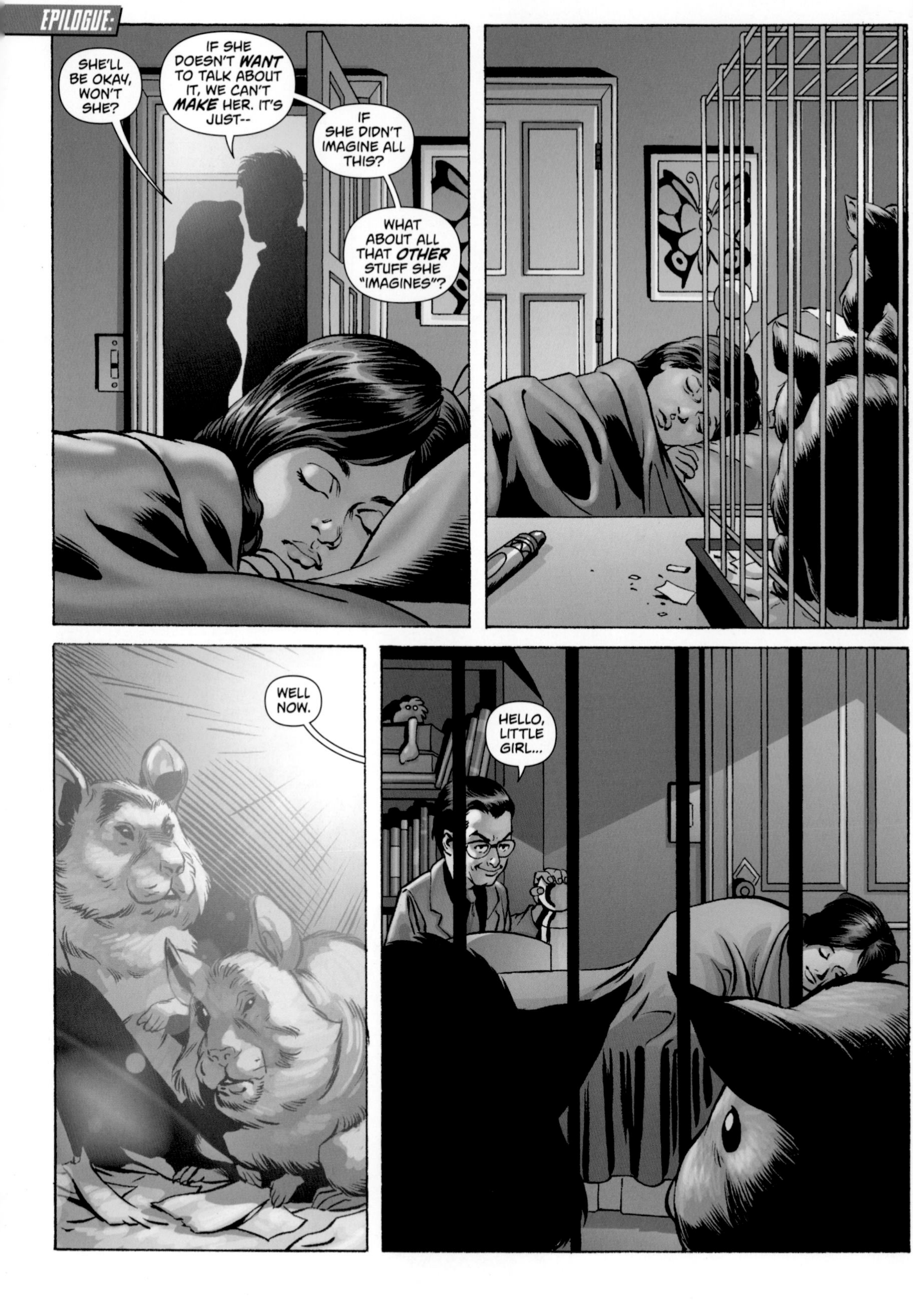
EPILOGUE:
SHE'LL BE OKAY, WON'T SHE?
IF SHE DOESN'T WANT TO TALK ABOUT IT, WE CAN'T MAKE HER. IT'S JUST--
IF SHE DIDN'T IMAGINE ALL THIS?
WHAT ABOUT ALL THAT OTHER STUFF SHE "IMAGINES"?
WELL NOW.
HELLO, LITTLE GIRL...

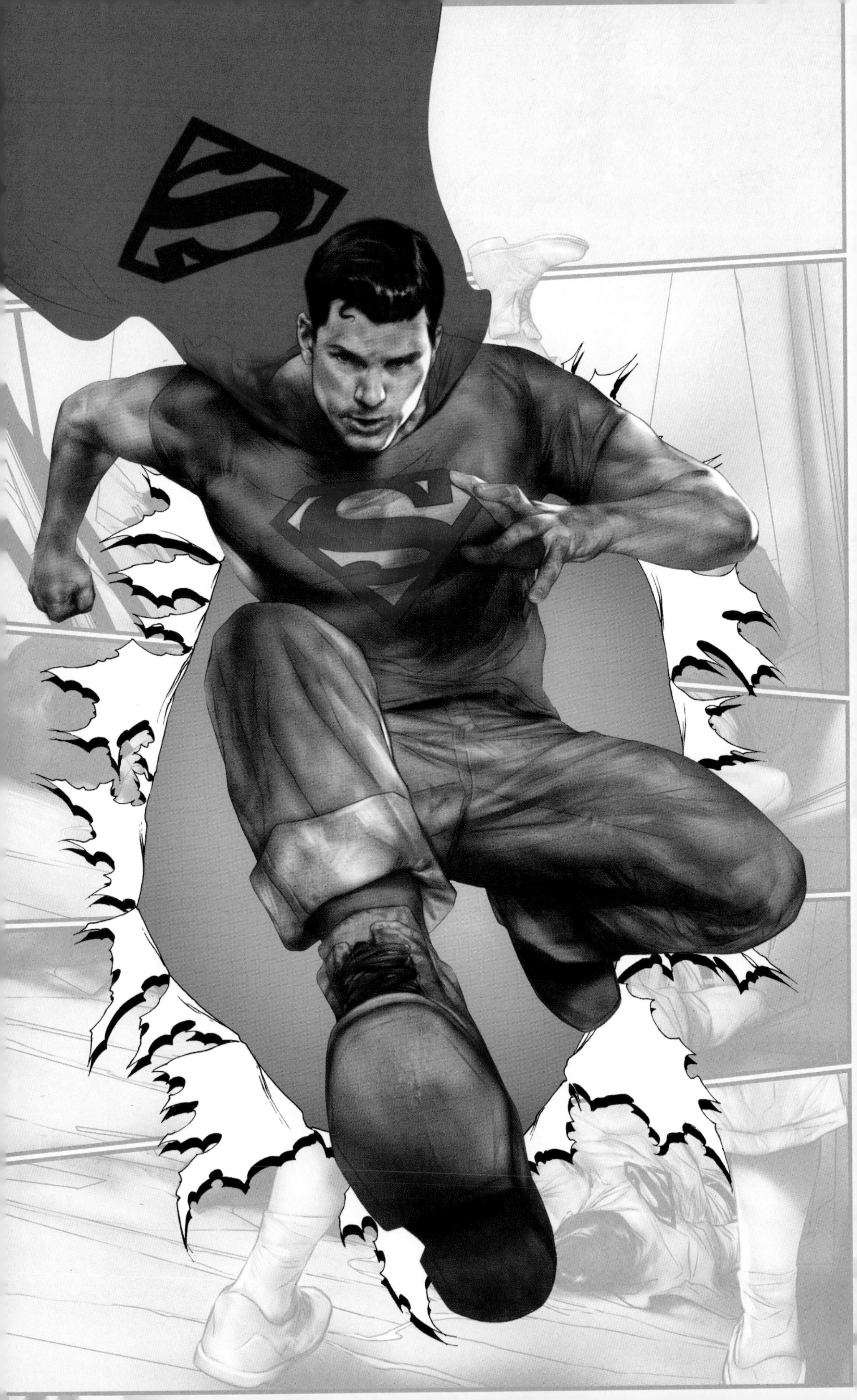

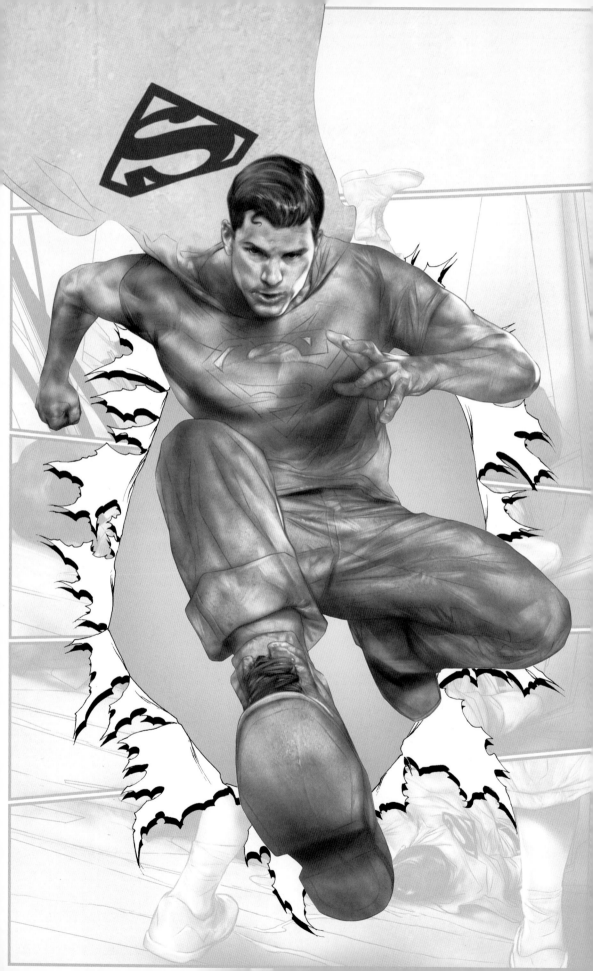

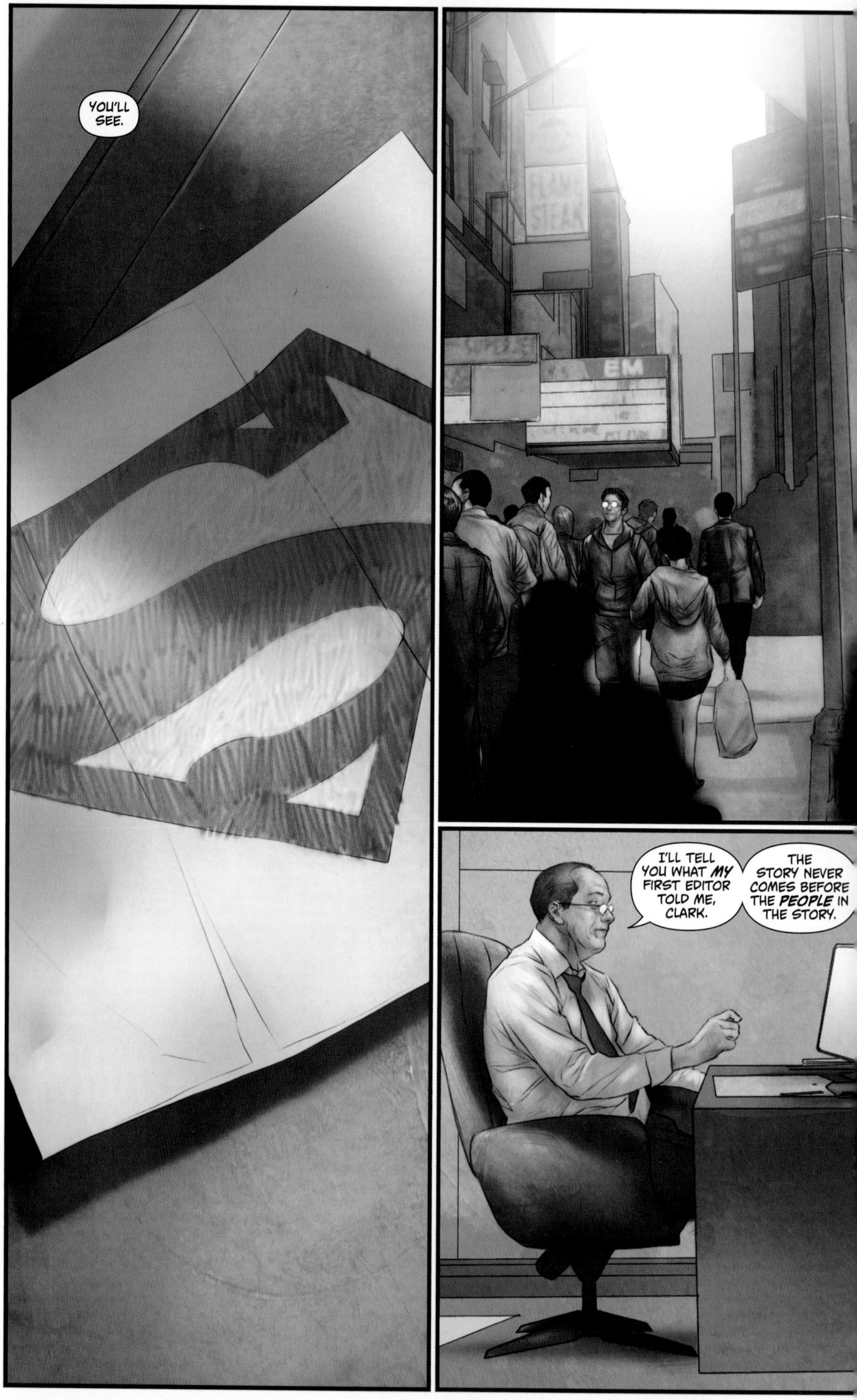

YOU'LL SEE.
FLAME STEAK
EM
I'LL TELL YOU WHAT *MY* FIRST EDITOR TOLD ME, CLARK.
THE STORY NEVER COMES BEFORE THE *PEOPLE* IN THE STORY.

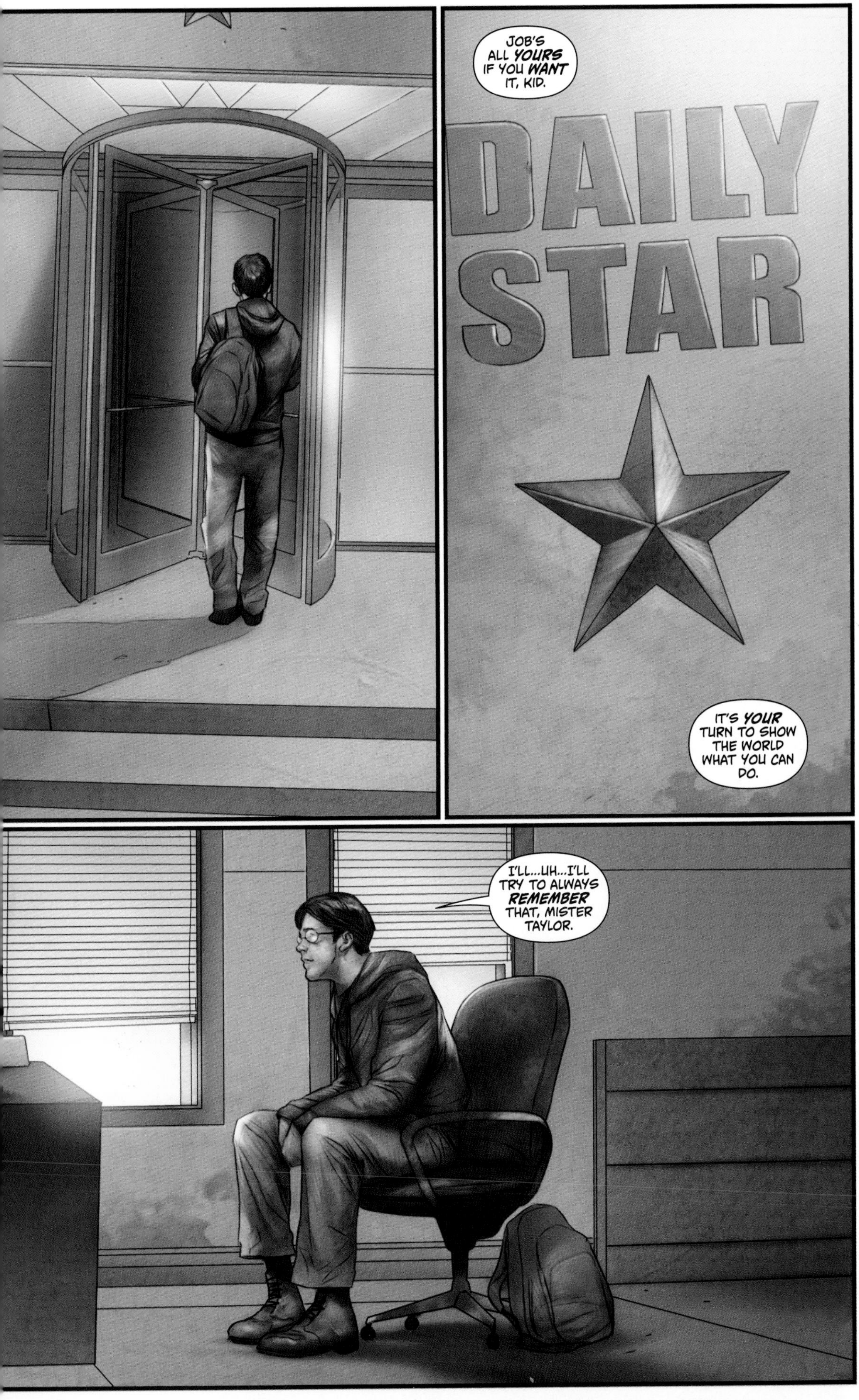
JOB'S ALL YOURS IF YOU WANT IT, KID.
DAILY STAR
IT'S YOUR TURN TO SHOW THE WORLD WHAT YOU CAN DO.
I'LL...UH...I'LL TRY TO ALWAYS REMEMBER THAT, MISTER TAYLOR.

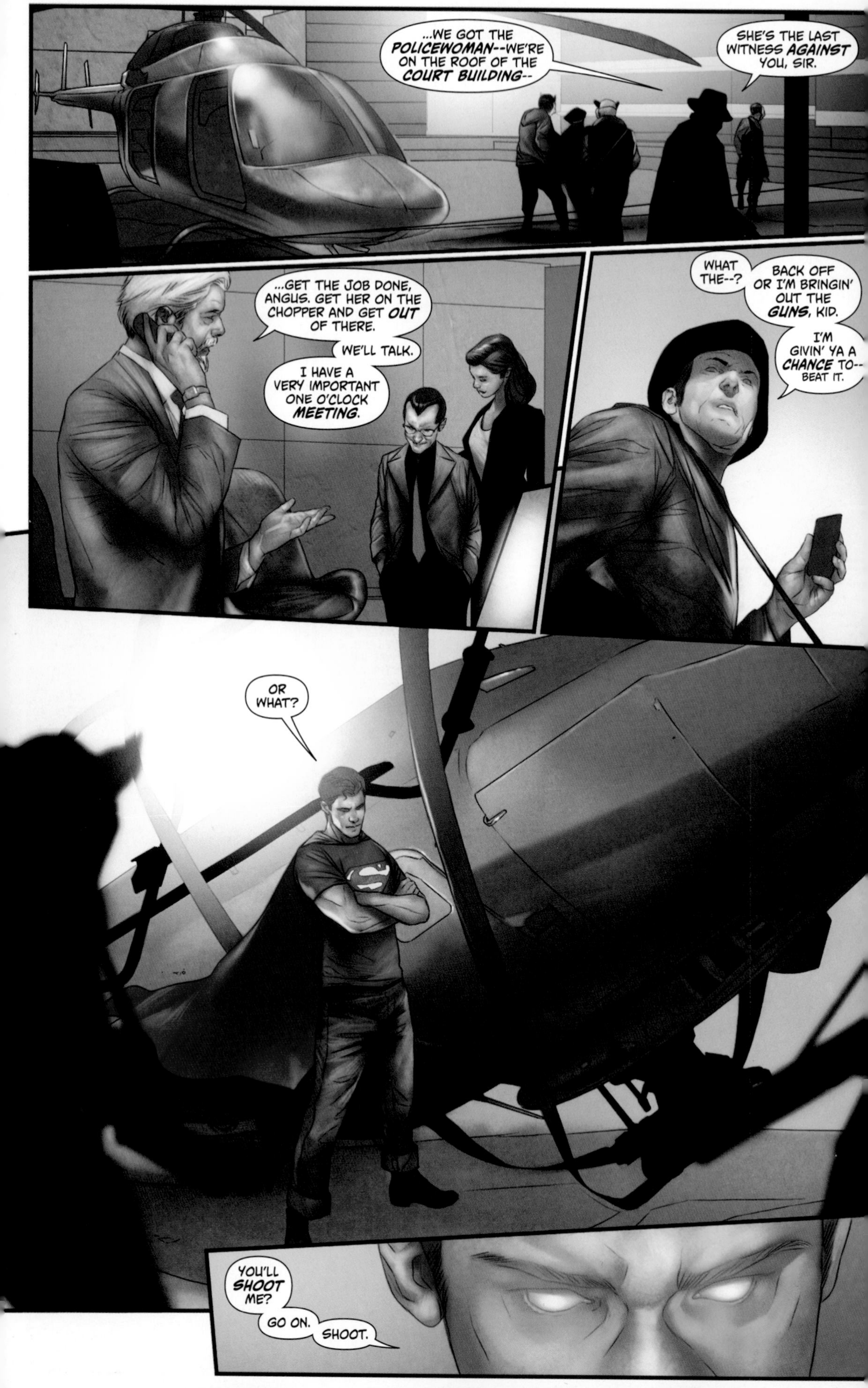
...WE GOT THE POLICEWOMAN--WE'RE ON THE ROOF OF THE COURT BUILDING--
SHE'S THE LAST WITNESS AGAINST YOU, SIR.
...GET THE JOB DONE, ANGUS. GET HER ON THE CHOPPER AND GET OUT OF THERE.
WE'LL TALK.
I HAVE A VERY IMPORTANT ONE O'CLOCK MEETING.
WHAT THE--?
BACK OFF OR I'M BRINGIN' OUT THE GUNS, KID.
I'M GIVIN' YA A CHANCE TO--BEAT IT.
OR WHAT?
YOU'LL SHOOT ME?
GO ON.
SHOOT.

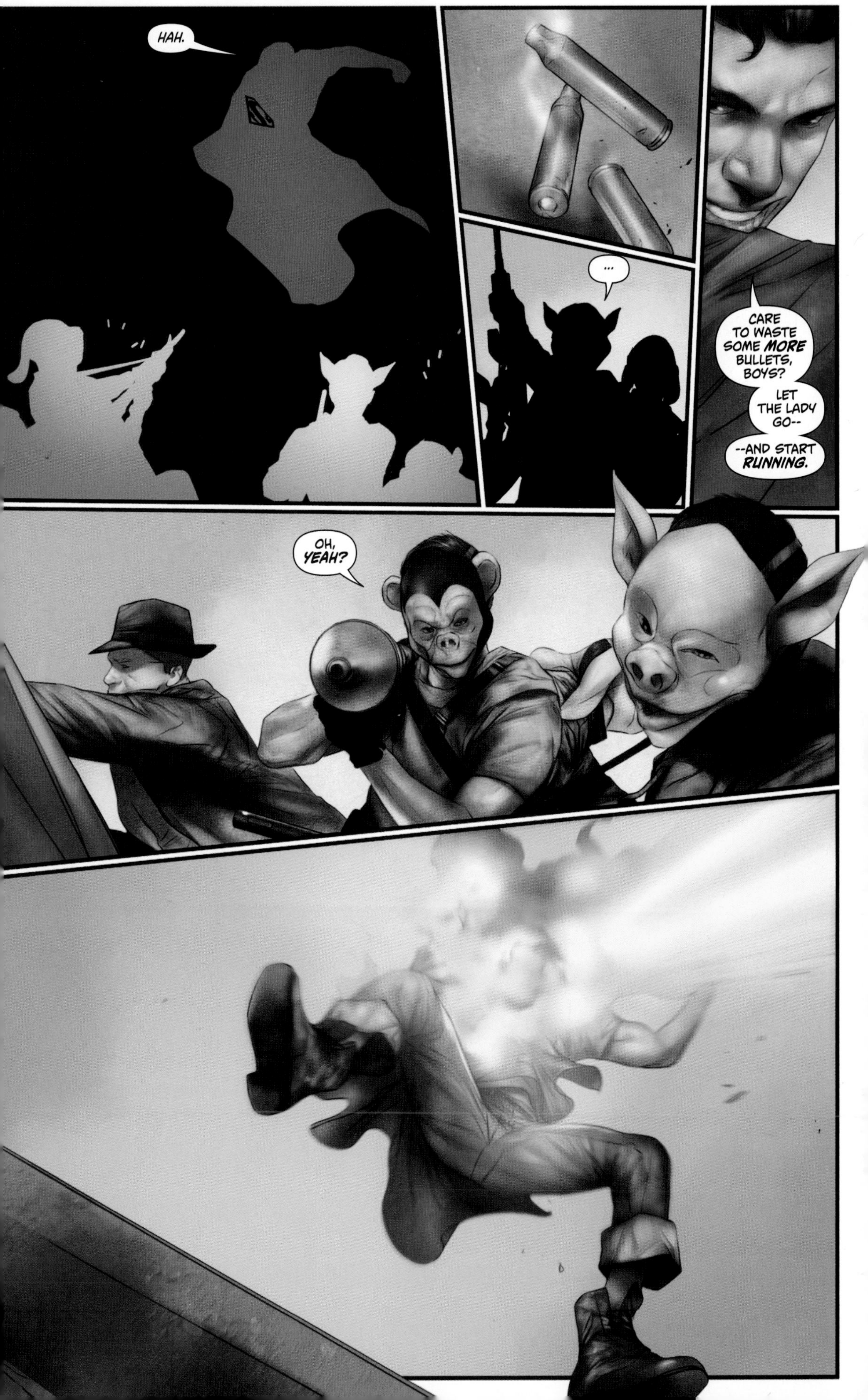
HAH.
...
CARE TO WASTE SOME MORE BULLETS, BOYS?
LET THE LADY GO--
--AND START RUNNING.
OH, YEAH?

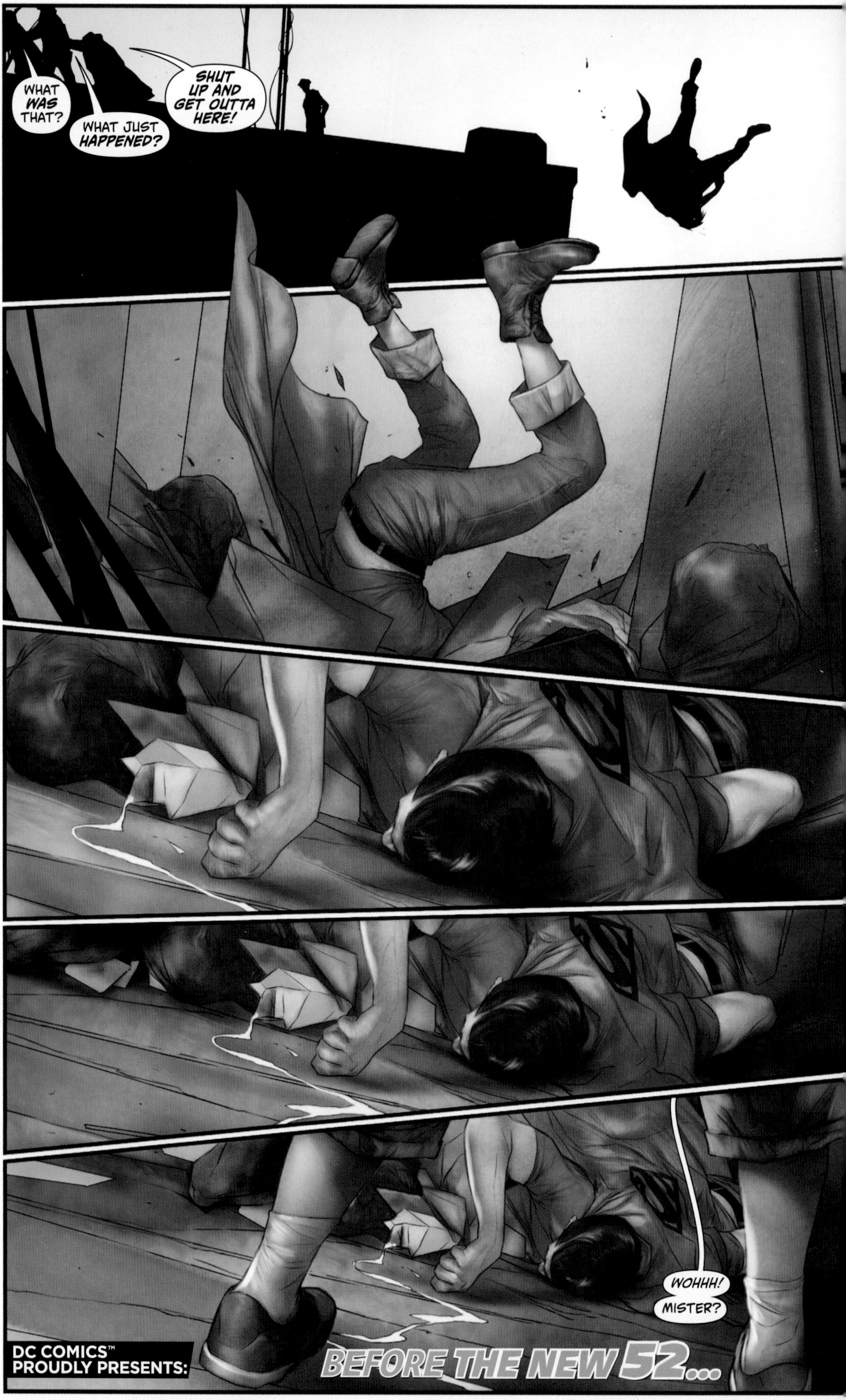
WHAT WAS THAT?
WHAT JUST HAPPENED?
SHUT UP AND GET OUTTA HERE!
WOHHH!
MISTER?
DC COMICS™ PROUDLY PRESENTS:
BEFORE THE NEW 52...

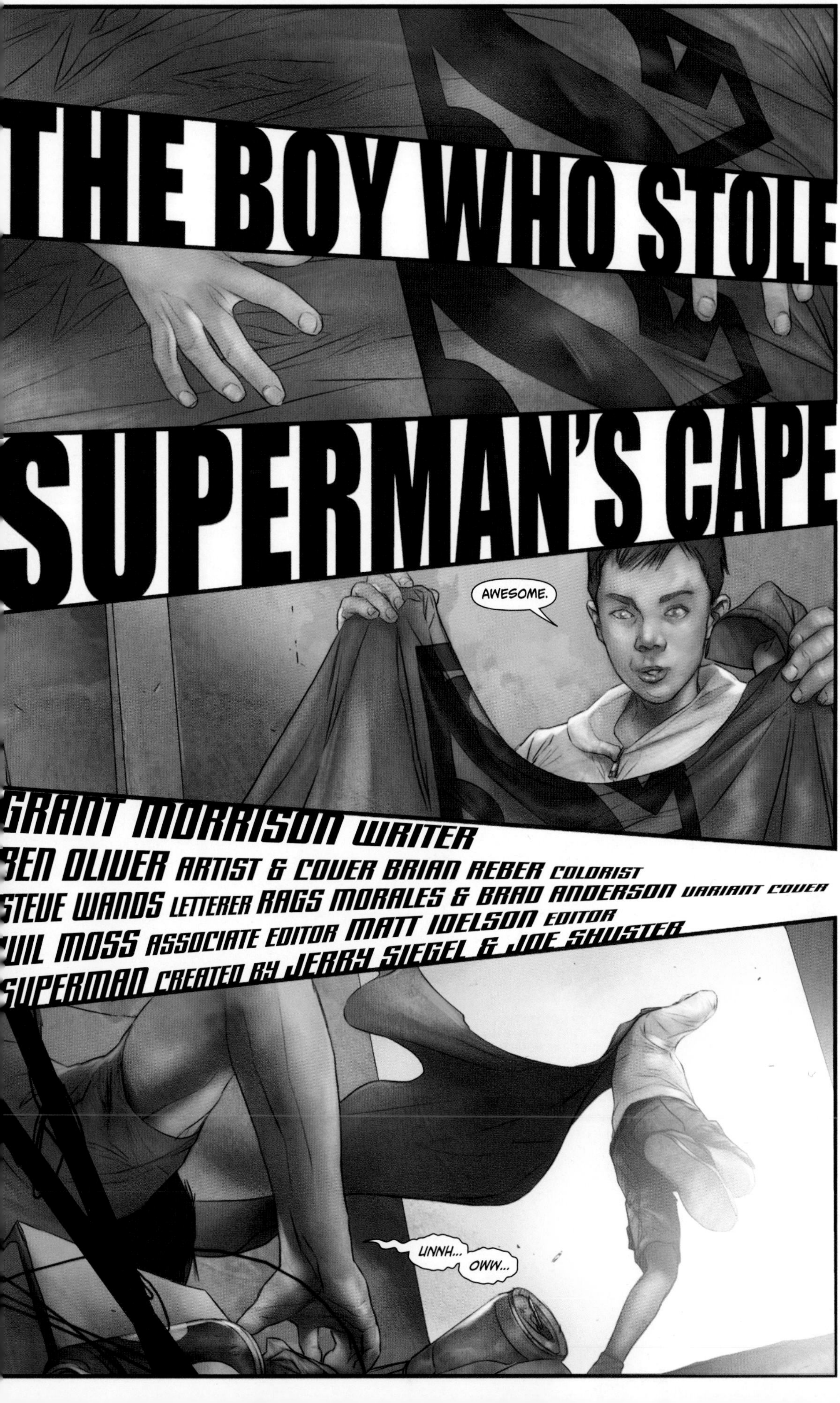
THE BOY WHO STOLE SUPERMAN'S CAPE
AWESOME.
GRANT MORRISON WRITER
BEN OLIVER ARTIST & COVER BRIAN REBER COLORIST
STEVE WANDS LETTERER RAGS MORALES & BRAD ANDERSON VARIANT COVER
WIL MOSS ASSOCIATE EDITOR MATT IDELSON EDITOR
SUPERMAN CREATED BY JERRY SIEGEL & JOE SHUSTER
UNNH... OWW...

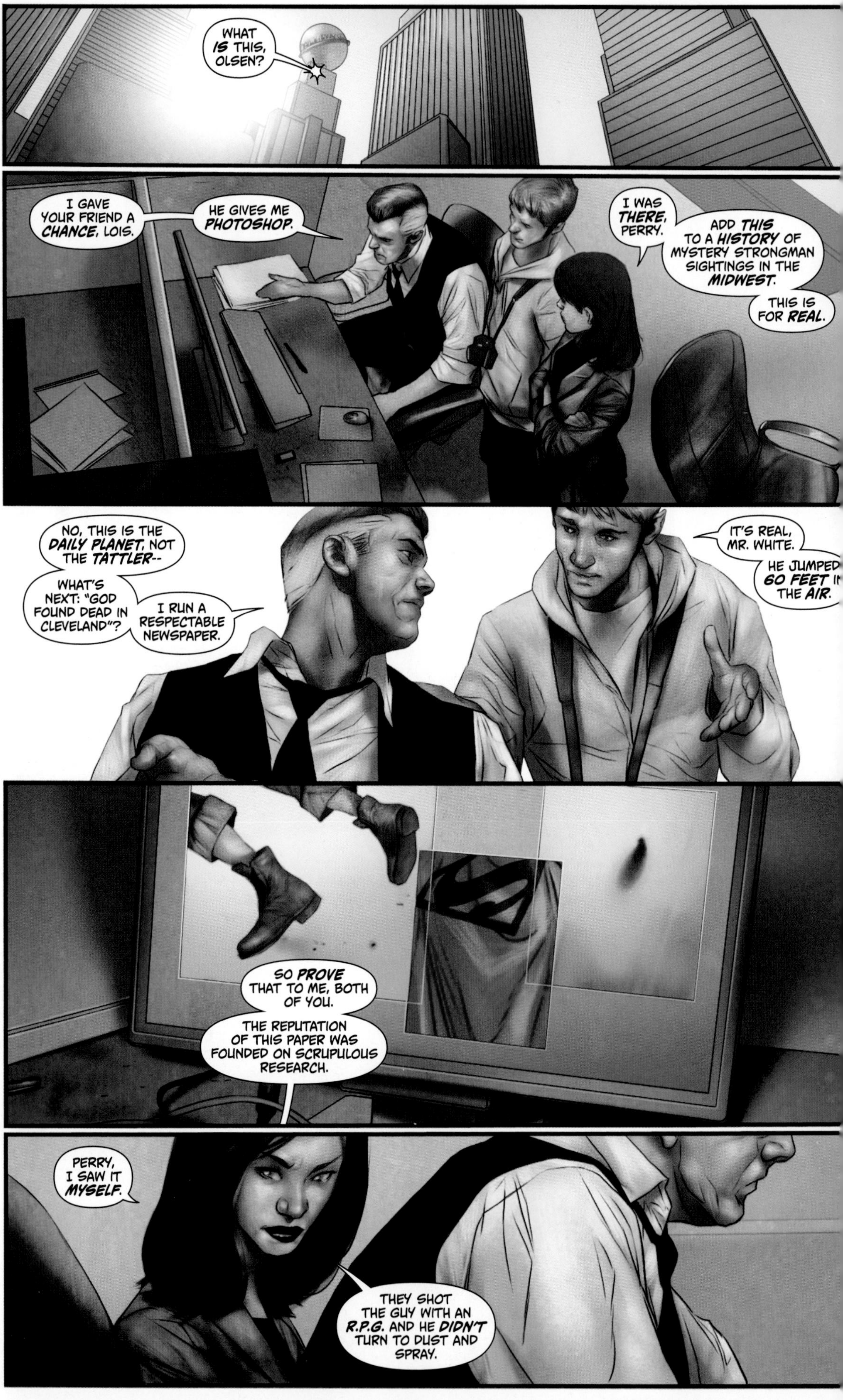
WHAT *IS* THIS, OLSEN?
I GAVE YOUR FRIEND A *CHANCE*, LOIS.
HE GIVES ME *PHOTOSHOP*.
I WAS *THERE*, PERRY.
ADD *THIS* TO A *HISTORY* OF MYSTERY STRONGMAN SIGHTINGS IN THE *MIDWEST*.
THIS IS FOR *REAL*.
NO, THIS IS THE *DAILY PLANET*, NOT THE *TATTLER*--
WHAT'S NEXT: "GOD FOUND DEAD IN CLEVELAND"?
I RUN A RESPECTABLE NEWSPAPER.
IT'S REAL, MR. WHITE.
HE JUMPED *60 FEET* IN THE *AIR*.
SO *PROVE* THAT TO ME, BOTH OF YOU.
THE REPUTATION OF THIS PAPER WAS FOUNDED ON SCRUPULOUS RESEARCH.
PERRY, I SAW IT *MYSELF*.
THEY SHOT THE GUY WITH AN *R.P.G.* AND HE *DIDN'T* TURN TO DUST AND SPRAY.

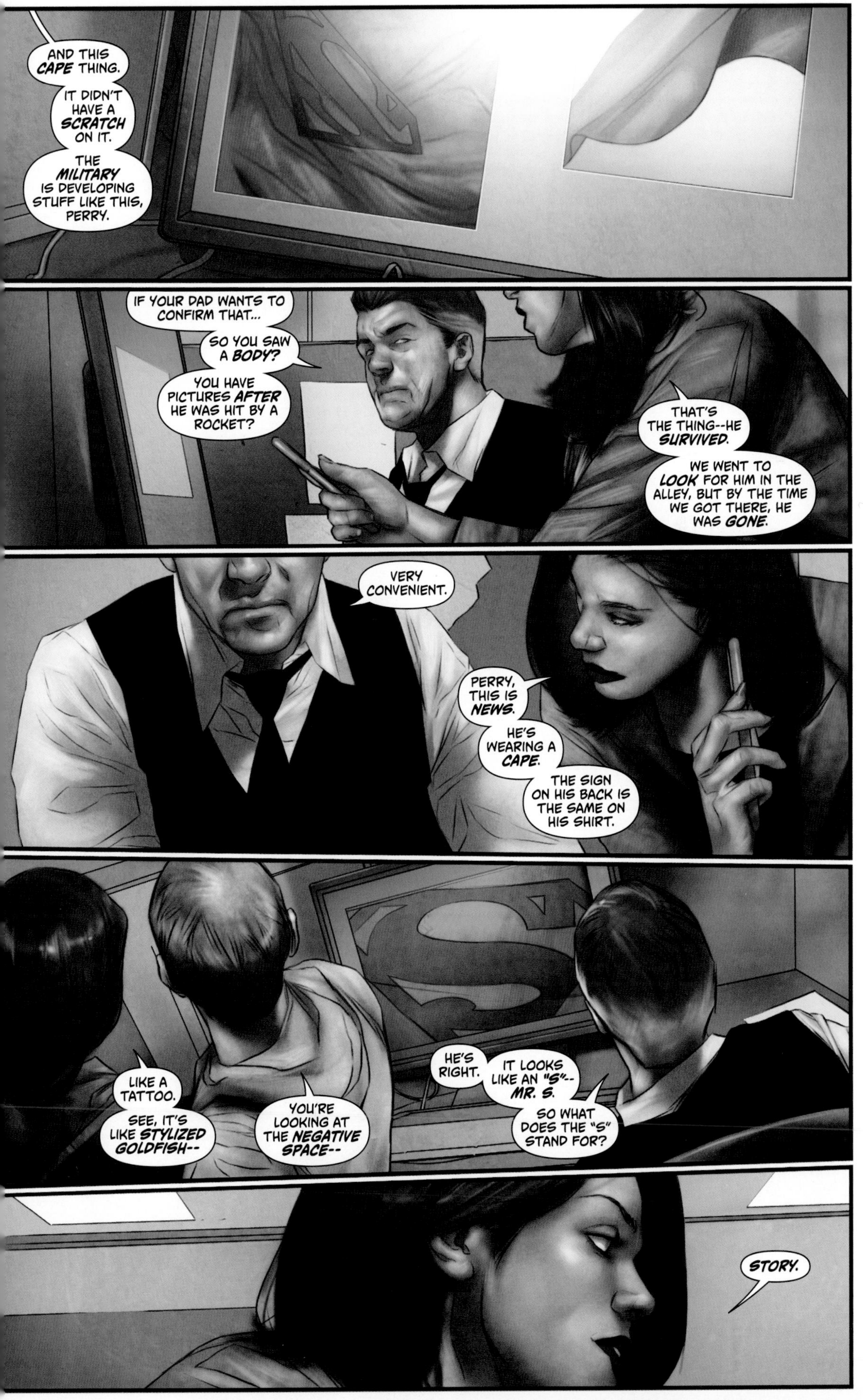
AND THIS CAPE THING.
IT DIDN'T HAVE A SCRATCH ON IT.
THE MILITARY IS DEVELOPING STUFF LIKE THIS, PERRY.
IF YOUR DAD WANTS TO CONFIRM THAT...
SO YOU SAW A BODY?
YOU HAVE PICTURES AFTER HE WAS HIT BY A ROCKET?
THAT'S THE THING--HE SURVIVED.
WE WENT TO LOOK FOR HIM IN THE ALLEY, BUT BY THE TIME WE GOT THERE, HE WAS GONE.
VERY CONVENIENT.
PERRY, THIS IS NEWS.
HE'S WEARING A CAPE.
THE SIGN ON HIS BACK IS THE SAME ON HIS SHIRT.
LIKE A TATTOO.
SEE, IT'S LIKE STYLIZED GOLDFISH--
YOU'RE LOOKING AT THE NEGATIVE SPACE--
HE'S RIGHT.
IT LOOKS LIKE AN "S"--MR. S.
SO WHAT DOES THE "S" STAND FOR?
STORY.

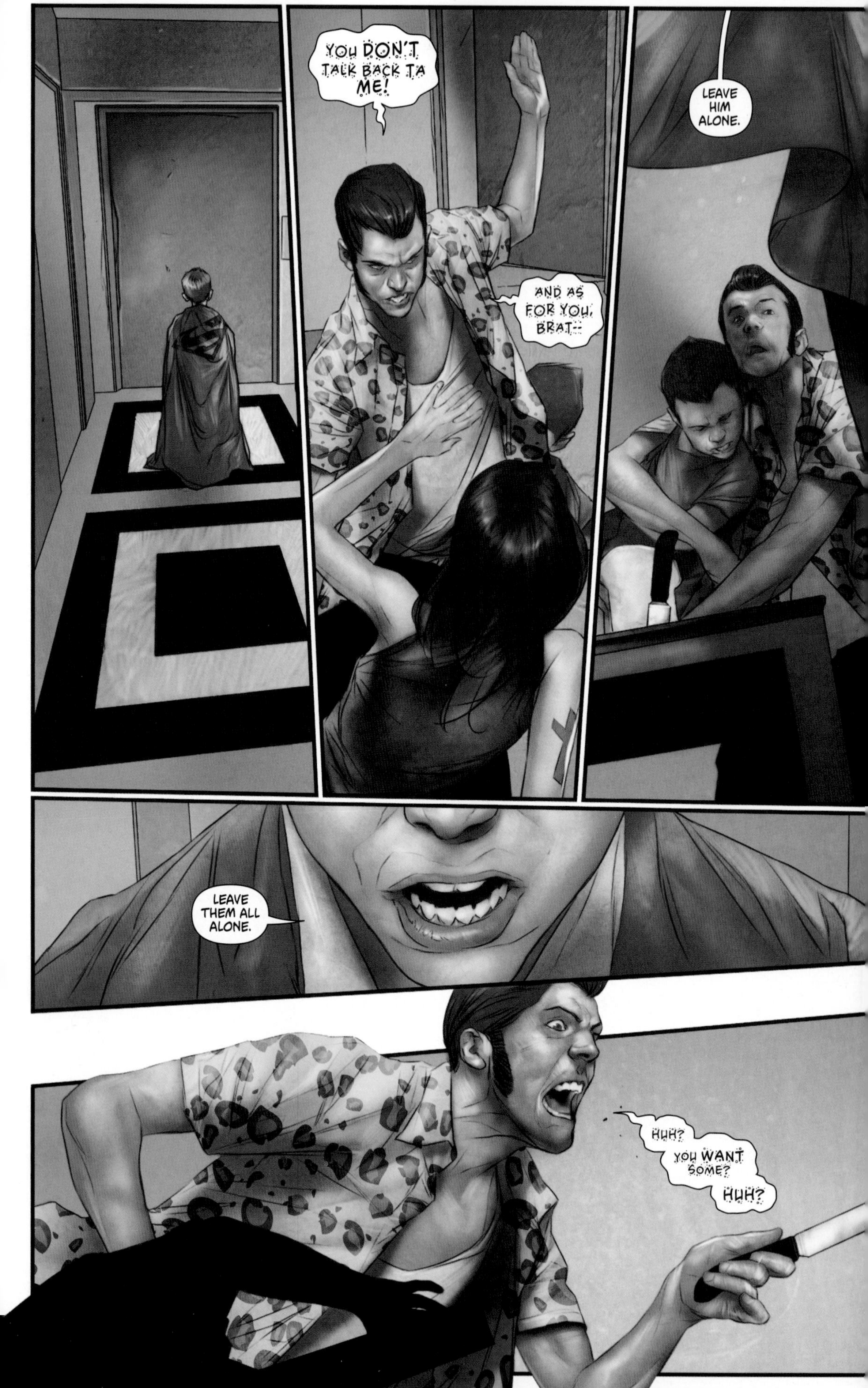
YOU DON'T TALK BACK TA ME!
AND AS FOR YOU, BRAT--
LEAVE HIM ALONE.
LEAVE THEM ALL ALONE.
HUH?
YOU WANT SOME?
HUH?

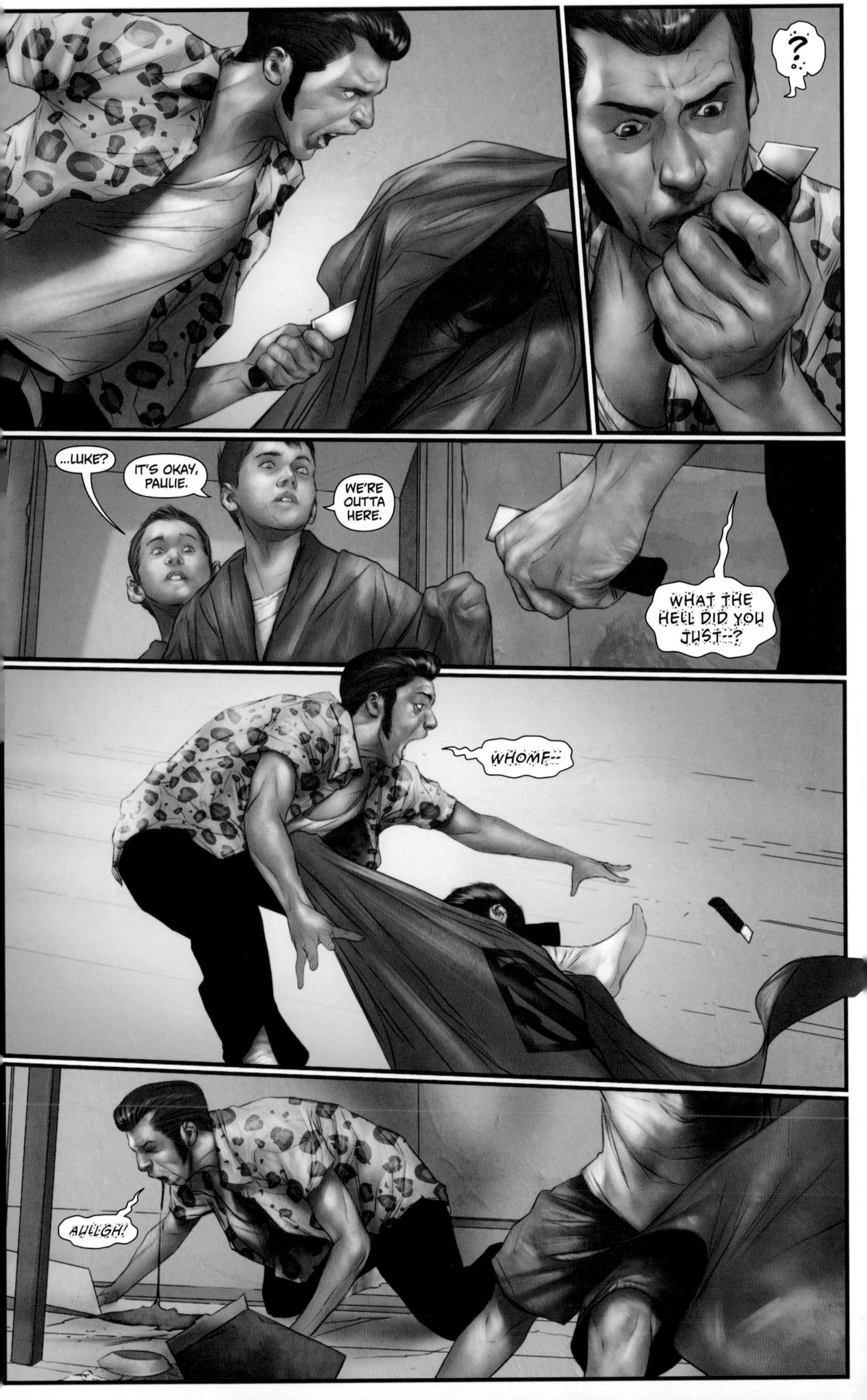
?
...LUKE?
IT'S OKAY, PAULIE.
WE'RE OUTTA HERE.
WHAT THE HELL DID YOU JUST--?
WHOMF--
AULLGH!

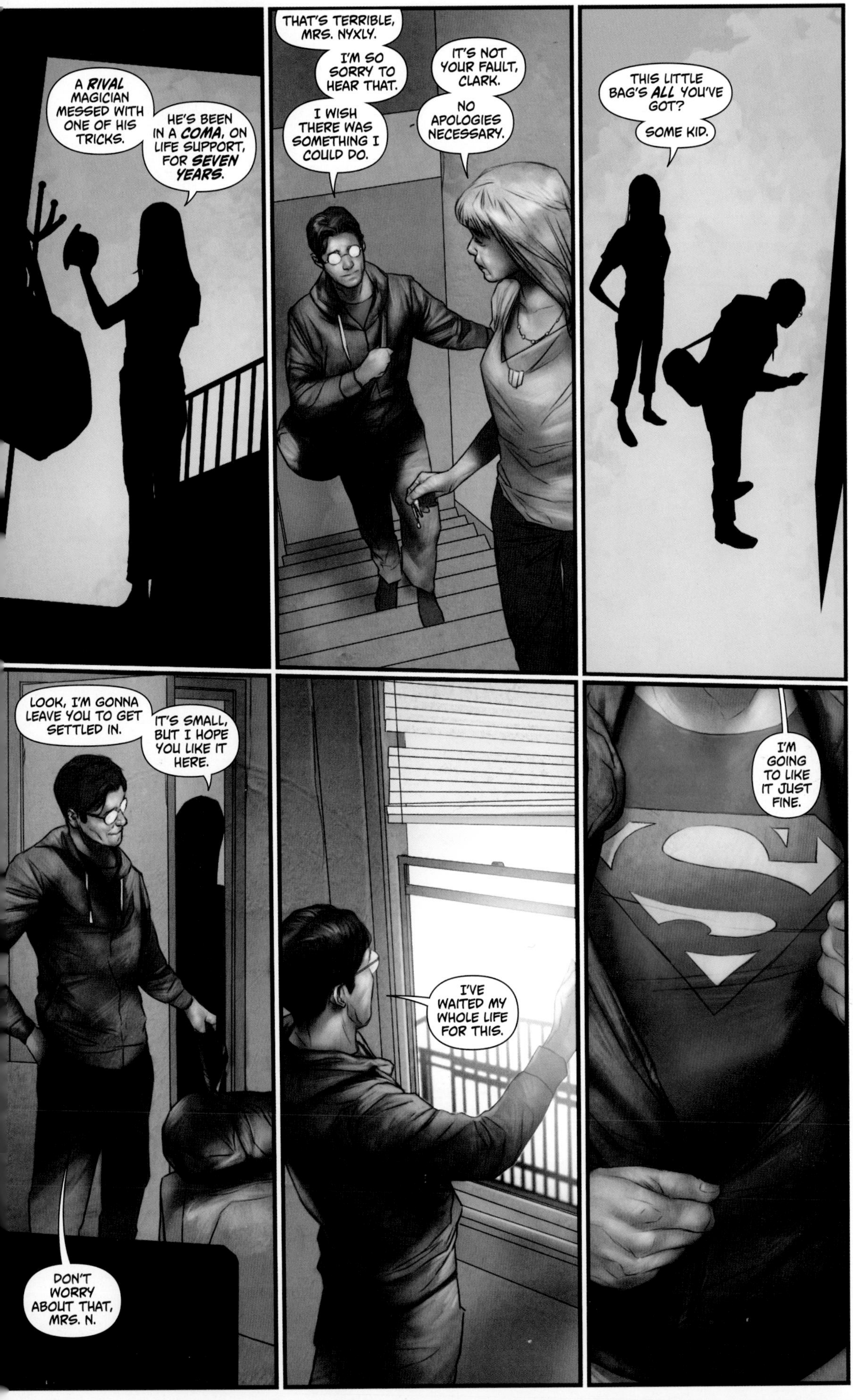
A RIVAL MAGICIAN MESSED WITH ONE OF HIS TRICKS.
HE'S BEEN IN A COMA, ON LIFE SUPPORT, FOR SEVEN YEARS.
THAT'S TERRIBLE, MRS. NYXLY.
I'M SO SORRY TO HEAR THAT.
I WISH THERE WAS SOMETHING I COULD DO.
IT'S NOT YOUR FAULT, CLARK.
NO APOLOGIES NECESSARY.
THIS LITTLE BAG'S ALL YOU'VE GOT?
SOME KID.
LOOK, I'M GONNA LEAVE YOU TO GET SETTLED IN.
IT'S SMALL, BUT I HOPE YOU LIKE IT HERE.
DON'T WORRY ABOUT THAT, MRS. N.
I'VE WAITED MY WHOLE LIFE FOR THIS.
I'M GOING TO LIKE IT JUST FINE.

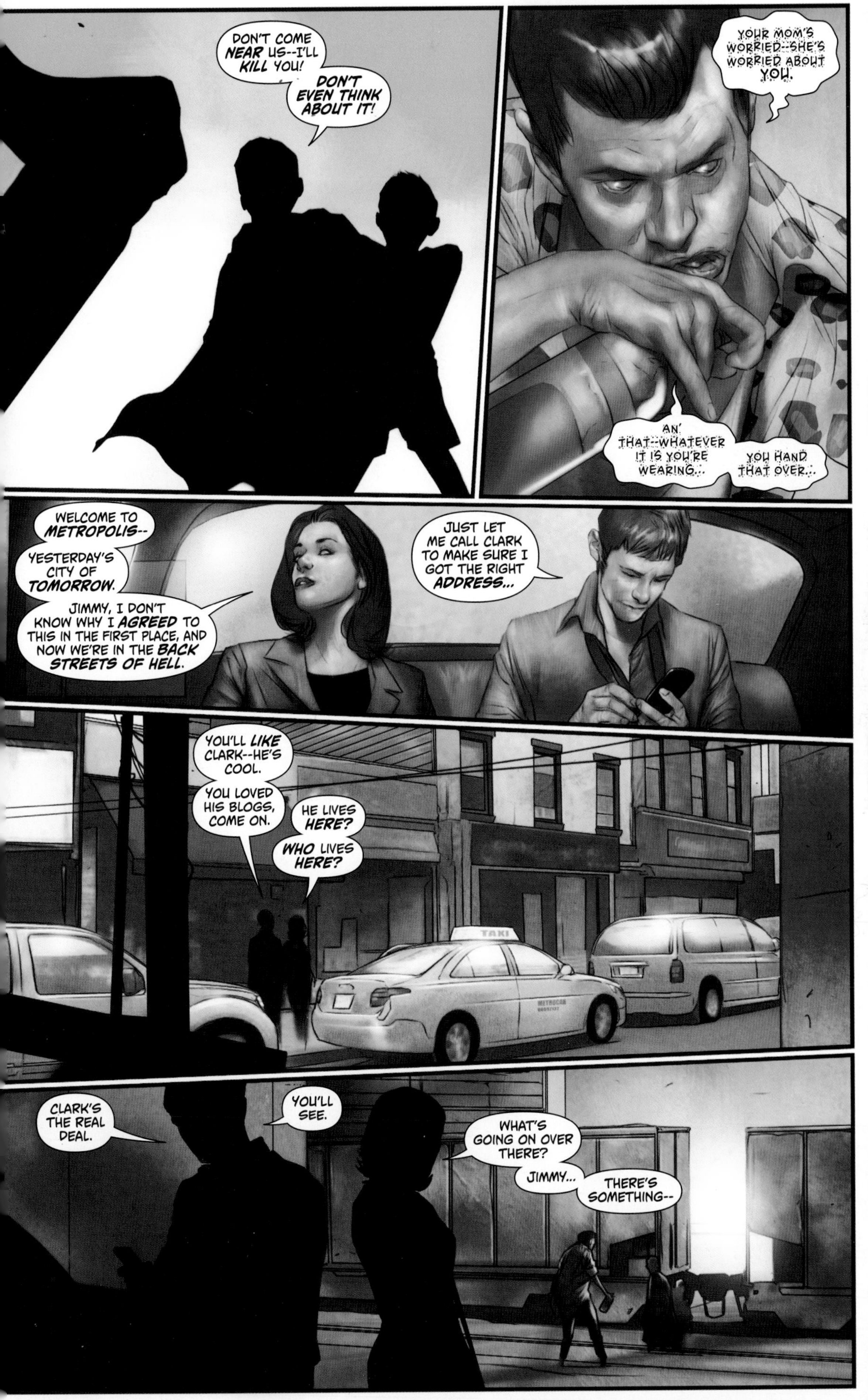
DON'T COME NEAR US--I'LL KILL YOU!
DON'T EVEN THINK ABOUT IT!
YOUR MOM'S WORRIED--SHE'S WORRIED ABOUT YOU.
AN' THAT--WHATEVER IT IS YOU'RE WEARING...
YOU HAND THAT OVER...
WELCOME TO METROPOLIS--
YESTERDAY'S CITY OF TOMORROW.
JIMMY, I DON'T KNOW WHY I AGREED TO THIS IN THE FIRST PLACE, AND NOW WE'RE IN THE BACK STREETS OF HELL.
JUST LET ME CALL CLARK TO MAKE SURE I GOT THE RIGHT ADDRESS...
YOU'LL LIKE CLARK--HE'S COOL.
YOU LOVED HIS BLOGS, COME ON.
HE LIVES HERE?
WHO LIVES HERE?
TAXI
CLARK'S THE REAL DEAL.
YOU'LL SEE.
WHAT'S GOING ON OVER THERE?
JIMMY...
THERE'S SOMETHING--

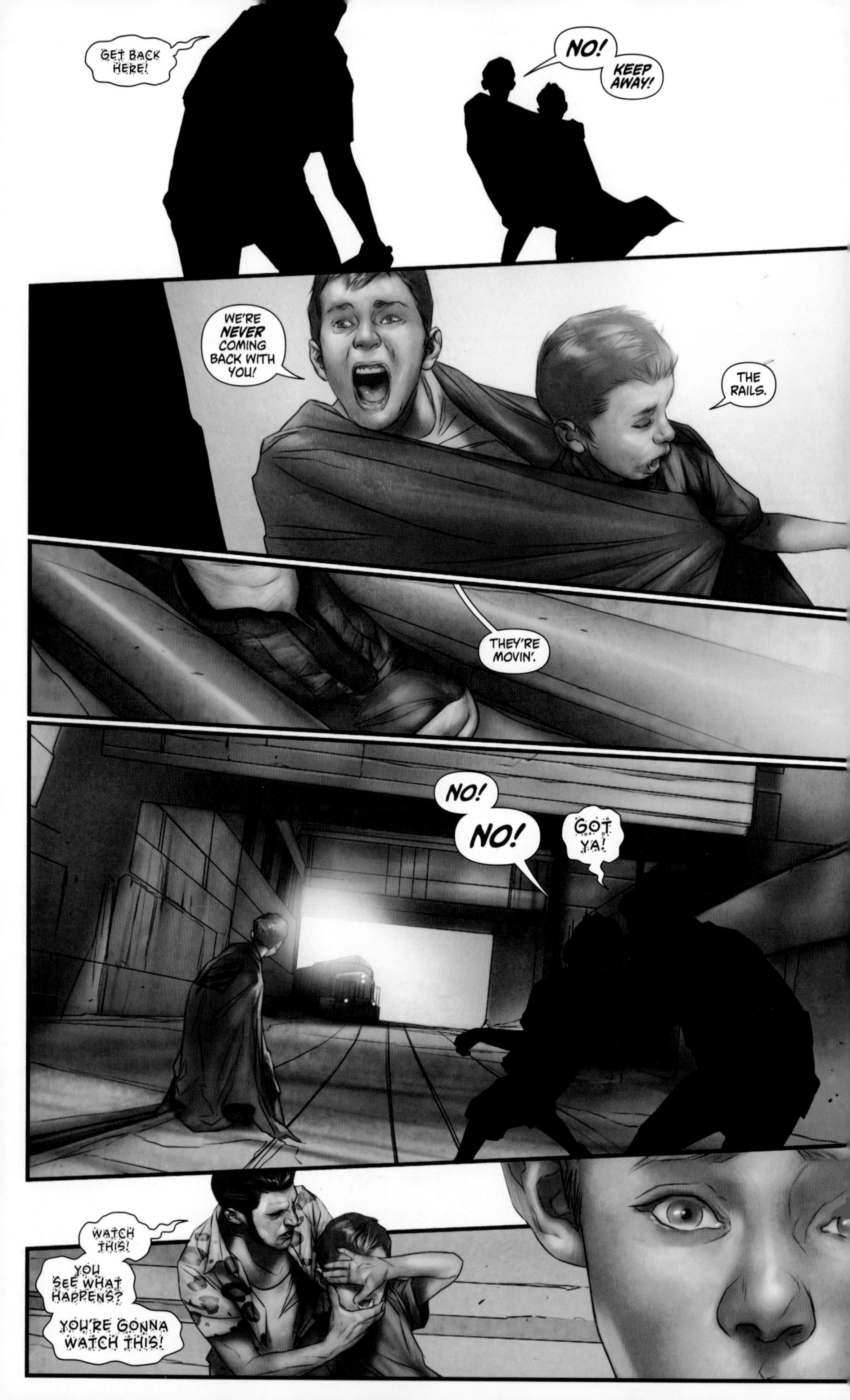
GET BACK HERE!
NO! KEEP AWAY!
WE'RE NEVER COMING BACK WITH YOU!
THE RAILS.
THEY'RE MOVIN'.
NO!
NO!
GOT YA!
WATCH THIS!
YOU SEE WHAT HAPPENS?
YOU'RE GONNA WATCH THIS!

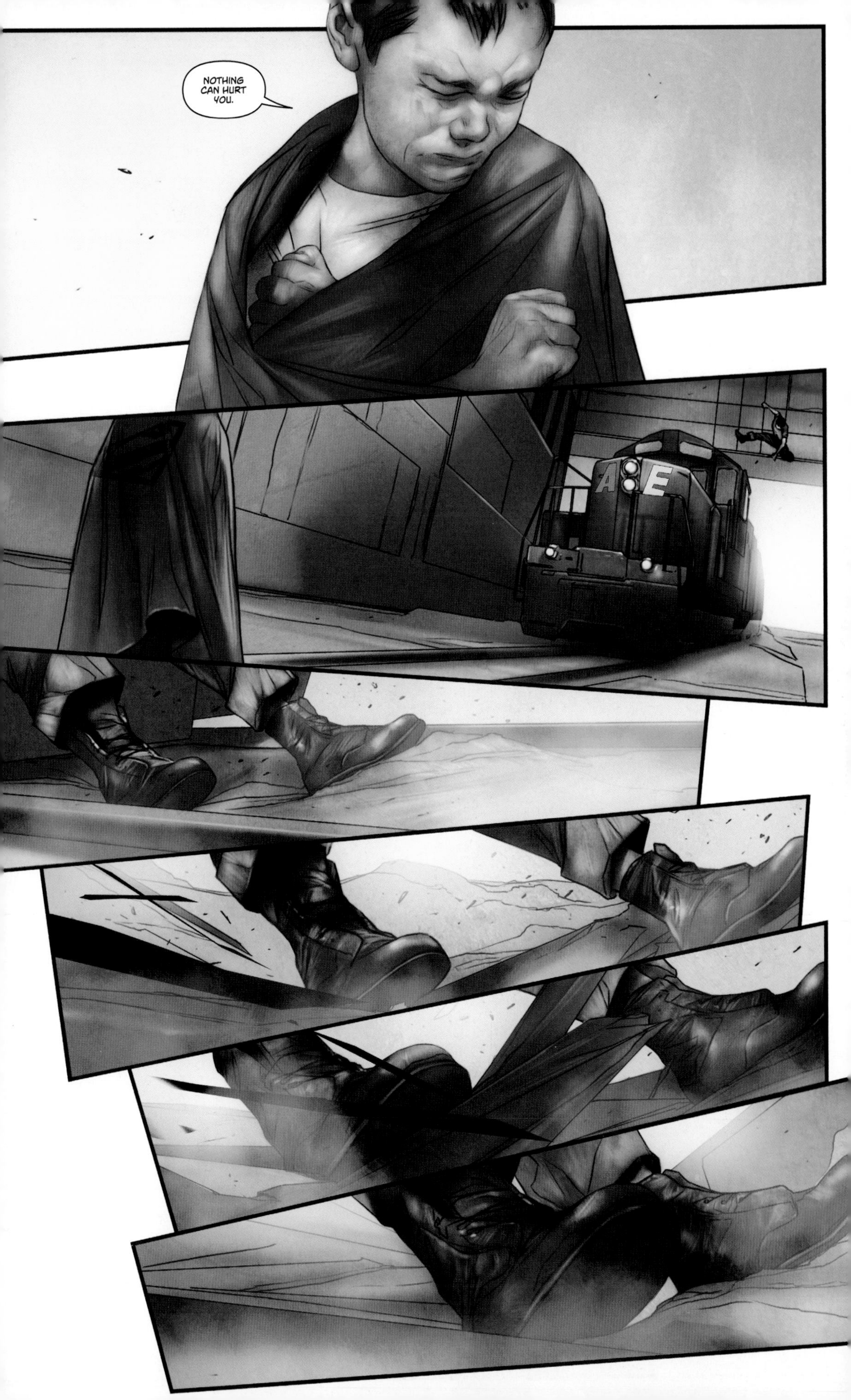
NOTHING CAN HURT YOU.

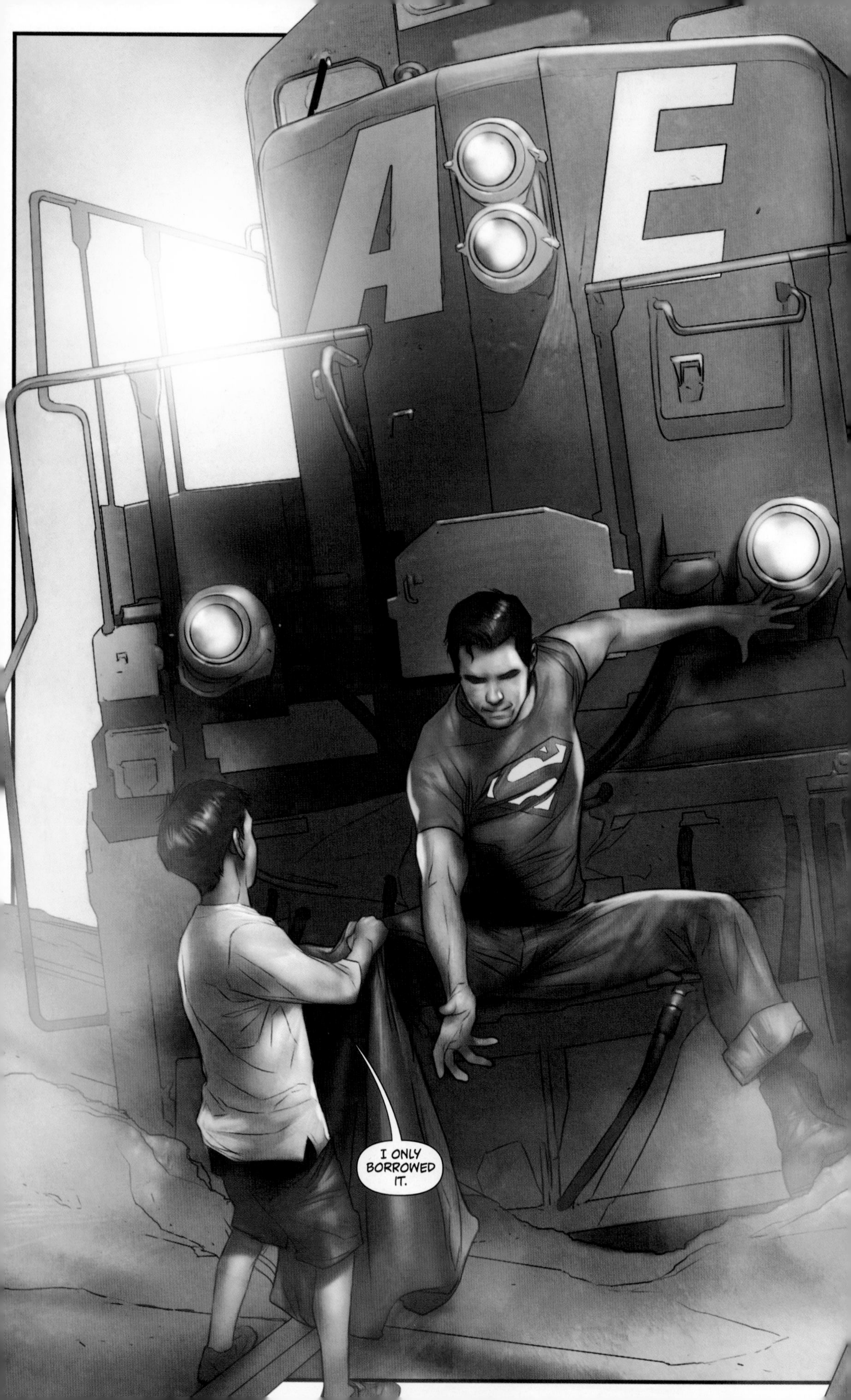
I ONLY BORROWED IT.

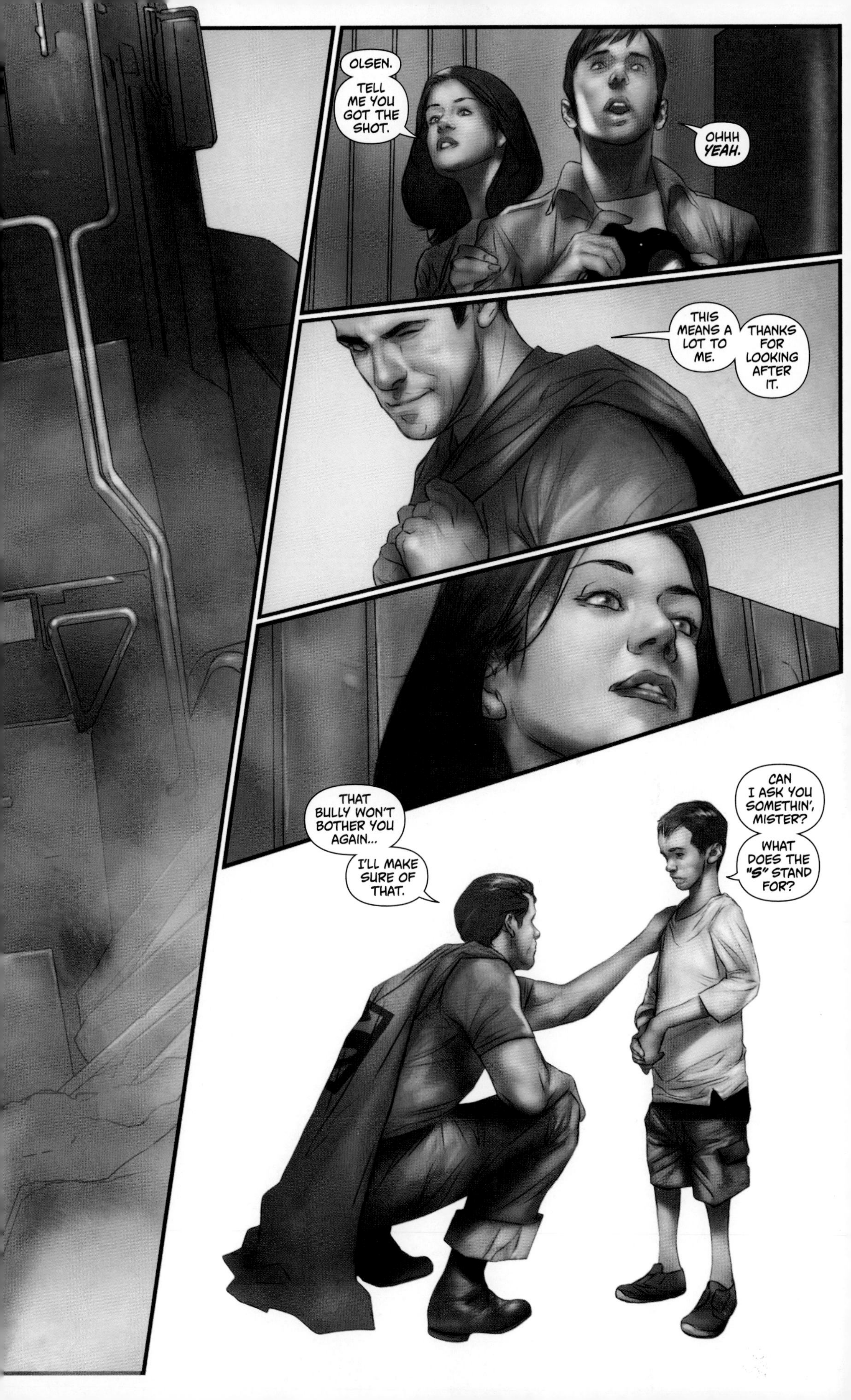
OLSEN.
TELL ME YOU GOT THE SHOT.
OHHH YEAH.
THIS MEANS A LOT TO ME.
THANKS FOR LOOKING AFTER IT.
THAT BULLY WON'T BOTHER YOU AGAIN...
I'LL MAKE SURE OF THAT.
CAN I ASK YOU SOMETHIN', MISTER?
WHAT DOES THE "S" STAND FOR?

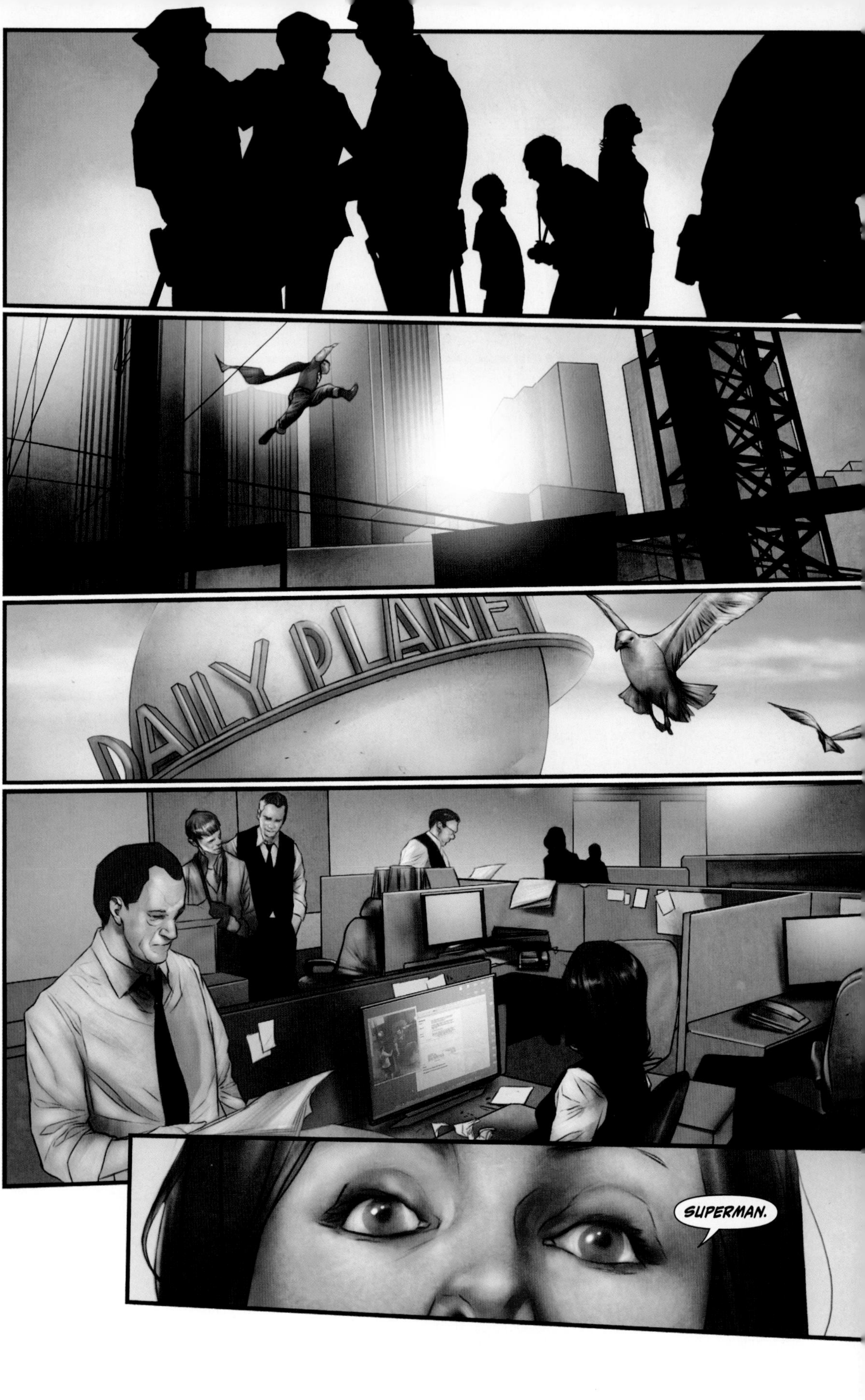
DAILY PLANET
SUPERMAN.

EXECUTIVE POWER

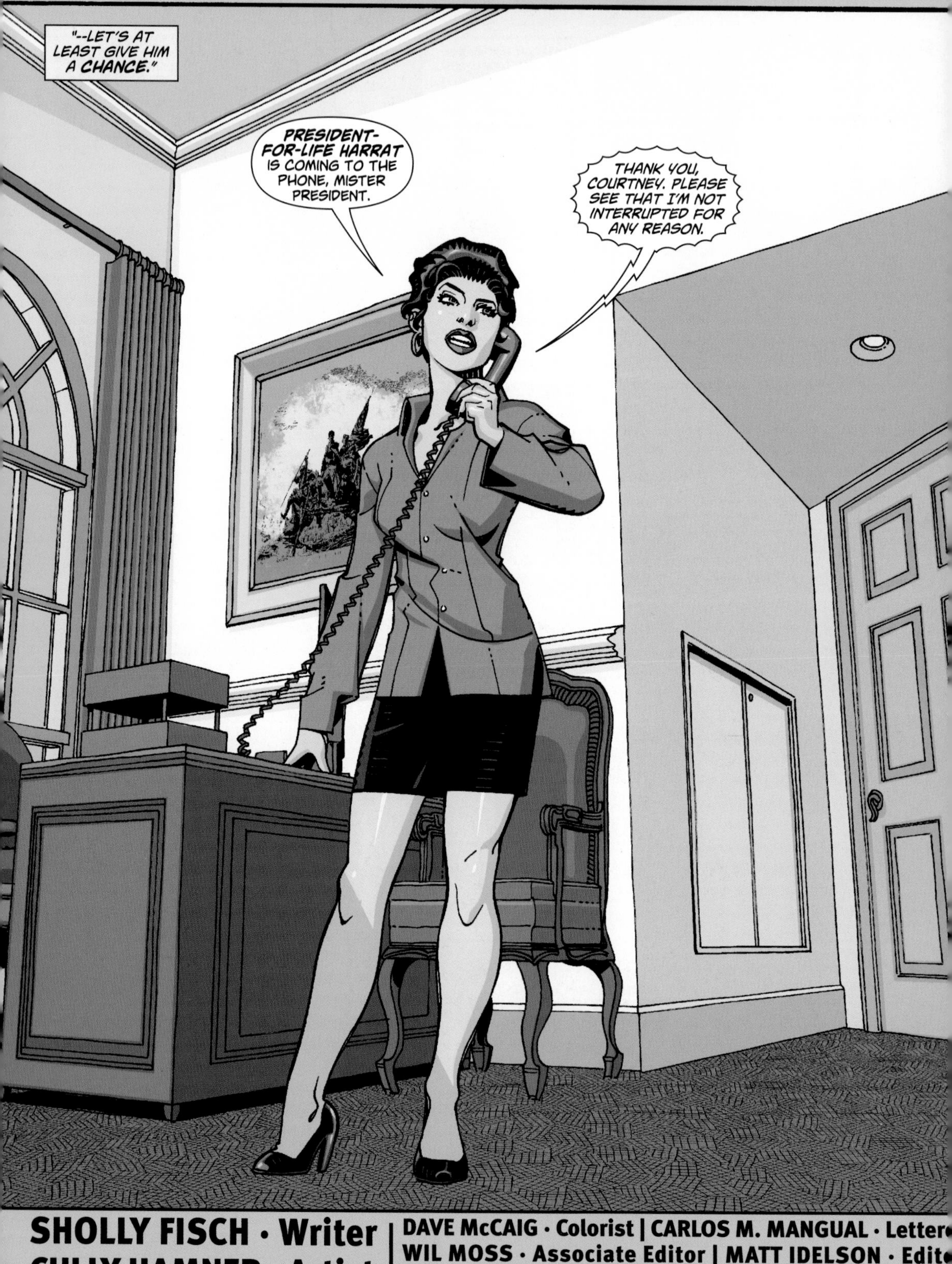
"--LET'S AT LEAST GIVE HIM A CHANCE."
PRESIDENT-FOR-LIFE HARRAT IS COMING TO THE PHONE, MISTER PRESIDENT.
THANK YOU, COURTNEY. PLEASE SEE THAT I'M NOT INTERRUPTED FOR ANY REASON.

SHOLLY FISCH • Writer
CULLY HAMNER • Artist

DAVE McCAIG • Colorist | CARLOS M. MANGUAL • Lettere
WIL MOSS • Associate Editor | MATT IDELSON • Edito
SUPERMAN created by JERRY SIEGEL & JOE SHUSTE

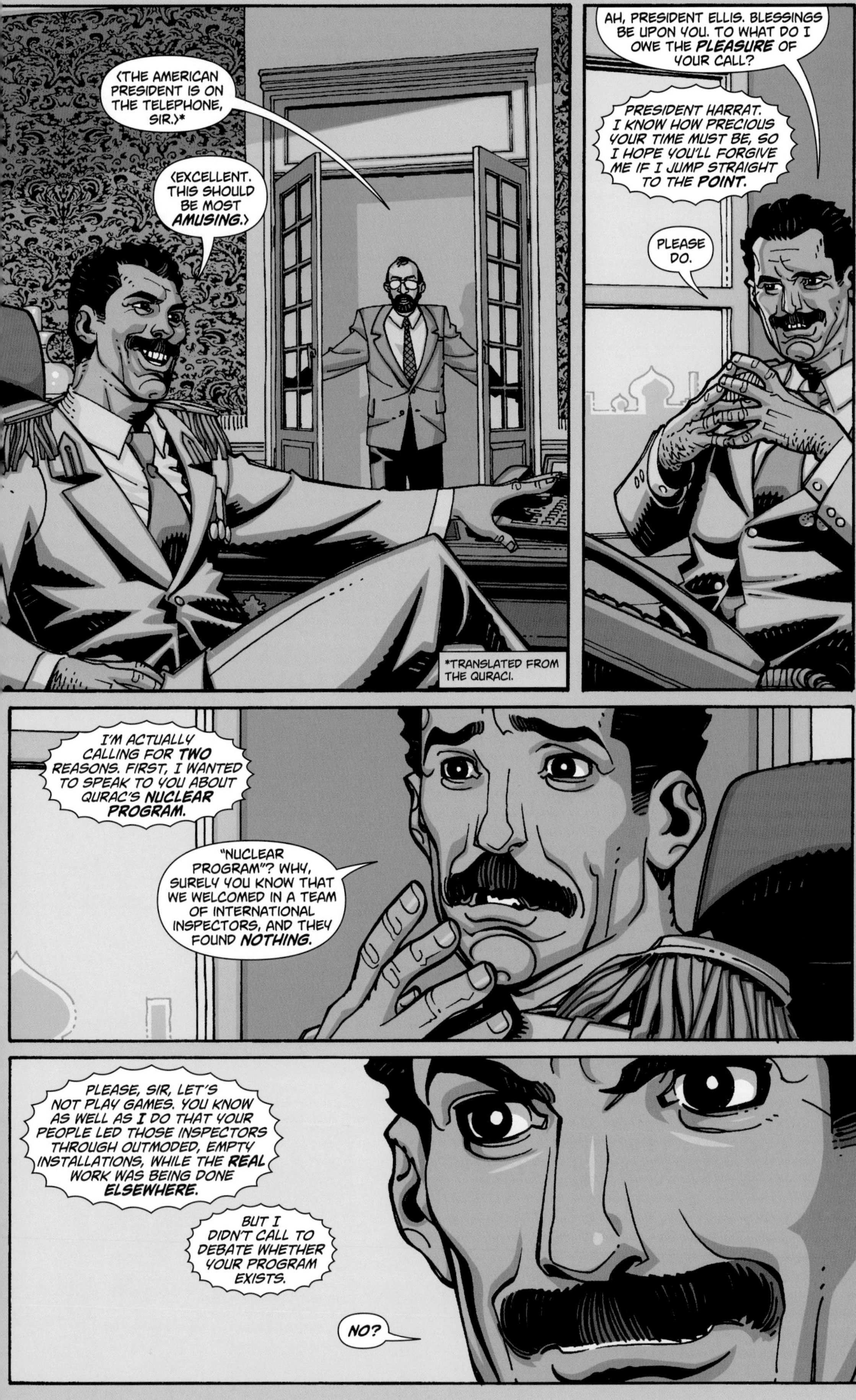

‹THE AMERICAN PRESIDENT IS ON THE TELEPHONE, SIR.›*
‹EXCELLENT. THIS SHOULD BE MOST AMUSING.›
*TRANSLATED FROM THE QURACI.
AH, PRESIDENT ELLIS. BLESSINGS BE UPON YOU. TO WHAT DO I OWE THE PLEASURE OF YOUR CALL?
PRESIDENT HARRAT. I KNOW HOW PRECIOUS YOUR TIME MUST BE, SO I HOPE YOU'LL FORGIVE ME IF I JUMP STRAIGHT TO THE POINT.
PLEASE DO.
I'M ACTUALLY CALLING FOR TWO REASONS. FIRST, I WANTED TO SPEAK TO YOU ABOUT QURAC'S NUCLEAR PROGRAM.
"NUCLEAR PROGRAM"? WHY, SURELY YOU KNOW THAT WE WELCOMED IN A TEAM OF INTERNATIONAL INSPECTORS, AND THEY FOUND NOTHING.
PLEASE, SIR, LET'S NOT PLAY GAMES. YOU KNOW AS WELL AS I DO THAT YOUR PEOPLE LED THOSE INSPECTORS THROUGH OUTMODED, EMPTY INSTALLATIONS, WHILE THE REAL WORK WAS BEING DONE ELSEWHERE.
BUT I DIDN'T CALL TO DEBATE WHETHER YOUR PROGRAM EXISTS.
NO?

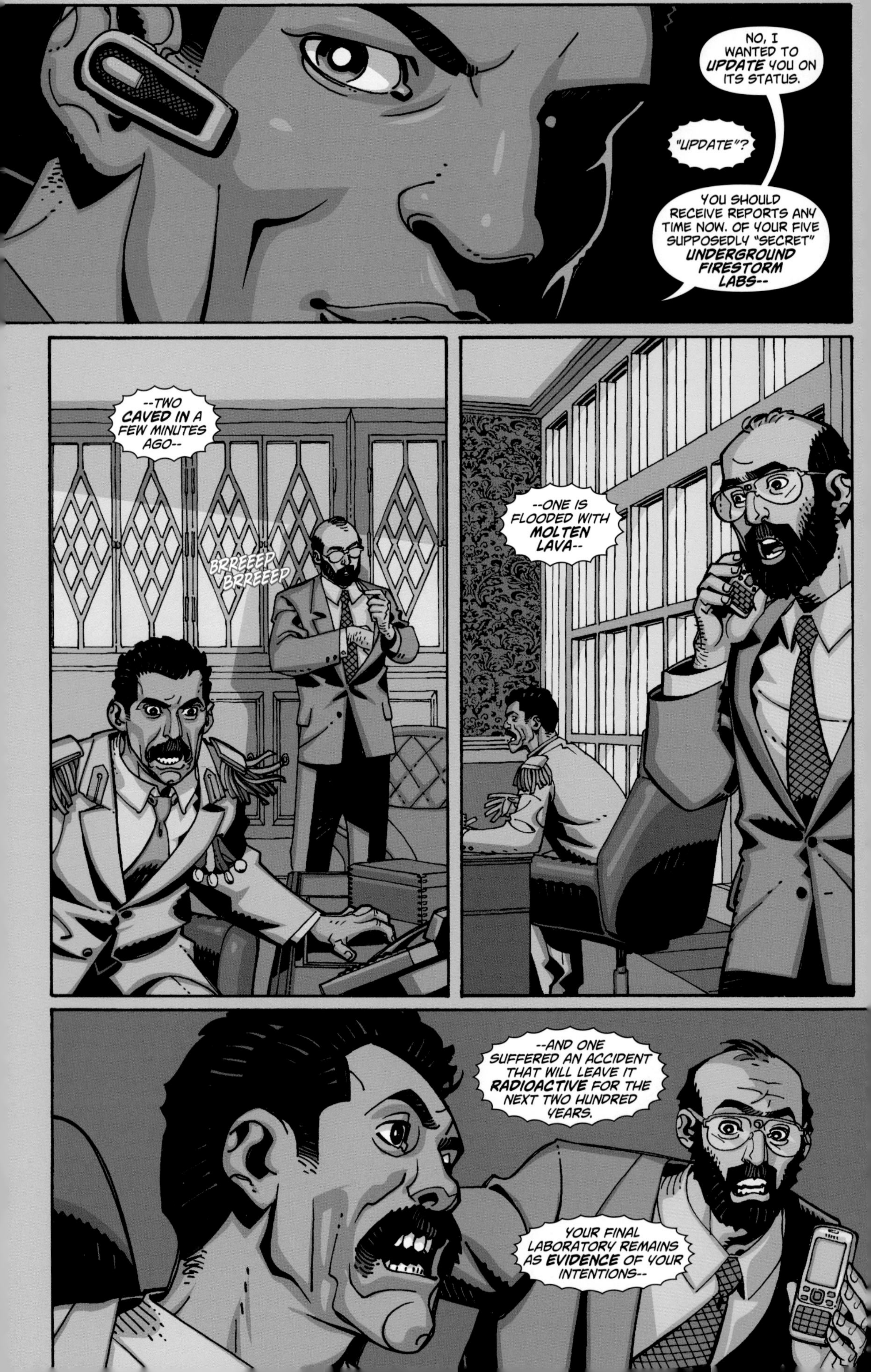
NO, I WANTED TO UPDATE YOU ON ITS STATUS.
"UPDATE"?
YOU SHOULD RECEIVE REPORTS ANY TIME NOW. OF YOUR FIVE SUPPOSEDLY "SECRET" UNDERGROUND FIRESTORM LABS--
--TWO CAVED IN A FEW MINUTES AGO--
BRREEEP BRREEEP
--ONE IS FLOODED WITH MOLTEN LAVA--
--AND ONE SUFFERED AN ACCIDENT THAT WILL LEAVE IT RADIOACTIVE FOR THE NEXT TWO HUNDRED YEARS.
YOUR FINAL LABORATORY REMAINS AS EVIDENCE OF YOUR INTENTIONS--

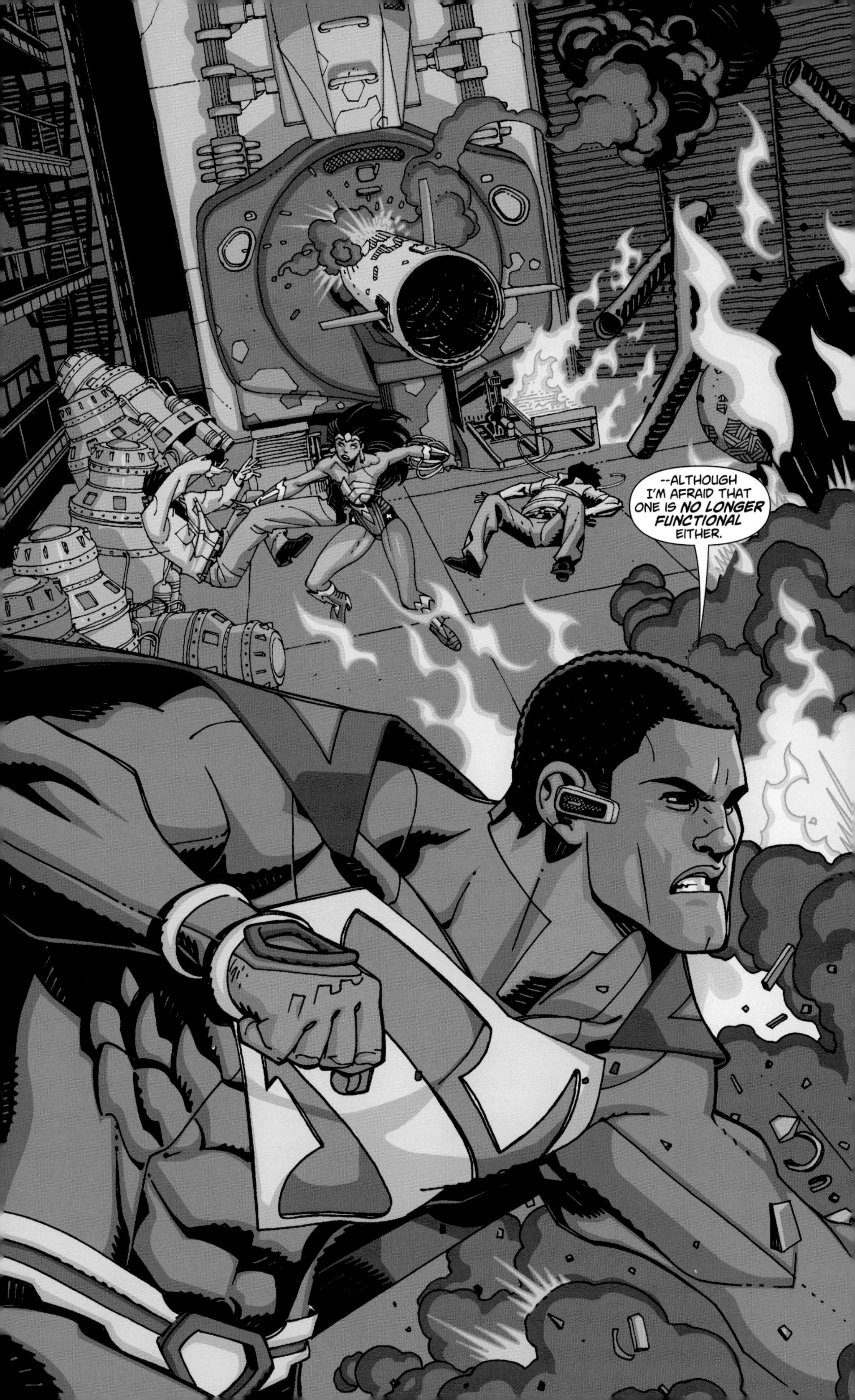
--ALTHOUGH I'M AFRAID THAT ONE IS NO LONGER FUNCTIONAL EITHER.

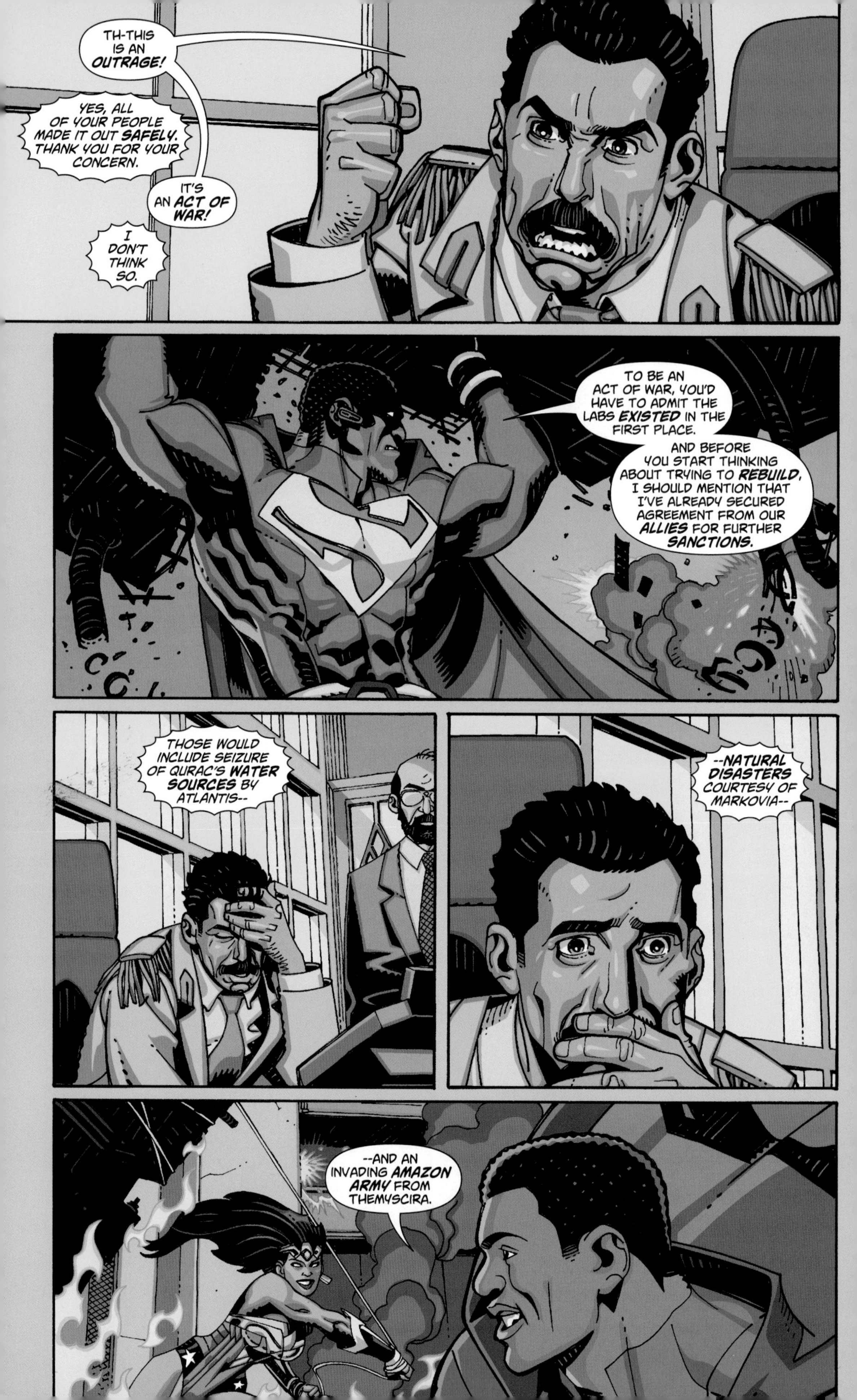

TH-THIS IS AN OUTRAGE!
YES, ALL OF YOUR PEOPLE MADE IT OUT SAFELY. THANK YOU FOR YOUR CONCERN.
IT'S AN ACT OF WAR!
I DON'T THINK SO.
TO BE AN ACT OF WAR, YOU'D HAVE TO ADMIT THE LABS EXISTED IN THE FIRST PLACE.
AND BEFORE YOU START THINKING ABOUT TRYING TO REBUILD, I SHOULD MENTION THAT I'VE ALREADY SECURED AGREEMENT FROM OUR ALLIES FOR FURTHER SANCTIONS.
THOSE WOULD INCLUDE SEIZURE OF QURAC'S WATER SOURCES BY ATLANTIS--
--NATURAL DISASTERS COURTESY OF MARKOVIA--
--AND AN INVADING AMAZON ARMY FROM THEMYSCIRA.

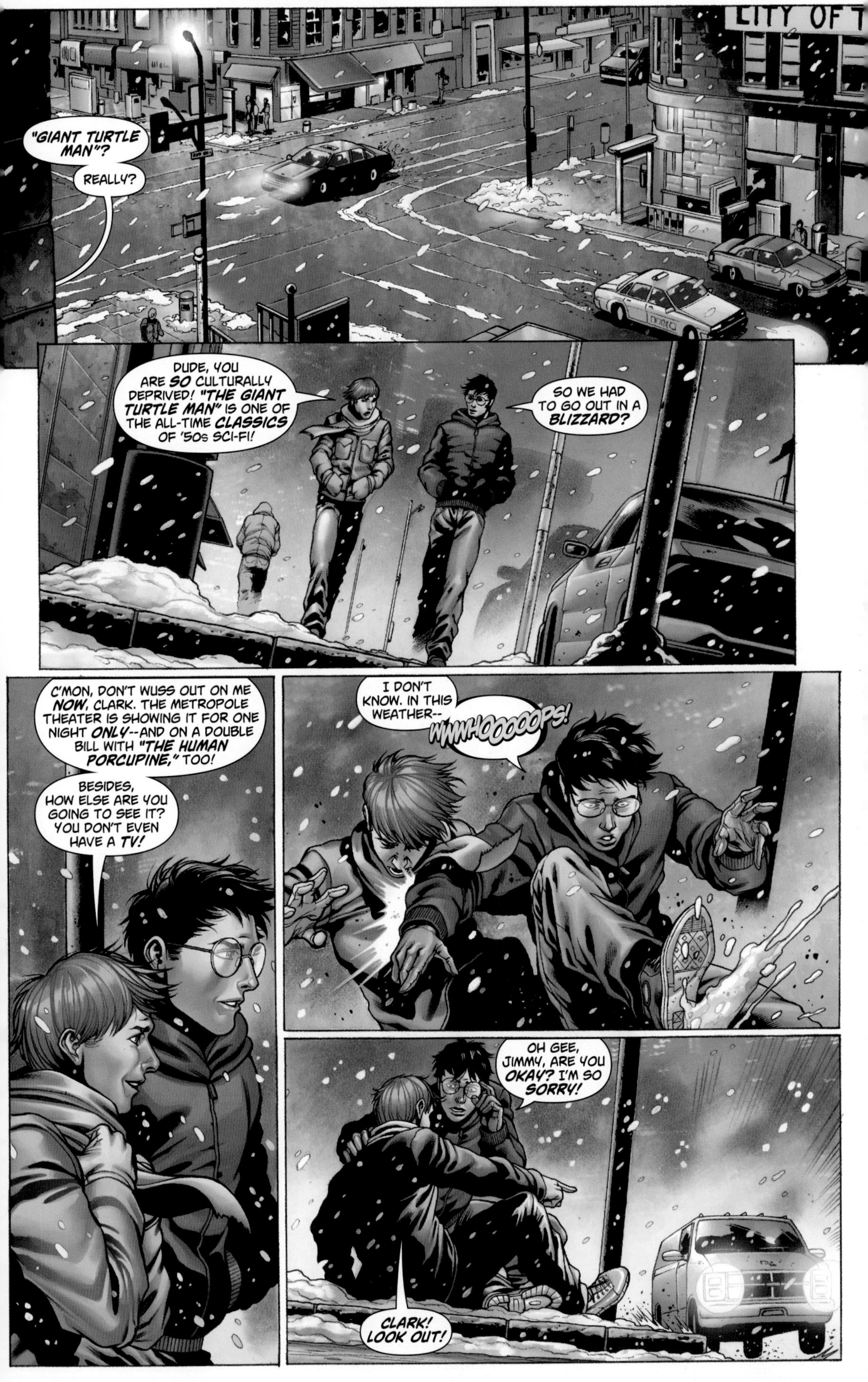
"GIANT TURTLE MAN"?
REALLY?
LITY OF T
DUDE, YOU ARE SO CULTURALLY DEPRIVED! "THE GIANT TURTLE MAN" IS ONE OF THE ALL-TIME CLASSICS OF '50s SCI-FI!
SO WE HAD TO GO OUT IN A BLIZZARD?
C'MON, DON'T WUSS OUT ON ME NOW, CLARK. THE METROPOLE THEATER IS SHOWING IT FOR ONE NIGHT ONLY--AND ON A DOUBLE BILL WITH "THE HUMAN PORCUPINE," TOO!
BESIDES, HOW ELSE ARE YOU GOING TO SEE IT? YOU DON'T EVEN HAVE A TV!
I DON'T KNOW. IN THIS WEATHER--
WWWHOOOOOPS!
OH GEE, JIMMY, ARE YOU OKAY? I'M SO SORRY!
CLARK! LOOK OUT!

KRRRUUUUNNNNCCCCHHH

HEY, ARE YOU ALL RIGHT?

I-I THINK SO. THERE WAS THIS PATCH OF ICE...

MAN...

CLARK...IF YOU HADN'T SLIPPED...

...WE'D BE *UNDER* THERE.

CLASSIC CLARK KENT MOMENT. HE *SLIPS* AND SAVES BOTH OUR LIVES BY *ACCIDENT*.

THAT KIND OF STUFF HAPPENED AROUND CLARK ALL THE TIME. HE HAD TO BE THE *LUCKIEST* GUY ON EARTH.

WELL, UNTIL, UH...

...YOU KNOW.

IT'S OKAY, JIM.

YOU KNOW, METROPOLIS NEWSMEN--YES, LOIS, AND NEWS*WOMEN*, TOO--HAVE BEEN GATHERING HERE AT SWAN'S TAVERN FOR NEARLY TWO HUNDRED YEARS.

I'VE LOST COUNT OF THE NUMBER OF TIMES I'VE SAT AT THAT BAR. BUT IT'S ALWAYS *HARDEST* WHEN WE GET TOGETHER--

--TO SAY *GOODBYE* TO ONE OF OUR OWN.

ABSENT FRIENDS

SHOLLY FISCH - Writer **CAFU** - Artist
JAY DAVID RAMOS - Colorist **CARLOS M. MANGUAL** - Letterer
WIL MOSS - Associate Editor **MATT IDELSON** - Editor
SUPERMAN created by JERRY SIEGEL & JOE SHUSTER

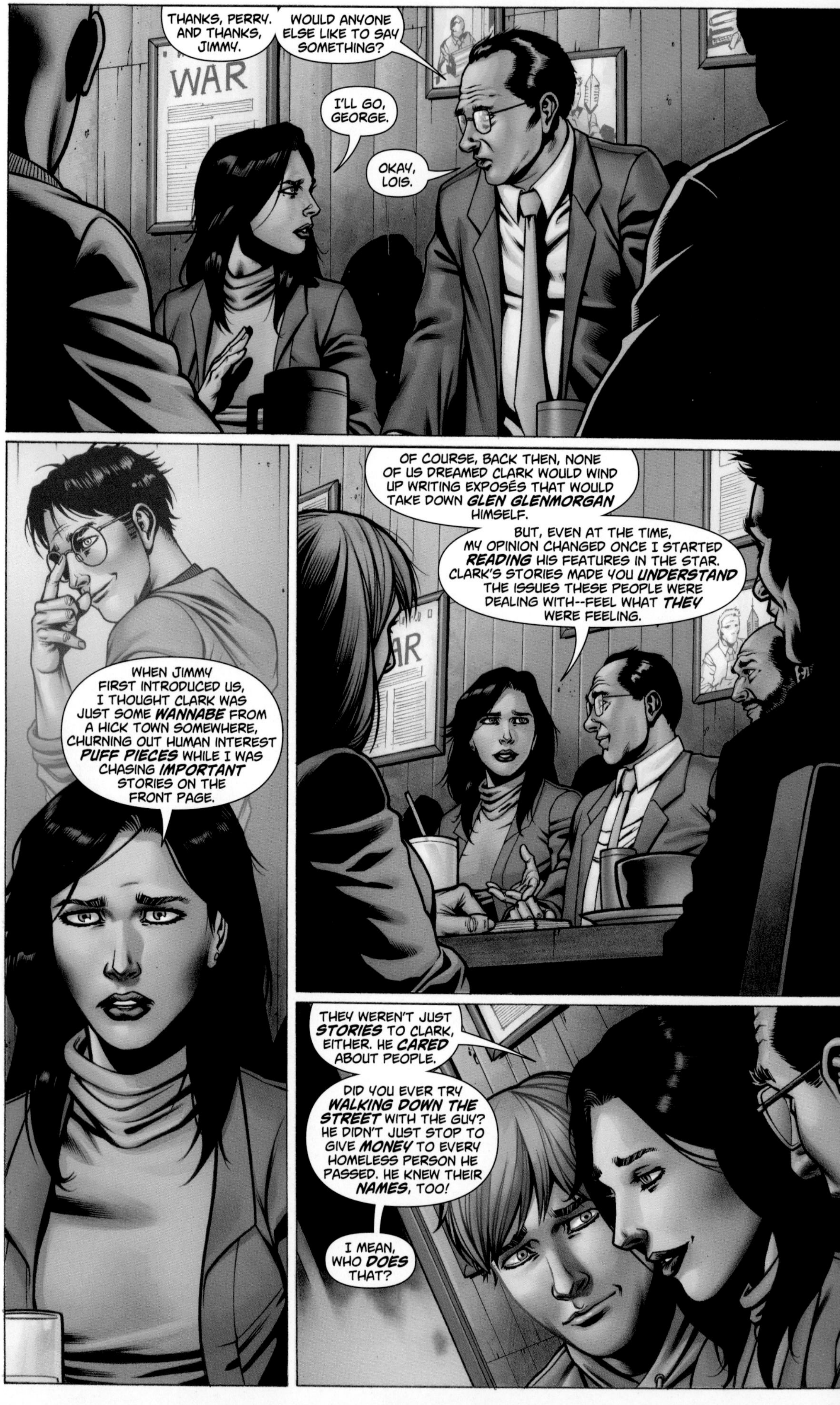
THANKS, PERRY. AND THANKS, JIMMY.
WOULD ANYONE ELSE LIKE TO SAY SOMETHING?
WAR
I'LL GO, GEORGE.
OKAY, LOIS.
WHEN JIMMY FIRST INTRODUCED US, I THOUGHT CLARK WAS JUST SOME WANNABE FROM A HICK TOWN SOMEWHERE, CHURNING OUT HUMAN INTEREST PUFF PIECES WHILE I WAS CHASING IMPORTANT STORIES ON THE FRONT PAGE.
OF COURSE, BACK THEN, NONE OF US DREAMED CLARK WOULD WIND UP WRITING EXPOSÉS THAT WOULD TAKE DOWN GLEN GLENMORGAN HIMSELF.
BUT, EVEN AT THE TIME, MY OPINION CHANGED ONCE I STARTED READING HIS FEATURES IN THE STAR. CLARK'S STORIES MADE YOU UNDERSTAND THE ISSUES THESE PEOPLE WERE DEALING WITH--FEEL WHAT THEY WERE FEELING.
THEY WEREN'T JUST STORIES TO CLARK, EITHER. HE CARED ABOUT PEOPLE.
DID YOU EVER TRY WALKING DOWN THE STREET WITH THE GUY? HE DIDN'T JUST STOP TO GIVE MONEY TO EVERY HOMELESS PERSON HE PASSED. HE KNEW THEIR NAMES, TOO!
I MEAN, WHO DOES THAT?

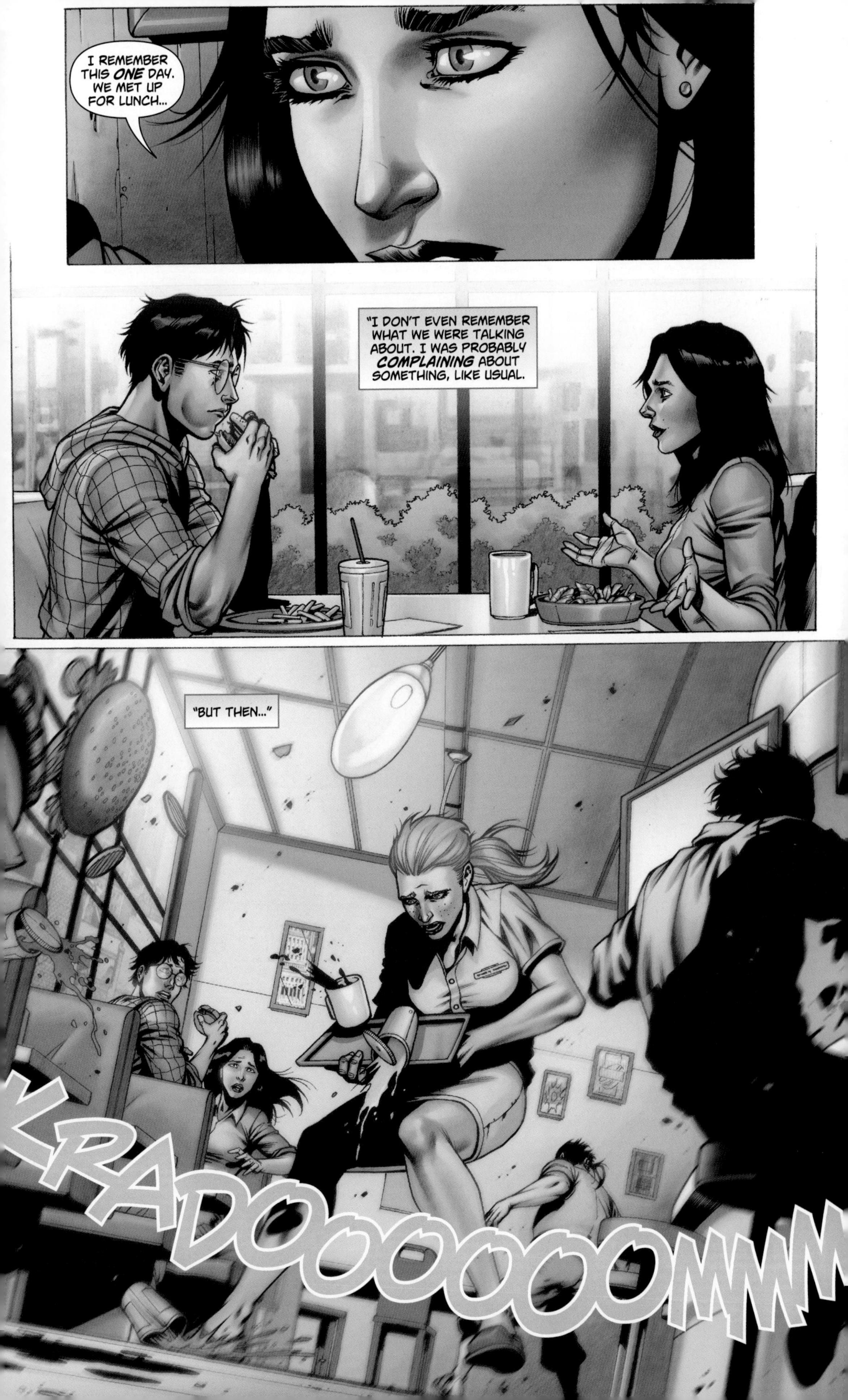
I REMEMBER THIS ONE DAY. WE MET UP FOR LUNCH...
"I DON'T EVEN REMEMBER WHAT WE WERE TALKING ABOUT. I WAS PROBABLY COMPLAINING ABOUT SOMETHING, LIKE USUAL.
"BUT THEN..."
KRADOOOOOOMM

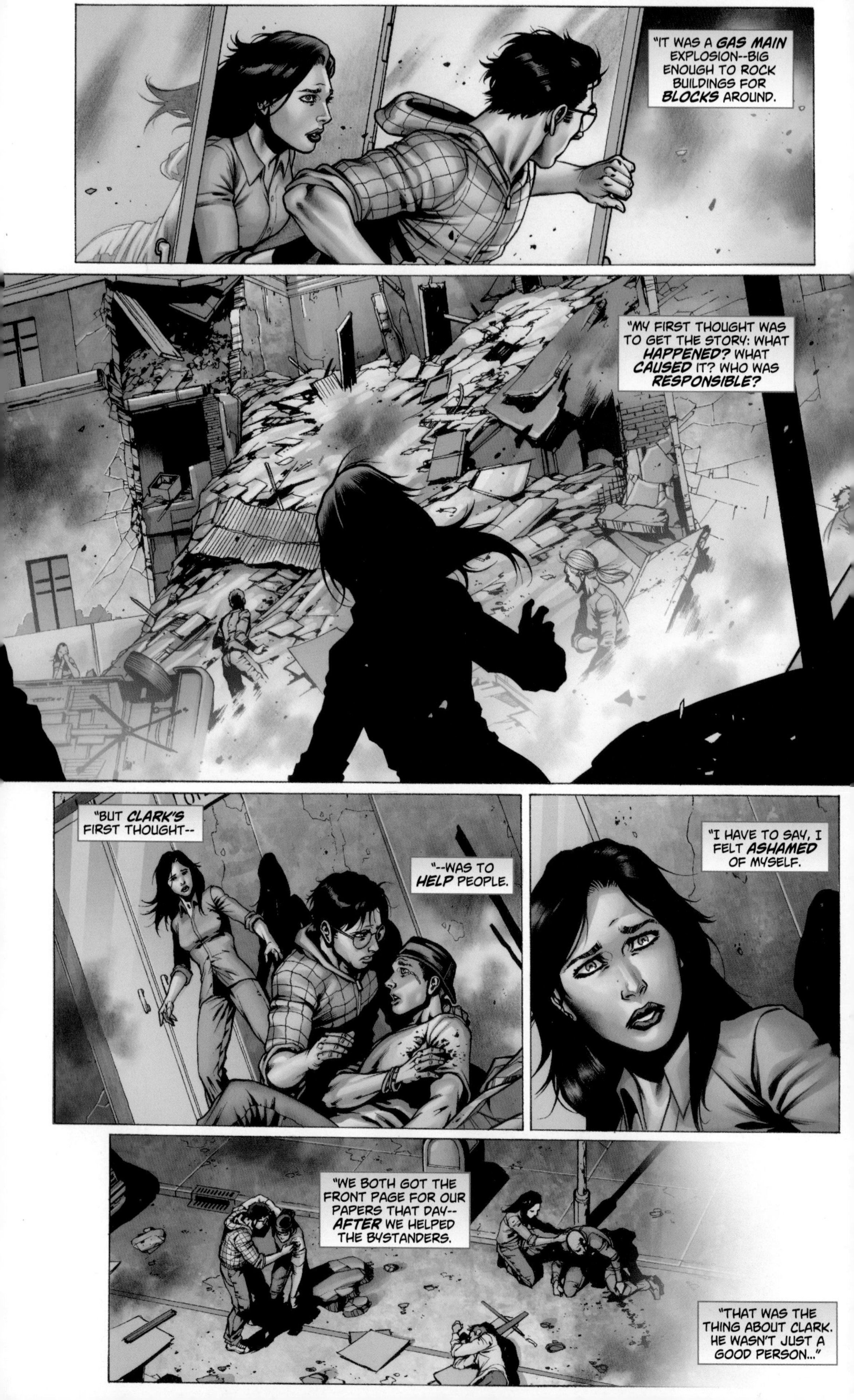
"IT WAS A GAS MAIN EXPLOSION--BIG ENOUGH TO ROCK BUILDINGS FOR BLOCKS AROUND.
"MY FIRST THOUGHT WAS TO GET THE STORY: WHAT HAPPENED? WHAT CAUSED IT? WHO WAS RESPONSIBLE?
"BUT CLARK'S FIRST THOUGHT--
"--WAS TO HELP PEOPLE.
"I HAVE TO SAY, I FELT ASHAMED OF MYSELF.
"WE BOTH GOT THE FRONT PAGE FOR OUR PAPERS THAT DAY--AFTER WE HELPED THE BYSTANDERS.
"THAT WAS THE THING ABOUT CLARK. HE WASN'T JUST A GOOD PERSON..."

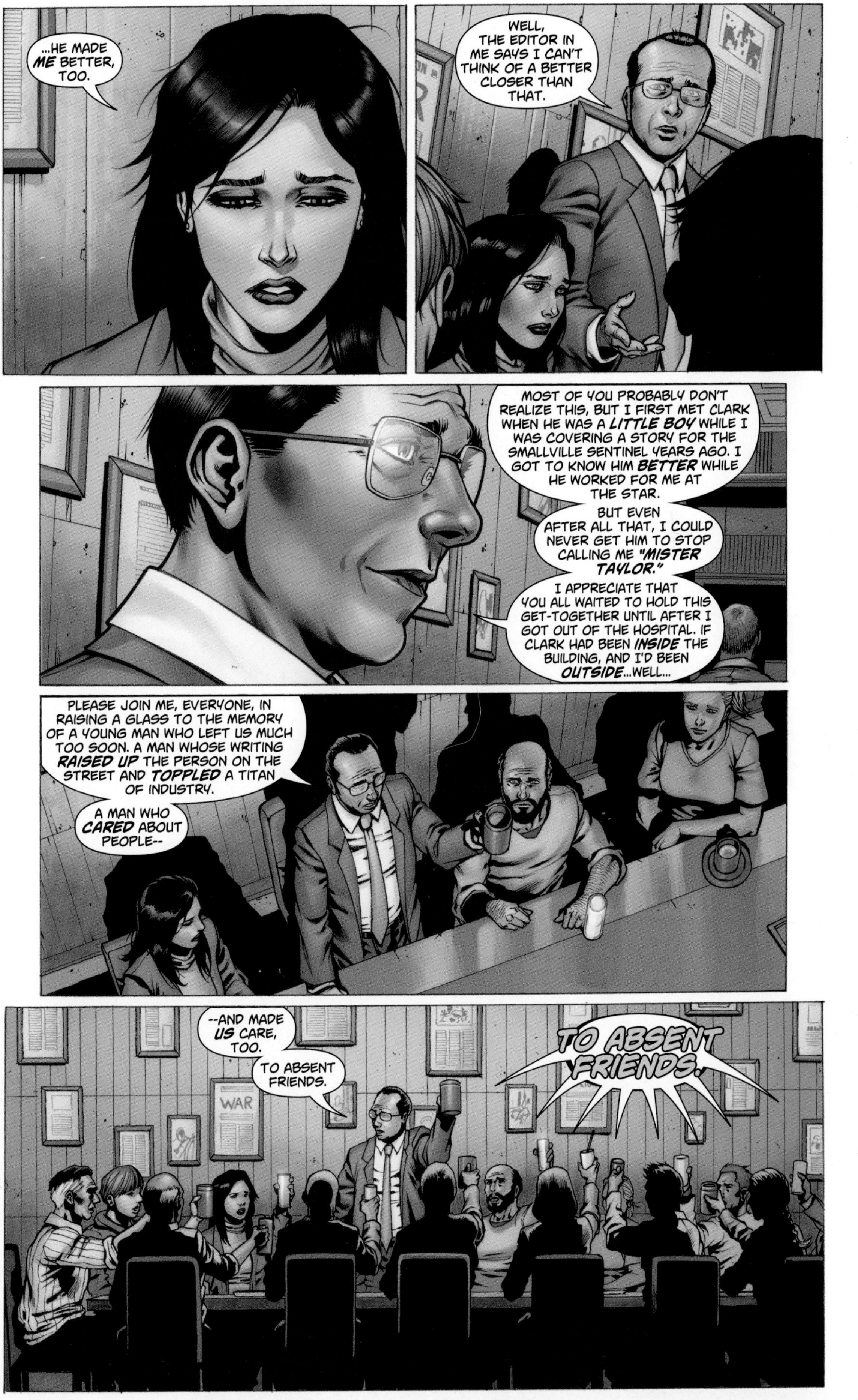
...HE MADE *ME* BETTER, TOO.
WELL, THE EDITOR IN ME SAYS I CAN'T THINK OF A BETTER CLOSER THAN THAT.
MOST OF YOU PROBABLY DON'T REALIZE THIS, BUT I FIRST MET CLARK WHEN HE WAS A *LITTLE BOY* WHILE I WAS COVERING A STORY FOR THE SMALLVILLE SENTINEL YEARS AGO. I GOT TO KNOW HIM *BETTER* WHILE HE WORKED FOR ME AT THE STAR.
BUT EVEN AFTER ALL THAT, I COULD NEVER GET HIM TO STOP CALLING ME *"MISTER TAYLOR."*
I APPRECIATE THAT YOU ALL WAITED TO HOLD THIS GET-TOGETHER UNTIL AFTER I GOT OUT OF THE HOSPITAL. IF CLARK HAD BEEN *INSIDE* THE BUILDING, AND I'D BEEN *OUTSIDE*...WELL...
PLEASE JOIN ME, EVERYONE, IN RAISING A GLASS TO THE MEMORY OF A YOUNG MAN WHO LEFT US MUCH TOO SOON. A MAN WHOSE WRITING *RAISED UP* THE PERSON ON THE STREET AND *TOPPLED* A TITAN OF INDUSTRY.
A MAN WHO *CARED* ABOUT PEOPLE--
--AND MADE *US* CARE, TOO.
TO ABSENT FRIENDS.
TO ABSENT FRIENDS.
WAR

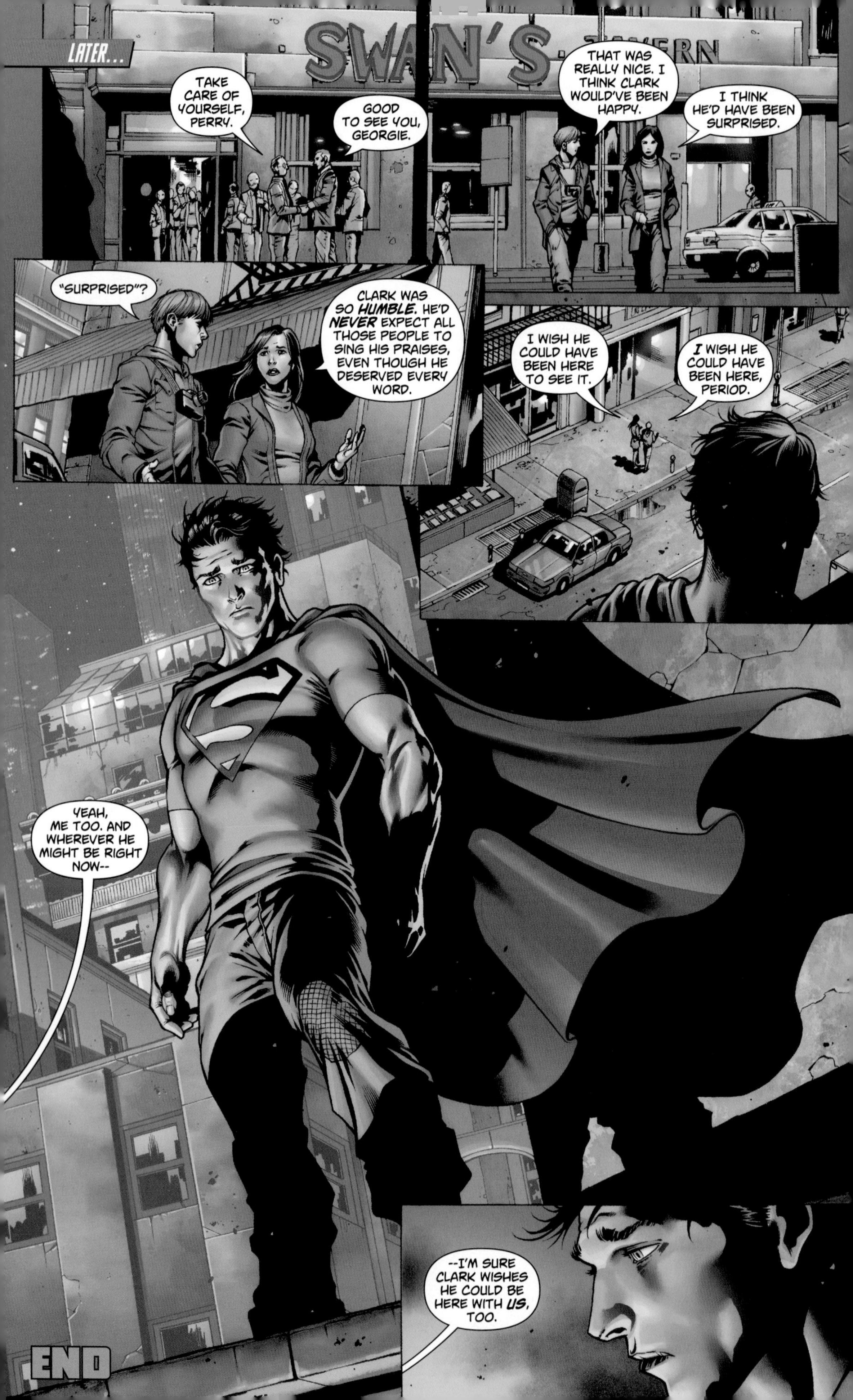
LATER...
SWAN'S TAVERN
TAKE CARE OF YOURSELF, PERRY.
GOOD TO SEE YOU, GEORGIE.
THAT WAS REALLY NICE. I THINK CLARK WOULD'VE BEEN HAPPY.
I THINK HE'D HAVE BEEN SURPRISED.
"SURPRISED"?
CLARK WAS SO HUMBLE. HE'D NEVER EXPECT ALL THOSE PEOPLE TO SING HIS PRAISES, EVEN THOUGH HE DESERVED EVERY WORD.
I WISH HE COULD HAVE BEEN HERE TO SEE IT.
I WISH HE COULD HAVE BEEN HERE, PERIOD.
YEAH, ME TOO. AND WHEREVER HE MIGHT BE RIGHT NOW--
--I'M SURE CLARK WISHES HE COULD BE HERE WITH US, TOO.
END

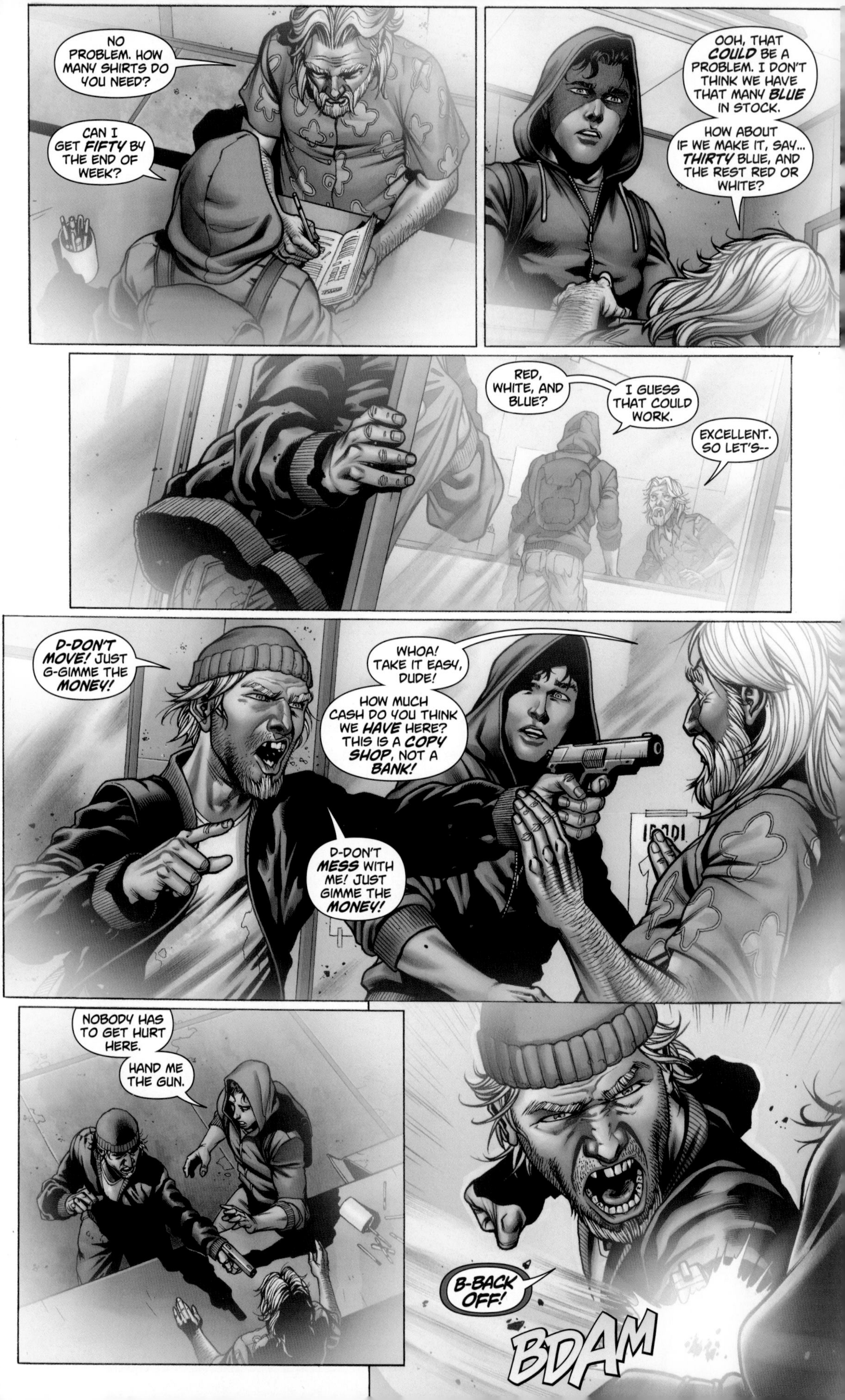
NO PROBLEM. HOW MANY SHIRTS DO YOU NEED?
CAN I GET FIFTY BY THE END OF WEEK?
OOH, THAT COULD BE A PROBLEM. I DON'T THINK WE HAVE THAT MANY BLUE IN STOCK.
HOW ABOUT IF WE MAKE IT, SAY... THIRTY BLUE, AND THE REST RED OR WHITE?
RED, WHITE, AND BLUE?
I GUESS THAT COULD WORK.
EXCELLENT. SO LET'S--
D-DON'T MOVE! JUST G-GIMME THE MONEY!
WHOA! TAKE IT EASY, DUDE!
HOW MUCH CASH DO YOU THINK WE HAVE HERE? THIS IS A COPY SHOP, NOT A BANK!
D-DON'T MESS WITH ME! JUST GIMME THE MONEY!
NOBODY HAS TO GET HURT HERE.
HAND ME THE GUN.
B-BACK OFF!
BDAM

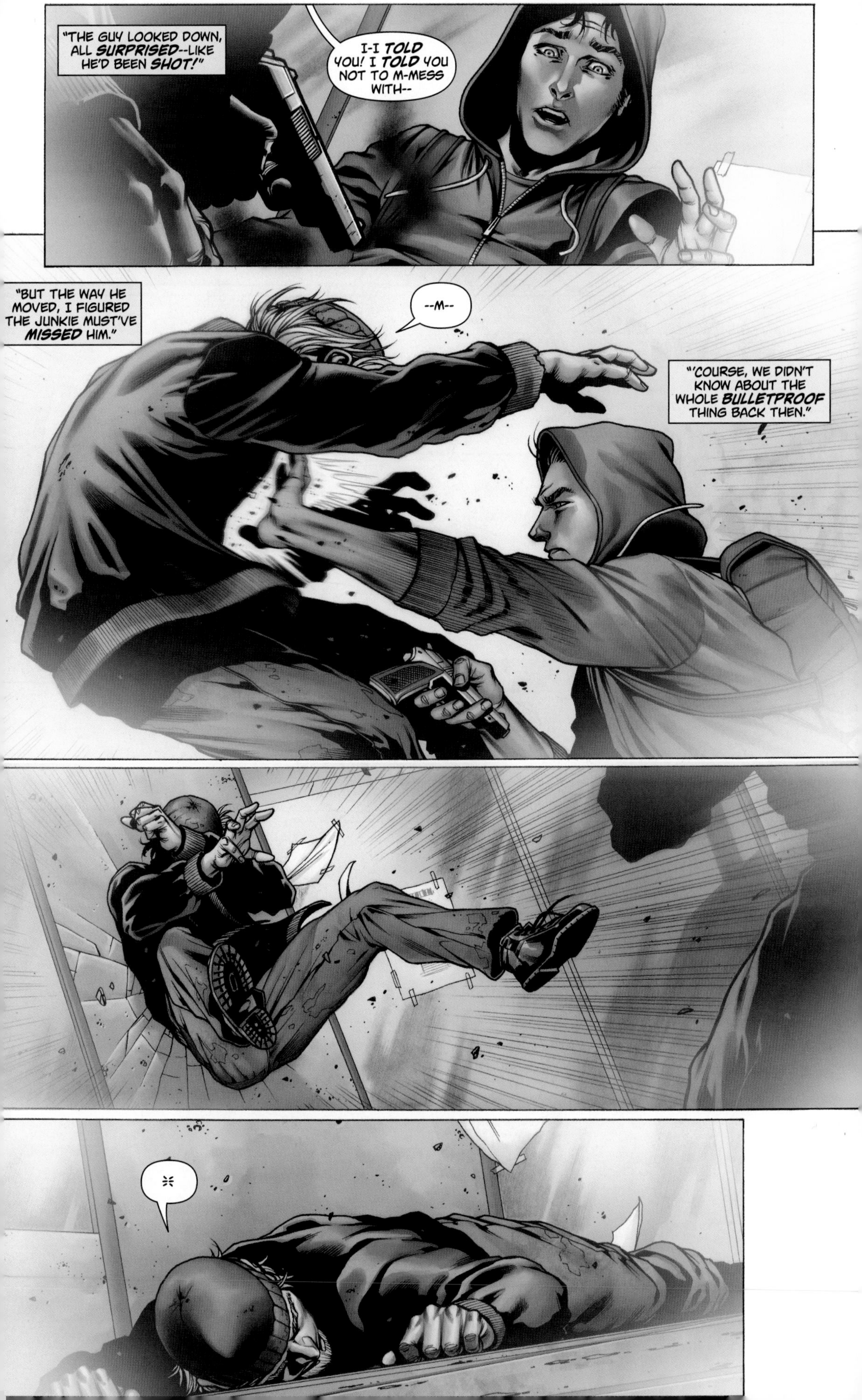
"THE GUY LOOKED DOWN, ALL SURPRISED--LIKE HE'D BEEN SHOT!"
I-I TOLD YOU! I TOLD YOU NOT TO M-MESS WITH--
"BUT THE WAY HE MOVED, I FIGURED THE JUNKIE MUST'VE MISSED HIM."
--M--
"'COURSE, WE DIDN'T KNOW ABOUT THE WHOLE BULLETPROOF THING BACK THEN."

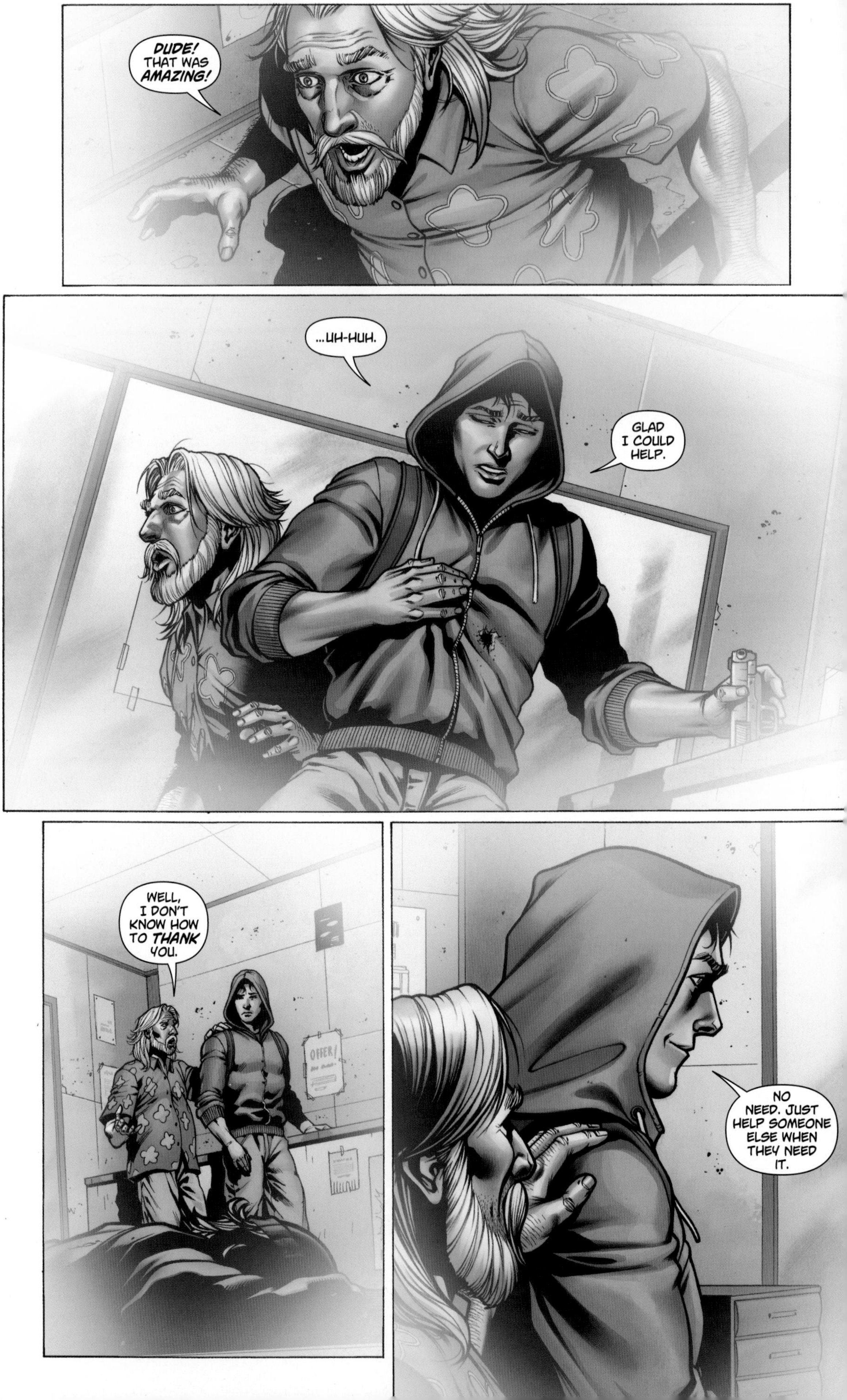
DUDE! THAT WAS AMAZING!
...UH-HUH.
GLAD I COULD HELP.
WELL, I DON'T KNOW HOW TO THANK YOU.
OFFER!
NO NEED. JUST HELP SOMEONE ELSE WHEN THEY NEED IT.

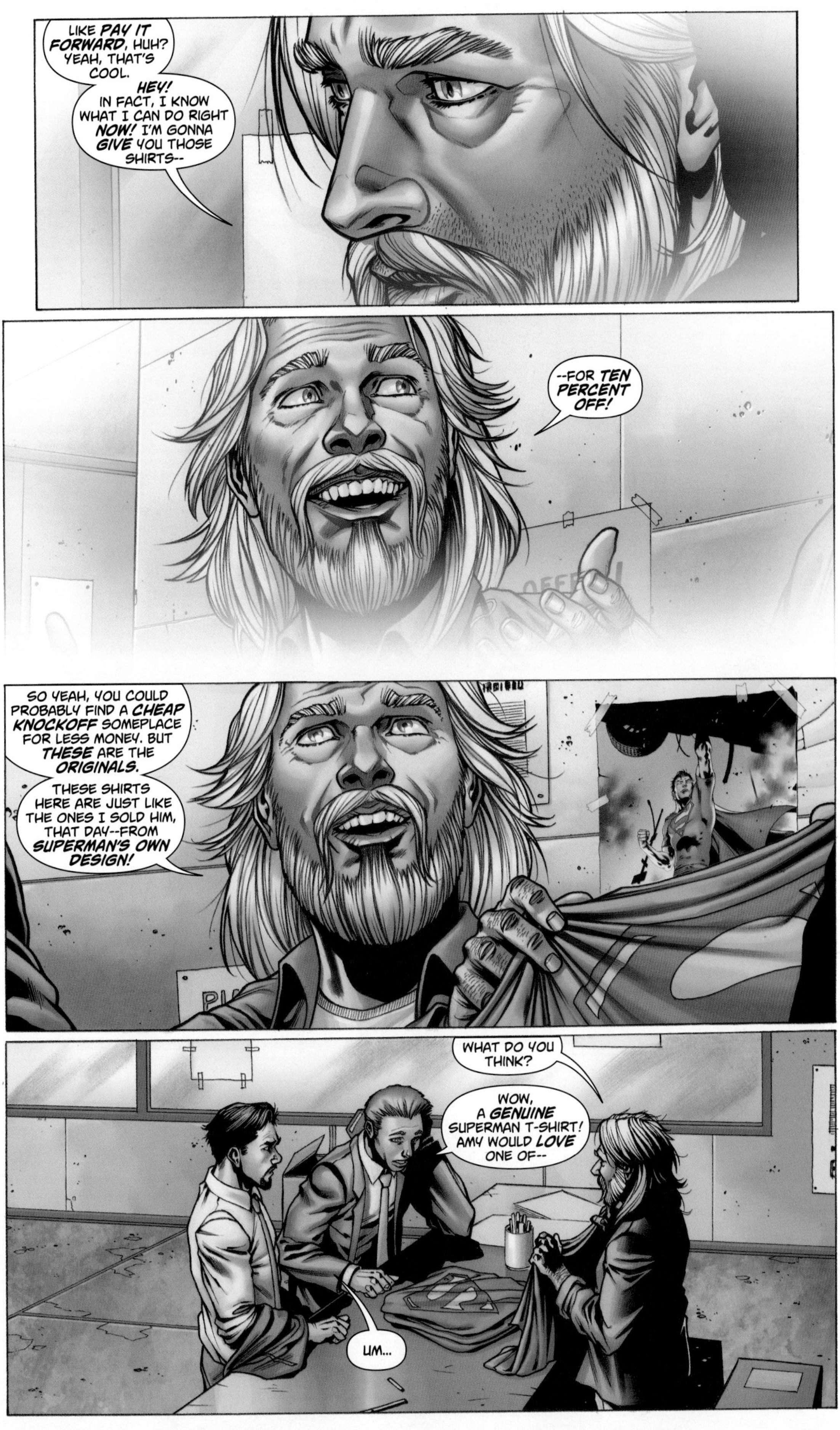
LIKE PAY IT FORWARD, HUH? YEAH, THAT'S COOL.
HEY! IN FACT, I KNOW WHAT I CAN DO RIGHT NOW! I'M GONNA GIVE YOU THOSE SHIRTS--
--FOR TEN PERCENT OFF!
SO YEAH, YOU COULD PROBABLY FIND A CHEAP KNOCKOFF SOMEPLACE FOR LESS MONEY. BUT THESE ARE THE ORIGINALS.
THESE SHIRTS HERE ARE JUST LIKE THE ONES I SOLD HIM, THAT DAY--FROM SUPERMAN'S OWN DESIGN!
WHAT DO YOU THINK?
WOW, A GENUINE SUPERMAN T-SHIRT! AMY WOULD LOVE ONE OF--
UM...

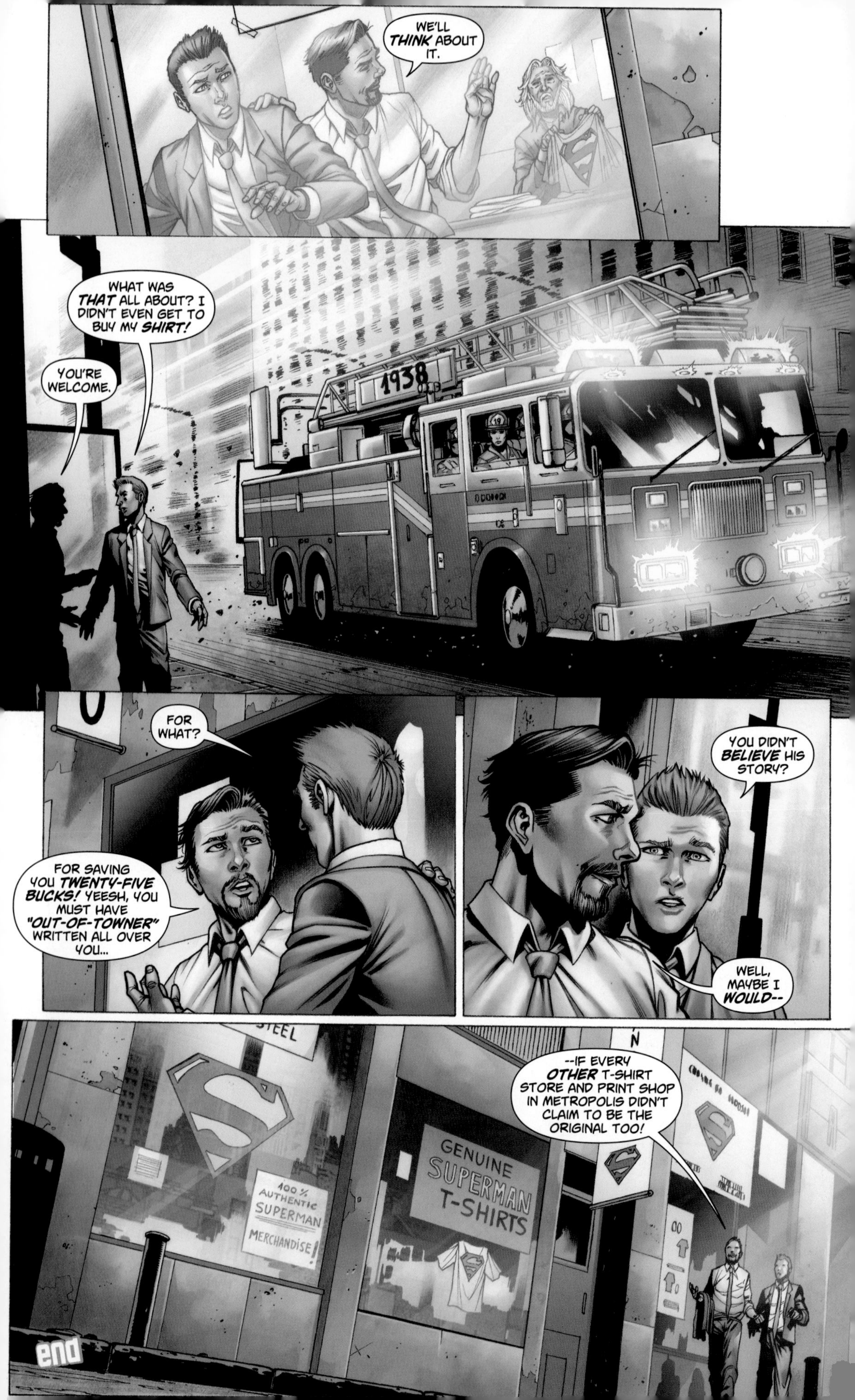
WE'LL THINK ABOUT IT.
WHAT WAS THAT ALL ABOUT? I DIDN'T EVEN GET TO BUY MY SHIRT!
YOU'RE WELCOME.
1938
FOR WHAT?
FOR SAVING YOU TWENTY-FIVE BUCKS! YEESH, YOU MUST HAVE "OUT-OF-TOWNER" WRITTEN ALL OVER YOU...
YOU DIDN'T BELIEVE HIS STORY?
WELL, MAYBE I WOULD--
--IF EVERY OTHER T-SHIRT STORE AND PRINT SHOP IN METROPOLIS DIDN'T CLAIM TO BE THE ORIGINAL TOO!
STEEL
GENUINE SUPERMAN T-SHIRTS
100% AUTHENTIC SUPERMAN MERCHANDISE!
end

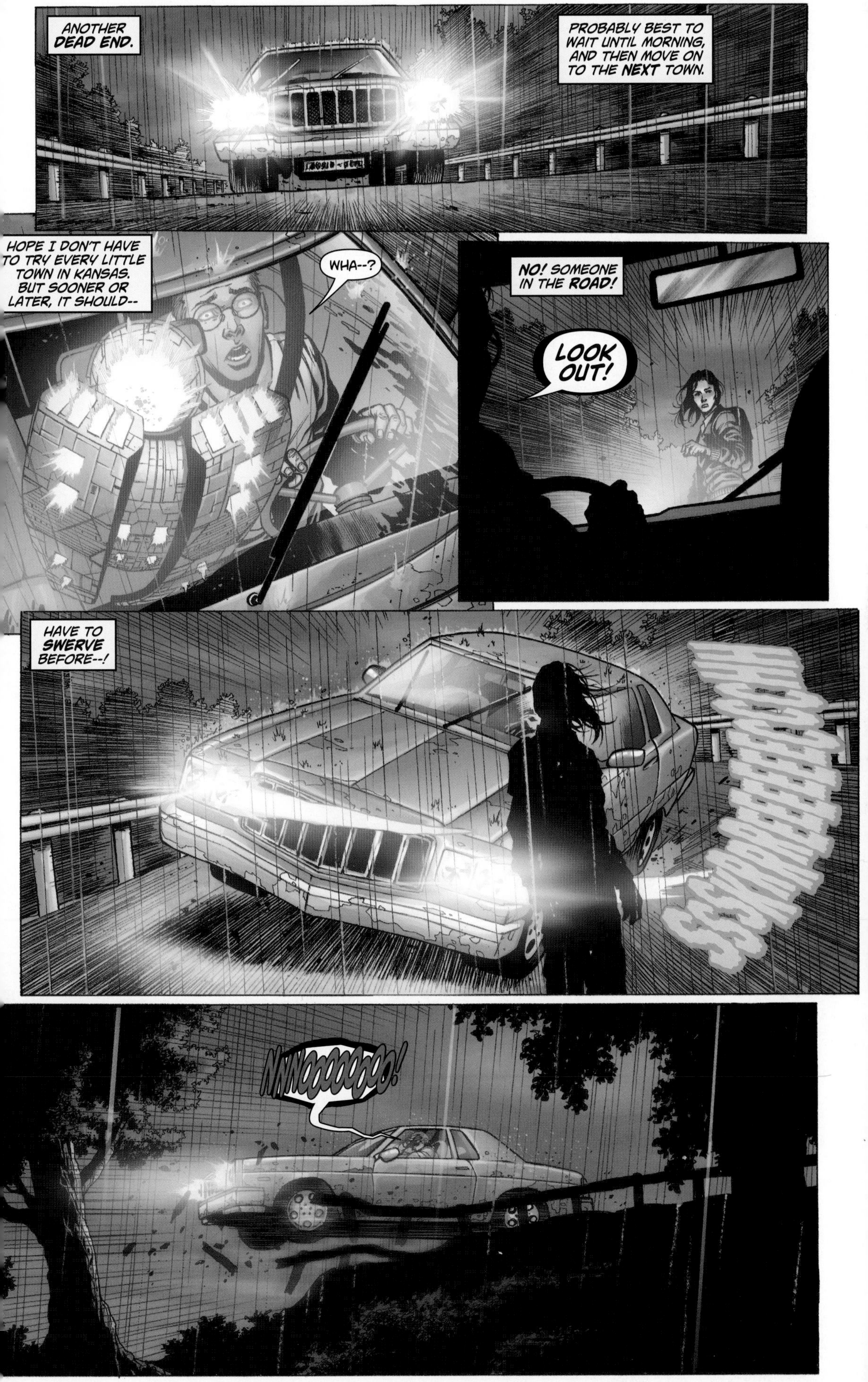
ANOTHER DEAD END.
PROBABLY BEST TO WAIT UNTIL MORNING, AND THEN MOVE ON TO THE NEXT TOWN.
HOPE I DON'T HAVE TO TRY EVERY LITTLE TOWN IN KANSAS. BUT SOONER OR LATER, IT SHOULD--
WHA--?
NO! SOMEONE IN THE ROAD!
LOOK OUT!
HAVE TO SWERVE BEFORE--!
NNNOOOOOOOO!

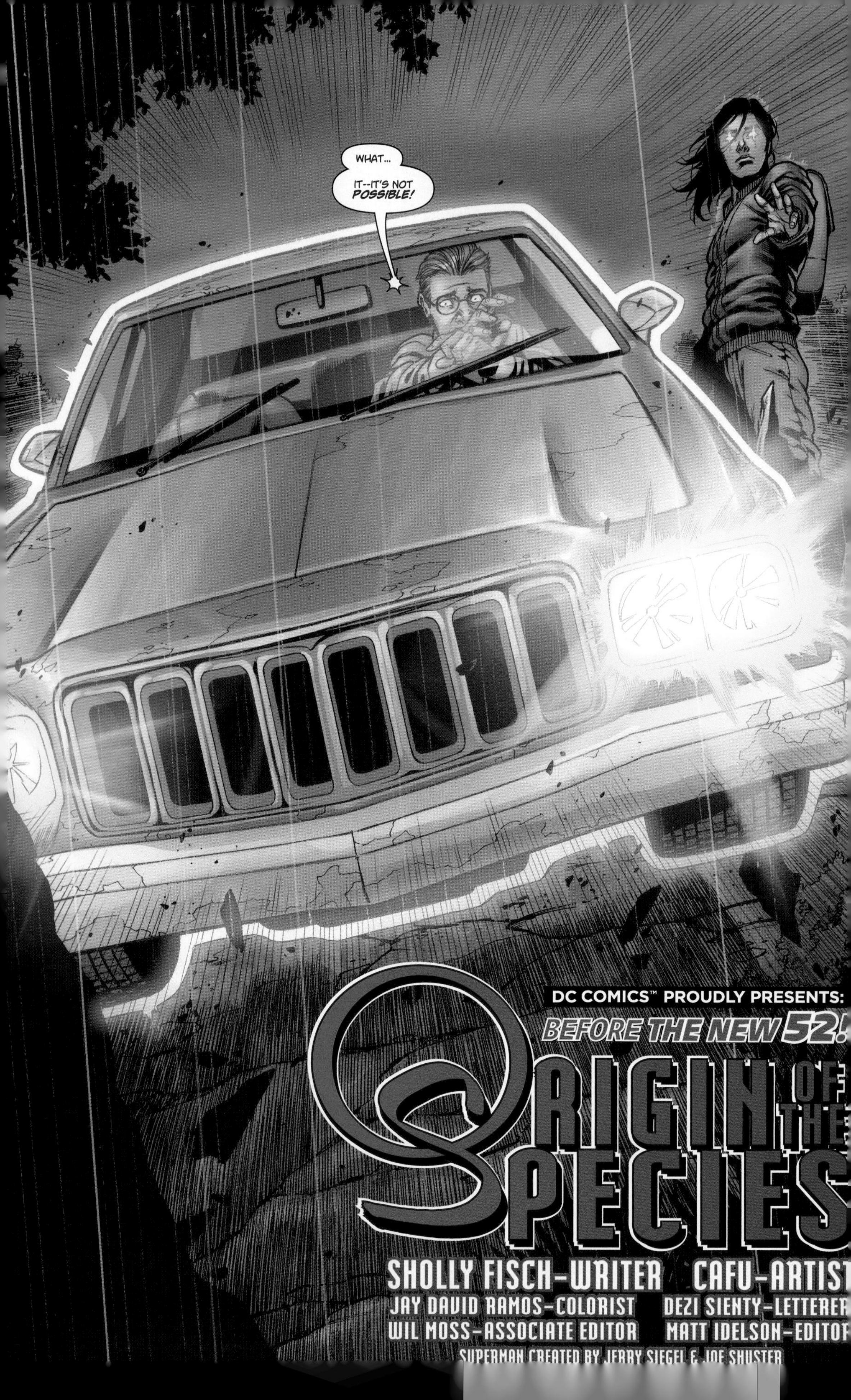
WHAT...
IT--IT'S NOT POSSIBLE!
DC COMICS™ PROUDLY PRESENTS:
BEFORE THE NEW 52!
ORIGIN OF THE SPECIES
SHOLLY FISCH-WRITER CAFU-ARTIST
JAY DAVID RAMOS-COLORIST DEZI SIENTY-LETTERER
WIL MOSS-ASSOCIATE EDITOR MATT IDELSON-EDITOR
SUPERMAN CREATED BY JERRY SIEGEL & JOE SHUSTER

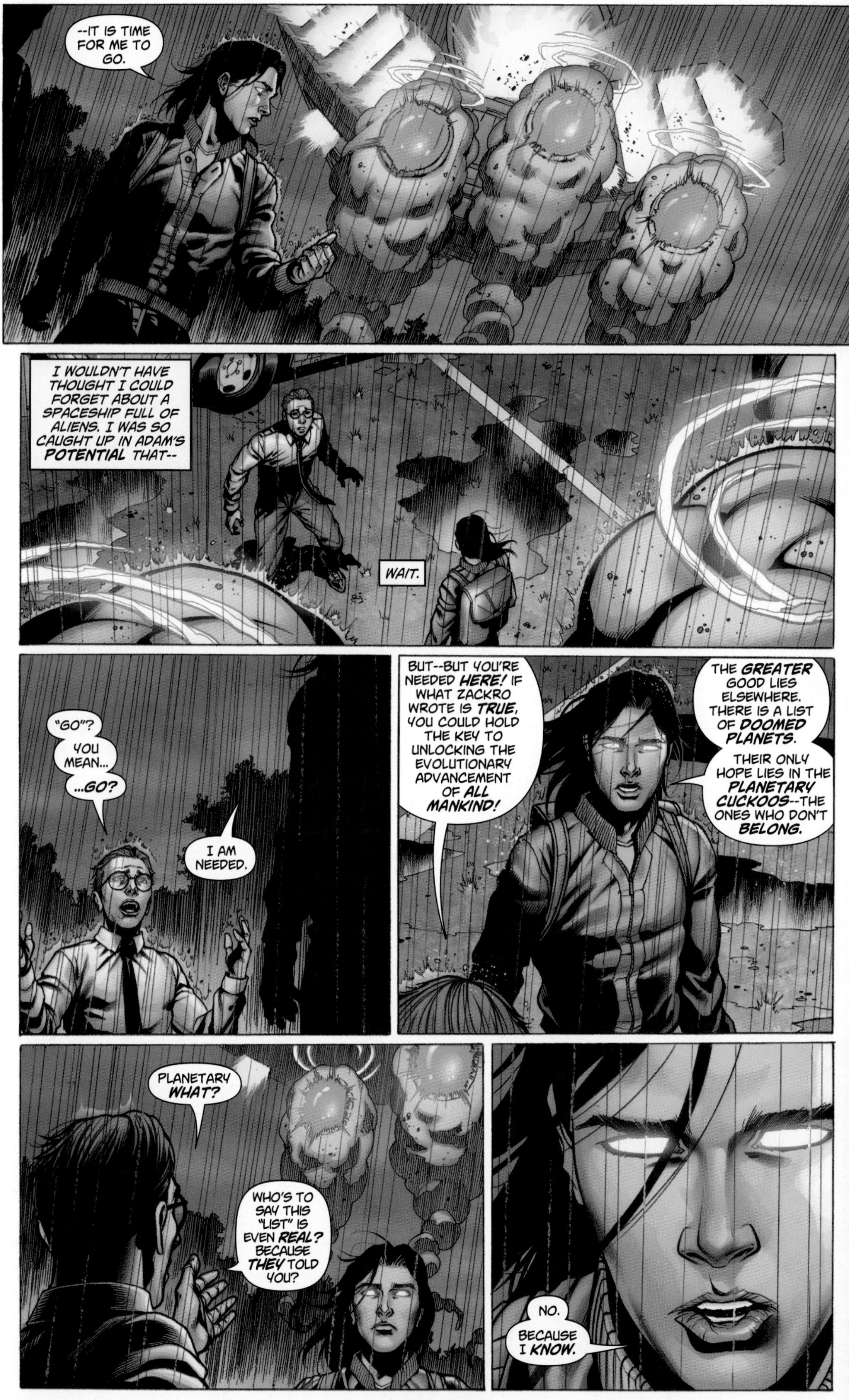
--IT IS TIME FOR ME TO GO.
I WOULDN'T HAVE THOUGHT I COULD FORGET ABOUT A SPACESHIP FULL OF ALIENS. I WAS SO CAUGHT UP IN ADAM'S **POTENTIAL** THAT--
WAIT.
"GO"? YOU MEAN... ...GO?
I AM NEEDED.
BUT--BUT YOU'RE NEEDED **HERE!** IF WHAT ZACKRO WROTE IS **TRUE**, YOU COULD HOLD THE KEY TO UNLOCKING THE EVOLUTIONARY ADVANCEMENT OF **ALL MANKIND!**
THE **GREATER** GOOD LIES ELSEWHERE. THERE IS A LIST OF **DOOMED PLANETS**.
THEIR ONLY HOPE LIES IN THE **PLANETARY CUCKOOS**--THE ONES WHO DON'T **BELONG**.
PLANETARY **WHAT?**
WHO'S TO SAY THIS "LIST" IS EVEN **REAL?** BECAUSE **THEY** TOLD YOU?
NO. BECAUSE I **KNOW**.

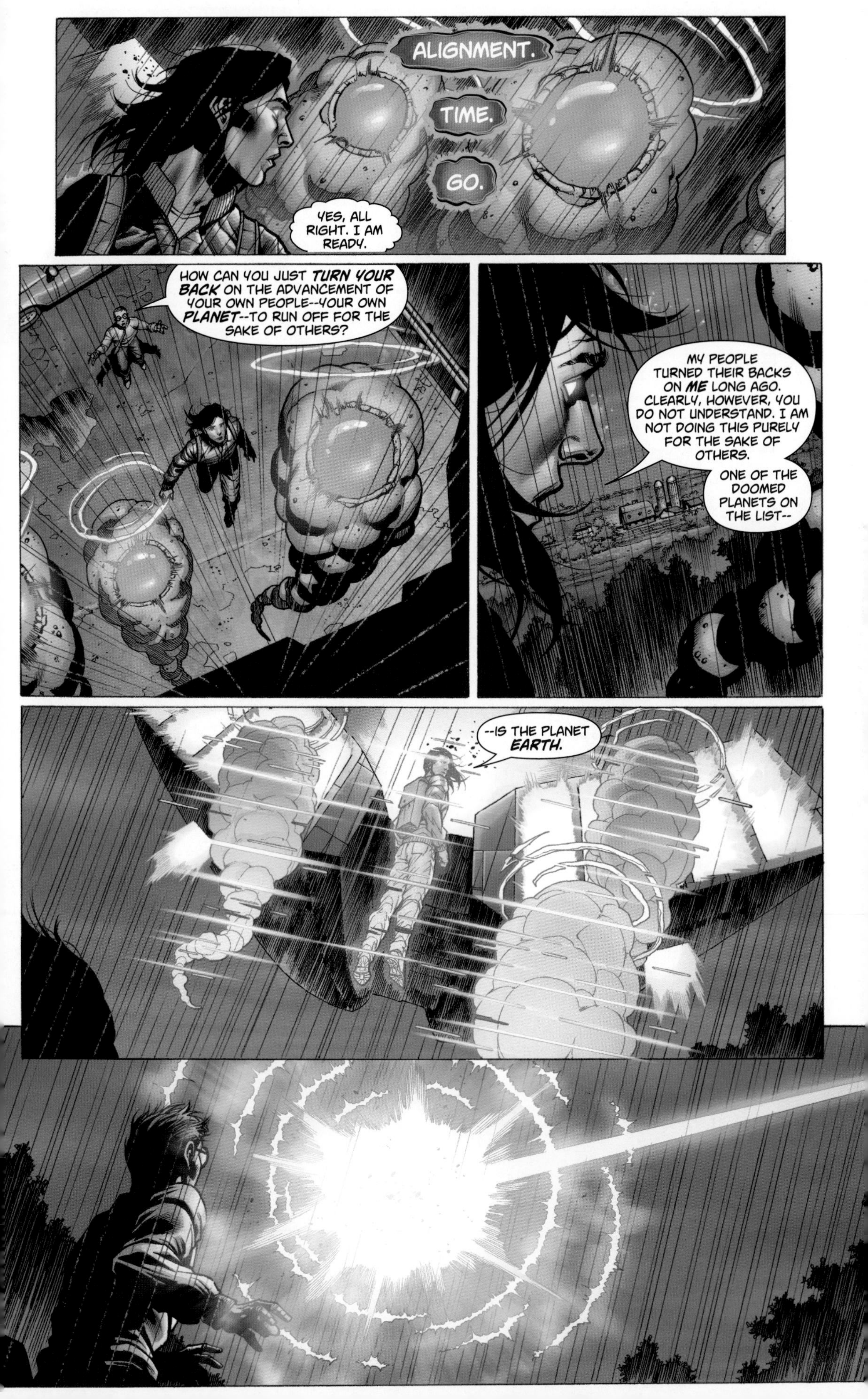
ALIGNMENT.
TIME.
GO.
YES, ALL RIGHT. I AM READY.
HOW CAN YOU JUST TURN YOUR BACK ON THE ADVANCEMENT OF YOUR OWN PEOPLE--YOUR OWN PLANET--TO RUN OFF FOR THE SAKE OF OTHERS?
MY PEOPLE TURNED THEIR BACKS ON ME LONG AGO. CLEARLY, HOWEVER, YOU DO NOT UNDERSTAND. I AM NOT DOING THIS PURELY FOR THE SAKE OF OTHERS.
ONE OF THE DOOMED PLANETS ON THE LIST--
--IS THE PLANET EARTH.

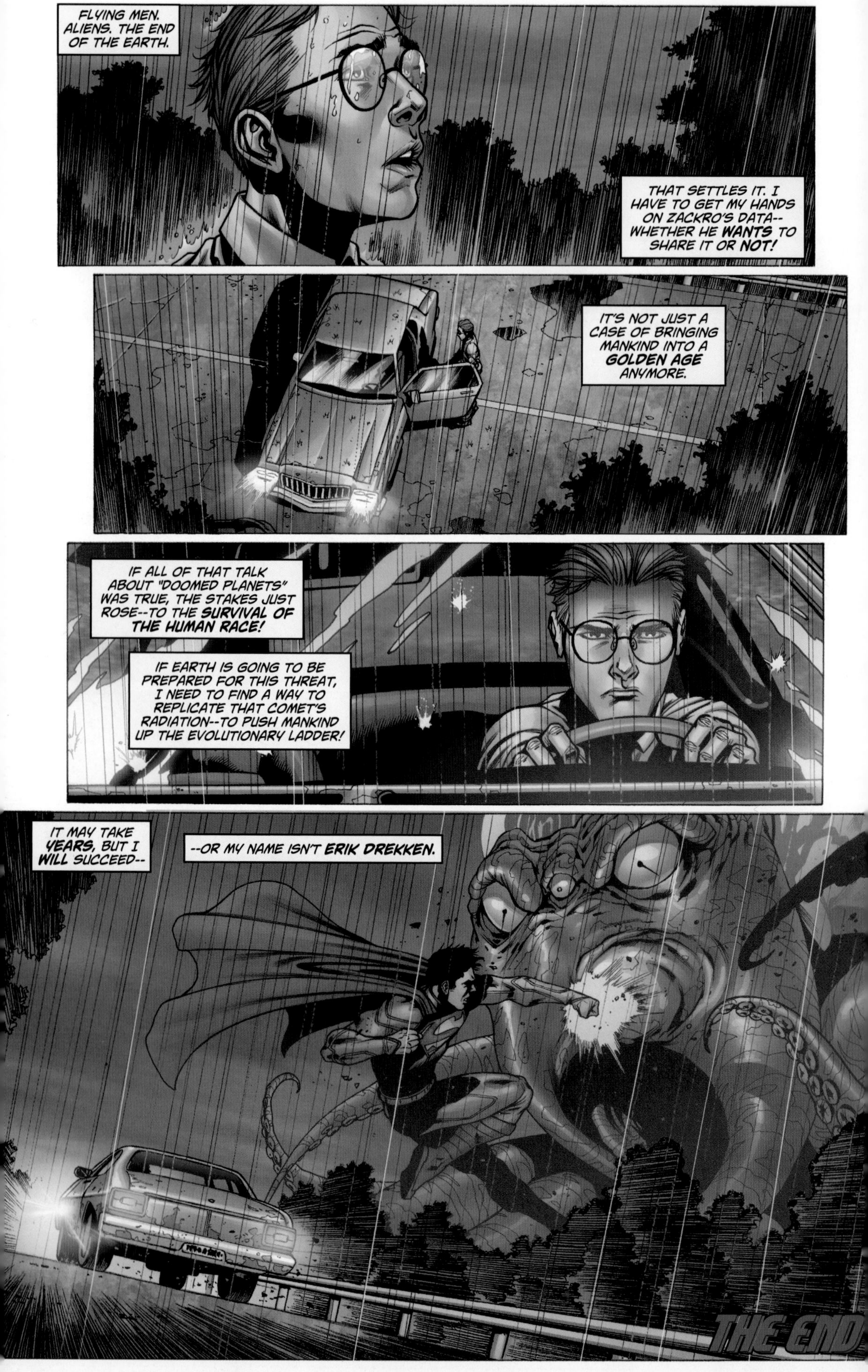

FLYING MEN. ALIENS. THE END OF THE EARTH.
THAT SETTLES IT. I HAVE TO GET MY HANDS ON ZACKRO'S DATA--WHETHER HE **WANTS** TO SHARE IT OR **NOT!**
IT'S NOT JUST A CASE OF BRINGING MANKIND INTO A **GOLDEN AGE** ANYMORE.
IF ALL OF THAT TALK ABOUT "DOOMED PLANETS" WAS TRUE, THE STAKES JUST ROSE--TO THE **SURVIVAL OF THE HUMAN RACE!**
IF EARTH IS GOING TO BE PREPARED FOR THIS THREAT, I NEED TO FIND A WAY TO REPLICATE THAT COMET'S RADIATION--TO PUSH MANKIND UP THE EVOLUTIONARY LADDER!
IT MAY TAKE **YEARS**, BUT I **WILL** SUCCEED--
--OR MY NAME ISN'T **ERIK DREKKEN**.
THE END

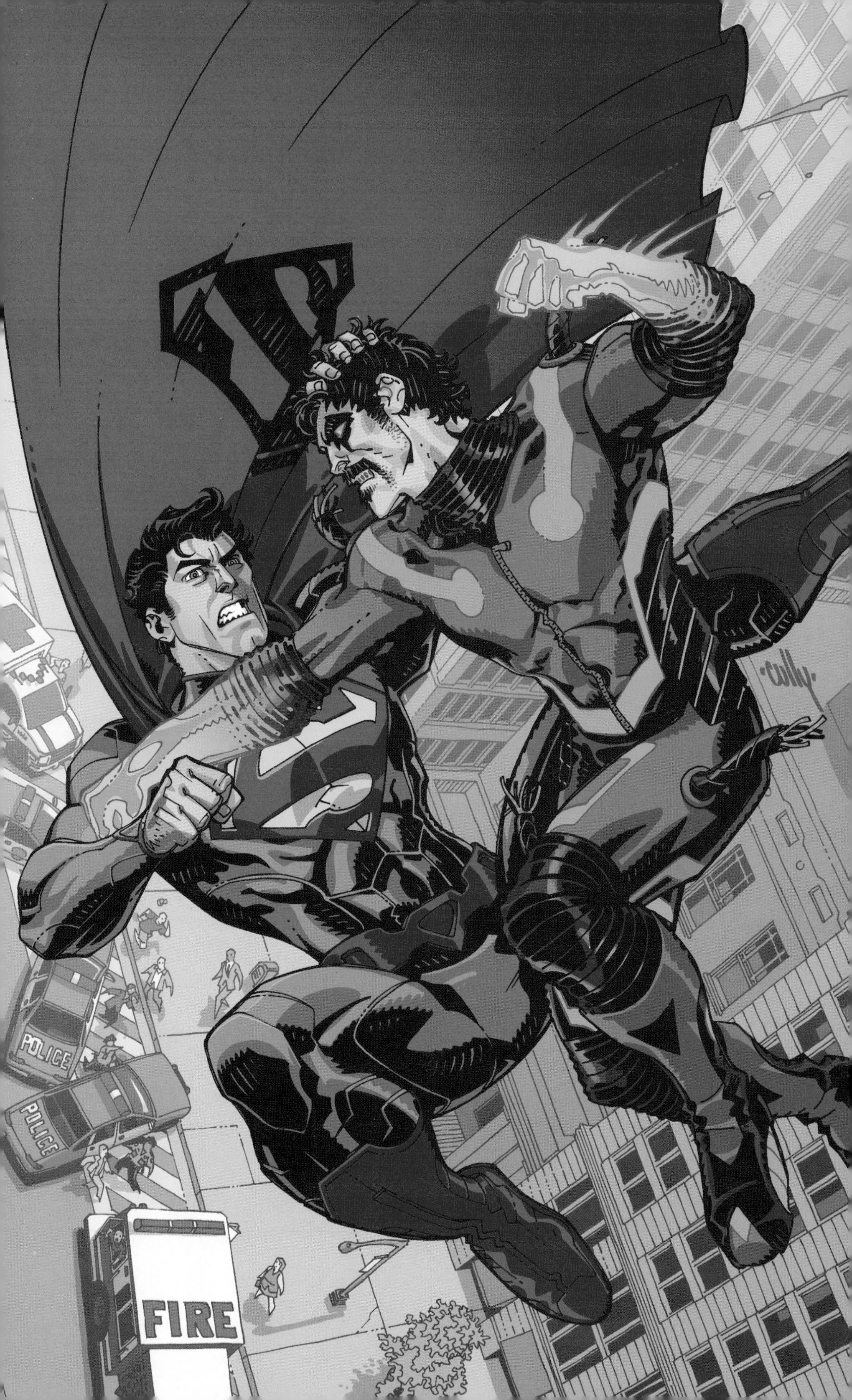
POLICE
POLICE
FIRE

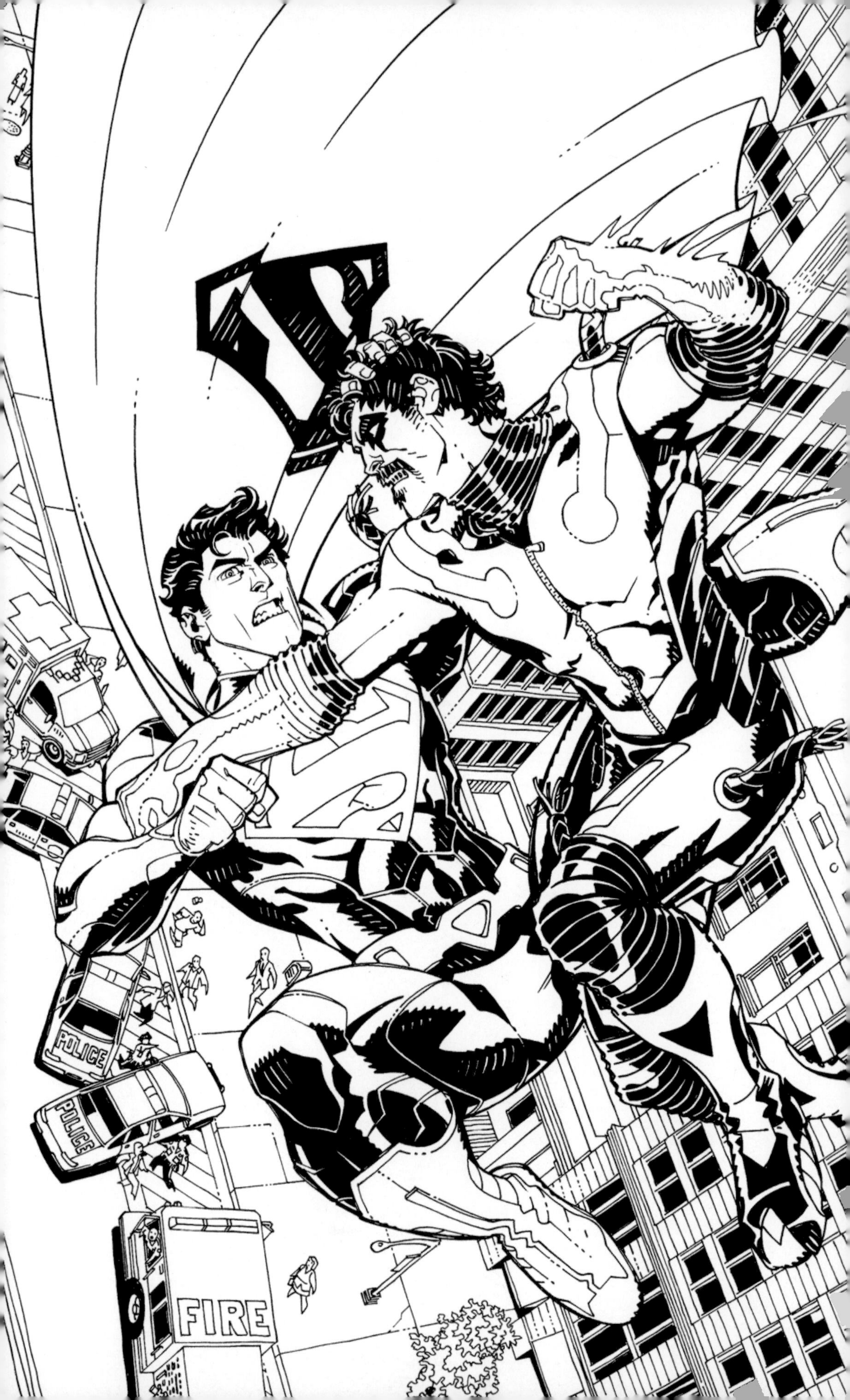
POLICE
POLICE
FIRE

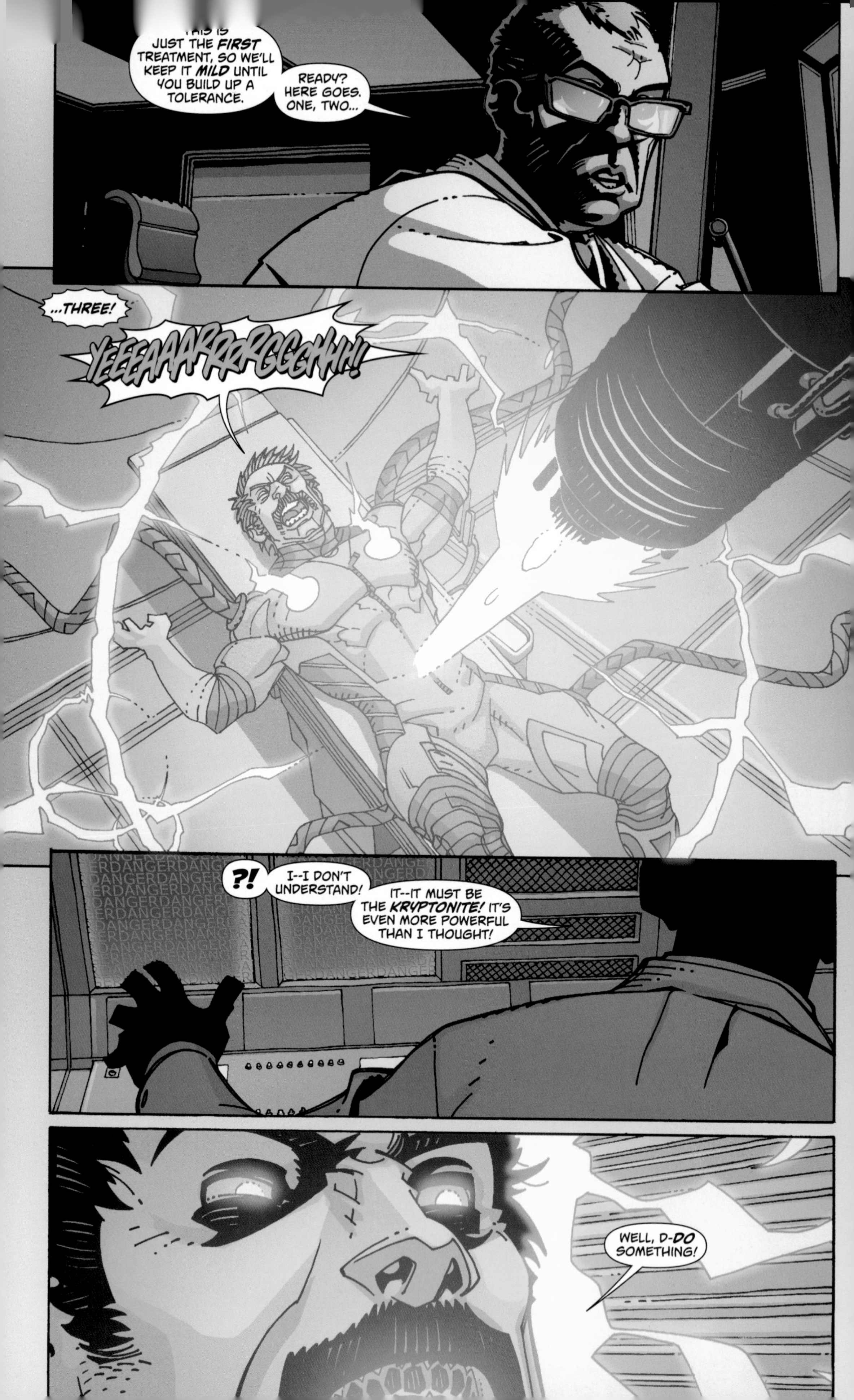
JUST THE FIRST TREATMENT, SO WE'LL KEEP IT MILD UNTIL YOU BUILD UP A TOLERANCE.
READY? HERE GOES. ONE, TWO...
...THREE!
YEEEAAARRRRGGGHHH!
?!
I--I DON'T UNDERSTAND!
IT--IT MUST BE THE KRYPTONITE! IT'S EVEN MORE POWERFUL THAN I THOUGHT!
WELL, D-DO SOMETHING!

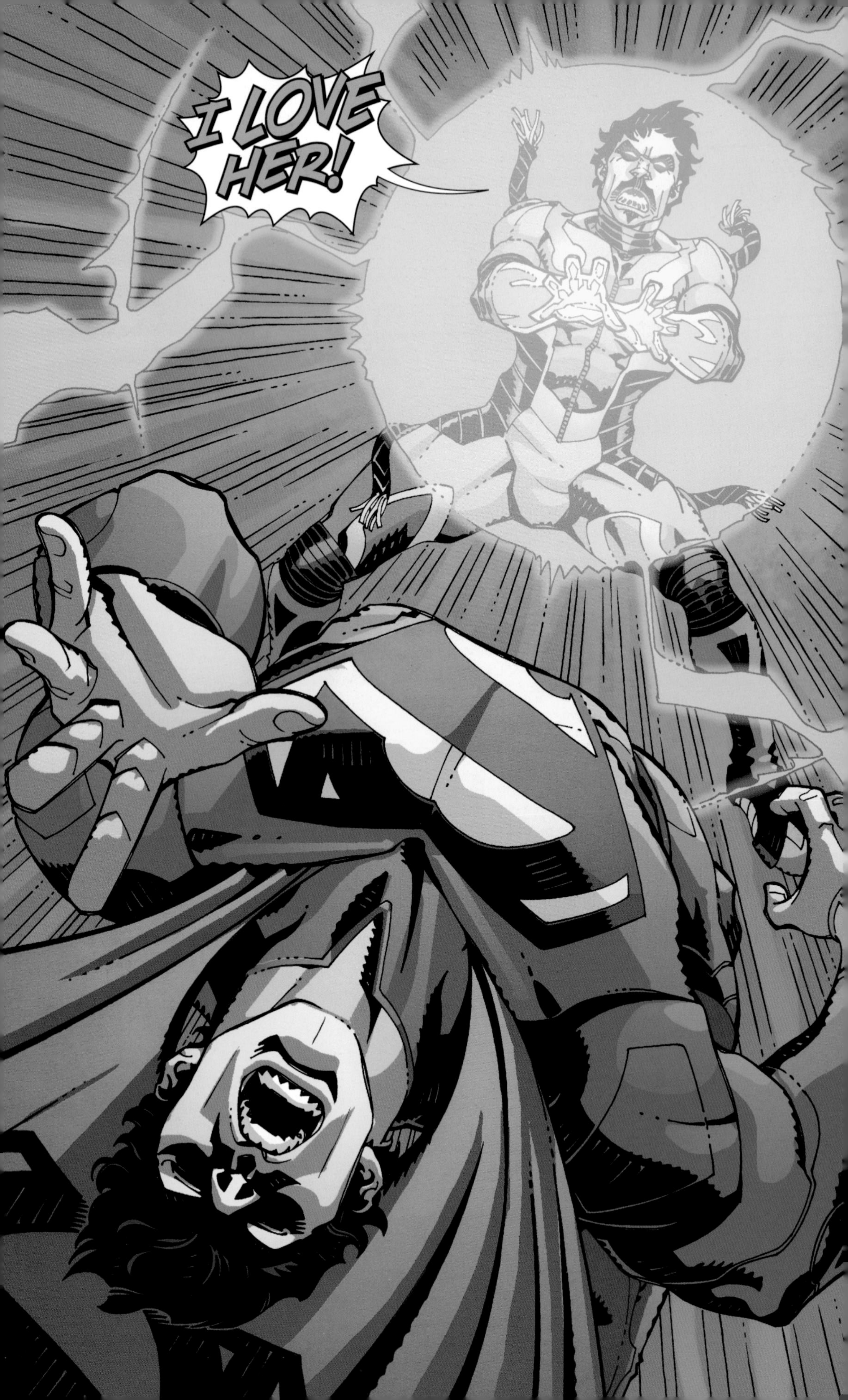
I LOVE HER!

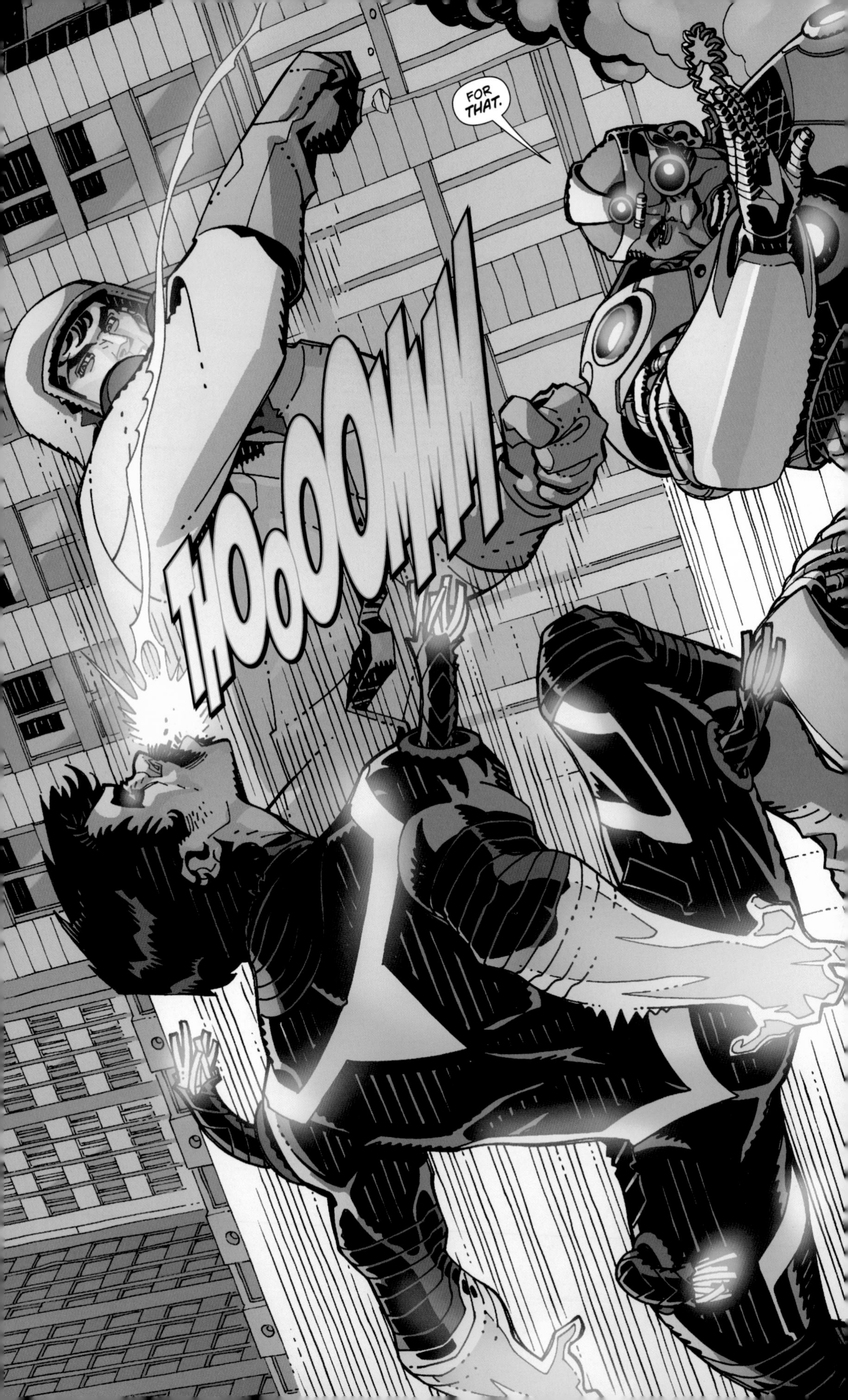
FOR THAT.
THOOOOMMM

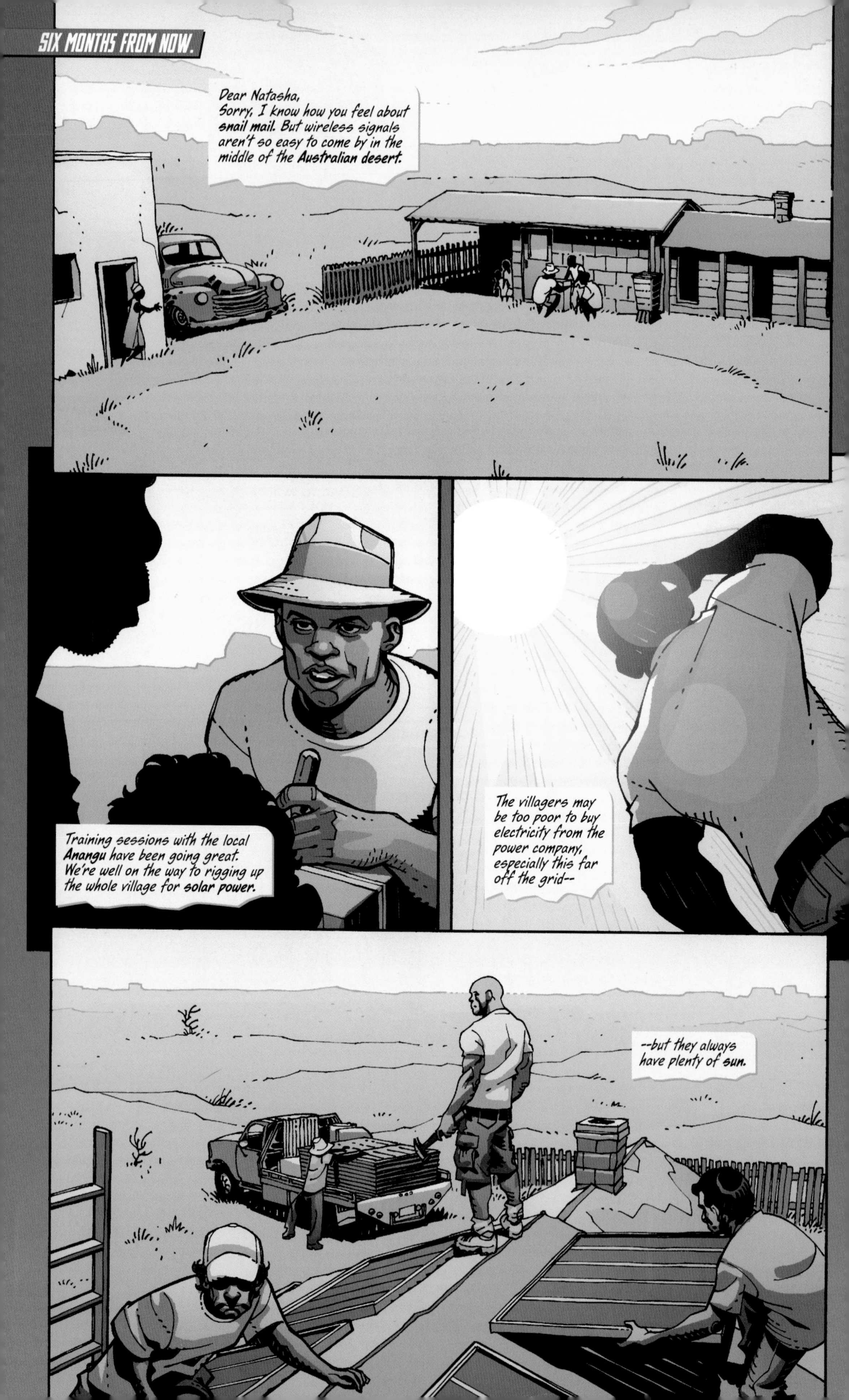
SIX MONTHS FROM NOW.
Dear Natasha, Sorry, I know how you feel about snail mail. But wireless signals aren't so easy to come by in the middle of the Australian desert.
Training sessions with the local Anangu have been going great. We're well on the way to rigging up the whole village for solar power.
The villagers may be too poor to buy electricity from the power company, especially this far off the grid--
--but they always have plenty of sun.

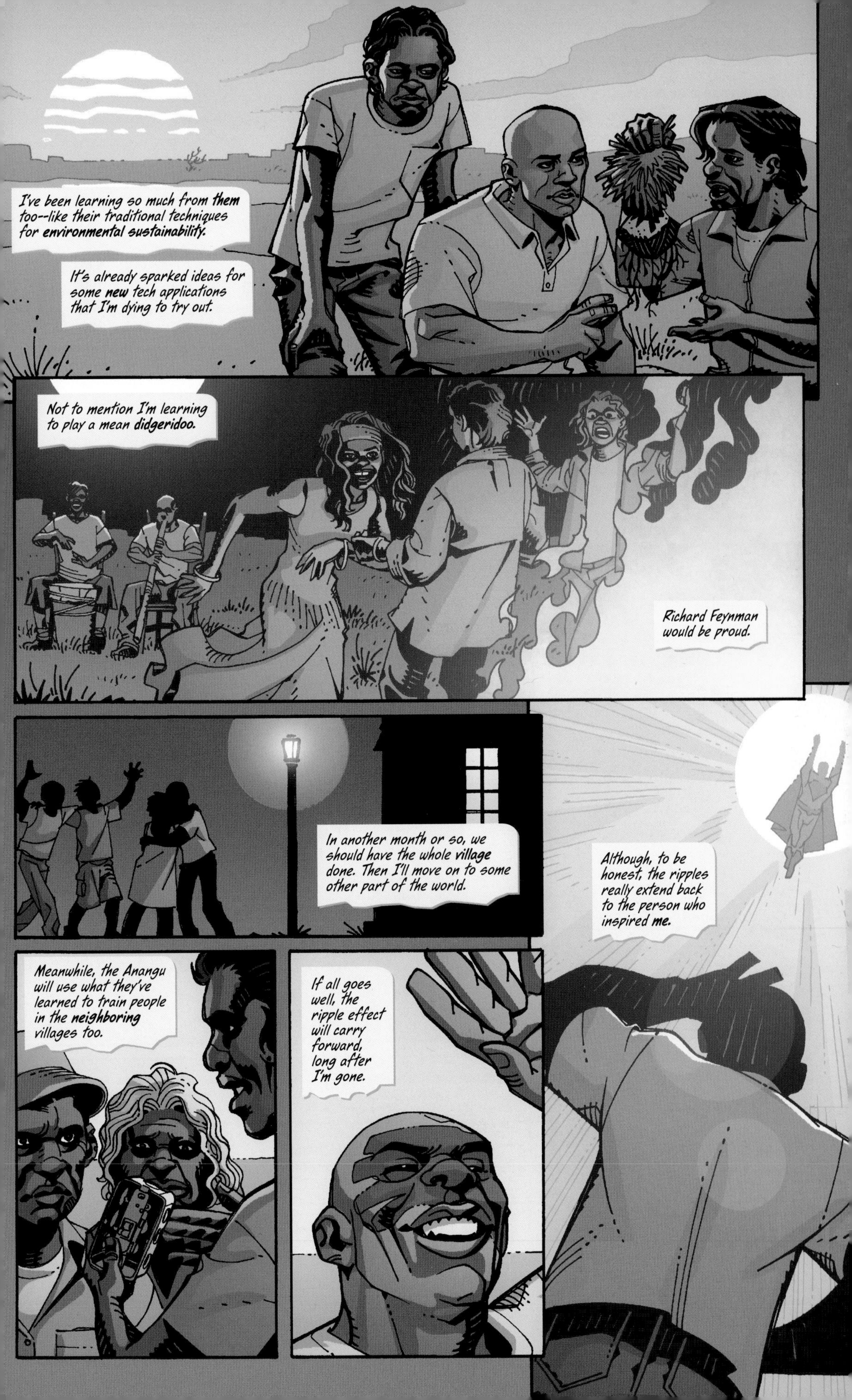
I've been learning so much from them too--like their traditional techniques for environmental sustainability.
It's already sparked ideas for some new tech applications that I'm dying to try out.
Not to mention I'm learning to play a mean didgeridoo.
Richard Feynman would be proud.
In another month or so, we should have the whole village done. Then I'll move on to some other part of the world.
Although, to be honest, the ripples really extend back to the person who inspired me.
Meanwhile, the Anangu will use what they've learned to train people in the neighboring villages too.
If all goes well, the ripple effect will carry forward, long after I'm gone.

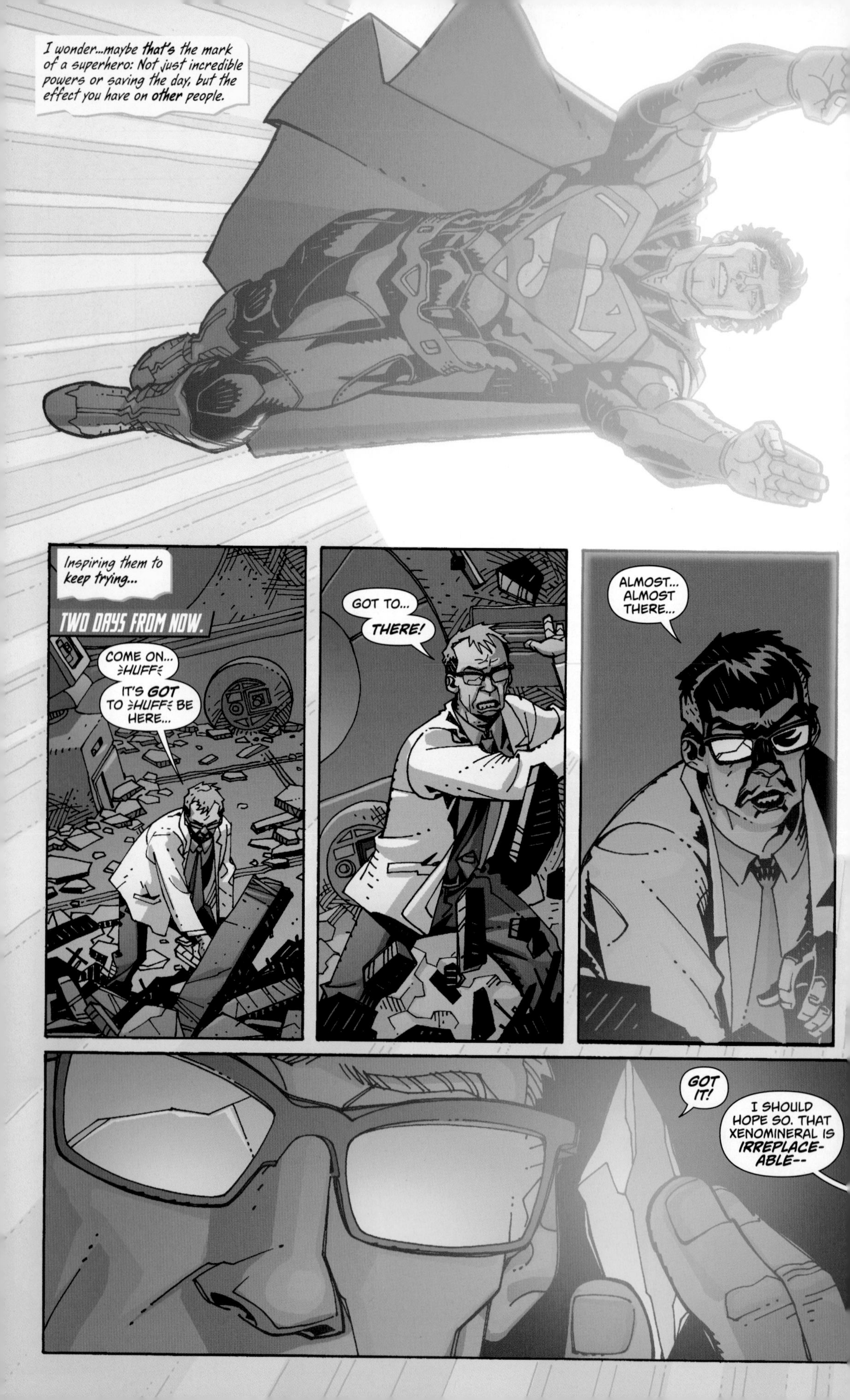
I wonder...maybe that's the mark of a superhero: Not just incredible powers or saving the day, but the effect you have on other people.
Inspiring them to keep trying...
TWO DAYS FROM NOW.
COME ON... HUFF
IT'S GOT TO HUFF BE HERE...
GOT TO... THERE!
ALMOST... ALMOST THERE...
GOT IT!
I SHOULD HOPE SO. THAT XENOMINERAL IS IRREPLACE-ABLE--

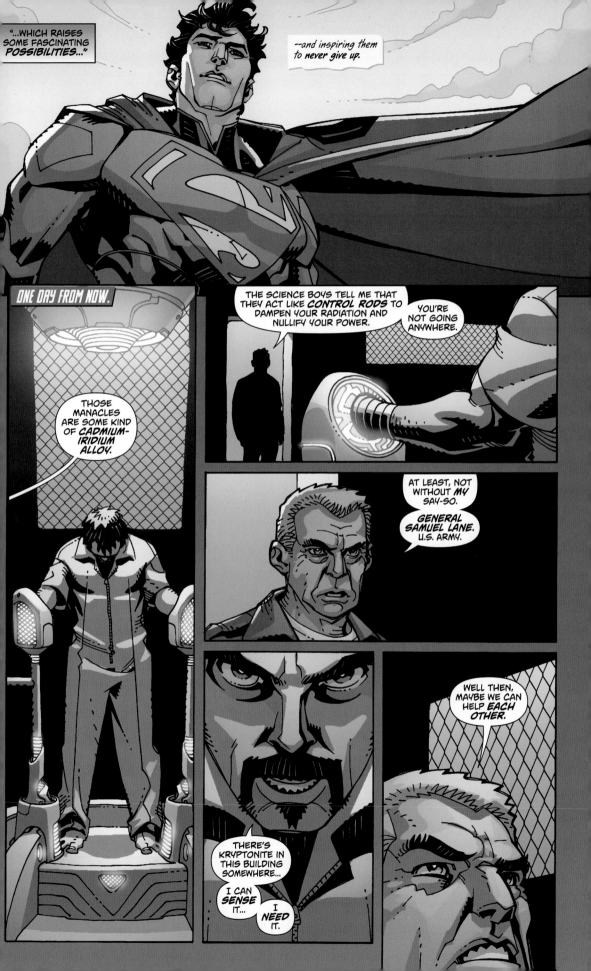

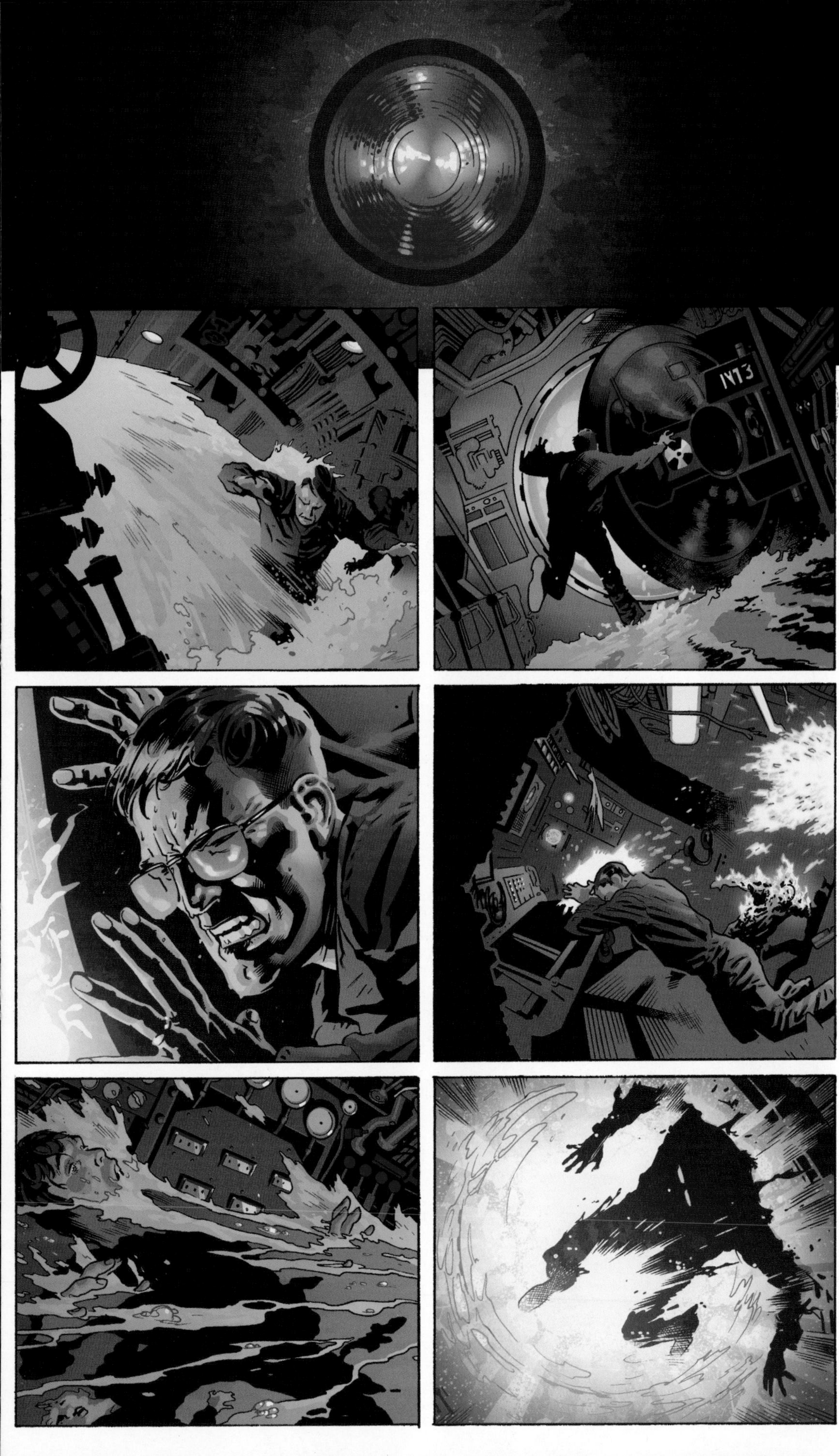

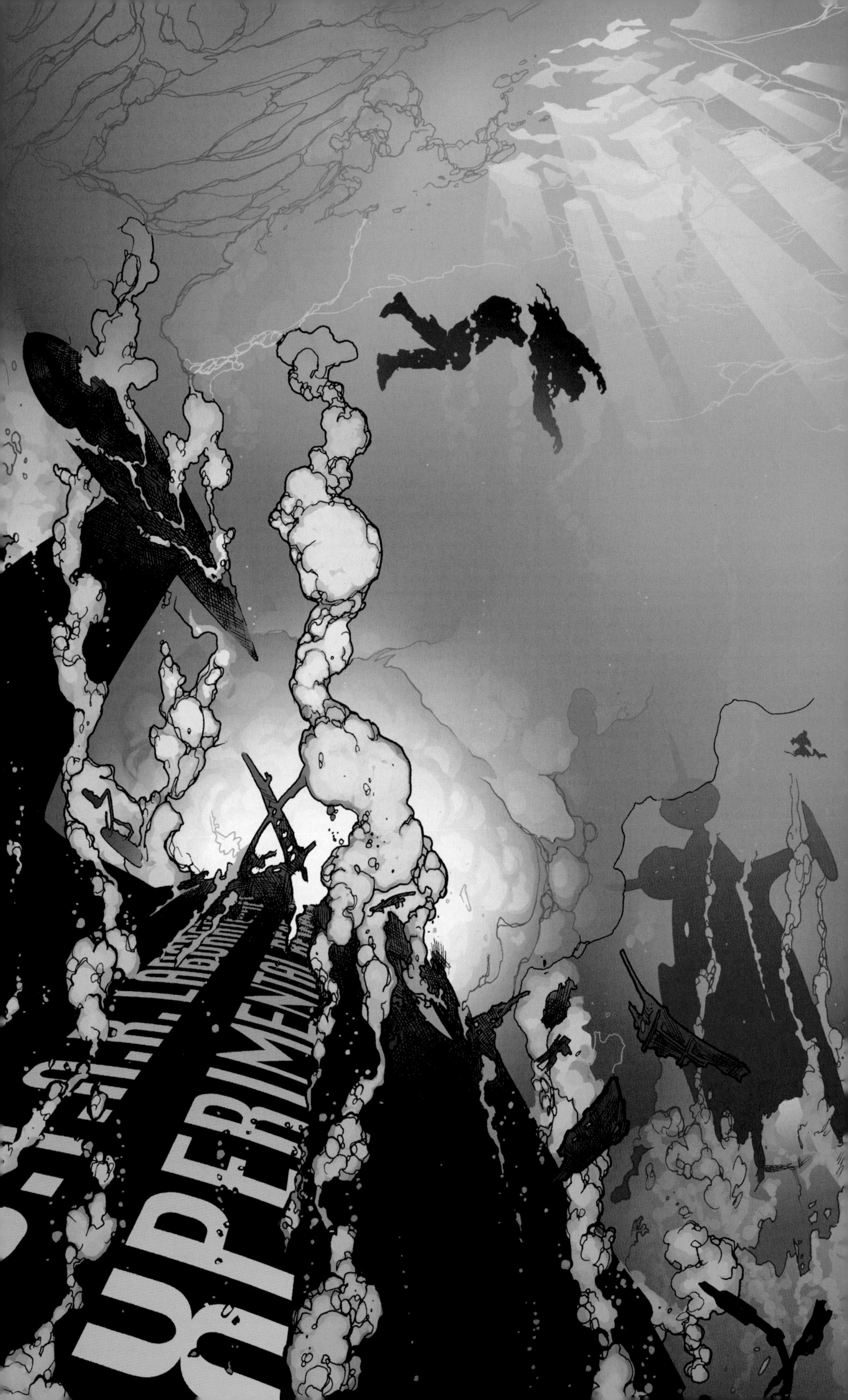

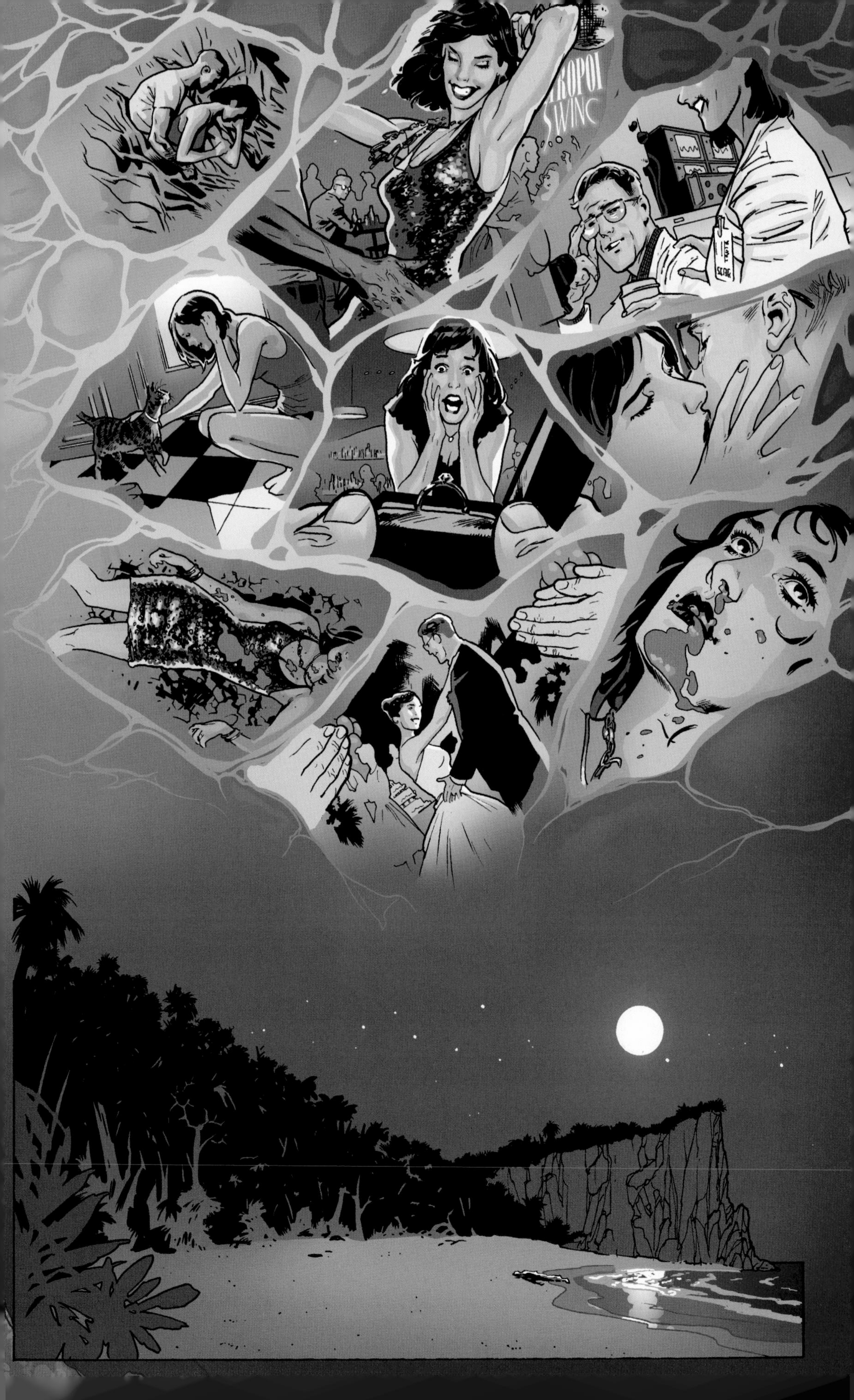
ROPOI
SWINC

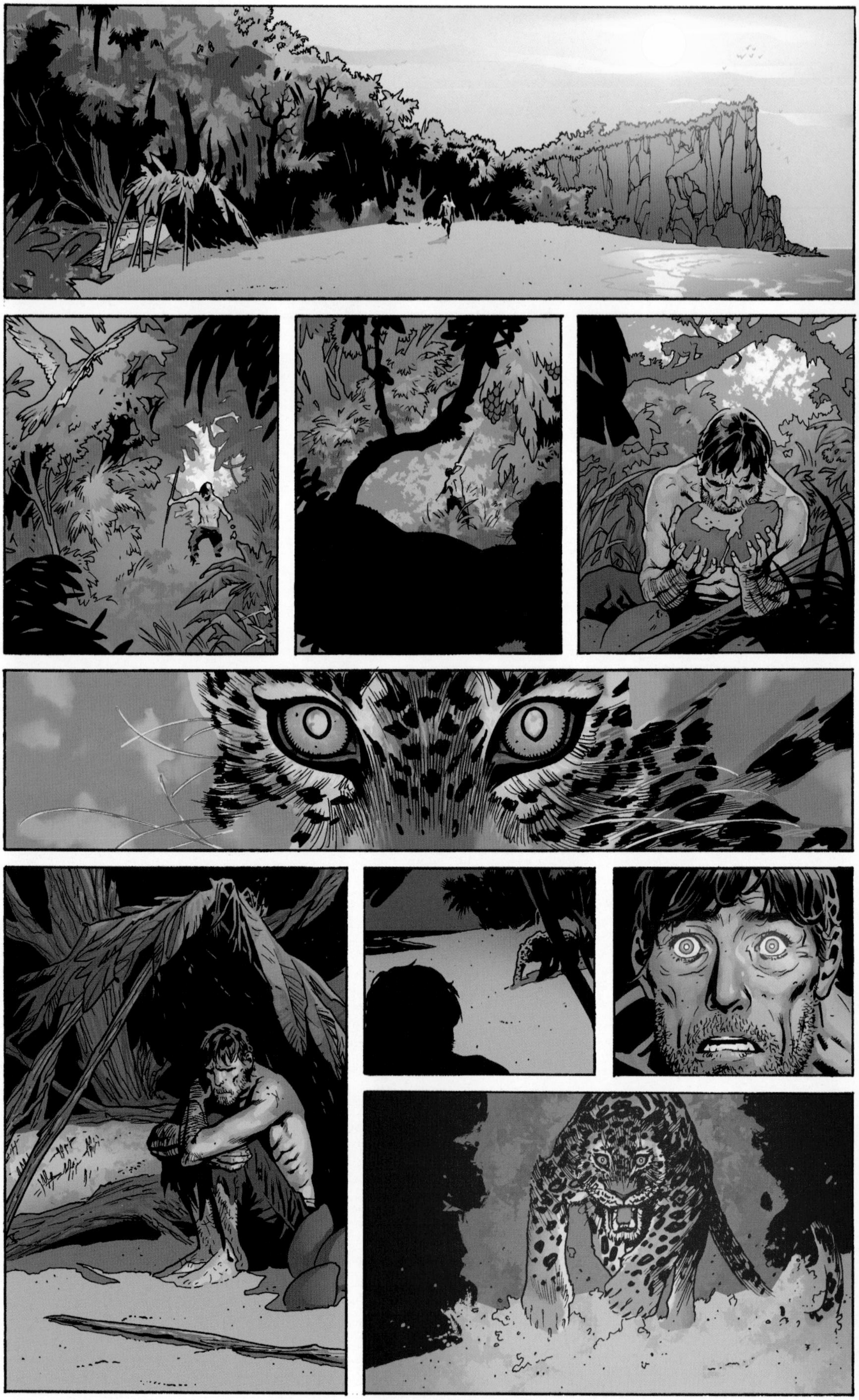

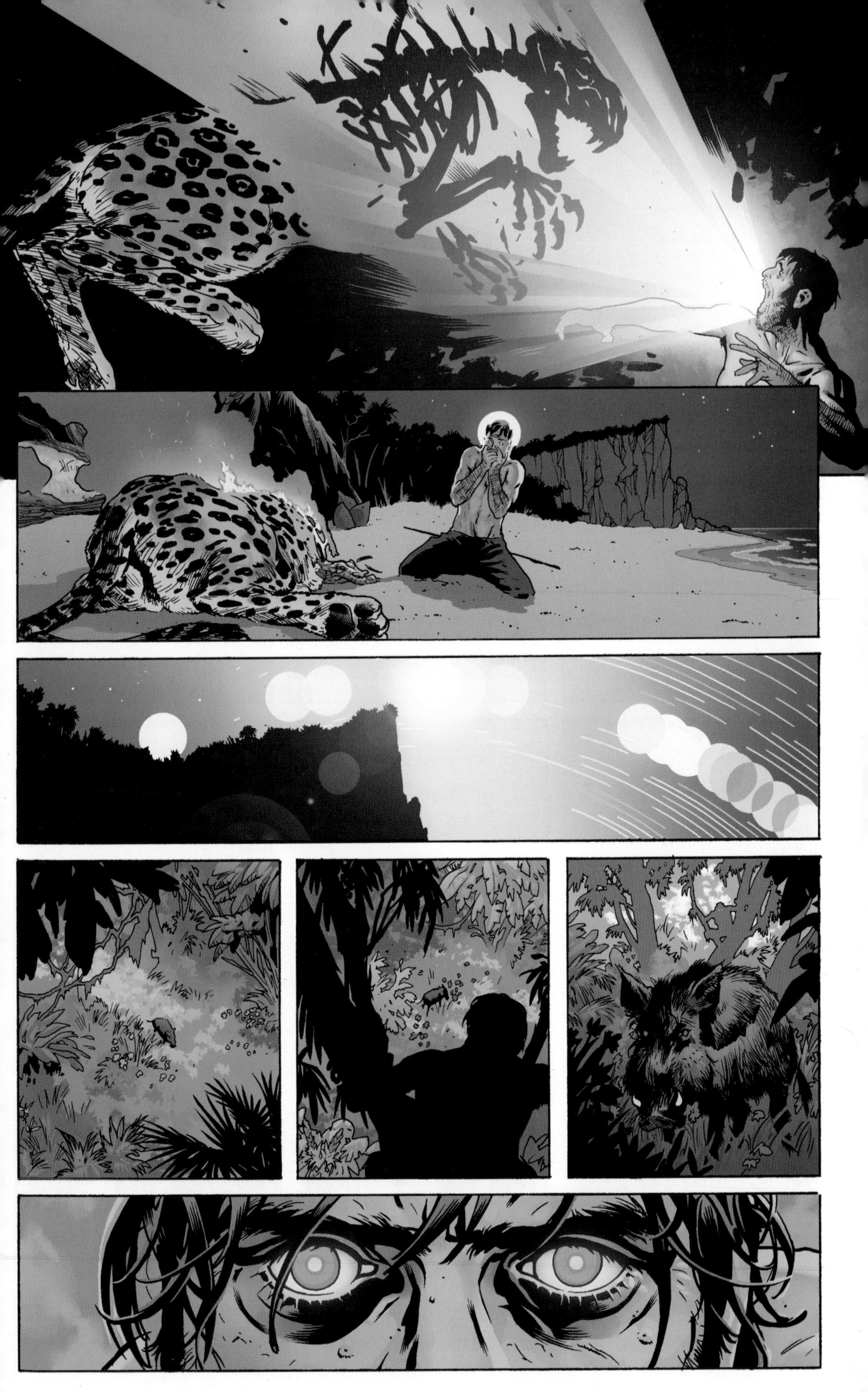

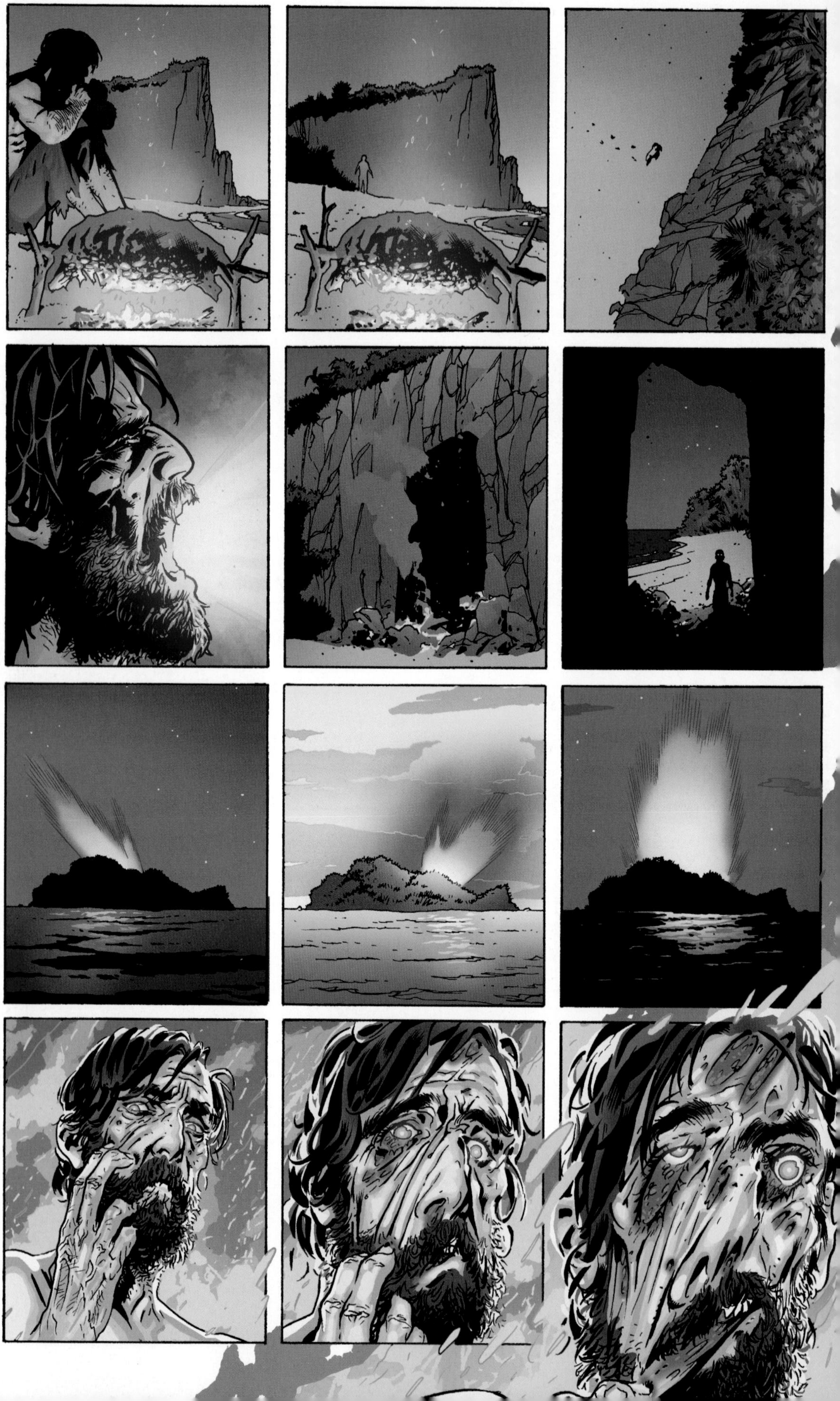

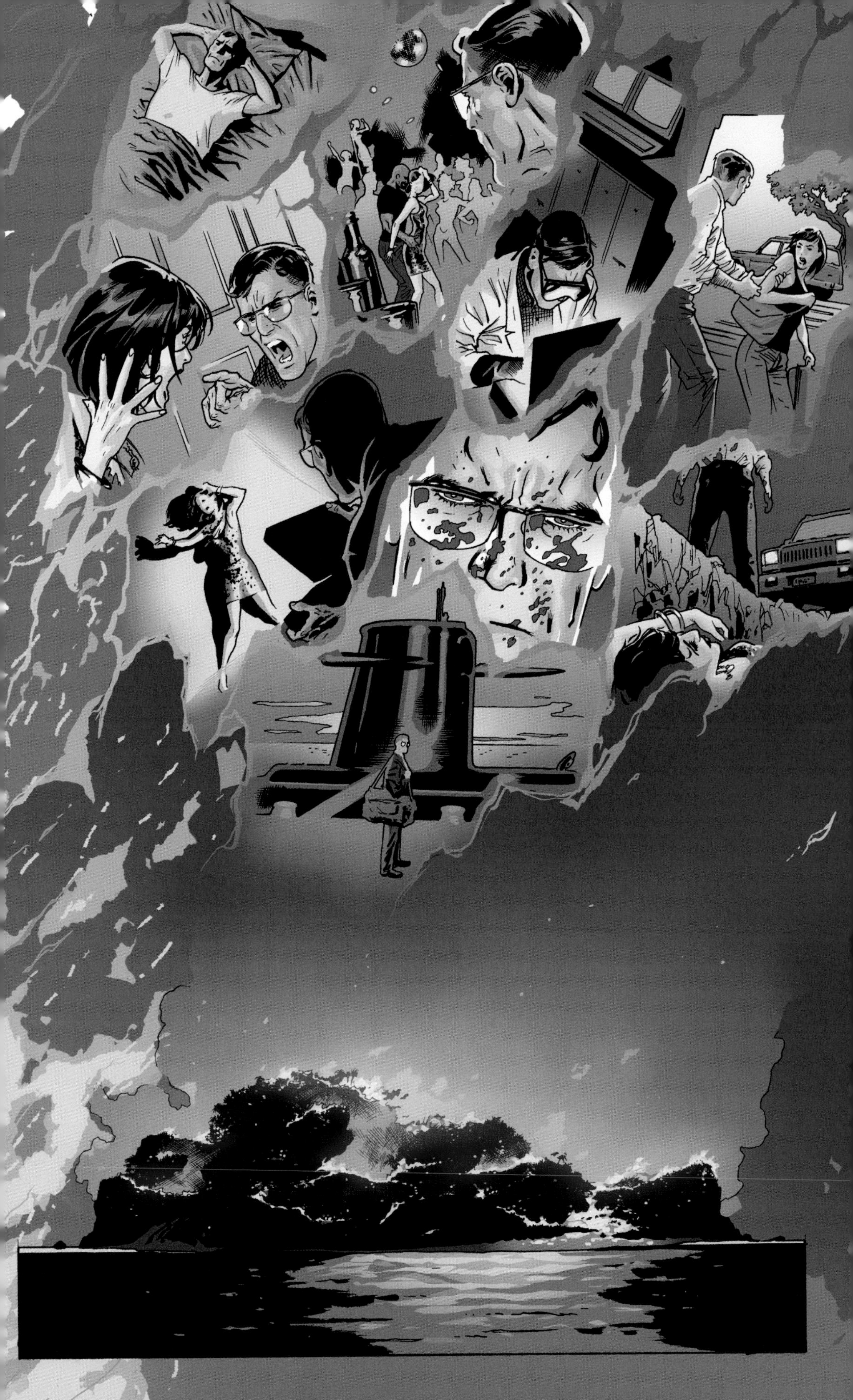

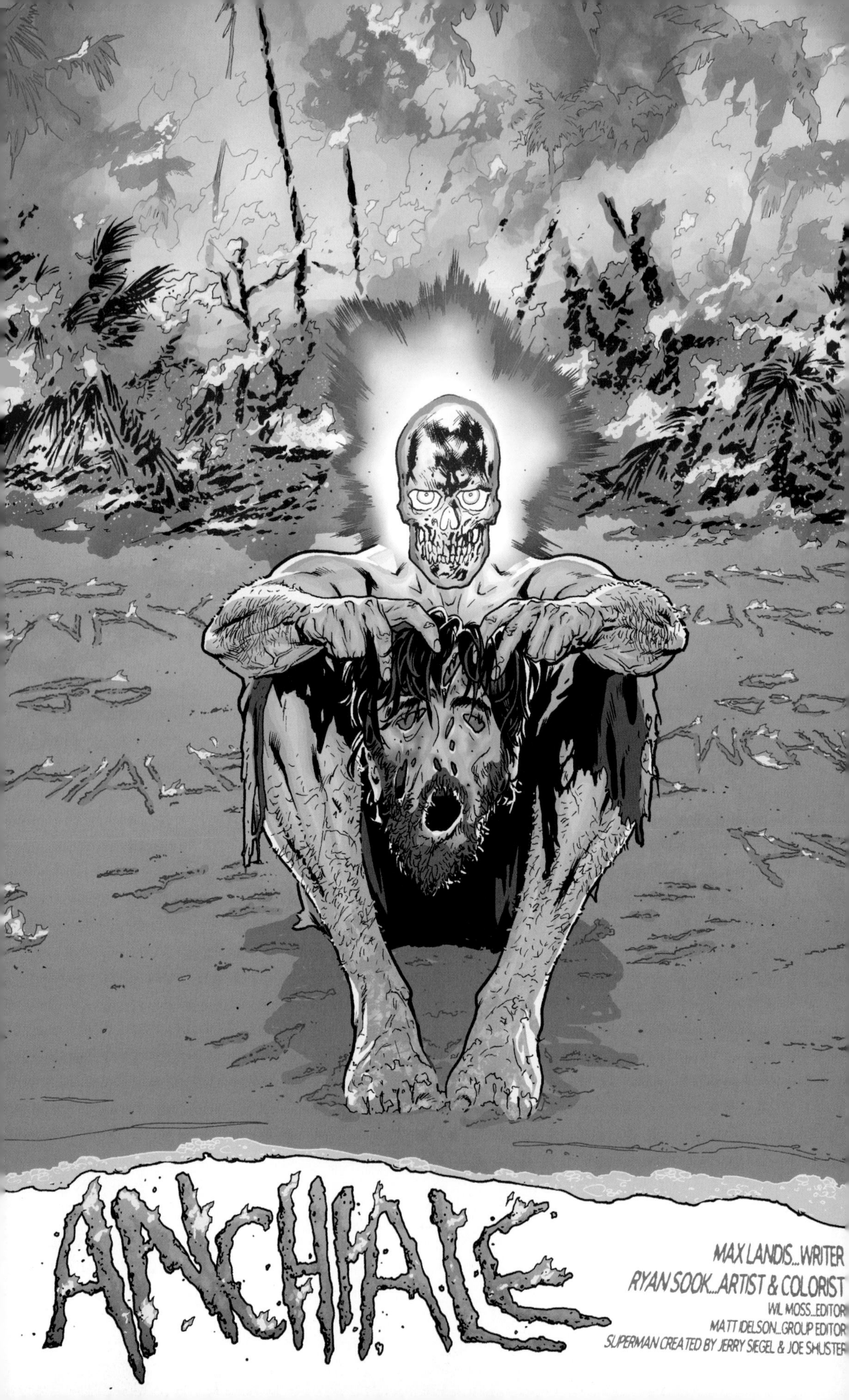
ANCHIALE
MAX LANDIS...WRITER
RYAN SOOK...ARTIST & COLORIST
WIL MOSS...EDITOR
MATT IDELSON...GROUP EDITOR
SUPERMAN CREATED BY JERRY SIEGEL & JOE SHUSTER

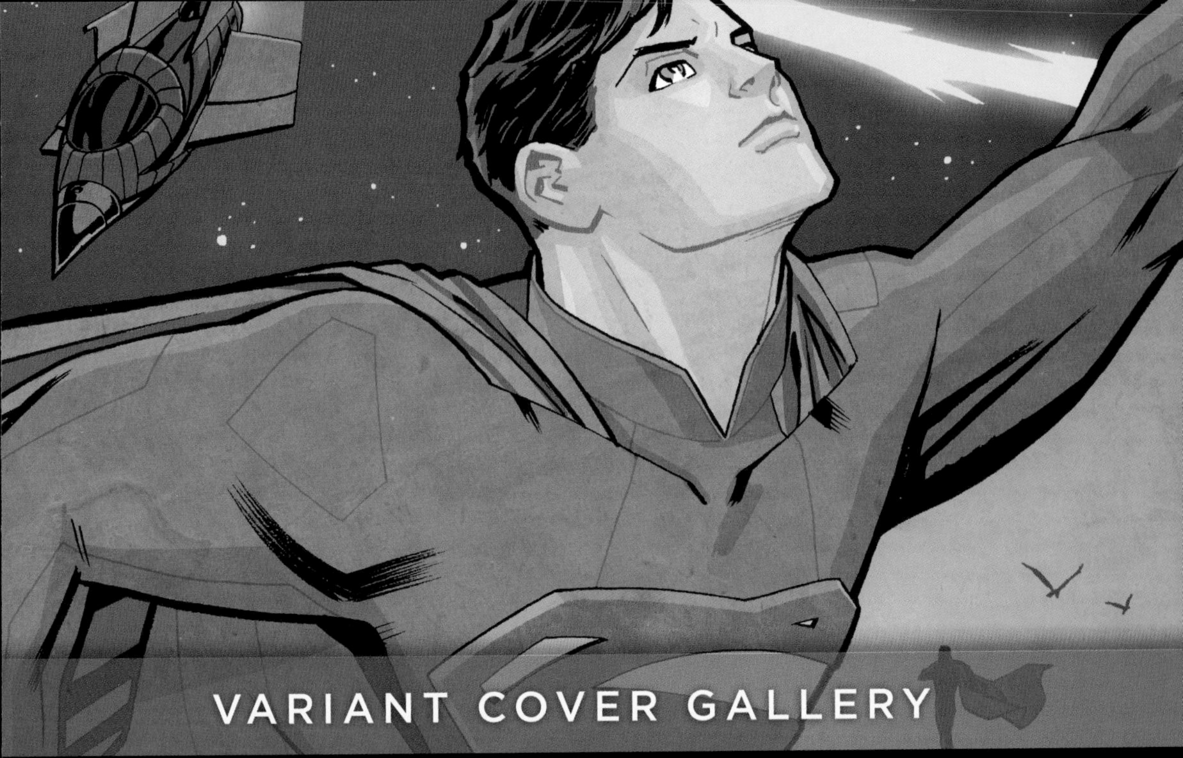

VARIANT COVER GALLERY

ACTION COMICS #9
Art by Rags Morales & Brad Anderson

ACTION COMICS #10
Art by Bryan Hitch & Paul Mounts

ACTION COMICS #11
Art by Cully Hamner & Val Staples

ACTION COMICS #12
Art by Cliff Chiang

ACTION COMICS #0
Art by Rags Morales & Brad Anderson

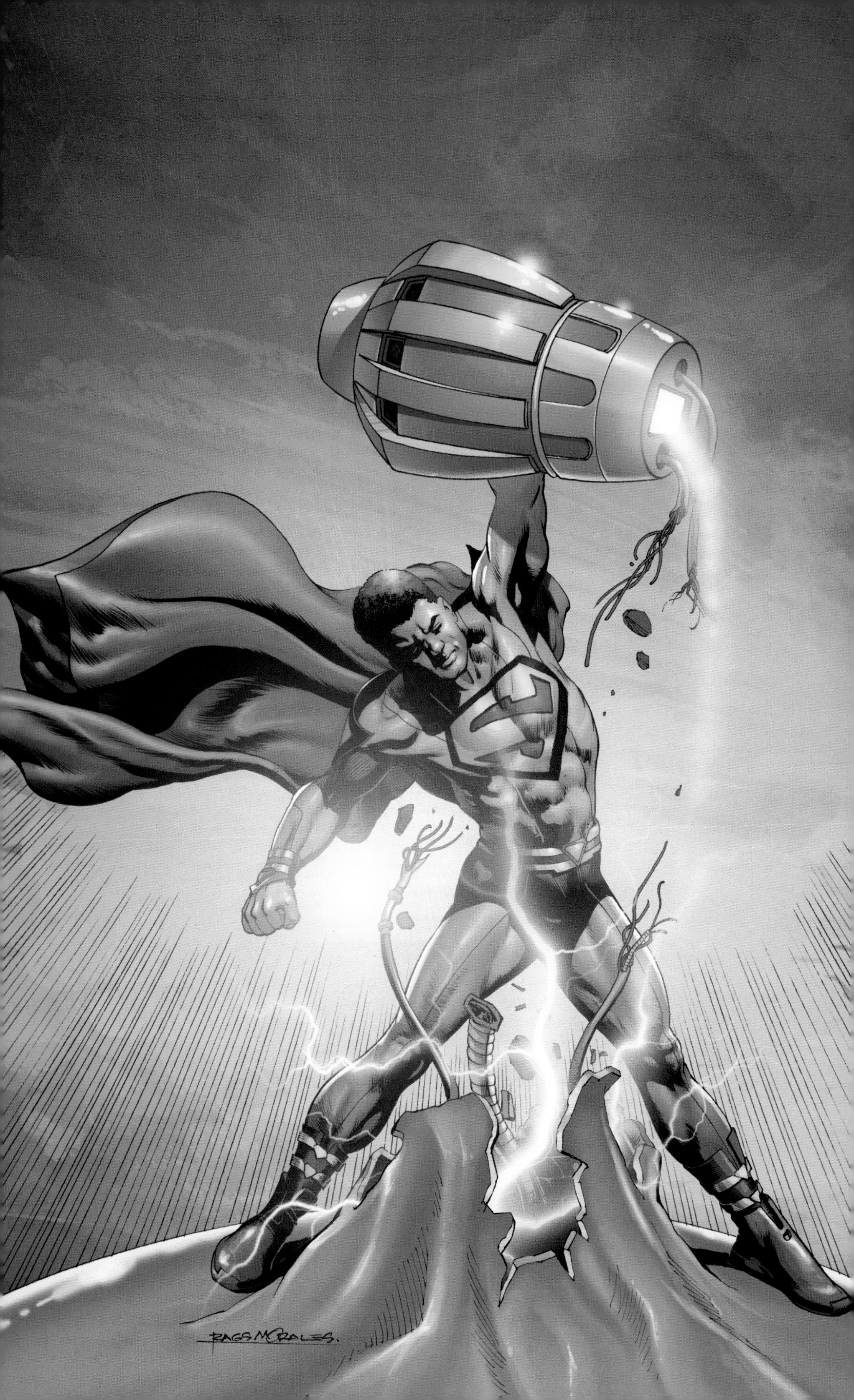
RAGS MORALES.

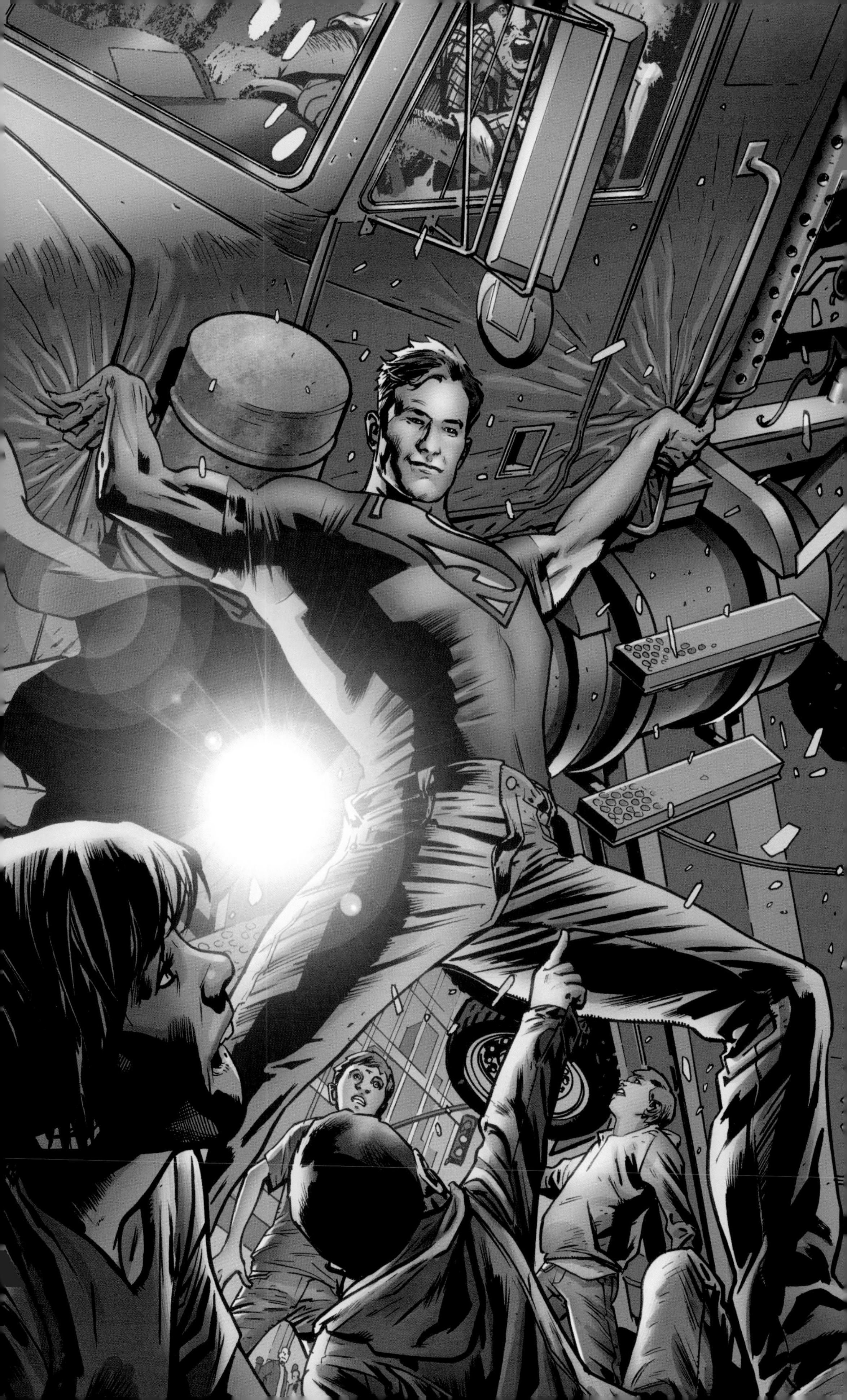

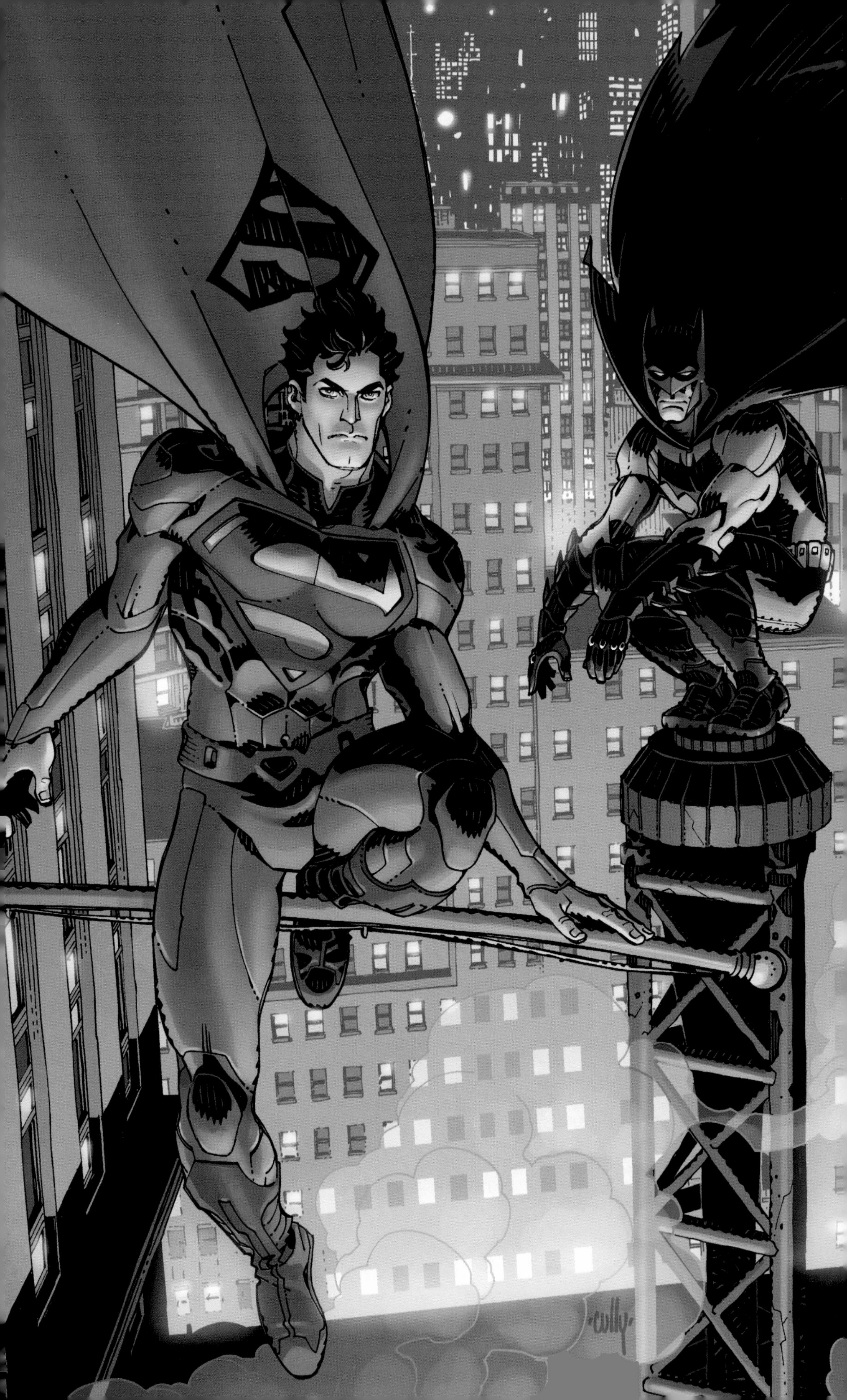

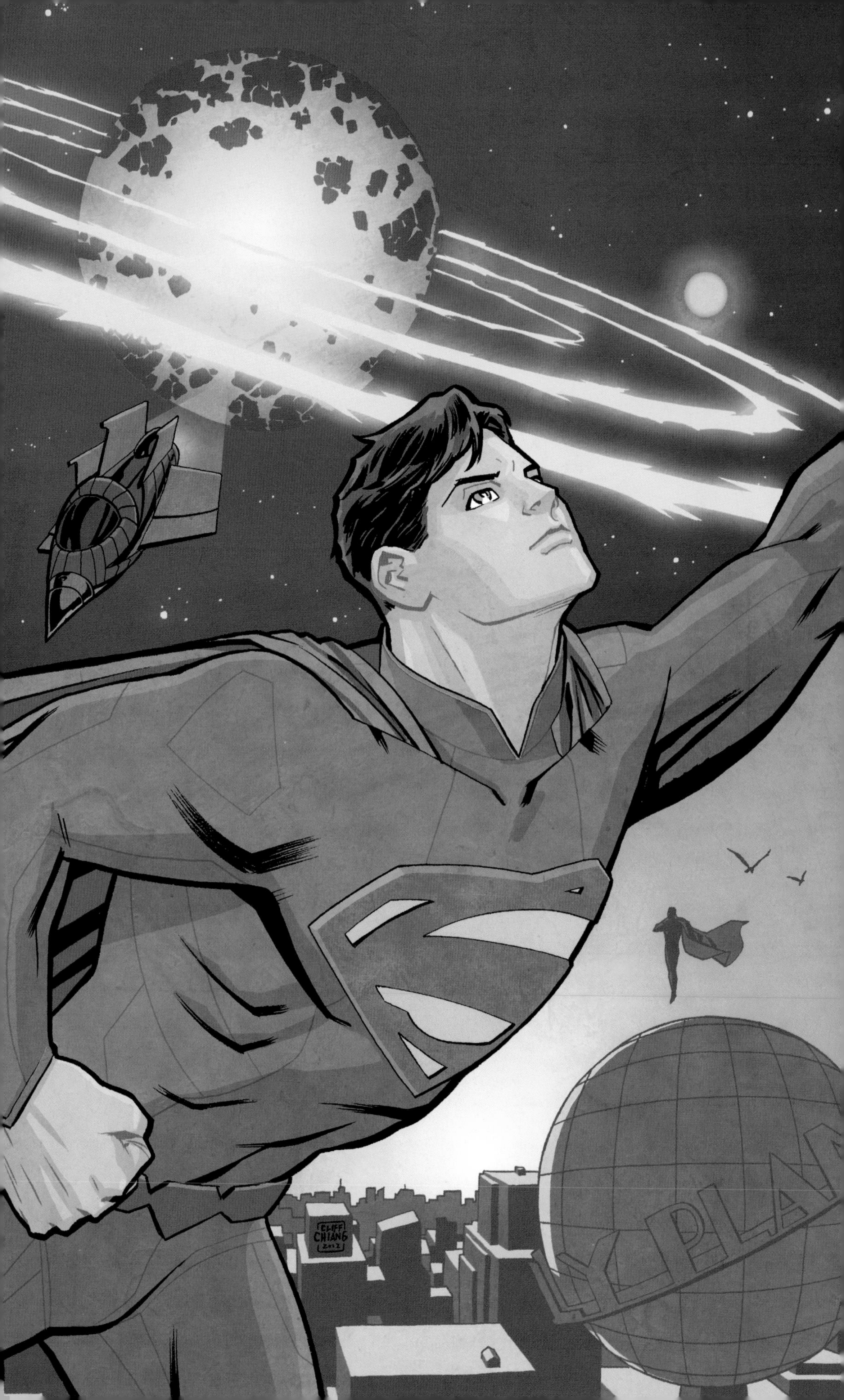
CLIFF CHIANG 2012

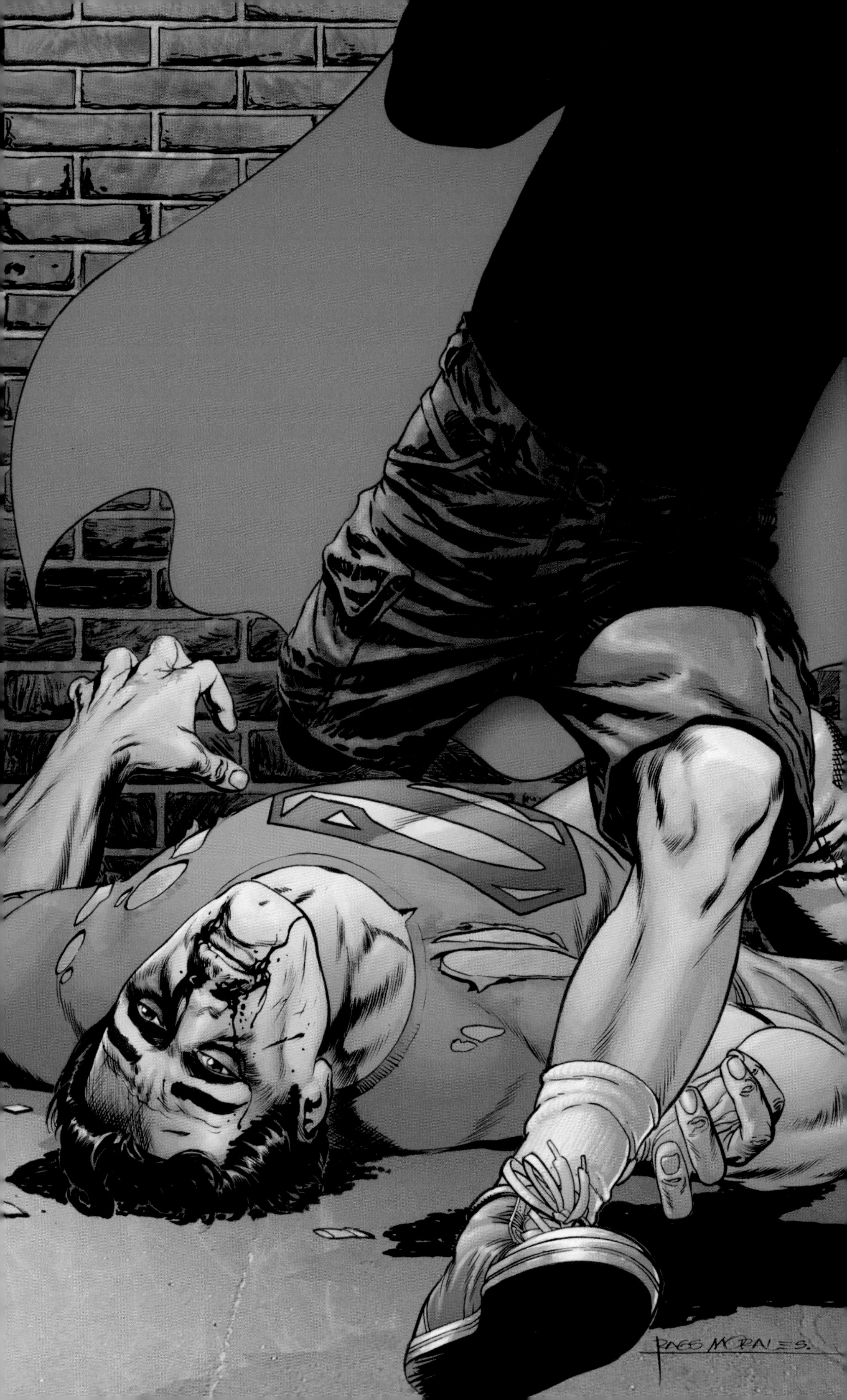
RAGS MORALES.

Designs for Superman of Earth 23 by Gene Ha

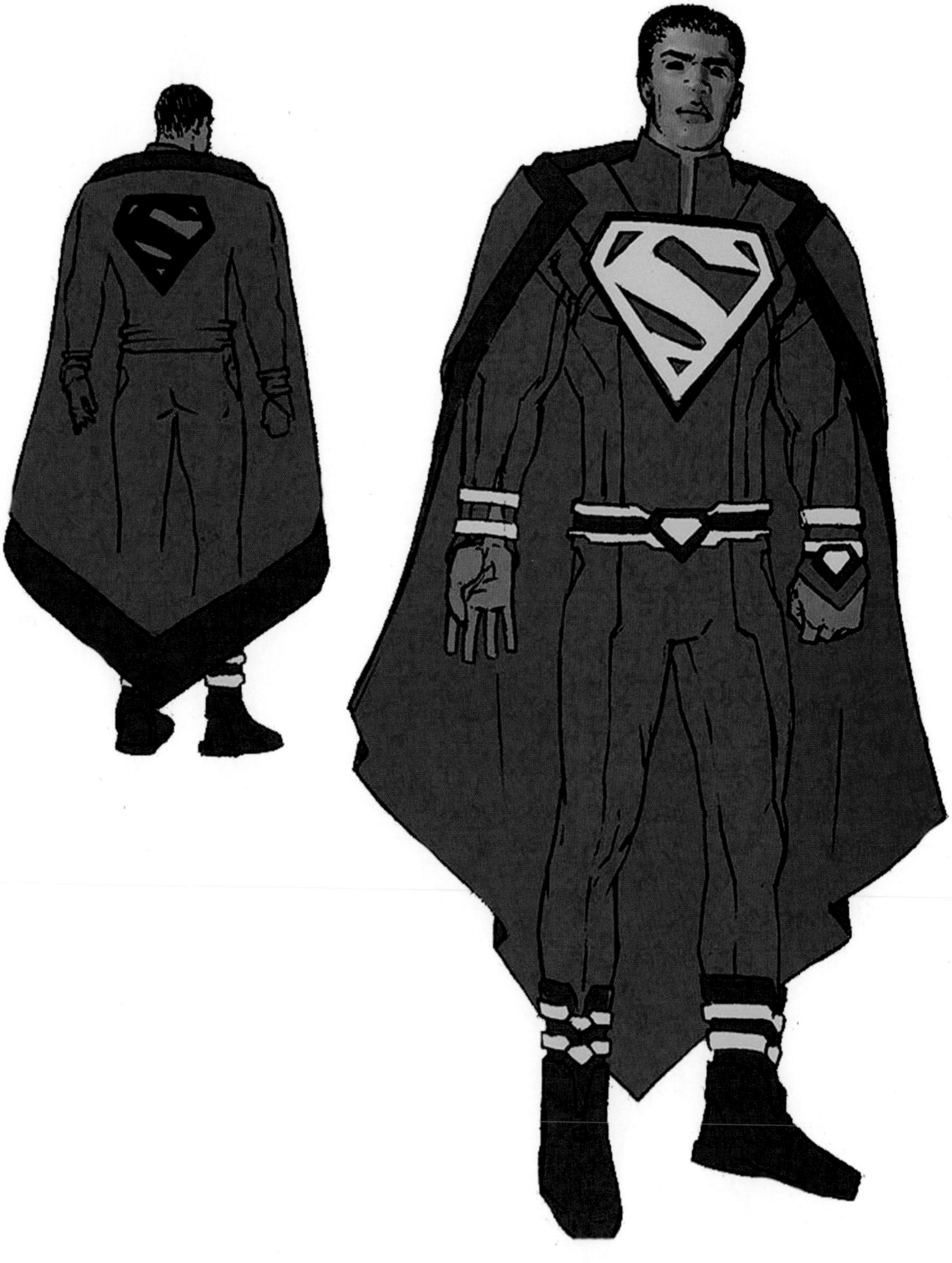

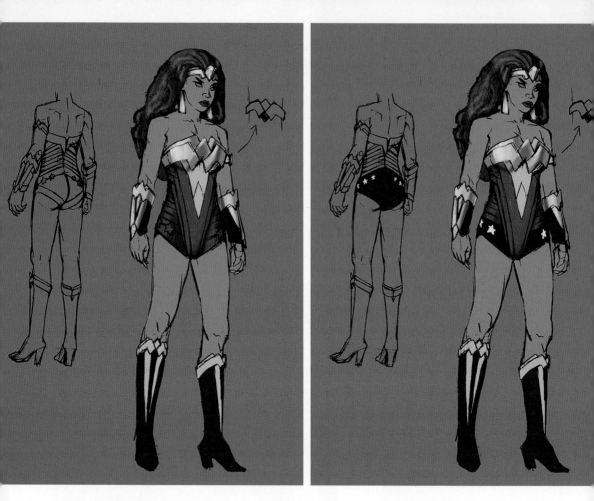

Designs for Wonder Woman of Earth 23 and Superdoom by Gene Ha

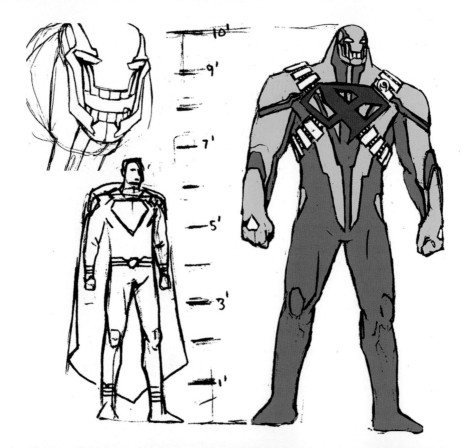

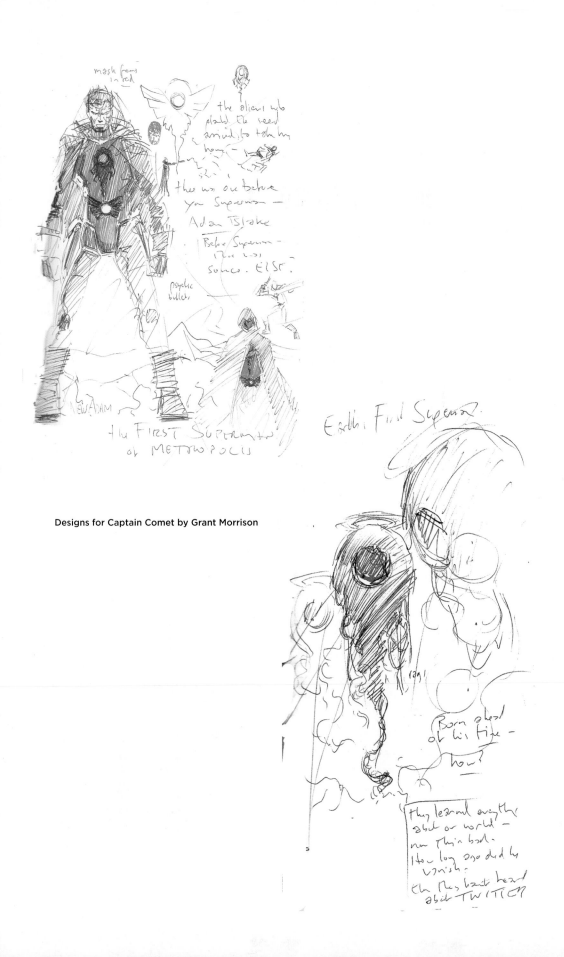

Designs for Captain Comet by Grant Morrison

Steel art by Cully Hamner

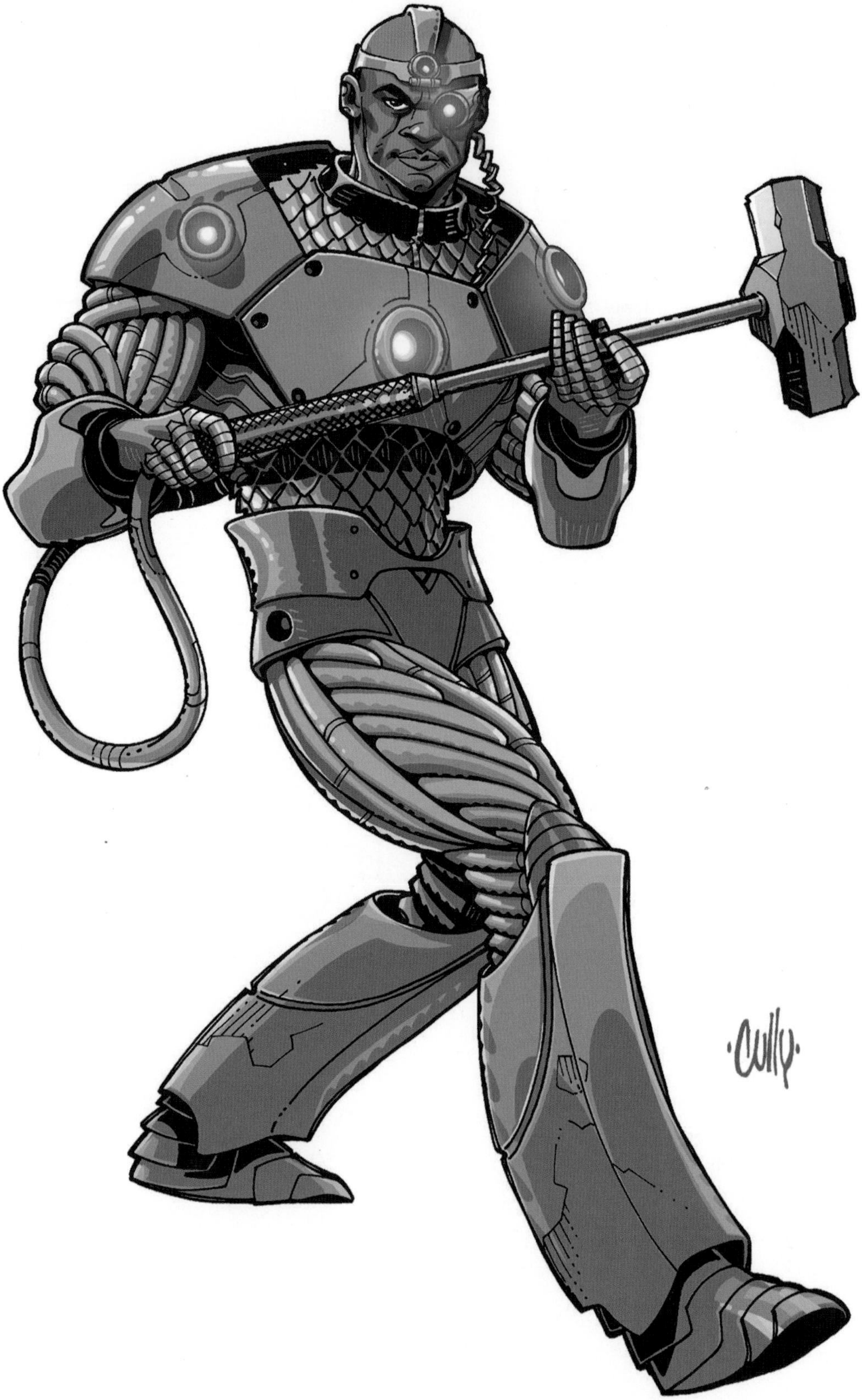
Cully

STEEL (REV)

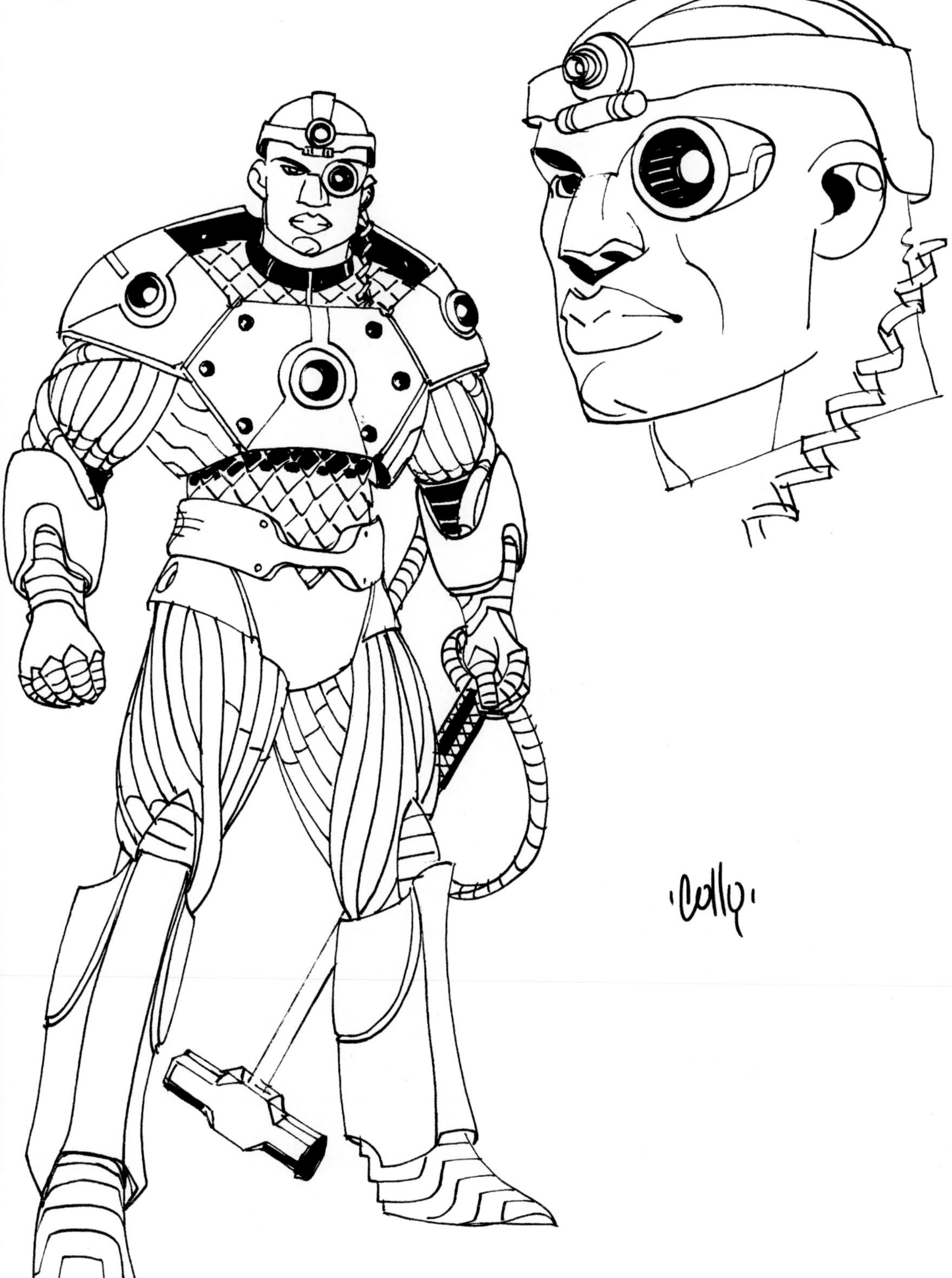
·Cully·

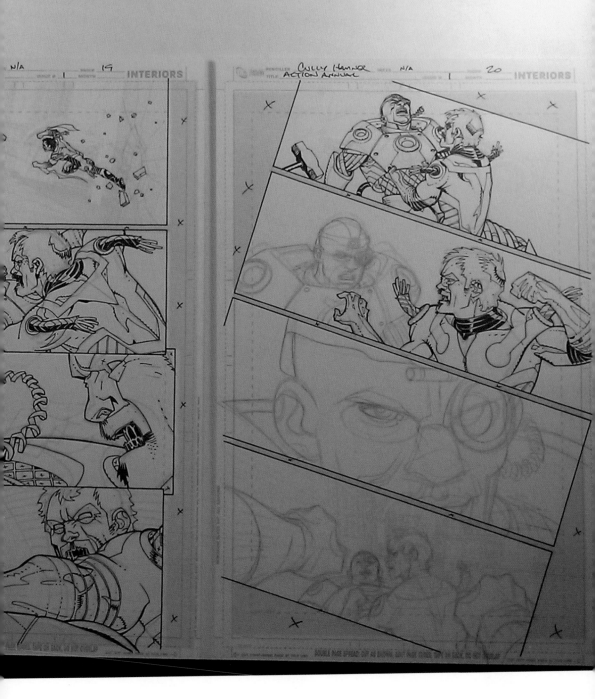

K-MAN
GREEN
(LAB SUIT)

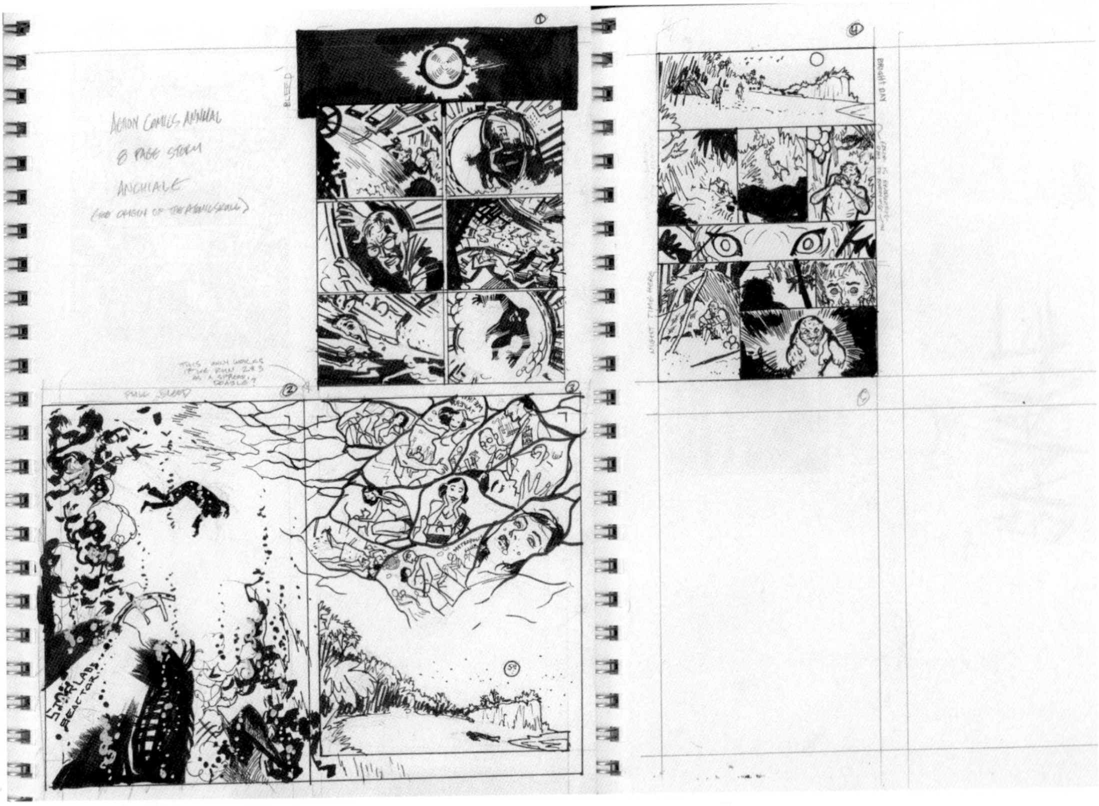
ACTION COMICS ANNUAL
8 PAGE STORY
ANCHIALE
FULL BLEED
BLEED
BRIGHT DAY
NIGHT TIME HERE

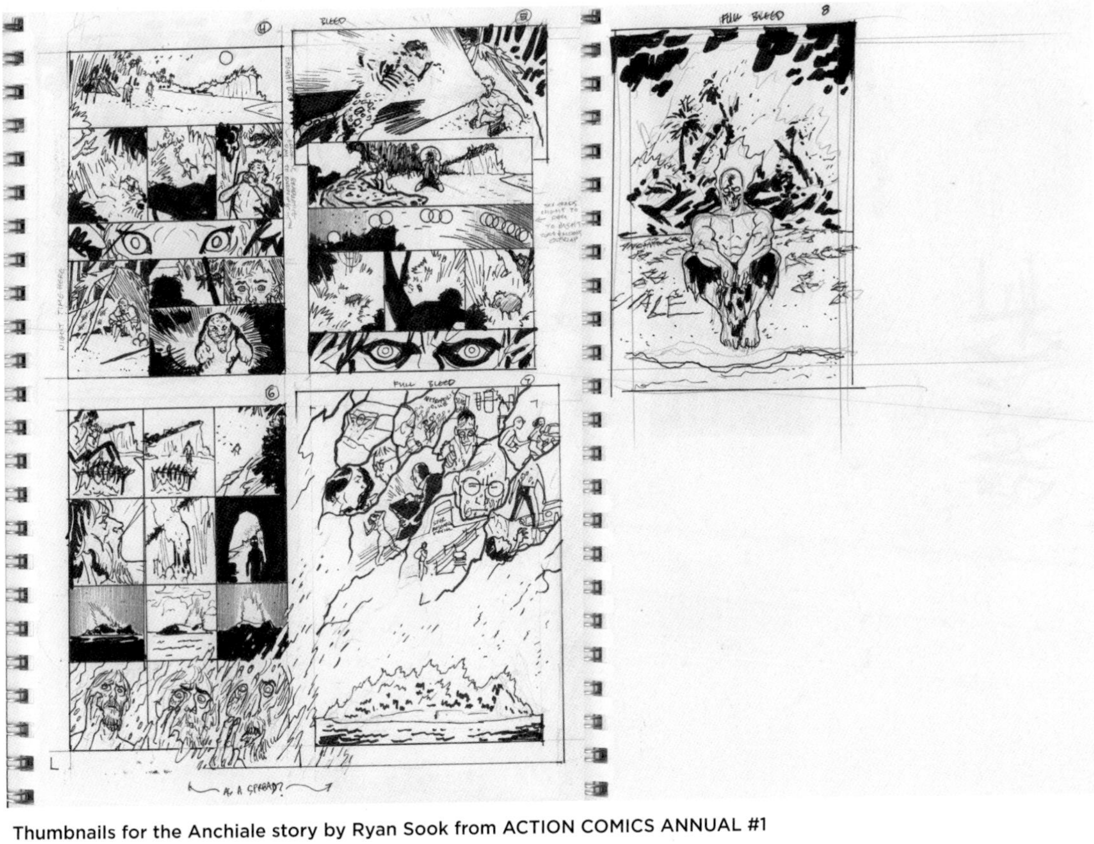
BLEED
FULL BLEED
BRIGHT DAY
NIGHT TIME HERE
AS A SPREAD?

Thumbnails for the Anchiale story by Ryan Sook from ACTION COMICS ANNUAL #1

Action Comics #9 cover sketches by Gene Ha

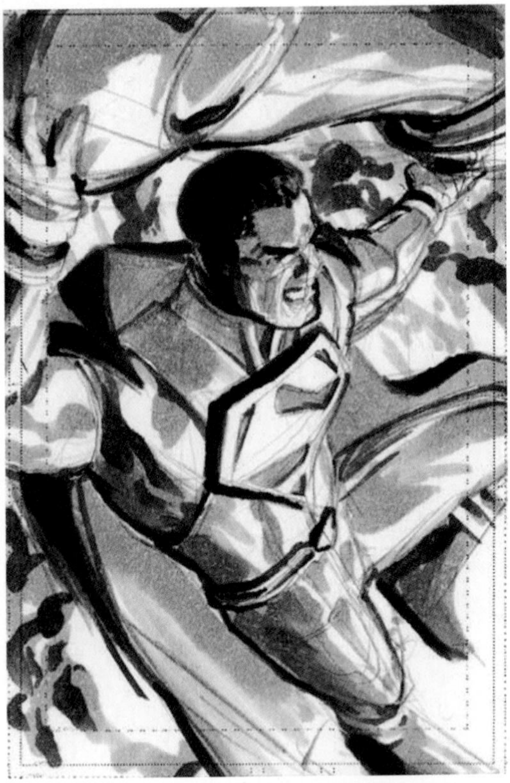
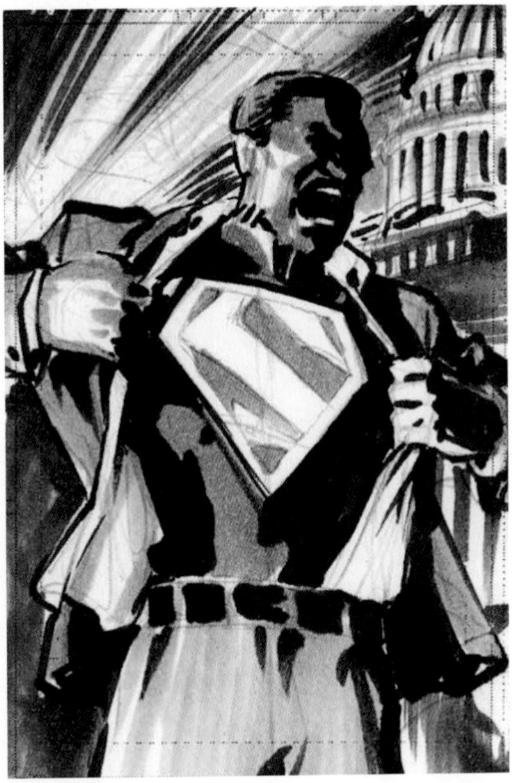
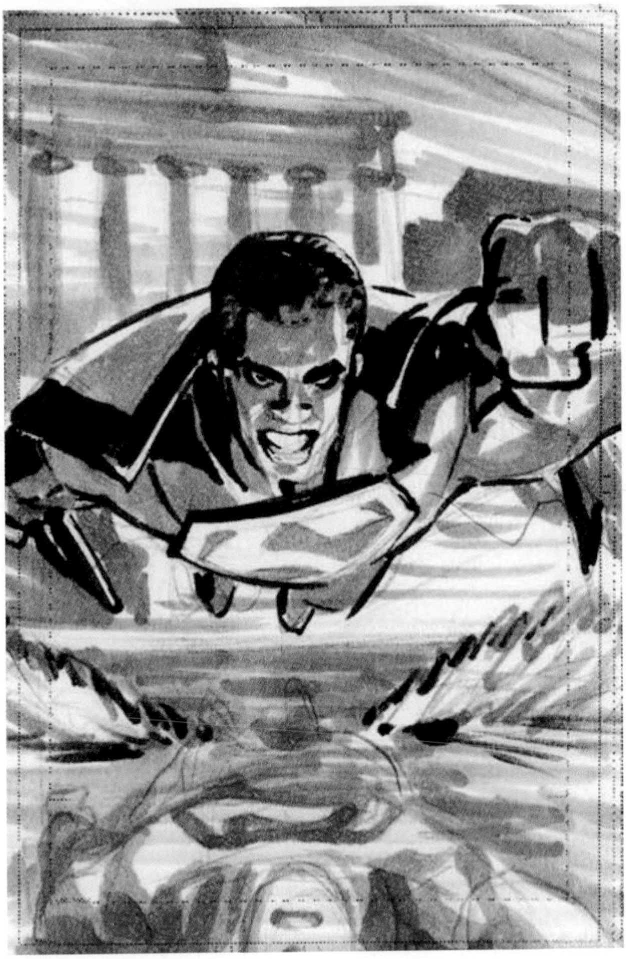

Action Comics #11 cover sketch by Grant Morrison

Action Comics #12 cover sketch by Grant Morrison

Action Comics Annual #1 cover sketch by Cully Hamner

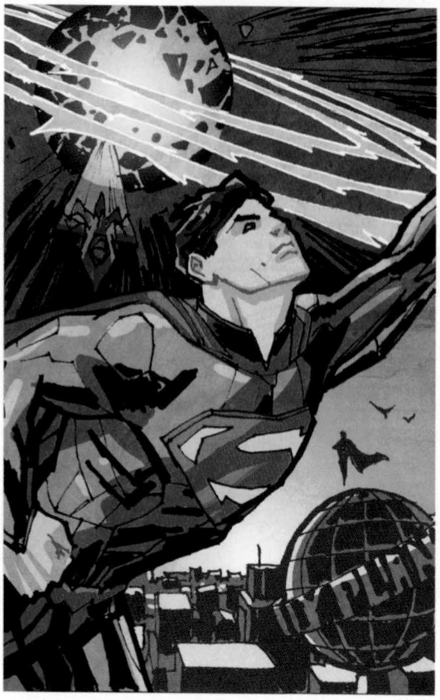

Action Comics #12 variant cover sketch by Cliff Chiang

Action Comics #11 cover sketch by Grant Morrison

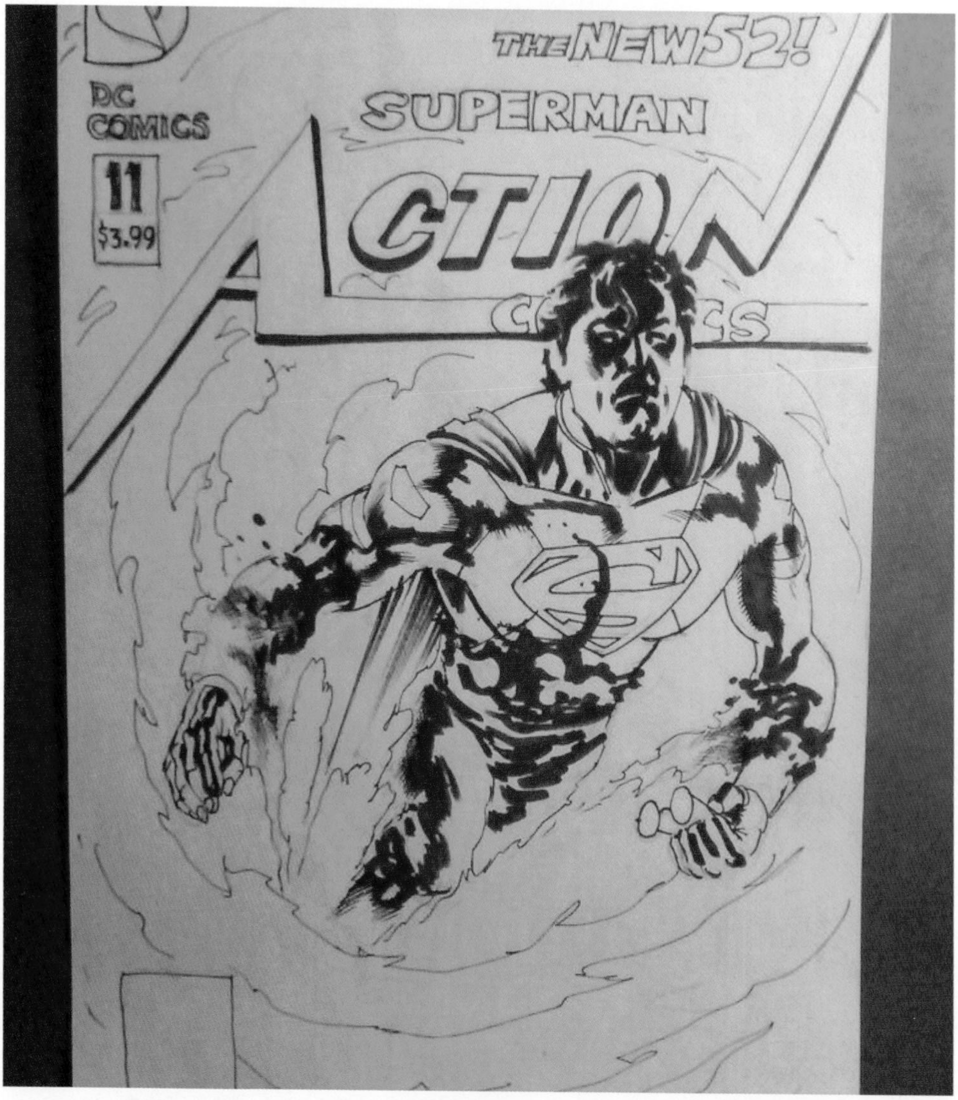
DC COMICS
11
$3.99
THE NEW 52!
SUPERMAN

DC COMICS™

"Maniacally brilliant."
—THE NEW YORK TIMES

"A stirringly mythic, emotionally resonant, and gloriously alternative take on the Man of Steel."
—ENTERTAINMENT WEEKLY

"Taking the Man of Steel back to his roots and into the future at the same time, All Star Superman is exciting, bold and supercool...all the makings of a classic."
—VARIETY

GRANT MORRISON

ALL-STAR SUPERMAN with FRANK QUITELY

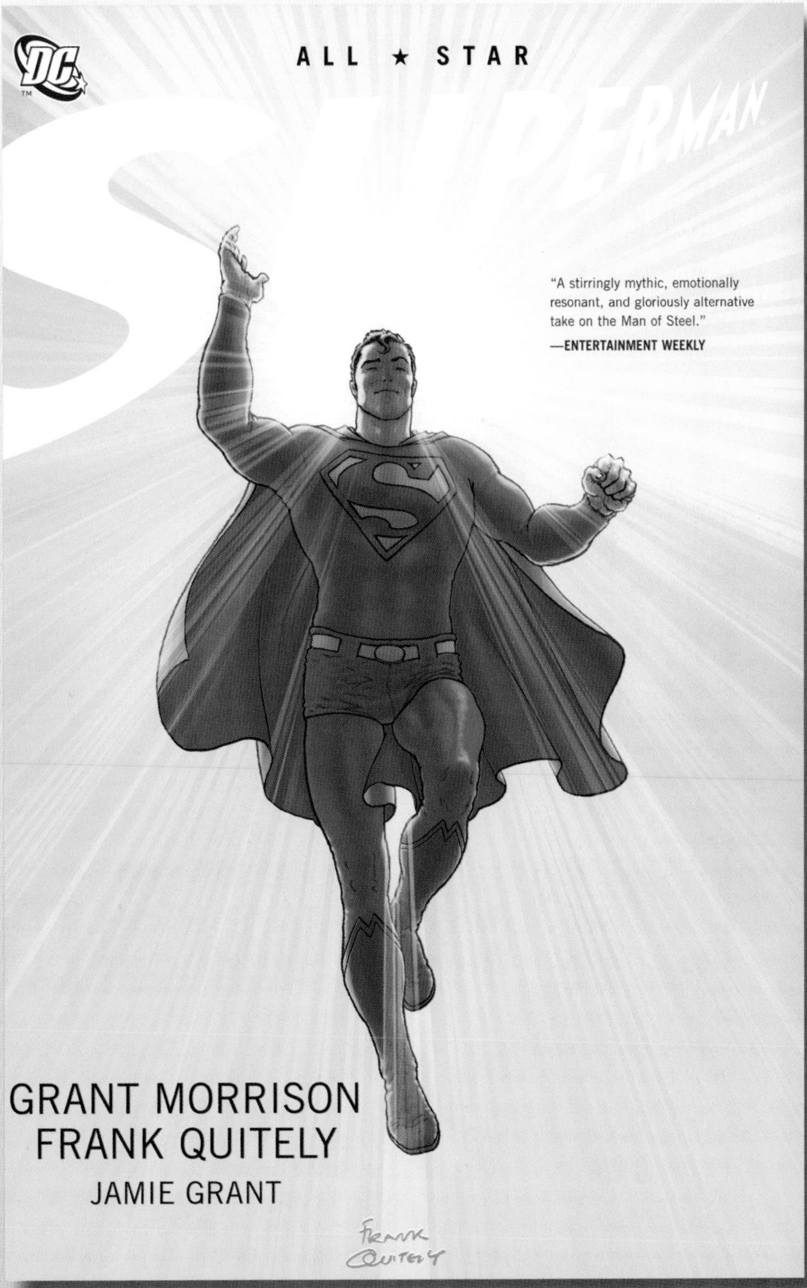
ALL ★ STAR
SUPERMAN
"A stirringly mythic, emotionally resonant, and gloriously alternative take on the Man of Steel."
—ENTERTAINMENT WEEKLY
GRANT MORRISON
FRANK QUITELY
JAMIE GRANT

FINAL CRISIS

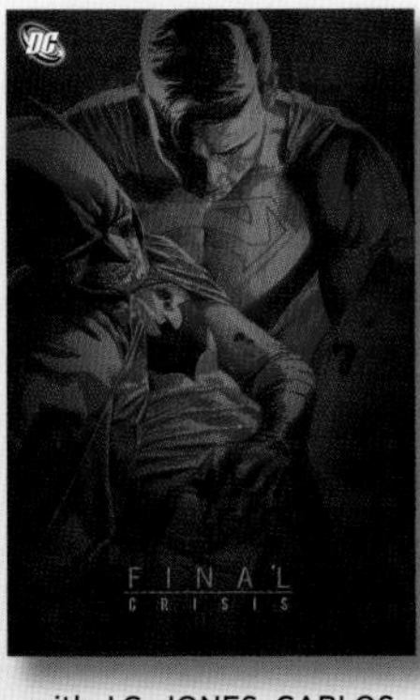
FINAL
CRISIS

with J.G. JONES, CARLOS PACHECO & DOUG MAHNKE

BATMAN: ARKHAM ASYLUM

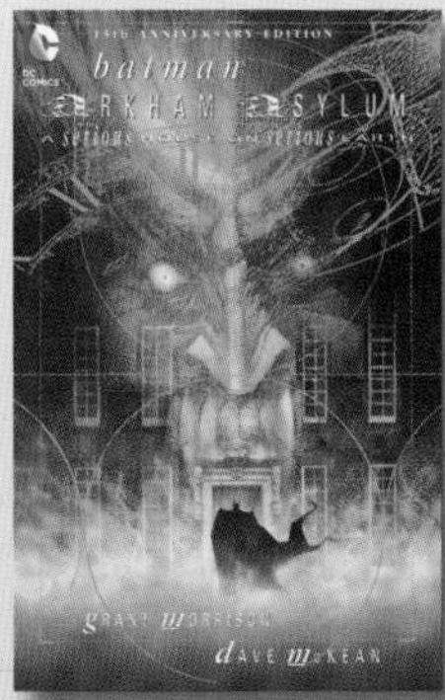
batman
ARKHAM ASYLUM
dave McKEAN

with DAVE McKEAN

SEVEN SOLDIERS OF VICTORY VOLS. 1 & 2

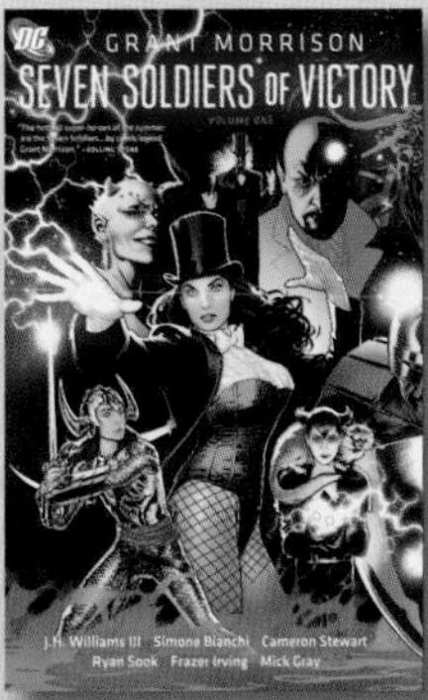
GRANT MORRISON
SEVEN SOLDIERS OF VICTORY
J.H. Williams III Simone Bianchi Cameron Stewart
Ryan Sook Frazer Irving Mick Gray

with J.H. WILLIAMS III & Various Artists

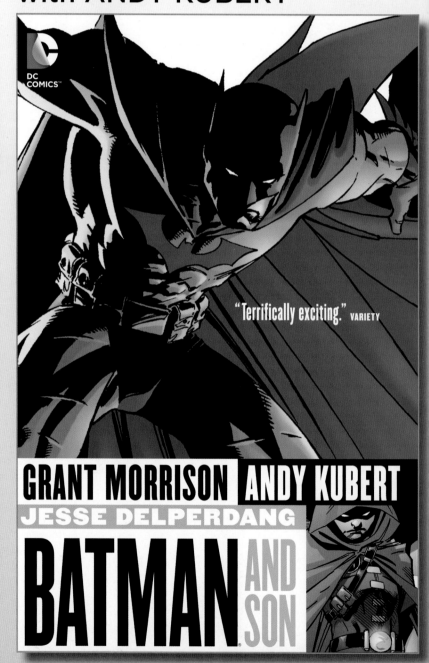

START AT THE BEGINNING!

JUSTICE LEAGUE VOLUME 1: ORIGIN

AQUAMAN VOLUME 1: THE TRENCH

THE SAVAGE HAWKMAN VOLUME 1: DARKNESS RISING

GREEN ARROW VOLUME 1: THE MIDAS TOUCH

GEOFF **JOHNS** JIM **LEE** SCOTT **WILLIAMS**

DC COMICS™

"It's fresh air. I like this all-too-human Superman, and I think a lot of you will, too."
—SCRIPPS HOWARD NEWS SERVICE

START AT THE BEGINNING!

SUPERMAN: ACTION COMICS VOLUME 1: SUPERMAN AND THE MEN OF STEEL

SUPERMAN VOLUME 1: WHAT PRICE TOMORROW?

SUPERGIRL VOLUME 1: THE LAST DAUGHTER OF KRYPTON

SUPERBOY VOLUME 1: INCUBATION

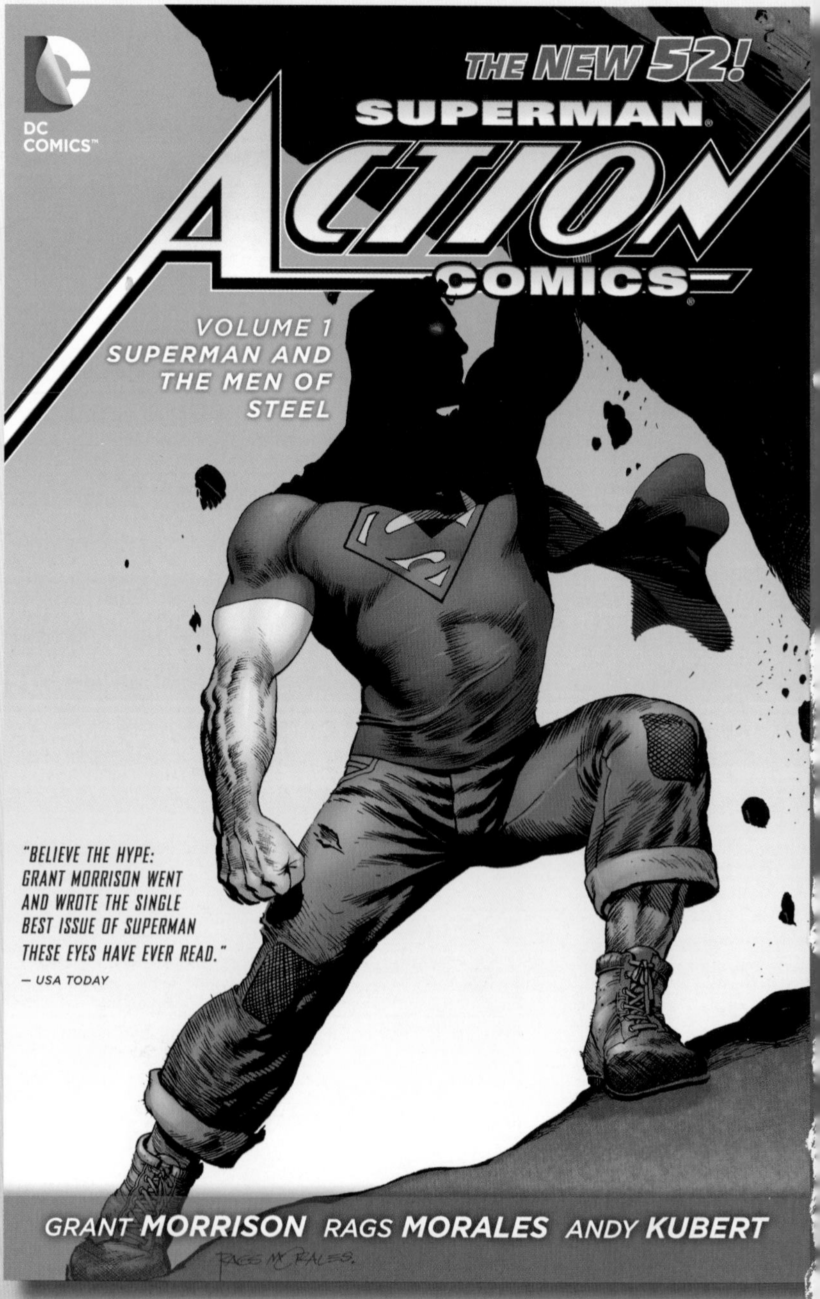

"BELIEVE THE HYPE: GRANT MORRISON WENT AND WROTE THE SINGLE BEST ISSUE OF SUPERMAN THESE EYES HAVE EVER READ." — USA TODAY

GRANT MORRISON RAGS **MORALES** ANDY **KUBERT**